The Development of Political Science

The study of the development of political science is a growing field. This book is the first comprehensive discussion of the subject in a comparative international perspective. Its distinguished contributors, all of whom are leading scholars in their respective countries, examine political science as a discipline and as a profession. They offer a wide-ranging account of the development of the subject and its dissemination across national borders and cultural divides. Opening with a study of the historiography of the discipline in the United States, a country which has been at the forefront of the field, the book broadens to emphasize Western Europe as a focus for discussion and comparison, and presents studies of further areas of interest such as China and Africa. This particular approach emphasizes the book's vision of political science as a growing transnational body of knowledge.

In presenting their critical analysis of the state of the field, the contributors aim to further the study of the development of the discipline in the countries discussed, and to provide a work that is interesting not only to political scientists, but to all those concerned with the development of the social sciences.

David Easton is Andrew Macleish Distinguished Service Professor Emeritus at the University of Chicago and Distinguished Professor of Political Science at the University of California at Irvine. **John G. Gunnell** is Professor of Political Science at the Rockefeller College of Public Affairs and Policy at the State University of New York at Albany. **Luigi Graziano** is Professor of Comparative Politics at the University of Turin in Italy, and is Recurrent Visiting Professor of Italian Civilization at New York University.

The Development of Political Science

A Comparative Survey

Edited by
David Easton, John G. Gunnell
and Luigi Graziano

London and New York

First published 1991
by Routledge
11 New Fetter Lane, London EC4P 4EE

Simultaneously published in the USA and Canada
by Routledge
a division of Routledge, Chapman and Hall, Inc.
29 West 35th Street, New York, NY 10001

Typeset by Amy Boyle Word Processing
Printed and bound in Great Britain by
Mackays of Chatham plc, Chatham, Kent

British Library Cataloguing in Publication Data
The Development of Political Science: A Comparative Survey
  1. Political science
  I. Easton, David II. Gunnell, John G. (John Gilbert) 1933–
  III. Graziano, Luigi
  320
  ISBN 0-415-05623-3

Library of Congress Cataloging in Publication Data
The Development of Political Science: A Comparative Survey.
  Edited by David Easton, John Gunnell and Luigi Graziano.
  p.   cm.
  Includes bibliographical references and index.
  ISBN 0-415-05623-3
  1. Political science – History. I. Easton, David, 1917-
  II. Gunnell, John G. III. Graziano, Luigi, 1939-
  JA83.D47 1991
  320'.09–dc20

Contents

Contributors

Dag Anckar is Professor of Political Science at Abo Academy University at Abo in Finland. His research interests include central government institutions, political theory and the history of political science.

Erkki Berndtson is currently a Research Fellow of the Academy of Finland at Helsinki in Finland. His research interests include democratic theory and the history of political science.

David Easton is Andrew Macleish Distinguished Service Professor Emeritus at the University of Chicago and Distinguished Professor of Political Science at the University of California at Irvine. He has published extensively on many aspects of political science. He is Vice-President of the American Academy of Arts and Sciences and co-chairs the International Committee for the Study of the Development of Political Science.

Zhengyuan Fu is a former Fellow at the Center for Advanced Study in the Behavioral Sciences at Stanford University and is Professor of the Chinese Academy of Social Sciences.

Luigi Graziano is Professor of Comparative Politics at the University of Turin in Italy and is Recurrent Visiting Professor of Italian Civilization at New York University in the US. His research interests include Italian politics and the development of political science in Italy.

John G. Gunnell is Professor of Political Science at the Rockefeller College of Public Affairs and Policy of the State University of New York at Albany. He has published extensively on the theory and philosophy of political science.

Jack Hayward is Professor of Politics at the University of Hull in Britain. He is Vice-President of the Political Studies Association of the United Kingdom and editor of *Political Studies*.

L. Adèle Jinadu is a Professor of Political Science at Lagos State University and was Secretary General of the African Association of Political Science (AAPS) between 1985-90. He has published extensively on politics in Africa, and is currently on leave as Member of the National Electoral Commission in Nigeria.

Hans Kastendiek is currently teaching British and American politics at the University of Giesen in West Germany. His research interests include state theory, corporatism, West German and British politics and the development of political science in West Germany.

Jean Leca is Professor of Political Science at the Institute of Political Studies, University of Paris, France. His research interests include comparative politics, Middle East and North African political systems and the evolution of citizenship in contemporary democracies.

Michael Stein is Professor of Political Science at McMaster University in Hamilton, Ontario, Canada. His research interests include the development of political science in Canada and other Western countries, and constitutional reform in Canada.

John E. Trent is Professor of Political Science and head of department at the University of Ottawa in Canada. His research interests include the development of political science in Canada.

Josep M. Vallès is Professor of Political Science at the Universitat Autònoma de Barcelona at Catalonia in Spain. His research interests include electoral behaviour, electoral systems and local government.

Preface

In 1985 the Finnish Political Science Association, on the occasion of its fiftieth anniversary, in collaboration with the International Political Science Association, sponsored a symposium in Helsinki on The Development and Institutionalization of Political Science: Centre-Periphery Relations and Other Crucial Concepts. Twenty-one papers were presented dealing with the history of political science within various countries as well as disciplinary relations between different countries. A selection of revised papers from that meeting was published in *Political Science Between Past and Future* (1988), edited by Dag Anckar and Erkki Berndtson, and several additional papers were published in the January 1987 issue of the *International Political Science Review*.

During the Helsinki conference, on the initiative of David Easton and John Trent, a committee was formed for the purpose of facilitating a more systematic and continuing historical and comparative study of the discipline and profession of political science. In 1988, this committee, designated as the International Committee for the Study of the Development of Political Science (ICSDPS), became a permanent subcommittee of the International Political Science Association's Research Committee for the Study of the Discipline of Political Science. The original research programme of the ICSDPS called, first, for a comparative examination of the history of political science and, second, for an assessment of the extent to which political science had produced a body of political knowledge that transcended regional and national fields. In order to follow through on the work commenced at the Helsinki conference and to encourage additional specific-country studies of the evolution of political science, the first international conference of the ICSDPS was held in Cortona, Italy in September of 1987.

The conference, organized by David Easton and Luigi Graziano, was sponsored by the Centre of Political Science at the Fondazione Giangiacomo Feltrinelli and by the Citta di Cortona. Thirteen papers were presented. Most of the papers focused on the evolution of political science in a specific country, but some papers also addressed methodological issues in the historiography of political and social science. Eight of the twelve chapters in this volume are revised versions of presentations from the Cortona conference while three chapters are based on presentations at Helsinki and reprinted from the 1987 volume of the *International Political Science Review*. The concluding chapter, by David Easton, was originally published in the 1985 volume of the *International Political Science Review*.

The chapters in this book are the product of leading scholars of political science in their respective countries. In all cases, the authors are practising political scientists rather than historians of social science, and, in many instances, the essays are unique in that they represent the first attempt to give an informed account of the history of the discipline in particular countries. While each chapter reflects the perspective of the individual author and the relevant historical and cultural context, this project has evolved in a collegial atmosphere where both the initial drafts and the revised contributions reflect continual communication and interaction among the participants with respect to general concerns and objectives.

We wish especially to thank the International Political Science Association, the Finnish Political Science Association, the Centre of Political Science at Fondazione Giangiacomo Feltrinelli, and the Citta di Cortona for the support that facilitated the creation of the material in this volume.

Introduction

John G. Gunnell and David Easton

During the past thirty years political science, as an academic discipline, has experienced an enormous growth throughout the world — in the number of persons involved, in the research tools available and in the sheer volume of productivity. Since World War Two, along with the other social sciences, it has undergone what can legitimately be called an extraordinary expansionist revolution. But there has been little systematic attention devoted to the historical development of the field as a whole and to the peculiarities of its evolution in specific countries — particularly outside the United States.

Although prior to World War Two most industrialized countries, especially in the West, boasted a scattered, handful of scholars in the field, the United States alone had an established institutionalized political science profession. In 1949, only four countries had political science associations that could join the newly founded international association. Today there are more than fifty national associations, and the discipline is actively promoted in many more countries. The number of journals, books, conferences, and research institutes has multiplied many times over.

Although this expansion has led to depth and diversity it has also fostered fragmentation, communication overload, multiple approaches, conflicting schools, and, one suspects, considerable overlap and duplication. Political scientists as a whole are no longer as certain about their 'progress' as they were formerly or as imbued with as confident a sense of direction.

Many scholars recognize the present as an opportune and legitimate moment to take stock of the process of development in our knowledge and of our objective understanding of the functioning of political systems, to assess our achievements to date, to identify major current problems, and from all this to speculate about future orientations. We turn to the history of the discipline worldwide as a way of shedding light on such issues as well as on the way that the character of the discipline has been determined by the varying forces at work in different countries.

HISTORY AND SCIENTIFIC EXPLANATION

Systematic study of the history of the social sciences is a relatively recent academic endeavour, and among these disciplines, historical reflection on the field of political science may well be the least developed. The principal concern of the ICSDPS, and its organizing meeting at Helsinki and its subsequent conference at Cortona, was not only to produce substantive comparative studies of the evolution of political science in various countries but to foster more focused work on the history of political science in general. To some extent, this was conceived as an end in itself, with a sense that self-consciousness about the history of the field and an account of that history was a worthy scholarly goal in its own right.

However for most of the contributors, who are practising students of politics, there were two additional desiderata. There was a desire to understand the factors, both internal and external to the discipline, that have shaped it in the past and, therefore, should enable us better to anticipate and guide its future development. There was also a distinct belief about the possible existence of important connections between historical reflection, both indigenous and comparative, and the enhancement and assessment of social scientific practice. Although, for the most part, the present essays do not overtly address the issue of social scientific practice, the concern is manifest in various ways in the distribution of emphasis. It is assumed that historical awareness is relevant to decisions about the progress of research and teaching in political science.[1] We are sensitive to the fact that this assumption raises a central issue about the explanatory as against the purely descriptive character of historical research. If we know the origins of some present state of affairs, does this really lead to a better understanding, at least in a scientific sense, of the present?

As true products of the historical centuries since the French Revolution, we are intuitively inclined to answer in the affirmative. Logically, however, the matter is not so easy to demonstrate. For example, if a bridge collapses, we can take one of two tacks in seeking an explanation. We may examine it, locate the construction defects from current evidence and thereby arrive at a satisfactory answer about its collapse. Alternatively, however, if the bridge were too large and complex or if the whole structure had been miraculously swept away, we could, given a precise and detailed historical record of the construction of the bridge, search it to pinpoint the moment when some fatal defect entered into the construction. Thereby history could give us a causal explanation. At times, of course, both current and historical analysis might be necessary as the quickest and best way for locating the source of the trouble.

The same alternatives hold true for society. We may try to understand current political relationships through observation of data and their direct analysis. Typically contemporary scientific research in political studies leans in this direction. Alternatively, we may try to trace out the antecedents of some present problem as a way of accounting for its current state. Thus an outbreak of ethnic violence may be analyzed with the data we have about existing ethnic relationships — mutual perceptions of the ethnic groups, present memories of past conflicts or persecution, ongoing exclusion of one or another ethnic group from social values, and the like. Where, however, these explanations may not seem to give an adequate explanation, we may look to the historical record to demonstrate the way in which past decisions and policies, at critical junctures, have laid down practices which, when handed down from generation to generation, serve to keep alive and even inflame intergroup hostilities.

We know, however, some of the difficulties in the path of historical analysis as a method for explaining the present. Often accurate records of the past are hard to come by. Events of the past are always too numerous to recapture in their entirety even by those who see history as simply a recounting of what has happened. A selection from the universe of all past events must be made. This opens the door to presentism, a bias that comes from the conscious or unconscious selection of historical facts in terms of present objectives. On the other hand, current analysis may itself be so involved and complex as to defy satisfactory resolution. Caught in this dilemma, there may be good reason to seek insight and help from historical analysis as an adjunct to contemporary research in the hope that a kind of triangulation can be achieved to give us a better understanding of the present reality than either approach alone. Inquiry into the history of the development of political science as a discipline and a profession worldwide by the ICSDPS adopts this dual strategy.

SELECTION OF ESSAYS IN THIS BOOK

In most instances, the essays in this book represent the first formal excursion into the history of political science in a specific country, and they are breaking new ground through such an initial exploration. Although comparative analysis is an ultimate objective, as well as a primary concern, most of the essays are not in themselves comparative in approach. The goal in this initial volume of the ICSDPS has been more to provide a basis for later critical and comparative analysis.

What may, more than anything else, require clarification is the concrete composition of the volume. Our goal in selecting and commissioning the essays included here was comprehensiveness but by no means completeness and definitiveness. In some cases, as already suggested, this was the first attempt to discuss the evolution of the field. There was by no means an effort to include a study of every country where it would be worth investigating the development of political science. To some extent, choices were dictated by the physical limits of one volume as well as by the interest, willingness, and availability of qualified scholars. In some instances, as in the case of the United States and larger European countries, it was clear that we assumed it important to represent the 'centre' of disciplinary development. In other instances, we aimed at significant but representative cases of the more peripheral examples of the evolution of political science. What constitutes centre and periphery, as our discussions in Helsinki had demonstrated,[2] is surely a contentious matter, but our judgment was based on the extensiveness of the field rather than on an assessment of the quality of political studies.

It will be apparent from the table of contents that Third World countries are vastly under-represented. Although the subject was discussed in papers presented at the conferences, it was in the end not possible to acquire chapters on Latin America and Japan in time for inclusion in this volume. Although an interesting paper on Poland was presented at Cortona, the Soviet Union and Eastern European nations have been excluded altogether. The latter decision reflects neither ethnocentrism nor political prejudice but, quite to the contrary, the fact that the development of political inquiry in these countries demands special treatment in its own right and would simply require more than can be accomplished in this volume. To understand a significant part of the character of political studies in much of the developing world involves an analysis of the transplantation and transformation of American and European modes, and the reactions to such influences. In the Eastern world, on the other hand, what might be called political science often has had little direct kinship with the concrete traditions of theory and practice that constitute Western political science. It is important to distinguish between political science as a generic category referring to any form of political inquiry and political science as a more specific institutionalized historical entity with a rather definite career. The latter is the subject of the endeavour represented in this book, although the former is included within the long-range objectives of the ICSDPS.

THE BEGINNING OF POLITICAL SCIENCE AS A DISCIPLINE

It was apparent, from the beginning of our discussions, that there were problems in attempting to specify when political science actually began, or the extent to which it actually existed, in a particular country. In most countries there was, before what we might designate as the specific institution of political science, some earlier form of political studies or a functional equivalent. Questions relating to the autonomy and identity of political science tended to be increasingly controversial.

What are the criteria for indicating such things as the beginning of the field, the dividing line between old and new political science (its periodization or stages in development), and the difference between political science and other fields such as sociology? And, equally important, are these criteria internal or external, that is, matters to be settled in terms of the perceptions of the actors or matters involving external analysis? What might be called political science in a particular country might not have anything to do with any identifiable tradition of scholarship elsewhere. In one case, Poland, it appeared to be merely a name attached to regime-supported ideological studies, while the functions associated with what we might normally term political science were performed by other disciplines such as sociology. Although it was noted that there were extreme cases with respect to the degree that political science was ideologically implicated, there were few instances in which the politicization of the field was not to some degree a matter to be taken into account in explaining its evolution.

It was clear that these issues were in many countries tied to indigenous debates about what was authentic political science, its national origin, its relationship to other fields such as law and philosophy, and concerns about biases that inhibited its evolution and institutionalization. There was some question about whether the beginning of political science in a country could be distinguished from its institutionalization and whether, for example, theory could be understood as preceding institutionalization as an academic practice.

INFLUENCES ON DEVELOPMENT: AUTONOMY AND CONTEXT

With respect to the evolution and institutionalization of political science, the initial papers and subsequent conference discussions, at Cortona as well as Helsinki, tended to focus on both the method and substance of disciplinary practice. In addition, we found, from the beginning, that the emphasis of investigators centred on the manner in which the development of political science had been influenced by its academic, social, and political contexts and on the extent to which it, in turn, influenced those contexts. It soon became evident, however, that the concepts of context and influence were far from clear and unproblematical.

The question of the autonomy of political science surfaced in two distinct but related ways. Not only was there the issue of its relationship to other fields, or its academic ecology, but its relationship, as well as that of the social scientific enterprise as a whole, to the political regime, to political culture, and to political practices in general. Issues respecting the integrity and identity of political science were widespread and continuing matters of concern at the centre as well as the periphery of the field.

The issue of the autonomy of political science also raised methodological questions with respect to understanding the history of the field. To what degree were internal or external approaches to the study of the development of political science preferable, and to what extent were such choices pragmatic and reflective of the situation of political science in a particular country? How much of the character of the field and the nature of its development is a function of factors in its milieu and how much can be attributed to intrinsic intellectual dynamics or even historical accident? To what extent has the development of the field depended on institutional factors as opposed, for example, to the efforts and creativity of particular individuals? The diverse histories of political science in different contexts suggested that it was difficult to generalize about development and arrive at explanations that transcended historical particularities.

Although often not directly confronted, it seemed that there was a general assumption that political science in large measure took shape and defined itself in response to the configuration of politics in a particular society. But a recognition of this fact also raised a question about the relationship between the two principal concerns of the conferences. If political science reflects its political context and if the criteria of knowledge are relative to the historical evolution of fields, to what extent is it possible to conceive of a universal body of political knowledge? Is, for example, a politically and socially detached community of scholars with its own standards of judgment conceivable? Politics at any time tends to impose a discourse which political science seeks in some respects to transcend through the language of the field and its methodologies. To what extent can or does political science transcend the culture in which it is imbedded? To what extent can it do so if it strives for universality in its theories and methods of inquiry? These were central questions that were raised in discussion but fundamentally went unanswered in the papers. In striving for universality, we would also be left with the ancillary issue as to whether the specialized languages necessary for this purpose might create difficulties both for keeping in touch with political reality and for communicating with those engaged in politics.

Circumscribing the concept of context became increasingly complicated in the course of attempting to determine what constituted, in principle or circumstantially, actual (as opposed to perceived) and relevant contexts and how they related to the field of political science and its development — and to each other. A context might be understood as narrowly as the nature of academic institutions and the university or a particular set of social and political events, but it was often construed as widely as a type of political culture or political system. At its broadest, it might include the whole society — its social structure and mode of production in the broadest sense. And exactly how does some approach, such as the sociology of knowledge, either in theory or practice, postulate, specify, and make explanatory connections between dependent and independent variables? Simply alluding to external factors is not sufficient. Finally, the synchronic dimension of explanation was not the only issue. How, in diachronic terms, as we have already noted, might the past, thought of now as part of the context, constitute an explanation of the present?

With respect to the relationship between political science and its context, it was not just a matter of explaining the development of the field in terms of its surroundings but also one of judging the extent, possibility, and kind of impact that political science might or should have on politics and the way this might react back on the discipline.

In other words, political science may help to shape the context by which it itself is influenced. But many of the terms used in talking about all these relationships were as difficult to define as the notion of context itself: influence, impact, reflection, recognition, contribution, cause, education, interaction, feedback, etc. It was generally agreed that it was crucial to map the connections between the discipline and relevant contextual variables, but it was difficult to determine just how to conduct such a cartographic exercise.

One significant issue involved the transfer of knowledge from one country to another. How in fact, for example, does a presumed centre influence the peripheries, and may there not be a reverse flow? Equally important — although the issue did not loom large in our discussions, nor was it phrased in quite this way — could the transfer of concepts, methods, theories, and general approaches to the study of politics from one culture to another suppress insights and creativeness that might otherwise have arisen from the study of politics indigenous to a particular culture? In other words, does the so-called imperialism of the idea manage to so dominate the indigenous political science, in countries where it is less developed, that theoretical and empirical practices of inquiry inappropriate to the host society displace those in process of forming locally?

Implicit in these questions is a challenge to the assumption that political science in those areas of the world, such as the United States — where the richness of resources has permitted a high degree of specialization which, in turn, has encouraged the vast growth of political science — must necessarily provide the basis for a universal body of knowledge and practices. To what extent is scientific practice itself culture-bound so that Western political science is just that, namely, a product of a particular culture at a particular place and time, losing thereby its claim to universality?

If political science were indeed culture-bound and in this way contextually constrained, would there be room for those cultures, in which political science has been developing more slowly, to 'catch up', as it were, to formulate their own practices for acquiring reliable knowledge, and to fold those into any emerging internationalized body of political research? Out of this, it is sometimes said, may emerge a truly universal set of standards, methodological practices and accepted theories about political behaviour and institutions. This position assumes, therefore, that we ought to be alert to the presence of other conceptions of science or ways of obtaining reliable knowledge. Such variations of what we have in the West might in the end affect the nature of any developing worldwide corpus of political knowledge. Such a perspective suggests that the development of political science in a particular country cannot be fully understood without some effort to sort out the differential effects of influences external to a culture from those indigenous to it as well as the possible influence of such latter elements on any emerging body of knowledge.

DEVELOPMENT AND SPECIALIZATION

In speaking about the history of political science in various countries, it was common to refer to the process as one of 'development', but as in the case of attempting to assess the extent of knowledge achieved, the criteria of development were less than easily agreed upon. Does development, for example, mean progress? If so, by what criteria is the evolution of political science to be assessed?

Or does development mean just growth in numbers of political scientists and in volume of production? If that were the case, would it translate into specialization among the disciplines as a way of increasing numbers together with specialization among subfields within the discipline? Development in this sense would suggest then the need to see it as a product of industrialization with its powerful and ever increasing pressures toward the division of intellectual labour.

Although we did not pursue the subject in any depth, specialization in political science clearly raises the spectre of one of the major and critical issues of our time. If knowledge becomes increasingly specialized and thereby fragmented, how is it brought together, if at all, for application in the solution of social problems? Who, in a particular educational establishment, assumes this responsibility and how is it handled? Even within political science itself, in those countries in which specialization has gone on apace, scholars in the burgeoning subfields have increasing difficulty in keeping up with their own research output, let alone talking to each other across subfields. In the diffusion of methods of specialized inquiry and their products, do they create a context for the development of political science in other less highly industrialized countries that may not be appropriate for the level of development of knowledge there, or for that matter, for the kinds of political problems they face? If so, it would be incumbent on any inquiry into the history of political science in such countries to be alert to difficulties that premature overspecialization might create.

EFFECTS OF REGIME TYPES

Another issue, one that did occasion considerable discussion, involved the degree to which the growth of political science and its sense of identity depends on a political context in which there is wide access to information and even to the inner councils of political decision-making. The diverse views on this subject may reflect in part different perceptions of the locus of politics as well as varying methodological perspectives. It was generally agreed in this respect that it is important to distinguish between governmental secrecy and closed or repressive regimes. It seemed possible to come to quite different hypotheses about the relationship between the vitality and autonomy of political science on the one hand and the degree of authoritarianism in the political regime on the other hand. Despite obvious examples to the contrary, there was some evidence to suggest that even though one might expect weak political systems to allow the growth of social knowledge, repressiveness could under certain conditions be an impetus to the development of political science. Also authoritarian regimes, for various reasons, did not always seek to stifle political inquiry. It was considered important, however, to distinguish between authoritarian and totalitarian regimes in this respect, since the latter were more apt to eliminate any meaningful form of social science.

It was clear that political science has at various times and places played dissident as well as legitimating roles in both closed and open societies, and it was repeatedly indicated that the origin of political science was practical and often tied to efforts at political change and reform as well as various modes of political education. In our discussions in Cortona we noted that the experience of the two overlapping disciplines, political science and public administration, had been somewhat different in that the latter had been traditionally viewed as less threatening to the political regime.

CASE STUDIES VS COMPARATIVE ANALYSIS

The problems of arriving at generalizations, and even categories of comparative analysis, appeared increasingly difficult as case studies of the history of the discipline in various countries were presented. We found that substantive discussions of the history of political science seemed inexorably linked with methodological issues involved in writing about such history. It was noted that in attempting to make comparisons, it is necessary to take account of the problem of the limiting character of certain concepts developed in one context of political science. Was, for example, American political science, as Bernard Crick argued,[3] really only an *American* science which reflected and reinforced American political culture? If so, was this, at least to some degree, necessarily the case? Although the discussions for the most part centered on questions about the development of political science, the matter of comparative generalization was critical with respect to the question of the possibility of some universal body of political knowledge. Does such a body of knowledge imply a universal language for talking about politics? It is at this point that questions involved in studying the history of political science merge with issues in the philosophy of science.

DIFFUSION VS PARALLEL DEVELOPMENT

Finally, the importance of distinguishing between parallel independent development and diffusion from one country to another emerged as a central theme. It touched matters that provoked considerable controversy.

It has often been suggested, as already noted, that, unlike sociology, for example, contemporary political science is, historically and conceptually, a peculiarly American social science. The argument is sometimes made that to a very large extent the development of political science in various countries must be explained in terms of the emigration and syncretic adaptation of American approaches to political inquiry. Although there was clearly a concern about the imperialism of American political science, and thus to some degree an acceptance of this proposition, there was also a concern with demonstrating the existence of an autonomous tradition of political inquiry in various countries. While some suggested that the American origins of the field were essential for understanding its character and development in foreign settings, others argued that as a weak thesis the claim that political science was an American invention is true but trivial, and as a stronger thesis it was simply incorrect.

Even if various countries have imported the assumptions, methods, findings and theories of American political science, some discussants at Cortona felt that this has not led to the cloning of the discipline in the host country. When imported, various aspects of political science often undergo significant modification in both content and application which while sometimes viewed as distortions by the country of origin might be seen in the receiving country as necessary cultural adaptations to local conditions. The nature of the international exchange of knowledge cannot be assessed in the abstract, and part of the task of writing the history of political science is precisely to illuminate this process.

Furthermore, it is sometimes forgotten that exchanges do not flow one way only, that is, from centre to periphery. American political inquiry, for example, was, from the beginning substantially influenced by European scholarship. Indeed, the whole educational system to this day continues to exhibit these origins as well as the effect of subsequent waves of the immigration of ideas. And although it may seem in the mid-twentieth century that the arrow points from the United States to Europe with respect to the development of mainstream political science, it is important to note the concurrent reversal of the direction of flow in such areas as existentialism, phenomenology, hermeneutics, neo-statism, neo-Marxism, structuralism, and other transformational influences on contemporary social scientific inquiry.

METHODOLOGY AND TECHNIQUES

It seemed evident that undertaking studies of the history of political science in various countries raised a series of methodological issues that were shared by the history of social science in general. Although two papers at the Cortona conference (both included in this volume), those by Gunnell and Berndtson, focused especially on these problems, such matters as the general nature of historical understanding as well as the relative value of internal and external approaches, that is, approaches emphasizing the theoretical and conceptual development of a field as opposed to attempts to explain it in terms of reference to its political and social context, continually surfaced during the course of the discussions.

The current status of historical studies and historiography in the social sciences did not suggest any easy solution. And we could expect little more from the much less developed state of historical studies in political science which have heretofore largely been tied to critical and legitimating disciplinary arguments. It was apparent that future work in the history of political science must come to grips with a wide range of historiographical problems and hermeneutical claims which extend to general matters of historical explanation and which transcend the regional concerns of political scientists.

THE FOCUS OF THE PAPERS

Although the study of the history of political science in the United States may not be as highly developed as that of certain other social sciences in that country, it has nevertheless reached a point of specialization where any single work, let alone book chapter, would be inadequate for encompassing the field, and where many of the issues have become increasingly methodological in character. At the same time, we wished to avoid offering a contribution on the United States that was excessively narrow and of interest to a limited audience or that duplicated prior work. The chapter, by John Gunnell, reviews the major literature on the history of American political science and analyses some of the principal historiographical issues which have become salient in this field of research and which will undoubtedly become a focus of concern in studies of the history of political science in other countries. The concluding chapter, by David Easton, presents a substantive interpretative overview of the history of political science in the United States that is addressed to a general international audience.

More general methodological and philosophical problems of historical and comparative inquiry are discussed by Erkki Berndtson before the focus shifts to specific country studies. Each of these studies speaks for itself and proceeds from indigenous concerns and perspectives, but certain common themes do emerge. To a very great extent, the development of political science as a distinct discipline has, outside the United States, been a post-World War Two phenomenon. Whatever interpretation we put on this matter, it has involved, in varying degrees, as we have already stressed, the export and import of American approaches to inquiry. This issue was evident in many of the discussions, and it is an important part of the distribution of emphasis in the chapters on Italy (Luigi Graziano), Great Britain (Jack Hayward), and the Nordic countries (Dag Anckar). Questions of centre and periphery are much at issue. As we have noted earlier, much of the discussion at the conferences focused on the political context of political science, and although most of the chapters reflect that concern, John Trent and Michael Stein's study of Canadian political science and Hans Kastendiek's study of West Germany deal most explicitly with the relationship between state and discipline.

Jean Leca's extensive and intensive examination of the study of politics in France and Joseph Vallès's unique analysis of political study in contemporary Spain round out the contributions to the history of political science in the West. L. Adèle Jinadu's comprehensive account of political science in 'Anglophone' Africa exemplifies the evolution of the field in one major segment of the post-colonial world. Finally, Zhengyuan Fu traces political studies in China from ancient times through recent events in the People's Republic of China. This original analysis offers an interesting contrast with the story of political science presented in the other chapters.

Whether readers are satisfied with the scope and content of the investigations represented here, it is our hope that these studies will encourage other political scientists in various countries to reflect historically on their discipline. What is contained in this volume is hardly the last word on the history of political science in the respective countries, but in many instances, it may represent virtually the first word.

NOTES

1 See John S. Dryzek and Stephen T. Leonard, 'History and discipline in political science', *American Political Science Review* 82 (1988):1243-60.
2 See Dag Anckar and Erkki Berndtson (eds) (1988) *Political Science between Past and Future*. Finnish Political Science Association; and *International Political Science Review* 8 (1987).
3 Bernard Crick (1959) *The American Science of Politics*, Berkeley: University of California Press.

1 The Historiography of American Political Science

John G. Gunnell[1]

> Having a historical sense is to conquer in a consistent manner the natural naivete which makes us judge the past by the so-called obvious scales of our current life, in the perspectives of our institutions, and from our acquired values and truths.
>
> (H-G. Gadamer)

The history of American political science is a field of study that, despite its problems, is considerably more developed than comparable endeavours in other countries. This should not be surprising, given the longer history of political science in the United States, but, at the same time, the reasonably large, and increasing, body of literature in this area has given rise to a number of methodological issues. Many of these issues will inevitably be encountered in other country studies of political science, and rather than offer a substantive contribution to the history of American political science, my concern is a critical analysis of the existing literature.

The purposes of this essay are, first, to explore the historiography of political science, that is, both the writing of the history of the field and the methodological principles embodied and asserted in that writing; and, second, to examine these in terms of the substance and method of the history of the social sciences in general. The principal claim attaching to this investigation is that, while accounts of the past of political science have heretofore been primarily instruments of disciplinary legitimation and critique, they must now, even to serve these functions successfully, develop a more adequate 'historical sense' and confront issues of historical validity.

During the last two decades, the history of the social sciences has become an increasingly autonomous and circumscribed activity. It has taken on many of the characteristics of a professional field, albeit a somewhat interdisciplinary one shared by both historians and practioners of particular social scientific disciplines. This has in some measure been a consequence of growing attention to the history of science in general, but it has also been the result of increased interest in this domain on the part of scholars in intellectual history and the history of ideas. These trends have coincided with an accentuated introspectiveness within the social sciences which has also involved an increase in historical reflection. This can be attributed to a number of causes including the demise, or at least the transformation, of certain perennial debates and the appearance of new crises of disciplinary identity.

All of this pertains to the particular case of political science, yet the situation in this field remains somewhat anomalous and idiosyncratic. While, for example, *The Journal of the History of the Behavioral Sciences* began publication in 1965, discussions of political science have been conspicuously absent, even with the expansion of focus represented in the creation of CHEIRON (the International Society for the History of the Behavioural and Social Sciences). The most obvious explanations may be necessary but they are not sufficient.

There is a sense in which, even as late as the 1960s, political science, despite all its attention to becoming a behavioural science, had not quite achieved that status — either in its own eyes or those of the social science community. But for the past two decades, it must be counted, both in terms of its self-image and institutional position, among those disciplines. In addition, even if the community of scholars that the *Journal* has most directly served, and that was most instrumental in founding it, was more closely associated with psychology and what might be conceived of as the 'harder' sciences, this has not been the case in recent years. The history of sociology has been well represented, and there is now an entire journal devoted to this subject. And certainly if anthropology, which was central to the enterprise from the beginning, features as a behavioural science, political science must qualify.

Political science has simply devoted less attention to a systematic investigation of its past, and we must seek the principal explanation in structural characteristics of the field and its history. One such factor involves the study of the history of political theory.

From its earliest disciplinary and professional beginnings in the United States, political science had a 'built in' historical self-image and one that provided it with a distinctive past that was an essential aspect of its identity. This was the interpretation of the canon of classic texts from Plato to Marx. Even as late as the mid-1970s, a systematic and highly objective account of the evolution of political science presented it as the lineage of the 'great tradition' of political theory (Waldo 1975). Modern academic political science was characteristically perceived as the latest stage in the development of systematic thought about politics, and this was not simply a prejudice of historians of political theory. The behavioural revolution, which understood itself as effecting a paradigmatic shift in political studies and as transforming the discipline into a truly scientific enterprise, retained this hagiolatry and the image of organic continuity with the great tradition.

If political scientists were not always inclined to seek their ancestors quite as far back as ancient Athens, they found an equally impressive, or supplementary, Pantheon and set of progenitors in the more practical and domestic version of the science of politics represented by Madison, Hamilton, Jefferson, Calhoun, and other putative founders of the principles and practice of American politics. The lack of attention to the 'real' history of the field cannot, however, be explained by suggesting simply that the study of the history of political thought preempted such an enterprise and insulated us from our actual past. The relationship between the discipline and its historical image, as Gene Poschman has so forcefully demonstrated (Poschman 1982), is a much more complicated matter.

Think, he suggests, if you can, of the works of Burgess, Goodnow, and Willoughby and try to picture their faces — as opposed to Locke, Marx, and Madison. Some members of the profession today might not even recognize the names, and for many the response would not be 'dissimilar from how we react at family reunions to the mention of the names of never seen, long dead, and many times removed uncles' (Poschman 1982). The mythical history has, to be sure, been much easier to study and probably a good deal more romantic, and it has served rhetorical functions with respect to conflicts within the discipline. But other fields, such as sociology and anthropology, where the names of Small or Boas might be as familiar as Aristotle or Rousseau, have paid more attention to their actual forebears.

To explain fully the ahistoricism of political science is a complex task, since the causes must in the end be located in the very history that has not been adequately pursued. Poschman suggests some subtle explanations, relating to the subject matter of politics and the characteristic attitudes of those who have wished to study it scientifically, which deserve careful consideration, but he also indicates some less elusive constraints.

The epic style of writing often associated with accounts of the history of political thought does not lend itself to the more labour-intensive type of investigation required for digging into the past of political science where, it might not be untoward to suggest, there has often been more quantity than quality. This kind of excavation requires more 'a method which at best resembles the extraction of crude ore through crushing and sifting' or dredging and an attempt 'to assay the mountain' rather than cutting, polishing, and weighing particular gems and nuggets. And the archaeology of political science sometimes indicates that what we might find upon close inspection is that it resembles 'those other products which we are warned not to look too closely at in their makings (sausages and legislation), if we do not wish to become disillusioned about our enterprise' (Poschman 1982). After all, John W. Burgess, who is usually accepted as one of the principal founders of the discipline, was, by today's standards, an outspoken racist and imperialist.

Finally, the most obvious, but maybe the most significant, inhibiting factor is that most existing contributions to the history of political science have not freed themselves from the partisanship associated with intellectual struggles within the field. Although there is no clear evidence that the establishment of autonomous historical studies of natural science and the other social sciences automatically created 'good' history, it may in some respects have been the precondition of serious attention to questions about the criteria of such history.

Although the history of political science is, then, not a very advanced enterprise, there is no doubt that it is much more developed than it was two decades ago at the apex of the behavioural movement. Between Bernard Crick's critical essay on *The American Science of Politics: Its Origins and Conditions* (1959) and Albert Somit and Joseph Tanenhaus' comprehensive account of *The Development of American Political Science* (1967), it might well have seemed that a single book was indeed a sufficient vehicle for encompassing the subject. Today, as one recent writer has suggested, it may be that 'no sane person . . . could possess the patience or sustain the inclination to write a "complete" history of political science' (Seidelman 1985, xix). An entire book could be devoted to exploring the methodological issues involved, and the literature has expanded to the point where research must be framed in terms of the particular problems addressed, the perspectives employed, the substantive themes explored, and the periods studied.

Until World War Two, the discipline of political science was, for the most part, committed to the fact and value of the complementary progress of science and democracy. To the extent that it reflected on its history, it was largely to tell a story of what had been accomplished and how much more must be done to achieve a scientific understanding of politics that could contribute to the development of liberal democracy. History was primarily either a celebration of the present or a justification for some prospective path. With the advent of the behavioural revolution, historical discussions still largely continued to serve the functions of criticism and apology as behaviouralists and anti-behaviouralists advanced accounts of the development of the discipline which legitimated their respective positions.

Although current research is still mortgaged by the terms of the old debate, the post-behavioural era has engendered an atmosphere in which the project of a more authentic historical account of the field could at least be contemplated. The differentiation of the discipline has encouraged more internal reflection on various elements of the field (for example Finifter 1983) and their place in the discipline as a whole. Historical study has become acceptable and popular, because mainstream political science has become more secure in its identity and thus more willing to eschew rhetorical history. And in the case of the cognitive dissidents within the field, the popularity of deconstructionism, hermeneutics, and other post-modernist philosophical approaches has legitimized history and narrative as a mode of critique. By the late 1980s, it would not be an exaggeration to suggest that the history of political science is on the threshold of becoming a distinct research specialty.

To talk about studies in the 'history' of political science prior to the behavioural movement requires putting the subject in quotation marks. There simply was no such genre. Although many early studies in the history of political theory were presented or understood as accounts of the development of political science (for example Pollock 1890; Dunning 1902, 1905, 1920; Murray 1925), the sense of disciplinary optimism did not encourage critical historical reflection. When it did occur, it was in the service of furthering some particular research programme as in the case of Merriam's survey of 'Recent Tendencies in Political Thought' (chapter in Merriam and Barnes 1924) and his well-known (1925) account of the four-stage development of the field, culminating in the psychological treatment of politics.

The first systematic study of an aspect of the history of the discipline was Anna Haddow's still very useful survey of *Political Science in American Colleges and Universities 1636-1900* (Haddow 1939). But apart from certain isolated and specialized works such as Bernard Brown's study of Lieber and Burgess (Brown 1951), there is little, before Crick's book, that can be distinctly identified as a history of political science. The controversy over behaviouralism, however, with the attending images of its decline and regeneration, produced a kind of literature which had a significant impact on reflection about the history of the field — at least in that it focused attention on the past. The medium was historical even if the historicity of the message could be questioned.

Beginning as early as the 1940s, a number of political theorists, often emigré scholars, began to challenge the dominant American vision of a science of politics, but there was also a growing concern within the mainstream about the failure of traditional studies to realize — theoretically, practically, and reputationally — the scientific and liberal democratic promise of the field. This concern was evident in early claims associated with the behavioural revolution such as David Easton's historical overview of the field and his account of its deficiencies and possibilities (1953). And the behavioural arguments were countered by numerous attacks on the idea of a scientific study of politics as well as by less than favourable references to the pedigree of the discipline and the legitimacy of the modern age in general (for example Voegelin 1952; Arendt 1958; Strauss 1959, 1962; Morgenthau 1955).

By the early 1960s, behaviouralists had declared victory and were assessing the development of political science from that standpoint (for example Dahl 1961; Kirkpatrick 1962; Irish 1968; Eulau 1969). In a series of American Political Science Association presidential addresses during this decade, the cumulative progress of the discipline was proclaimed, often in the increasingly popular terms of Thomas Kuhn's theory of scientific revolutions (Redford 1961; Truman 1965; Almond 1966). By the late 1960s, the view of behaviouralism was less sanguine — even on the part of some of its strongest advocates.

Easton, for example, had scarcely finished an account of the development of the discipline that culminated in the successes of the behavioural movement (Easton 1968) when, in this era of volatility, both in the discipline and its context, he found it necessary to describe, and prescribe, a 'new revolution' in political science (Easton 1969). As the post-behavioural era was ushered in, new images of the evolution of the discipline would begin to emerge as political scientists struggled to keep ahead of their past.

Although these synoptic accounts served to keep political scientists concerned about their history, they also tended to obviate a careful investigation of the past. These accounts were the essence of history as rhetoric and were designed to support particular claims about the state of the discipline and its preferred future direction. They deserve attention primarily as events in the history of political science and as examples of the uses, and abuses, of history in disciplinary debates. But even within this context, there was the beginning of historical studies of a more comprehensive and autonomous character.

Crick's work has profoundly affected, structurally and thematically, thinking about the history of American political science. Although Crick expressly demurred with respect to writing a comprehensive history of the discipline and profession of political science, the book was the closest approximation that would be available for nearly a decade, and it forced its readers to come to grips with many of those obscure names already hardly known or remembered by either faculty or graduate students.

Originally offered as a doctoral dissertation for the London School of Economics and largely conceived and drafted while visiting the political science department at the University of California at Berkeley, the work looked backward from the early years of the behavioural movement and the end of the Cold War. The purpose was to demonstrate the degree to which the idea of a scientific study of politics was a uniquely American invention which, from its earliest beginnings in citizenship training to the methodological claims characteristic of behaviouralism, must be understood in the context of the tradition of American liberalism which it both reflected and reinforced. Despite its pretensions to an objective value-free study of politics, American political science, Crick maintained, manifested 'strong assertions of political doctrine' and presuppositions of an 'intense democratic moralism' (Crick 1959: v, vi) which made it more an example of American political thought than a science.

There is no doubt that Crick was less than sympathetic to the philosophical assumptions that had informed the dominant ideas about science in the American discipline, but he was more concerned to point out what he believed was the often paradoxical relationship between the commitments to science and democracy especially in the case of Merriam and the Chicago school. The belief in social control eventuated in what Crick suggested was the 'direct totalitarian implication in Lasswell's manner of thought', and it reflected 'a deeper derangement in the wider thought of American liberalism' that 'confused science with technology'. This, Crick argued, was 'profoundly at odds with almost all that is best in American political experience and expression' and threatened the very realm of politics itself (Crick 1959: 208-9, 233-4).

If Crick's work was history, it was history in the service of polemic, and he looked briefly but sympathetically at the moralistic critiques of political science by individuals like Leo Strauss. Crick was probably too close to the events of the early 1950s and the emergence of behaviouralism to gain much perspective on the period, and there can be little doubt that he was influenced by claims about the orthodoxy of liberalism in America that had been advanced by writers such as Louis Hartz and Daniel Boorstin. The book as a whole was the product of a rapidly ingested and digested corpus of material, and it was self-consciously offered as a kind of neo-Tocquevillean critique of the idea of a science of politics against a background of concern about contemporary liberalism and its problems.

An obscure study that has received relatively little attention, but deserves more, is Albert Lepawsky's monograph on 'The politics of epistemology' (Lepawsky 1964). Once more the Berkeley context, which was a microcosm of conflicts of the day, might be noted given the kind of concern reflected in the study. Much as is the case with Crick, the initiating premise was clearly derived from the intellectual climate created by the debate about behaviouralism. In Lepawsky's terms, it was the conflict between the growing hegemony of 'devout political scientists' seeking a science of 'universal validity' and those 'more sceptical' members of the profession who 'suspect that the criteria and methods of their discipline, and even its intrinsic content, are shaped by the values and politics of the culture in which they operate' (Lepawsky 1964:21).

Lepawsky wished to pursue the approach of the sociology of knowledge and explore the 'reciprocity between politics and epistemology', by which he meant political concerns as opposed to concerns about political knowledge. Following to some extent Haddow's classification, he suggested that there were five basic periods in the history of the discipline. The crucial break, however, occurred with the establishment of the American Political Science Association, (1903) which indicated that political science was 'clearly recognized as a distinct scientific discipline'. Lepawsky's initial project (a second was planned) was limited largely to an analysis of the first era when 'political science was somewhat more noticeably influenced by the politics of the day'. The twentieth century, on the other hand, was marked by 'the dominance of the epistemological influence over the political circumstances — when the "politics of epistemology" prevailed over the "epistemology of politics"'. And Lepawsky asked the reader to keep in mind the question of whether the discipline was 'more productive' before or after it became a 'science' (Lepawsky 1964:22,23).

This essay is important in several respects. Although limited in scope, it was the most careful and detailed piece of research on the general intellectual history of the discipline that had appeared. And it raised, much in advance of later research, the important questions of the impact of professionalism and specialization on the discipline and of its relationship to politics.

Although the story told by Somit and Tanenhaus was very much, at least structurally, a tale of the 'rise' of the profession and the evolution of political science, from its earliest American origins to behaviouralism, it was, despite some characterizations to the contrary, far from a historical apology. The authors were of somewhat different minds about behaviouralism, and although hardly a critique, it was not a celebration. It was, however, very much a discussion in which the authors decided to limit their 'attention to those aspects of the past which bear directly on the present state of the discipline'. The project had begun as a prospective textbook chapter, but the subject increasingly seemed too difficult to encompass within that scope. They did not pretend to be historians, and their intention was not to offer 'a full-blown history of political science' or even a 'short survey' of such a history but rather an overview of how political scientists have defined their professional responsibilities and goals and viewed the scope and method of their enterprise (Somit and Tanenhaus 1967:1).

The authors were probably too self-effacing. They produced something that was more than a short systematic account of the development of the discipline and profession. It provided a good deal of useful information for a field that, in general, was vague about its past. The study was divided between the pre-history of the field (up until 1880), 1880-1903, 1903-21, 1921-45, and 1945 to the present. And the second edition (1982) provided a short epilogue covering 1965-80. Again, the focus on behaviouralism was evident, and it was designated as 'the paramount development in the discipline's entire intellectual history' (Somit and Tanenhaus 1982:173).

Despite the discipline's cycles of enchantment with the 'idea' of a scientific study of politics', they suggested that behaviouralism could be treated, at least metaphorically, in Kuhnian terms, 'as an attempt to move political science from a pre-paradigmatic (or literally non-scientific) condition to a paradigmatic stage' (173, 175, 205). They believed that, as they wrote, behaviouralism was not yet a 'predominant paradigm', and they predicted, probably quite accurately, that although the discipline would become 'more behavioural in tempo', its '"scientistic aspirations" would become more modest' (Somit and Tanenhaus 1982: 208, 210).

Another useful and accessible monograph was Dwight Waldo's 'Political science: tradition, discipline, profession, science, enterprise' (Waldo 1975). This was not the longest but probably the most comprehensive and balanced discussion that had appeared. Waldo had long been a scholar of the field and its history (see his 1956 study) as well as a participant in some of the transformational debates. This 'attempt at ecumenicism' (1975:3) followed the struggle over behaviouralism and traced the idea of a science of politics from ancient Greece through the travails of the American field and the days of the New Caucus. Waldo emphasized the need to distinguish between different internal dimensions of the field, such as profession and discipline, as well as to locate its development within relevant historical contexts.

It would be nearly a decade before a new wave of historical concern about the discipline would appear. This wave was linked to such factors as the reflective and eclectic atmosphere of the post-behavioural era; the increasing awareness of work in the history of both the natural and social sciences; and the impact of certain developments in the study of intellectual history. But before turning to this literature, it is worthwhile saying something about methodological issues with respect to the earlier work.

What constitutes proper historical analysis is indeed, and deservedly, a contentious issue, but no matter how one might choose to define it, a case can be made, without taking an unduly puritanical stance, that much of the literature that had appeared by the mid-1970s was historical primarily in the broad sense that it talked about the past. It was not simply that it largely reflected what Michael Oakeshott (1962) has termed a 'practical' (as opposed to a 'historical') attitude where the principal concern was in effect largely to say something about the present. It did not pose for itself, at least in any apparently articulate way, such questions as what kind of phenomena (both empirically and theoretically considered) it was looking at; what criteria are appropriate for judging a historical account; what kind of explanation was being advanced; and what was the relationship between disciplinary history and the practice of a discipline.

My argument is neither that later studies would always, or ever, deal adequately with such issues nor that these earlier studies should have dealt with them. Many of the earlier studies, even to some extent those of Crick and Somit and Tanenhaus, could not, even by their own lights, be defined in any differentiated sense as historical. They were too tightly immeshed in the 'politics of epistemology'. What distinguishes later studies is not that they would extricate themselves from these disciplinary debates but rather that they faced the burden of dealing with the problem of an increased consciousness of the difference between history and instrumental narrative.

Whatever judgmental stance and critical approach that subsequent work might assume, innocence of the difference between the language of political science, and language about the history of political science, had been lost. Where political science and historical accounts of the discipline represent, at least in principle, two different modes of discourse, questions of the integrity of the latter and its relationship to the former cannot be avoided. This is not to suggest that the two can in practice be neatly compartmentalized but, quite the opposite, that to speak of relationship implies a distinction. This is an issue which other social sciences had confronted somewhat earlier.

In the first volume (1965) of the *Journal of the History of Behavioural Sciences*, George Stocking wrote an editorial 'On the limits of "presentism" and "Historicism" in the historiography of the behavioural sciences' which sought to raise certain 'questions of motive and method'. Although noting the varieties and vagaries of historical study, he stressed that, after all, 'history remains a discipline of sorts' (211) and its practice requires reflection. In the case of the subject matter of the social sciences, the choice between the (admittedly overdrawn) poles of presentism (the study of the past for the sake of the present — what Herbert Butterfield (Butterfield 1931) had dubbed 'Whig history') — and historicism (the study of the past for the sake of the past) was particularly salient.

Although, as in the case of Oakeshott's distinction between the 'practical' and 'historical' attitude, the issues in practice could never be posed so starkly, there was an analytical distinction and a difference in distribution of emphasis. Was it possible to study the history of social science from a perspective that was not primarily informed by 'normative commitment' and a partisan concern but rather a concern, at least in the first instance, with understanding the past on its own terms? For Stocking, these ideal typical attitudes broke somewhat along disciplinary lines. He suggested that since presentism was 'virtually built into . . . the history of the behavioural sciences', the professional behavioural scientist was likely to be Whiggish.

Stocking, however, was not pushing for some absolutist position, and he recognized that the perspective of the social scientist, who was interested in achieving generalized knowledge as well as involved with contemporary social issues, would always have a somewhat presentist viewpoint. He was simply urging a more 'enlightened' perspective and a realization of the need to throw off the assumption of cumulative progress which, despite the work of Kuhn and others, still governed the social scientist's vision of history. He suggested that because social science was still largely pre-paradigmatic, its 'historiography is more open to certain vices of presentism'. The manifold 'sins of history written "for the sake of the present" insinuate themselves' (Stocking 1965:215) and must to some degree be repressed if we are to achieve a realistic understanding of the history of these disciplines — even for present purposes.

A great deal of metatheoretical discussion of these matters, both in general and with respect to the intellectual history of the social sciences, has taken place since Stocking's article was published, but the definition of the fundamental problem has changed little. And it is a problem to keep in mind as we consider the recent work of political scientists writing about the history of their discipline. The latter surely have not cast off the bonds of presentism even when the concern has hardly been to celebrate the progress of the field.

Before turning to these studies, it is instructive to consider one recent historical investigation that was informed by a distinct wish to avoid the practical attitude toward history and to reject writing history backward as a teleology in support of a present value. This is the exploration of nineteenth century English political science in *That Noble Science of Politics* (1983) by Stefan Collini, Donald Winch, and John Burrow.

It has been claimed, with some justification, that 'contextualization is the strongest feature in the area of the history of ideas that has made the strongest progress during the last decade: the history of political thought' (Darnton 1980). It might, however, be more accurate to say that during the 1970s, the study of the history of political thought was profoundly influenced by a neo-contextualist and neo-historicist approach in the history of ideas (Boucher 1985; Condren 1985). But there can be no doubt that the methodological claims, as well as the substantive research, associated with the 'new history of political theory' and represented by the work of individuals such as Quentin Skinner (Skinner 1969, 1978) and J.G.A. Pocock (Pocock 1971, 1975) has begun to exercise a significant influence outside its original sphere of discussion. The history of sociological theory is a case in point (Seidman et al 1985; Seidman, Merton, and Jones 1985; Jones 1977). It is somewhat ironic that this work, which has been closely tied to the field of political science, has had the least effect in writing about the history of this discipline.

The claims associated with the 'new historicism' have been appealing for those who, in theory and practice, have, for various reasons, been anxious about presentism. It has offered a new and stronger epistemological grounding for the notion that historical investigation and interpretation could and should reject an understanding of the past from the perspective of present values. And it tends, at least ostensibly, to complement the efforts of sociologists of knowledge who often find it 'unexceptionable' (Kuklick 1983:296). The aim is to recover the meaning of texts by understanding the intentions of the authors in terms of the context in which they wrote. The methodological claims have been the subject of extensive controversy and commentary, but *That Noble Science of Politics* is a deliberate attempt to approach the history of the science of politics in terms of these premises.

The book is not, strictly speaking, a disciplinary history but rather a series of essays on prominent aspects of, and figures involved with, the nineteenth century British pursuit of a science of politics. It aims, quite successfully for a work of less than one piece, at reconstructing this segment of intellectual history and sorting out the entwined political and methodological motives that informed this vision of a comparative political/historical science. It is significant in its own right, and it aids in illuminating contemporaneous, similar, and sometimes intellectually related developments in American political science.

Although this work is pointedly methodologically self-conscious, it implicitly raises unanswered questions with respect to the relationship between a philosophical argument about historical understanding and the practice of inquiry. And although the particular historical subject is well specified, the subject of history (ideas, events, texts, discourse) is more ambiguous. Finally, it is tempting to ask if the authors do not protest too strongly with respect to the lack of presentist purpose. This is a complicated issue, but the passionate attack of the new historicism on the distortions of presentism involves more than merely an academic dedication to objectivity and historical purity. Part of the concern has been the particular philosophical and ideological positions of those who have most often written presentist history — such as the Marxists.

Two recent studies of the history of American political science are, in purpose and execution, very different from *That Noble Science. The Tragedy of Political Science: Politics, Scholarship, and Democracy* (1984) by David Ricci and *Disenchanted Realists: Political Science and the American Crisis* (1985) by Raymond Seidelman (with the assistance of Edward J Harpham) are important and controversial books which have already done much to galvanize a renewed concern about the history of political science. They have been widely discussed and reviewed, but my concern is less with the substance of their claims than with the historiographical issues that are raised by their projects. Given the level of contemporary discussion about historical interpretation, and even the history of the social sciences, both books are strikingly methodologically unreflective. But to label them as presentist and practical would not be to categorize them in other than a self-ascribed manner.

These works are thematically quite similar even though structurally different. They both deal with the issue of the relationship between political science and politics or, more specifically, with the relationship between the discipline's scientific pretensions and its attachment to American liberal democratic culture as well as the tension between its scientific and political commitments. Although they participate in an agenda that had been set by Crick and contemporary debates about liberalism, the issues may be inherent in the structure of the discourse of American political science. What is more problematical is the manner in which they emplot the story that they tell. Although, as Hayden White (White 1973, 1987) has so forcefully pointed out, we may in the end find it impossible to discern the epistemological boundary between historical and fictional discourse, it is clear that both of these works gain much of their force from narrative structures that are more imposed than discovered.

Ricci's approach is still rooted in the now somewhat primitive terms of the 1960s controversy between behaviouralism and the study of the history of political theory. He posits a fundamental break between the 'great tradition' from Plato to Marx and modern political science and then attempts to give a historical explanation of that very unhistorical 'fact'. Relying on the recent literature on the rise of professionalism and the place of the modern university in this process, Ricci suggests that it is more than a coincidence that 'the line of the first-rate thinkers in the Western tradition came to an end' with the appearance, in the late nineteenth century, of university-based professional social science and its emphasis on 'a scientific approach to natural and social affairs'. He claims that the 'old tradition of political thought' and the 'aggregate wisdom of the ages' was replaced by the narrow learning of modern political science (Ricci 1984: ix,x) — which hopefully might be mitigated by the academic revival of political theory in recent years.

There can be little quarrel with Ricci's presumption that contemporary political science can and does play a significant role in political education, and there are many grounds for criticizing both its form and content as well as how well it performs this role. But the general plot that informs Ricci's story, that is, the replacement of an old wisdom by a sterile new science, is neither one that he attempts to sustain evidentially nor one that could be so sustained. It is in fact an argument that is less a historical account of political science than one that has been part of the history of the discipline and has been most characteristically associated with the claims of individuals such as Sheldon Wolin (Wolin 1969) and Strauss.

What might be considered the sub-plot, which is actually the principal focus of the work, the tragedy of political science, revolves around a claim very much like that of Crick with respect to the interpenetration of political science and American liberalism. The argument is certainly more historical in that it points up a problem that few observers or participants would deny has shaped the discursive universe of American political science, but now Ricci's explanation of this historical fact is quite unhistorical.

Ricci specifies the fact well in saying that 'the discipline is committed to two ends which, from time to time, turn out to be incompatible' — 'the study of public life in scientific fashion' and 'devotion to democratic politics. . . . It is between these two commitments of the discipline — acceptance of scientific techniques and attachment to democratic ideals — that trouble begins' (Ricci 1984: 23, 24). He emplots the story of the development of the discipline, quite literally, as a tragic tale with the protoganist's flaw in its 'stubborn insistence on studying politics scientifically, even though inquiry in that mode cannot insure the health of a democratic society' (25). This is not an unappealing and unrevealing rhetorical strategy in support of a long-standing complaint within the field, but it also keeps us a bit at arm's length from the actual history of political science and the dynamics of its internal conceptual development.

Although Ricci's book brings together much relevant information and argument and may provide the most comprehensive critical overview of the history of the discipline that we possess, it is difficult to specify exactly what could be construed as new in terms of either argument or information. Finally, although thematically well unified, the book is topically diverse and loosely structured. Some attempts to explain intellectual influence, such as the extended analysis of the assumptions of behaviouralism in terms of the philosophy of Karl Popper (which is in fact directly in conflict with some of the most basic of those assumptions) while declining a concern with any actual 'intellectual pedigree' (Ricci 1984:115) is at best odd.

Seidelman provides us with concise and compelling intellectual portraits of some of those oft forgotten 'uncles' of political science such as Bentley, Beard, Merriam, and Lasswell (and grandfathers such as Lester Frank Ward and Woodrow Wilson) as well as of those who he suggests are their most legitimate progeny — V.O. Key, Theodore Lowi, and Walter Dean Burnham. Although Seidelman does not use the term 'tragedy', the plot is not unlike that of Ricci's work, and attempting to assess the arguments as history presents many of the same problems.

Seidelman's claim is that running through the history of professional political science is a 'tradition' of liberal scientific realism which has nevertheless represented a disenchantment with conventional liberal politics. These individuals have constituted 'a consistent and critical perspective' which he dubs a 'third tradition' (in addition to 'institutionalist' and 'radical democratic') which has 'blended scholarship and political advocacy' and viewed 'political science as a non-revolutionary alternative to outdated ideologies and practices'. Seidelman suggests that this is a paradoxical tradition which 'embodies impossible contradictions and tensions'. Not the least of these is an attempt to fuse commitments to science, political reform, and professionalism (Seidelman 1985:2,12-13).

Academic professionalism, Seidelman argues, has obscured deep structural problems in the American liberal tradition, and the democratic aspirations of political scientists 'have always excluded and feared a future beyond liberalism' (241). Seidelman is not very specific about the content of that future, but he argues that, today, the third tradition has, in any event, petered out. Its peculiarly American vision of political science with its commitment to achieving social harmony through scientific state-building has, after generations of disenchantment, finally lost its impetus as political science and political reality go their separate ways.

While the individuals whom Seidelman discusses are, for the most part, distinctly situated within the actual historical tradition of American political science, the 'traditions' that he discusses are retrospective and analytical constructs. But even according to Seidelman's criteria, the members of the third tradition, which in many respects seems to represent mainstream political science, appear somewhat arbitrarily selected. Why not Easton or Robert Dahl, for example? Some of those discussed never pursued political reform, except mentally, and exactly how Ward and Bentley belong to the history of political science is not entirely clear. But the book does not claim to be a history of political science in any strict sense, and its rhetorical and ideological means and ends are not submerged.

Like Ricci's book, it is less a history of political science than a characterization and judgment of that history. The critical perspective on liberalism informed, and certainly preceded, any historical discovery, and historical research is selectively appropriated to support the case advanced. Although Seidelman, more so than Ricci, gets inside the texts and the discourse of American political science, the successive constructions of dual portraits representing periods (Progressivism, New Deal, behaviouralism, etc.) in the development of the field does not recover much sense of the diachronic dimension of the discourse and its internal development.

Although Seidelman does not put so much emphasis as Ricci on the tension between professionalism and political commitment, he is more successful in drawing out the dimensions of the intrinsic paradox involved in political science's journey from a reform movement to an establishment science. Political science sought scientific status within the university to legitimate and give authority to its challenge to political authority, but once separated from politics it faced the question of how to articulate public and academic discourse. Seidelman is sensitive to the manner in which political scientists struggled with this dilemma and looks carefully at the various strategies they adopted, albeit unsuccessfully, in seeking a solution.

After Ricci and Seidelman, the question of what writing the history of political science is all about, and how and why to conduct it, cannot be avoided. There are also other works that should be noted. A compendium on *Political Science: The State of the Discipline* (Finifter, ed., 1983) contains some historical and semi-historical essays. There is a specialized study of theory-change in political science (Janos 1986), and two collections of comparative studies in the history of political science contain essays on the history of American political science (Anckar and Berndtson 1987, 1988).

Although the history of political science is an essential aspect of critical reflection on the discipline, we have reached a point where we must also be self-conscious about both the form and content of historical claims. If such studies are to be a continuing endeavour and more than adjuncts to disciplinary disputes, it is necessary to give more systematic consideration to what should be done in the light of issues peculiar to this field as well as those relating to the broader realm of intellectual history and the history of the social sciences. Although the scope of this essay does not permit any comprehensive consideration of these complex theoretical and methodological problems, I want to make a plea for what I will call 'internalist' history and then to say something about the general relationship between history and criticism.

The arguments of Ricci and Seidelman relied heavily, both thematically and evidentially but often unreflectively and instrumentally, on a recent body of historical literature dealing with professionalism, the university, and the development of the social sciences in the United States during the late nineteenth century. Some of these works include Mary O. Furner, *Advocacy and Objectivity* (1975); Burton J. Bledstein, *The Culture of Professionalism: The Middle Class and the Development of Higher Education in America* (1976); Thomas L. Haskell, *The Emergence of Professional Social Science: the American Social Science Association and the Nineteenth Century Crisis of Authority* (1977); A. Oleson and J. Voss, eds, *The Organization of Knowledge in Modern America* (1979), and especially the essay by Dorothy Ross, 'The development of the social sciences'; and John Higham and Paul Conkin, eds, *New Directions in American Intellectual History* (1979). Much of this work was, in turn, influenced by earlier historical research on the rise of the middle-class, Progressivism, and the transformation in social authority during this period — maybe most notably, Robert Wiebe's *The Search for Order* (1967).

Works such as those of Furner and Haskell represent some of the best research available in the history of the social sciences, and they have opened up a window on the past of these disciplines that no one can ignore. Furthermore, they both focus on an issue that has been central to much of the work on the history of political science — and which may very well be the most significant dialectical element in the evolution of the field. This, broadly framed, might be understood as the problem of the relationship between political and academic discourse. As another recent work has suggested (Jacoby 1987), there may be good reason to argue that the American university and academic professionalism have contributed to a debilitation of intellectual and political life.

Ricci and Seidelman, however, tended to accept this literature quite uncritically, both methodologically and substantively, as setting an explanatory context for their claims about the history of political science. There are at least two problems involved in their reliance on this material. First, ironically, much of this work represents an attempt to extricate the history of social science from the genre of disciplinary presentism in which the Ricci and Seidelman books must ultimately be located. Second, it is not without its own problems as a model and resource for the study of the history of political science.

These books represent one aspect of the new wave of historicism and its emphasis on contextualist or externalist histories. First, they in part approach a certain subject matter and set of ideas and events, which might be relatively uncontentiously designated as the professionalization of early social science, in terms of certain models or constructs drawn from sociology. In the case of Furner, a sort of Weberian image of specialization and rationalization is used to explain the retreat of social science from political advocacy. For Haskell, the values of the old amateur social science were not functionally suited to the changing social conditions and capable of responding to a late nineteenth century 'crisis of authority'. Second, they posit general and somewhat abstractly conceived historical and social contexts (for example crisis of authority) that derive from other secondary historical accounts of the period — such as that of Wiebe (which in turn relied on sociological models and other secondary historical literature).

By the time that we reach a book such as Ricci's, this evolving historio-sociological story of the rise of the middle-class, the emergence of a distinct academic culture, and the development of professionalism has become an explanatory context which, in substance and method, has largely escaped critical scrutiny. What gets short shrift are details of the structure and content of the discourse of disciplines and their actual context. Haskell is looking for a deeper explanation than Furner advances. He does not want to see the issue as simply the retreat of radical politics in the face of conservatism and other threats to the increasingly comfortable sinecure of the ivory tower. But in distancing the explanation from the details of disciplinary practice, and the politics in and of the university, historical understanding may suffer.

It is time that we pull back from Lamarckian contextualism and inject a little Mendelian thinking into our investigations. I would suggest approaching the history of political science as the evolution of a discursive practice and conceiving of such an investigation as something on the order of a genealogy or archaeology of its internal conceptual development. While this requires taking account of relevant contexts and the perception of those contexts, digging into the past of political science involves excavating an evolving population of conventional, propositional, and conceptual artifacts which reveal themselves in a more or less stratified manner despite the transformational connections.

The history of political science is, at least in one important sense, the history of the internal evolution of arguments within the discipline. It is the details of this dialectical process that demand more attention. Although it is important to be sensitive to 'ecological' influences, not even in modern theories of biological evolution do investigators attempt to read off development against a determinative environment. It is the genetic capacities of past forms that are traced, and contexts play an important but ultimately random role.

'Context' is best conceived as a generic term for referring to a particular complex of contingent factors that emerge as relevant and concretely connected to a particular explanatory problem. While attention to general historical contexts is important, it is necessary to avoid positing contexts that are little more than reified sociological constructs and/or rapidly extrapolated and unexamined images from secondary literature that are no more knowable or given than what they purport to explain. Such external history often fails to establish concrete connections between such putative contexts and the object of investigation. It tends to assume that explanation is a matter of juxtaposition.

My last observation is that the historical investigation of political science, even with a critical or practical purpose, might think about setting aside rhetorically informed emplotment, or at least seek the plots intrinsic to the evolution of disciplinary practices. We may be too philosophically sophisticated to believe that there are any neutral narratives or that the historical attitude can be methodologically vouchsafed, but we are also too sophisticated to fail to distinguish between a historical and instrumental approach to the past. There is a certain inherent paradox in rhetorical history aimed at a primarily academic audience. It may confirm the views of those already committed to the message or irritate those who reject it, but in this reflective context, it is neither likely to persuade opponents nor convince those who examine it in terms of critical historical criteria.

The issue of the relationship of the study of the history of political science to the contemporary practice of political science is indeed complex (see Dryzek and Leonard 1988), but as Orwell and Arendt have suggested, there is something to be said for the idea that descriptive history and faithful genealogies, particularly when they emphasize the conventional and therefore the ephemeral, decisionist, and reversible character of social practices, can carry a persuasive force. The search for historical realism may be more effective than rhetorical fiction, and the historical attitude can serve a presentist purpose. There may be a lesson here for the history of political science which has for too long been overwhelmed by the plots of progress and decline.

NOTE

This is a revision of a paper presented at Cortona, Italy, September 1987.

REFERENCES

Almond, Gabriel (1966) 'Political theory and political science', *American Political Science Review* 60:869-79.

Anckar, Dag and Berndtson, Erkki (1987) 'The evolution of political science: selected case studies', *International Political Science Review* 8.

—— (1988) *Political Science: Between Past and Future*, Finnish Political Science Association.

Arendt, Hannah (1958) *The Human Condition*, New York: Doubleday.

Barnes, Harry E. *et al.* (1925) *The History and Prospects of the Social Sciences*, New York: Knopf.

Berndtson, Erkki (1987) 'The rise and fall of American political science', in D. Anckar and E. Berndtson (eds) *International Political Science Review* 8.

Bledstein, Burton J. (1976) *The Culture of Professionalism: The Middle Class and the Development of Higher Education in America*, New York: Norton.

Boucher, David (1985) *Texts in Context: Revisionist Methods for Studying the History of Political Theory*, Dordrecht, Netherlands: Martinus Nijhoff.

Brown, Bernard, (1951) *American Conservatives: The Political Thought of Francis Lieber and John W Burgess*, New York: Columbia University Press.

Burgess, John W. (1882) 'The study of political science at Columbia College', *International Review* 12:346-67.

— (1934) *Reminisences of an American Scholar*, New York: Columbia University Press.

Butterfield, Herbert (1931) *The Whig Interpretation of History*, New York: Penguin.

Collini, Stefan, Winch, Donald, and Burrow, John, (1983) *That Noble Science of Politics*, Cambridge: Cambridge University Press.

Condren, Conal, (1985) *The Status and Appraisal of Classic Texts*, Princeton, N.J.: Princeton University Press.

Crick, Bernard (1959) *The American Science of Politics: Its Origins and Conditions*, Berkeley: University of California Press.

Dahl, Robert, (1961) 'The behavioural approach in political science: epitaph for a monument to a successful protest', *American Political Science Review* 55:763-72.

Darnton, Robert, (1980) 'Intellectual and Cultural History', in Michael Kanmen, (ed.) *The Past Before Us: Contemporary Historical Writing in the United States*, Ithaca, N.Y.: Cornell University Press.

Diggins, John Patrick (1984) 'The oyster and the pearl: the problem of contextualism in intellectual history', *History and Theory* 23:151-69.

Dryzek, John and Leonard, Stephen (1988) 'History and discipline in political science', *American Political Science Review* 82:1245-60.

Dunning, William, (1902, 1905, 1920) *A History of Political Theories*, 3 vols, New York: Macmillan.

Easton, David (1953) *The Political System: An Inquiry into the State of Political Science*, New York: Knopf.

— (1968) 'Political science', in David Sills (ed.) *International Encyclopedia of the Social Sciences*, vol. 12, New York: Crowell Collier and Macmillan.

— (1969) 'The new revolution in political science', *American Political Science Review* 68:1051-61.

— (1985) 'Political science in the United States: past and present', *International Political Science Review* 6:133-52.

Eulau, Heinz (1969) 'Tradition and innovation: on the tension between ancient and modern ways in the study of politics', in Eulau (ed.) *Behavioralism in Political Science*, New York: Atherton.

Finifter, Ada (ed.) (1983) *Political Science: The State of the Discipline*, Washington, D.C.: American Political Science Association.

Furner, Mary O. (1975) *Advocacy and Objectivity: A Crisis in the Professionalization of American Social Science, 1865-1905*, Lexington Ky: University of Kentucky Press.

Graham, George and Carey, George, (eds) (1972) *The Post-Behavioral Era: Perspectives on Political Science*, New York: McCay.

Haddow, Anna (1939) *Political Science in American Colleges and Universities, 1636-1900*, New York: Appleton-Century.

Haskell, Thomas L. (1977) *The Emergence of Professional Social Science: The American Social Science Association and the Nineteenth Century Crisis of Authority*, Urbana, Ill.: University of Illinois Press.

Higham, John and Conkin, Paul, (eds) (1979) *New Directions in American Intellectual*

History, Baltimore, MD: Johns Hopkins University Press.

Hoxie, Ralph Gordon et al (1955) *A History of the Faculty of Political Science, Columbia University*, New York: Columbia University Press.

Irish, Marion, (ed.) (1968) *Political Science: The Advance of a Discipline*, Englewood Cliffs, N.J.: Prentice-Hall.

Jacoby, Russell (1987) *The Last Intellectuals*, New York: Basic Books.

Janos, Andrew C. (1986) *Politics and Paradigms: Changing Theories of Change in Social Science*, Stanford, CA: Stanford University Press.

Jones, Robert Alun (1977) 'On understanding a sociological classic' *American Journal of Sociology* 83:279-319.

Kirkpatrick, Evron (1962) 'The impact of the behavioral movement in traditional political science', in Austin Ranney (ed.) *Essays in the Behavioral Study of Politics*, Urbana, Ill.: University of Illionois Press.

Kuhn, Thomas S. (1962) *The Structure of Scientific Revolutions*, Chicago: University of Chicago Press.

Kuklick, Henrika (1980) 'Restructuring the past: toward an appreciation of the social context of social science', *Sociological Quarterly* 21:5-21.

Lasswell, Harold and Kaplan, Abraham (1950) *Power and Society*, New Haven, CT: Yale University Press.

Lepawsky, Albert (1964) 'The politics of epistemology', *Western Political Quarterly*, supp.: 21-52.

Merriam, Charles (1925) *New Aspects of Politics*, Chicago: University of Chicago Press.

Merriam, Charles and Barnes, Harry Elmer (1924) *A History of Political Theories: Recent Times*, New York: Macmillan.

Morgenthau, Hans (1955) 'Reflections on the state of political science', *Review of Politics* 17:431-60.

Murray, Robert H. (1925) *The History of Political Science from Plato to the Present*, New York: Appleton.

Oakeshott, Michael (1962) *Rationalism in Politics*, London: Methuen.

Oleson, Alexandra and Voss, John (eds) (1979) *The Organization of Knowledge in Modern America, 1860-1920*, Baltimore, MD: Johns Hopkins University Press.

Pocock, J.G.A. (1971) *Politics, Language, and Time: Essays in Political Thought and History*, New York: Atheneum.

—- (1975) *The Machiavellian Moment*, Princeton, N.J.: Princeton University Press.

Pollock, Frederick (1890) *An Introduction to the History of the Science of Politics*, London: Macmillan.

Poschman, Gene (1982) 'Emerging social science and political relevance: some extractions from a less than classic literature', Paper presented at the Annual Meeting of the American Political Science Association, Denver, Colorado.

Redford, Emmet (1961) 'Reflections on a discipline', *American Political Science Review* 55:755-62.

Ricci, David M. (1984) *The Tragedy of Political Science: Politics, Scholarship, and Democracy*, New Haven, CT: Yale University Press.

Ross, Dorothy (1978) 'Professionalism and the transformation of American social thought', *The Journal of Economic History* 38:494-99.

—- (1979) 'The development of the social sciences', in A. Oleson and J. Voss (eds) *The Origins of Knowledge in Modern America, 1860-1920*, Baltimore, MD: Johns

Hopkins University Press.
— (1984) 'American social science and the idea of progress', in Thomas Haskell (ed.) *The Authority of Experts*, Bloomington, Ind.: Indiana University Press.
Seidelman, Raymond (with the assistance of Edward J. Harpham) (1985) *Disenchanted Realists: Political Science and the American Crisis, 1884-1984*, Albany, N.Y.: State University of New York Press.
Seidman, Steven, (1983) 'Beyond positivism and historicism: understanding the history of social science', *Social Inquiry* 53:179-94.
Seidman, Steven *et al.* (1985) 'The historicist controversy: understanding the sociological past', *Sociological Theory* 3:11-28.
Seidman, Steven, Merton, Robert, and Jones, Robert Alun (1985) 'Debate', *History of Sociology* 6:121-60.
Skinner, Quentin, (1969) 'Meaning and understanding in the history of ideas', *History and Theory* 8:3-35.
— (1978) *The Foundations of Modern Political Thought*, 2 vols, Cambridge: Cambridge University Press.
Somit, Albert and Tanenhaus, Joseph, (1967) *The Development of American Political Science: From Burgess to Behavioralism*, Boston: Allyn and Bacon. Enlarged edition (1982), New York: Irvington.
Stocking, George (1965) 'On the limits of "Presentism" and "Historicism" in the historiography of the behavioral sciences', *Journal of the History of the Behavioral Sciences* 1:211-18.
Strauss, Leo (1959) *What is Political Philosophy?* Glencoe, Ill.: Free Press.
— (1962) 'Epilogue' in Herbert Storing (ed.) *Essays in the Scientific Study of Politics*, New York: Holt, Rinehart, Winston.
Truman, David (1965) 'Disillusion and regeneration: the quest for a discipline', *American Political Science Review* 59:867-73.
— (1967) 'The Implications for political science of the revolution in the behavioral sciences', in Heinz Eulau (ed.) *Behavioralism in Political Science*, Chicago: Atherton.
Voegelin, Eric (1952) *The New Science of Politics*, Chicago: University of Chicago Press.
Waldo, Dwight (1956) *Political Science in the United States of America: A Trend Report*, Paris: UNESCO.
— (1975) 'Political science: tradition, discipline, profession, science, enterprise', in Fred Greenstein and Nelson Polsby. (eds) *Handbook of Political Science*, vol. 1, Reading, MA.: Addison-Wesley.
White, Hayden, (1973) *Metahistory: The Historical Imagination in Nineteenth Century Europe*, Baltimore, MD: Johns Hopkins University Press.
— (1987) *The Content of Form: Narrative Discourse and Historical Representation*, Baltimore, MD: Johns Hopkins University Press.
Wiebe, Robert H. (1967) *The Search for Order, 1877-1920*, New York: Hill and Wang.
Wolin, Sheldon (1969) 'Political theory as a vocation', *American Political Science Review*, 62:1062-82.

2 The development of political science

Methodological problems of comparative research

Erkki Berndtson[1]

PERSPECTIVES ON THE STUDY OF SCIENCE

The new interest in the study of science in the last twenty years has given birth to different perspectives on the development of science. Generally these historical studies can be divided into 'historical writing' and 'theoretical research on history' (Lepenies 1977). The basic difference is that the former looks at history as a continuity and is written in a narrative form; theoretical research in history, on the other hand, tries to reconstruct different stages in history. While the former tries to present history 'as it happened', the latter claims that it is impossible to present everything in writing. However, there are many who have clearly used a narrative form stressing that theirs is only a partial picture and the whole is impossible to attain (e.g. Ricci 1984; Seidelman 1985). In that sense the difference is relative.

Without even trying to construct a definitive list of the approaches in the study of science and their applications to the history of science, one can refer at least to the following:

'Histories'

Most discipline histories come under this heading. Usually they have been written in order to legitimize the present (cf. Lepenies and Weingart 1983), or they are introductory accounts of the history of the discipline (for example, for students, the general public, foreign colleagues) or they are case-studies of 'important' figures in the history of the discipline.

Critical 'histories'

Sometimes these are written in the form of the history of 'losers': for example, the history of forgotten scholars and ideas (eg. Palonen 1978).

Philosophy of science

1 The analyses of the growth of science inspired by Karl Popper (Popper 1968).
2 Anarchistic theory of knowledge (Feyerabend 1975).

Sociology of knowledge inspired by Karl Mannheim

See Mannheim 1960.

Sociology of science

1 The analysis of external and internal factors affecting the development of science (e.g. Merton 1968).
2 Science as a bureaucracy. The classical analysis is William H. Whyte's '*The Organization Man*' (1956:190-223).
3 Science as a market — the foremost representative is Pierre Bourdieu and his analysis of science as a field where scientists try to add to their academic capital (Bourdieu 1979).

Psychology of science

For example Bärmark 1971.

Empirical analyses of science inspired by Thomas Kuhn

Kuhn 1962.

Theory of science

A theory of science which tries to synthesize the philosophical analysis of science with more sociological aspects of reality. Håkan Törnebohm's model of the growth of science is a good example in this category (e.g. Törnebohm 1973).

Politics of science

1 Dominance-models explaining the development of science, for example centre-periphery relations (Galtung 1981).
2 Analyses of science policies and their impact on the development of science (e.g. Andersson 1971); economics of science could also be placed in this category, because in spite of the utmost

importance of economics, it is usually linked to the problems of science policy (or to the sociology of science as an economic factor) (e.g. Elzinga, ed., 1971).

Hermeneutical studies

Studies on science which try to understand the texts on their own terms (e.g. Ricoeur 1981).

British intellectual history

British intellectual history (e.g. Skinner 1969; 1971-2) inspired by the works of R.G. Collingwood, Ludwig Wittgenstein and Peter Winch.

Semiotics

Semiotics of the text which reconstruct the meaning of the text (e.g. Eco 1981).

Archaeology of knowledge

Inspired by the studies of Michel Foucault (Foucault 1973; 1974).

Marxist analyses

Marxist analyses of the history of science, which can also be divided at least into three subcategories:

1 Marxist-Leninist historical materialism, which does not differ much from the traditional sociology of science. The main difference is that historical materialism uses as independent variables class relations and relations of production (e.g. Wiatr 1978).
2 Marxist structuralism explicated above all by Louis Althusser's analysis of the development of Marx's thinking (Althusser 1970), and applied to the analysis of whole disciplines, for example by Göran Therborn (Therborn 1974).
3 Analyses inspired by the capital-logical school of Marxism which often stand near functionalism by trying to give different functions to different existing disciplines (e.g. Nielsen 1975).

Feminist studies of science

For example Lovenduski 1981.

Theoretical treatises

Theoretical treatises which use history to substantiate their arguments (e.g. Parsons 1937).

These approaches may be applied to different aspects of scientific enterprise: disciplinary growth, problem areas, theories, concepts, individual scholars, or they may even try to understand science as a whole. Of course, it is also possible to 'cross-fertilize' these approaches with each other, producing countless species. This being the case, the possibilities for the study of the development of political science seem to be nearly infinite. It is easy to agree with David Ricci that no one has yet invented a way of studying entire disciplines. These studies must always be selective, and the only thing one can do is to select a perspective from which to look at the given discipline (Ricci 1988).

STUDIES ON THE DEVELOPMENT OF POLITICAL SCIENCE

In writing history or doing theoretical research on the development of political science one can be, for example (cf. Heiskanen 1988: 119-20):

— A scholar trying to legitimize the hegemonic paradigm of the discipline
— A researcher trying to convince financiers of the might of political science
— A professor writing an introductory chapter to his/her Introduction to Political Science
— A critic trying to reorient the study of politics
— A student of intellectual history trying to interpret history as well as possible
— A social theorist trying to formulate a theory of politics by reconstructing the historical modes of thinking in society.

The possibilities are many and all have been used by historians of political science. Of the various approaches outlined at the beginning of this chapter, political science has witnessed almost all of them, too. Works representing 'histories' are the largest group also in political science, from *Contemporary Political Science* (UNESCO 1950) to *International Handbook of Political Science* (Andrews, ed. 1982). More thorough works dealing with the history of one country are studies such as Albert Somit and Joseph Tanenhaus's *The Development of Political Science* (1967), Dwight Waldo's essay 'Political science; tradition, discipline, profession, science, enterprise' (1975) or the APSA's collection of articles *Political Science: The State of the Discipline* (Finifter, ed., 1983). Biographies of political scientists are also well represented either in the form of different articles (e.g. Rogow, ed., 1969; Beale, ed., 1954) or monographs (e.g. Karl 1974; Wiener 1971).

Kuhn has clearly been overused. It is a peculiar historical phenomenon that Kuhn's book came out at a time when there was a need for the analysis of the development of science, but few had done it empirically. As a result political scientists, too, were eager to adopt his ideas (e.g. Truman 1965) and he was soon coopted into the mainstream of political science (Ricci 1984: 199-201).

Critical analyses of the history of political science have also appeared in many forms. Bernard Crick's *The American Science of Politics* (1959) is one of the best examples of the critical reading of the history of political science, although it is difficult to say what is its methodology (cf. Crick 1980). However, it does not matter whether it is an example of early British intellectual history or a piece of unconscious hermeneutics, as it is a brilliant analysis in any case.

Of the what-went-wrong? tradition, the classic work is *Essays on the Scientific Study of Politics* (Storing, ed., 1962). The sociology of science (e.g. Petras 1967) is also well represented among the critical analyses, as are Marxist critiques from the scholars of the socialist countries (e.g. Gulijew, Löwe, and Röder 1978). David Ricci's *The Tragedy of Political Science* (1984) applies critical perspectives from the analysis of bureaucracy to the philosophy of science.

There are also good examples of other categories. British intellectual history is well represented in *That Noble Science of Politics* (Collini, Winch and Burrow 1983). A classic theoretical treatise which uses history as a help in constructing a framework for the theory of politics is David Easton's *The Political System* (Easton 1971).

What then is missing? It depends how one interprets the situation, but one could claim that those studies are few that apply hermeneutics, semiotics and/or the archaeology of knowledge in the study of the development of political science (cf. Gunnell 1987; see, however, Berndtson 1983). Clearly also missing are comparative analyses of the history of political science. In fact, there have been no comparative studies, except short articles dealing with limited areas (e.g. Anckar 1987).

The situation poses many problems for the comparative study of the development of political science. However, it would not be very fruitful to analyse the different approaches listed at the beginning of this chapter and to evaluate them by using some metatheoretical standard, and as a 'solution' present some methodological construction of one's own. At this embryonic stage of the study of the history of political science one should be humble and start with some of the problems which the comparative study of the development of political science has to deal with.

COMPARATIVE NOTES ON THE INSTITUTIONALIZATION OF POLITICAL SCIENCE IN NORTH AMERICA AND WESTERN EUROPE

It is difficult to tell when politics was taught for the first time in the universities, so different names have been given to the chairs which have been attributed to its teaching. Swedes usually refer to the fact that the Johan Skytte professorship of *discourse and politics* was established at the University of Uppsala as early as 1622, although the scholars holding the chair did not concentrate on the study of politics until the 1840s (Ruin 1982: 299). However, at the same time there were similar chairs also at the Dutch universities, sometimes called *politica* and *retorica* (Hoogerwerf 1982: 227) and politics was at the same time taught under different labels also in other countries (e.g. Haddow 1939).

Many have argued, however, that political science is a peculiarly American discipline (e.g. Friedrich 1947:978; Crick 1959). On the other hand, Samuel Huntington has written that 'there is not an *American* science of politics; there is a *democratic* science of politics, which developed first and fullest in the United States because the United States was the first and fullest democracy in the modern world' (Huntington 1988:6). Huntington's argument in fact substantiates the claim of political science being a peculiarly American discipline. Alexis de Tocqueville pointed out that 'a new political science is needed for a world itself quite new' (de Tocqueville 1966:6) and in that sense the widening of democracy with its attendant problems clearly was a prerequisite for the emergence of political science as a distinct discipline in the United States at the end of the nineteenth century (cf. Berndtson 1983), making it an 'American discipline' from the beginning.

There were also other reasons for the birth of a distinct American political science. The flexible American university system made possible the emergence of new social science disciplines (Veysey 1965). In Europe, social sciences were not as differentiated, and it was sociology that was often considered the general social science containing problems of culture and economics as well as those of politics. Both because of democracy and organizational possibilities in academia, political science was institutionalized in the United States at the end of the nineteenth century (one usually refers to the founding of The School of Political Science in Columbia University in 1880). The result was that even today the political science profession in the United States is massive compared to other political science communities around the world (Andrews 1982:3).

Political science as a peculiarly American discipline must be understood in this sense. Partly due to the early institutionalization, and partly because of the global hegemony of the United States after World War Two, American political science has influenced the institutionalization of political science around the world. To talk about the Americanization of political science does not mean that the study of politics did not exist elsewhere before the influence of American political science. The argument refers to certain historical constellations that have moulded the discipline in its emergence as a distinct academic discipline and its institutionalization around the world. Political science as a discipline will not necessarily continue to have an American label in future (cf. Berndtson 1987).

Many articles, for instance, in *International Handbook of Political Science* (Andrews, ed., 1982) illustrate plainly the American influence. The argument can also be substantiated by referring to evidence given by some close observers of the process. Quincy Wright, the first President of the International Political Science Association (the founding of the IPSA being an important event in itself in this process), wrote in 1949:

> One difficulty of course is that social science is a very recent growth and few people really believe in its possibilities. I was impressed at the recent meeting to form an International Political Science Association in Paris with the lack of political science associations in the world and the lack of belief among many people that a political science was possible. Really as disciplines seeking to utilize so far as possible the objective methods which have developed in the natural sciences, social science comes near to being an American phenomenon of the last fifty years. Little as there has been to spend on social sciences in the United States there has been infinitely more than in any other country. One of the tasks of the international associations in the social sciences therefore is to try to spread what we know about social science in the United States to the rest of the world. (Wright 1949b)

Maybe it was natural that Canada was one of the first countries to introduce political science on the model given by the United States. Although not all Canadians have seen that their discipline of political science has been imported from the United States (pointing to the domestic and British roots of the discipline in Canada), there have been, however, many who have written worriedly about the Americanization of the country's political science. This has been explained by factors such as the proximity to the United States, a common language for English-speaking Canadians, the extensive resort to American graduate schools, widespread use of American textbooks and the presence of American graduate students and American teaching in Canadian universities (Cairns 1975; cf. Trent 1987).

On the other hand, if one takes a look at the institutionalization of the modern political science in Western Europe after World War Two, several main lines of development may be noticed that prove the importance of democracy and academic organizations for the birth of the discipline. For instance, in the cases of the Federal Republic of Germany and Italy, socio-economic development which is linked to democratization and modernization (or a wish to modernize the political system) has been an important factor in this respect.

Although an intense debate on politics and the theory of the state had already emerged in Germany between 1890 and 1933 (Palonen 1985), the conditions for a distinct discipline of political science did not exist at that time (its seeds, however, could be seen in the founding of Deutsche Hochschule für Politik in 1920). The emergence of political science as an independent academic discipline was due to a specific political constellation: the failure of the Weimar Republic, the experience of National Socialism and World War Two, the collapse of the German state and the political development in a divided country which became involved in the Cold War (Kastendiek 1987; see also Chapter 5). The task of political science was explicitly defined as 'to build up democracy', and the support for the new discipline came from Social Democrats while resistance to it among the established sciences was considerable. Resistance arose among the conservatives because of their aversion to the 'science of re-education' sponsored by the American occupation forces (von Beyme 1982:169). In the case of West Germany one may clearly see what the spreading of the American political science to other countries meant in reality. One may again refer to a letter by Quincy Wright:

> At Paris we organized an International Political Science Association but discovered there were few national associations to organize . . . . Apparently political science as an academic discipline has been dead in Germany for a generation, but this group was anxious to reestablish it. Our colleague Karl Lowenstein of Amherst had organized the meeting under the auspices of the Military Government and emphasized the importance of creating an understanding in Germany of what we mean by political science. (Wright 1949a)

In post-war Italy the social and economic conditions affected the development of political science in another way. 'Scientific realism' was needed as an instrument for reform (voiced, among others, by Norberto Bobbio) and for the modernization of the political system (voiced, for example, by Giovanni Sartori). The development of political science was due to several factors: socio-economic needs, changes in the Italian university structure, the external influences (the impact of American behaviouralism) and the role of certain individuals. American funds and institutional cooperation seem to have been also readily available to help to introduce new methods and themes of investigation (Graziano 1987).

Political scientists in Italy had to face, however, a war on two fronts. Together with other social sciences they had to fight first against the disciplines of history and law. The second front was formed against sociology that presented itself as a general science of society. It is interesting that the problems of Italian political science in this respect seem to have been quite common elsewhere too. In Canada this 'war of two fronts' was waged already in the 1940s and 1950s (Cairns 1975:196); and in Finland, for example, in the 1950s and 1960s (see Jansson 1966).

The linkage to democratization and modernization seems to be quite evident in the cases of Italy and the FRG, two major European countries emerging from fascism to democracy. France and the United Kingdom, however, would have had all the prerequisites to develop a distinct discipline of political science earlier — except, it seems, for the right kind of university system. Pierre Favre writes about France:

> For a number of reasons political science could not appear in France at the end of the nineteenth century. Sociology, born in the Faculty of Letters, too absorbed in its conquest of legitimacy through its combat with philosophy and the humanities, left political science to the jurists at the very time that the latter were bringing the science of the state back to pure and simple study of juridical standards. (Favre 1982:154)

The French intellectual tradition remained relatively isolated from foreign influences, while, on the other hand, the seeds of 'American' political science were already contained in the French *sciences politiques*. Constitutional studies consisted of the comparative study and classification of political regimes and the functioning of political institutions, as well as the analysis of political doctrines, projects for the reform of the state and so forth. Electoral studies also had their own tradition of French electoral geography or sociology. In this context, 'French political scientists find their scientific serenity with difficulty, for they constantly encounter philosophers, sociologists, and historians who publicly announce their own claim to talk about politics and to talk about it with incomparably greater explanatory power' (Favre 1982:164).

Traditions of the study of politics and the system of higher education seem to have been a hindrance to the emergence of 'modern' political science in the United Kingdom also. The founding of the London School of Economics and Political Science in 1895 could have been a beginning, because the Webbs, Graham Wallas and Harold Laski had many common interests with American political scientists. However, in the strongholds of the English academic world, in Oxford and in Cambridge, the philosophical and traditional study of politics was favoured and after World War Two the British response to American behaviouralism was either lukewarm or outright critical. A 'modern' political science did not really develop in the United Kingdom until 1965 (Hayward 1982).

In spite of similarities, the development of political science in the four major European countries has been different in each. This heterogeneity of paths leading to a distinct political science discipline can also be seen in the smaller European nations. For instance, in the Nordic countries, too, the development was dependent on political constellations, scientific traditions and systems of higher education. Among these countries Finland was the first to develop a modern political science discipline (Anckar 1987). The key for this may be the internal political situation in Finland which was susceptible to the influence of American political science. Finland's internal politics (a struggle between the Right and the Communist Party) and the country's external problems (relations with the Soviet Union) made political scientists turn to the United States. The scientific relations were eagerly used as a way to form political ties with the West (Paakkunainen 1988).

In this respect, Finland may be compared to Switzerland, where political science did not develop until the 1960s:

> How can this lack of interest be explained in a country where it is well known that politics is everybody's affair? . . . To their eyes, practical experience made scientific analysis quite useless. Many saw in political science a passing fashion from abroad and held it in suspicion. There was a fear that the study of politics would lead to a politicization of science or to the 'scientification' of politics. It was considered unacceptable that politics which was everybody's affair, would become that of a few specialists, even if they were political scientists. . . the stability of the Swiss political system is another factor which accounts for the reticence of the Swiss toward political science. . . . Until very recently, law was considered a discipline both necessary and sufficient for a good understanding of Swiss politics. (Wemegah 1982:327)

PROBLEMS OF (COMPARATIVE) RESEARCH ON THE DEVELOPMENT OF POLITICAL SCIENCE AND SOME TENTATIVE PROPOSALS

'Variables' as a problem

As the brief survey in the previous section attempts to point out, there are similarities and dissimilarities in the development of political science worldwide. To compare is just to play with these differences and similarities. The subject matter of comparative historical research is always full of choices, from concepts to cases. The more general the concepts are the more cases one can subsume under them, but then the clarity of the analysis is in danger. On the other hand, the more narrow the concepts are, the clearer one can see, but the range will be smaller.

For instance, proximity to the United States and the presence of

American graduate schools and American faculty are important factors in studying the development in Canada, but possibilities to use the same factors in explaining the development elsewhere are clearly limited. Political constellations, the need for democratization and modernization of the political system, the usefulness of political science in the eyes of authorities, and the role of individuals, seem to be more general factors. The same seems to be the case with factors that have hindered the institutionalization of political science: the stability of the country (there has been no need for political science); the intellectual tradition (for example, isolationism); and organization of academic disciplines in universities (conservatism of scholars in other fields, intellectual traditions concerning the discourse on politics). Some of these factors also seem to be relevant for the study of the development of political science in non-European countries. For instance, in Nigeria the country's statist political economy and the logic of colonial nationalism have been important factors influencing the development of Nigerian political science (Jinadu 1987).

However, for comparative purposes, these factors may be too general, and, on the other hand, their influence has obviously varied. Furthermore, more 'factors' influencing the development could easily be invented (e.g. Trent 1987). It is also difficult to judge the nature of these factors. They cannot be measured exactly, and it is often impossible to say whether they are dependent, independent or intervening 'variables'. The Americanization of the study of politics in Europe, for instance, may have been the result of a conscious effort on behalf of the Americans, but it may also have been due to the changes in the style of politics in these countries, to the Americanization or democratization of politics itself.

The first conclusion is that the development of political science must be analysed in each country's own cultural context using methods of historical and cultural studies (cf. Jones 1983). Of course, the goals of research determine the methods. The concrete description of institutional development is another thing, compared to the analysis of theoretical development. It is important that there are concepts and 'variables' to guide research, but to compare theoretical achievements of political science needs special care, because in the comparative study of political ideologies or scientific theories 'one cannot hope to approach a psychological reality without going down to a level where universal scientific categories lose most of their sharpness. Fabian ideology or Russian nihilism are clearly very specific trends, not to be evaluated with objective measures' (Dogan and Pelassy 1984:108).

A good example of the meaning of cultural context is David Ricci's book *The Tragedy of Political Science* (1984) dealing with the development of political science in the United States. Ricci uses a model (that he constructed not before, but during his research) drawn from five different sources: studies dealing with the nature of organizations, the history of education, the liberal tradition, the philosophy of science, and the notion of tragedy (see also Ricci 1988).

These five perspectives are, however, suitable mainly for the study of American political science; there are countries where the application of the model would be totally misleading.

The second conclusion is a need for a plurality of methods. There is no single proper method of analysing the history of political science, but empirical surveys dealing with the organizational history are needed as well as case studies on prominent scholars in the field. Intellectual history, the analysis of discursive practices, or semiotics should be used according to situation (cf. Berndtson 1983). It is simply preposterous to think to achieve all possible aims by using a single method. To try to combine them into one coherent approach would, on the other hand, not be feasible.

A good example is that of the role of individual scholars in the history of science. Men are both subjects in history and objects of currents, institutions, functions and structures (Ricoeur 1983:180). Because of that there have been different attempts in the study of the development of science to face the problem of individuals as subjects and/or objects.

For instance, Quentin Skinner (1969; 1971-2) argues that in the historical study of ideas one should always study the intentions of a scholar by taking into account both the social and intellectual conditions of the idea. Ideas are answers to specific questions. On the other hand, the earlier writings on the subject must also be consulted in order to understand the theoretical context. It is important to study the literature of an era as a whole, not only those works which have remained known to posterity. For Skinner the history of ideas is not a narrative containing different and contradictory answers to the same and always relevant questions, but a narrative containing answers to always different questions. In this sense, intellectual history tries to take into account both the role of individuals and social structures. Some intellectual historians have also stressed the necessity of dealing with the sensibilities of the authors, their aesthetic emotions and their feelings towards contradictory pressures in work (Collini, Winch, and Burrow 1983:5-6).

On the other hand, it is also quite legitimate to leave the subject out totally. As Michel Foucault wrote:

> I do not wish to deny the validity of intellectual biographies, or the possibility of a history of theories, concepts, or themes. It is simply that I wonder whether such descriptions are themselves enough, whether they do justice to the immense density of scientific discourse, whether there do not exist, outside their customary boundaries, systems of regularities that have a decisive role in the history of science. I should like to know whether the subjects responsible for scientific discourse are not determined in their situation, their function, their perceptive capacity, and their practical possibilities by conditions that dominate and overwhelm them. (Foucault 1973:xiii-xiv)

Americanization as a problem

Skinner and Foucault represent two different strategies in focusing on the history of science. Both have their merits and problems. But in spite of dissimilarities between countries and the need for different methods, one must also have some guidelines for systematic analysis. Political science as a 'peculiarly American discipline' offers a starting point for this.

However, the nature of the Americanization process must still be specified. One of the major criticisms against American political science has been that using its theories and concepts makes a person define his or her own political system with concepts developed out of foreign political experience.

In analysing this kind of dominance, sometimes use has been made of the concepts of centre and periphery borrowed from theorists of imperialism (Galtung 1981). The framework of centre—periphery relations cannot, however, explain the spreading of theories and their reception in all cases. Political science communities tend to import only some chosen theories and approaches from other countries. There are many different kinds of 'Americanized' political science communities in the world. For instance, David Easton's systems analysis was accepted as a theoretical framework in Finland in the 1960s. At the same time hardly any Finnish political scientist referred to Robert A. Dahl's studies of power, although community studies were under heated debate in the United States at that time.

It has also been argued that the perspective of centre—periphery relations proceeds from a subjectless perspective. That is why it should be concretized by taking a look at individual scholars as paradigmatic exemplars or carriers connecting the centre and the periphery (Stolte-Heiskanen and Heiskanen 1985:166-7). Political scientists are linked to other countries in different ways. French-Canadians may be more interested in the work of French political scientists than in the work of American political scientists, Swedish-Finns more in the Swedish political science than in the Finnish, British feminist political scientists more in feminist political theory in Italy than in British electoral research, and Australian Marxists more in German Marxism than in Australian administrative studies. If one focuses on countries only as a single unit, important features will be overlooked. One should study subcultures and their linkages to other countries (e.g. Laponce 1988).

In addition, it is important to notice that theories and ideas often change in content (through active subjects) when they are transferred to other cultural contexts (Kanerva and Palonen 1987). The influence may be direct or indirect (for the latter, see Gunnell 1988), but in the case of the intellectual development of science, it is seldom direct, because that would deny the creativity of thinking.

One of the best articles, dealing with the issue, is Alan C. Cairns's 'Political science in Canada and the Americanization issue' (1975), where Cairns writes:

> One of the major factors contributing to tension in Canada, as elsewhere, has been what Shils labels the institutionalization of the social sciences. By this term Shils refers to the creation of specific structures by means of which the intellectual activity of the particular discipline takes place, its intellectual products are disseminated, its standards are maintained, new recruits are socialized, and incentives and disincentives are systematically given to intellectual work in accordance with evolving criteria of quality. The relevant structures include courses, departments, libraries and undergraduate and graduate programmes which give recognition and support to particular disciplines. To these university aspects of structure must be added professional journals, learned societies, publishers, funding agencies, and the 'invisible college' of colleagues working on related problems who use these instrumentalities to coordinate their efforts and to transmit cues to each other. In these terms it is clear that political science is far more institutionalized in the United States than in any other country, a fact possessed of crucial intellectual consequences. (Cairns 1975:203)

The message of Cairns's article is that the institutionalization and size of the American political science has had a mass-effect in moulding political science communities elsewhere. There has been no way of not taking the American political science into account. Its dominance in the world has been due mainly to the degree of institutionalization.

Because of the smallness of other political science communities, American political science has determined much that has been known about politics around the world. The situation has varied, of course. There have been, for instance, many developing countries that have had no political scientists of their own. Many times the interpretations concerning politics and society in those countries have been made by American scholars. This is a prime example of how the politics of those countries have been defined by American concepts and interests.

Cairns argues also that the imitation of American political science in smaller countries has led to other negative consequences. The flexibility of the American university system has made it possible to expand into hitherto unknown territories. The system has had a capacity to specialize and to form heterogeneous research groups with meetings and journals. Specialization in other countries has, however, often led to an unstable situation and changing fads, leaving many problems untouched. A good example is the spread of behaviouralism. It led to a situation where the basic structures and formal features of the political system were left unexplored in many countries, because young scholars were eager to follow international trends, not the needs of their own country.

However, according to Cairns, the Americanization of political science may also have had its positive sides. In countries with only a few political scientists the development of political science is sporadic in any case. Many interpretations go unchallenged for long periods of time and many features of the political system are not touched at all, because there are not enough scholars. In this situation it is possible to learn from American political science.

Because of the mixed situation the Americanization of political science around the world must be critically evaluated case by case. The process must be looked at from many angles and no simple theories of influence can be used. The comparative research must find a way to disperse the accidental from the history by constructing a concept or concepts which can be used as means of comparison. Max Weber's method of ideal types is one possible way of doing that. As Weber wrote:

> An ideal type is formed by the one-sided accentuation of one or more points of view and by the synthesis of a great many diffuse, discrete, more or less present and occasionally absent concrete individual phenomena, which are arranged according to those one-sidedly emphasized viewpoints into a unified analytical construct (*Gedankenbild*). In its conceptual purity, this mental construct (*Gedankenbild*) cannot be found empirically anywhere in reality. It is a utopia. Historical research faces the task of determining in each individual case, the extent to which this ideal-construct approximates to or diverges from reality (Weber 1969:90).

How to construct these ideal types for the comparative study of the development of political science is another matter. One possibility is through texts of American political science, because of its historical dominance. This would mean a construction of American political science, that is, as a science of democracy with certain basic concepts and research areas (Berndtson 1983). To resort to the American political science in constructing an ideal type of the development of political science and not to political science in general is due to the idea of Weberian ideal types, which is to make explicit not any average character but rather the unique individual character of cultural phenomena (Weber 1969:101).

Of course, there are different methods even for this undertaking, from Louis Althusser's strategy of 'symptomatic reading' by finding the crucial breaks (epistemological breaks) in the problematic of different sciences (Althusser 1970:249-57) to Paul Ricoeur's hermeneutical reading of the texts (Ricoeur 1981). To apply Ricoeur's analysis, for instance, would mean that the texts would have to be taken as different possible 'worlds'. How we, as readers, interpret these need not be contingent upon the author's original intentions. Texts are always open to different readings and the reader always reconstructs his/her own meanings and makes guesses. These guesses, however, are not arbitrary, because the texts themselves delimit the field of possible interpretations and the reader assumedly follows the logic of probability. Consequently the reader's pre-understanding, the reader's 'theory', necessarily gives the reading a subjective factor, and affects the interpretation of the text as a whole. On the other hand, the reading of the parts of a text (or a larger textual unity) offers procedures for testing and falsification. If a part of a text (or a text in a textual unity) does not 'fit' into the whole, the reader must reconsider the interpretation of the whole (cf. Whitaker 1982). There is no strict method or theory one can use in reading texts, because imagination has its own autonomy, but finding the internal logic of texts is one way of constructing ideal types for comparative research.

In this sense I have previously (Berndtson 1983; 1987) divided the history of American political science into four phases: 1 the formation of representative democracy (1880 to 1920); 2 the emergence of the problems of representative democracy (1900 to 1940); 3 pluralist democracy as a solution to the problems of democracy (1920 to 1965); and 4 the crisis of pluralist democracy (1945 to the present). These phases contain different concepts, research interests, goals of a discipline, research methodology, and so on. If democracy and American political science are linked, it should be possible to use these ideal-types as a starting point for comparative analysis of the development of political science. In this vein one would be able to see similarities and dissimilarities in the development and would also be able to evaluate the nature of the Americanization process in different countries.

Relations between scientific disciplines as a problem

Many have claimed that it is impossible to study the development of a single discipline in isolation from other disciplines (Collini, Winch, and Burrow 1983:4; Foucault 1973) and a prerequisite for understanding the nature of scientific growth would be to construct a theory of relations between scientific disciplines (Lepenies 1977:59-60). This task is also a prerequisite for understanding the nature of political science and its role in society.

However, there is an institutional 'bias'. Because political scientists are political scientists they tend to overlook certain things. The struggle against jurists, historians, and sociologists is a good example, as other disciplines have been seen mainly as competitors of political science. It has often been forgotten that there has also been cooperation between political scientists and scholars from other fields (such as sociologists) that has been fruitful for the development of discipline.

The early phase of American social science is an example of the many intertwining influences in science. At the beginning of its evolution American social science was based as much on French system building (Comte) and English evolutionary empiricism (Spencer, Booth) as on German sociology and psychology. When the ideas from these sources were applied in the United States, there emerged an American pragmatism and a Comtean positivism reinforced with a developing science of statistics. In the same way, it is impossible to understand the development of American political science if one does not consider developments in other sciences, such as in psychology and statistics (cf. Jensen 1969b). Furthermore, history and also geography were important for the development of all social sciences at that time. Frederick Jackson Turner's use of statistical graphs, for instance, helped to spread the use of statistics into social sciences (Jensen 1969a:232-5).

When one looks at the history of political science as an institutionalized discipline worldwide, one finds a general pattern of political science emerging from constitutional law, history and philosophy (the history of ideas) (cf. Andrews 1982:2). This has been the case, for example, both in Sweden (with three traditions before 1945: constitutional law, represented by Fredrik Lagerroth; history, represented by Axel Bruzewitz; and philosophy, represented by Herbert Tingsten) (Ruin 1982:299-300); and in the Netherlands (for example: 'In the nineteenth century and the first half of the twentieth century political phenomena were studied within the framework of disciplines such as public philosophy, constitutional law, and history', Hoogerwerf 1982:227).

The same was also the case in the United States. It must be remembered that the first scientific journal in political science, *The Political Science Quarterly*, founded in 1886 in Columbia University, was a review devoted to the Historical, Statistical and Comparative Study of Politics, Economics and Public Law. Even more clearly the intertwining of public law, history and philosophy can be seen in the works of the first generation of American political scientists (John W. Burgess — public law; William A. Dunning — history and political philosophy; and Woodrow Wilson — history). In that sense the early phase of American political science was not much different in content from the European study of politics at that time. Besides, many American political scientists did not yet adhere to the notion of science in the study of politics (e.g. Wilson 1911).

However, a change in American political science began in earnest at the beginning of the twentieth century. History, jurisprudence and philosophy were no longer alone adequate discourses on politics. Relations between the social science disciplines began to change. This did not happen in Europe, because there did not yet exist a distinct discipline of political science.

In the United States, however, methodologically political science came to resemble sociology at the same time as the interest of sociologists turned more towards apolitical problems. At the beginning of the century there was also a close interchange of ideas between scholars of different disciplines. Charles E. Merriam, for instance, had listened to Franklin H. Giddings's lectures in Columbia University and often referred to Giddings's teaching in his early writings, either defending American imperialism (Merriam 1903:328) or talking about the relationship of democracy to freedom and social laws. At the University of Chicago Harold F. Gosnell, on the other hand, used in his election studies ideas from sociologists' research on the city (Faris 1970:53).

Although the social sciences began to differentiate more and more in their research areas, many common thematic categories prevailed. For instance, in the 1920s there was a clear ideological standpoint from which they focused on people: the intelligent, non-deviant, good citizen. Intelligence was the central category in psychology (Ash 1983); in sociology the central category was success as a positive criterion and deviant behaviour as a negative one (cf. Vidich and Lyman 1985); and in political science, yes! a good citizen who used his or her vote (e.g. Merriam and Gosnell 1924).

What the above argumentation should point out, however, is that the relations between different social science disciplines are not eternal; they are as subject to change as society itself. This must also be taken into account when comparing the development of political science in different countries, because the relations between academic disciplines are not the same country by country. They may even be different university by university (cf. Barber 1988) which means that one should also try to break down countries as a single unit of study if necessary.

The problem is repeated if one cannot take a look at the development of political science also from the perspective of future possibilities. History is usually explained from the past or from the present. A third way is to try to understand it from the future. Political science was born as an American discipline and its history has been dependent on its role in the division of labour between social sciences. However, as the internal structures and politics of societies change, social science disciplines will also be rearranged (cf. Lyotard 1984). The globalization of political science is already pointing political science in new directions. There is a trend towards a new kind of fragmentation and disintegration at the same time as the criticism against the discipline has taken new forms. If this reorientation changes the nature of political science drastically, it is no use studying the history of the discipline from its present condition.

Writing the history of a given discipline from the present will direct the attention of a researcher only to certain questions, and the questions which would break the positive narrative are often tacitly ignored (Collini, Winch and Burrow 1983:4-5). If one is not ready to admit that political science as a distinct discipline is only one possible discourse on politics, and if the future transformations of the discipline are not considered, its past will not be understood either.

CONCLUSION: POLITICAL SCIENCE AS A PROBLEM

The argumentation of the chapter is based on the belief that the development and growth of science can be studied rationally. I do not believe in Popper's 'World Three' or the thesis of the ultimate illegibility of texts advanced by Jacques Derrida (e.g. Derrida 1981). Neither do I believe in mechanical explanations of the development of science by external or internal factors, such as 'class relations' or 'scientific crises'. There are causes that affect the development of political science, but one cannot analyse them in any single way.

However, a disciplinary historian should try to clear himself/herself from different biases that arise from the socialization process of political scientists. Few of them are ready to study their own behaviour rationally. Students of the history of political science have not usually applied to themselves the methods they may otherwise use in research. Some have applied class analysis (or even generational analysis) to explain the development of political science, but psychoanalysis or theories of political clientilism have hardly been used.

During the socialization of political scientists certain rules are learned regarding what it means to be a good political scientist. These rules include what to study, how to argue, to whom one should refer, and how to write in general (introduction, theory, methods, data, conclusions). The understanding of these rules would be of utmost importance for the study of the development of political science, because through them the discipline is linked to other disciplines and to the history of knowledge in general (Foucault 1974). These rules also affect the scientists' evaluation of the usefulness of their own discipline ('it must be useful because we are in it'). Few political scientists would be ready to deny themselves, to demand an end to political science.

To understand the nature of political theories and the role of political science in different countries, it would also be necessary to know what kind of personalities political scientists have possessed. Personalities have been important for the development of political science in the countries where there have been few political scientists. Even if there have been, say, one hundred of them in some country at a certain time, individuals have still been important, because not many of them have been influential scholars. Although American political science is an exception because of its size, even in the United States different personalities have evidently had an effect on the nature of political science (Berndtson 1987:97).

This leads to the problem of the recruitment of political scientists. Actually there are at least two connecting problems. First, what kind of people start to study political science, and secondly, who are recruited into the profession? It is difficult to say if there are any general motives among political scientists (even different generations seem to have their own motives and concerns), but it seems that money and fame are not usually among the prime ones. Instead there may be a fascination with power or a strong motive for reforming the system.

Pierre Bourdieu has claimed that many sociologists have started to study sociology because the discipline offers a possibility not to think of one's own social position. Sociologists are necessarily utopians trying to place themselves above social hierarchies. Whether they really are equipped to understand society better than some other professions is an interesting question (Bourdieu 1979:596; cf. Stinchcombe 1984). The same kind of questions should also be posed in regard to political science. It is an interesting fact from the recent history of the social sciences, that, for instance, when Marxism was revived in the 1960s, sociology students all over the world were usually more radical than students of political science. An explanation may be that these disciplines attract different personalities and, on the other hand, socialization processes within them are different, owing to the different histories of the disciplines.

Furthermore, socialization and recruitment mechanisms vary country by country. That is another reason why it is important to focus on them in the comparative study of the development of political science. If the worldwide development of the discipline is ever to be understood, the problems associated with its study should be rationally analysed. This paper suggests methodological innovations with different research techniques and an open mind for looking at political science as a changing institution. First it is necessary to identify the problems, before trying to tackle them.

NOTE

This is a revision of a paper presented at Cortona, Italy, September 1987.

REFERENCES

Althusser, L. (1970) *For Marx*, New York: Vintage Books.

Anckar, D. (1987) 'Political science in the Nordic countries', *International Political Science Review* 8:73-84.

Andersson, G. (1971) *Forskning och samhälle: En vetenskapsteoretisk debattanalys*, Institutionen för Vetenskapsteori, Göteborgs Universitet, Rapport 21.

Andrews, W.G. (1982) 'Introduction: freaks, rainbows, and pots of gold', in W.G. Andrews (ed.) *International Handbook of Political Science* pp. 1-6, Westport, CT: Greenwood Press.

— (ed.) (1982) *International Handbook of Political Science*, Westport, CT: Greenwood Press.

Ash, M.G. (1983) 'The self-presentation of a discipline: history of psychology in the United States between pedagogy and scholarship', in L. Graham, W. Lepenies, and P. Weingast (eds) *Functions and Uses of Disciplinary Histories* pp. 143-89,

Sociology of the Sciences Yearbook VII, Dordrecht: Reidel.

Barber, William J. (ed.) (1988) *Breaking the Academic Mould: Economists and American Higher Learning in the Nineteenth Century*, Middletown, CT: Wesleyan University Press.

Bärmark, J. (1971) 'Människobild som styrfaktor', in A. Elzinga (ed.) *Vetenskapen i samhället* pp. VI-5 to VI-11, Institutionen för Vetenskapsteori, Göteborgs Universitet, Rapport 23.

Beale, H.K. (ed.) (1954) *Charles A. Beard: An Appraisal*, Kentucky: University of Kentucky Press.

Berndtson, E. (1983) 'Political science and democracy. Four phases of development in American political science', in I. Heiskanen and S. Hänninen (eds) *Exploring the Basis of Politics: Five Essays on the Politics of Experience, Language, Knowledge, History* pp. 89-105, Ilmajoki: Finnish Political Science Association.

— (1987) 'The rise and fall of American political science: personalities, quotations, speculations', in *International Political Science Review* 8:85-100.

von Beyme, K. (1982) 'Federal Republic of Germany', in W. G. Andrews (ed.) *International Handbook of Political Science* pp. 169-176, Westport, CT: Greenwood Press.

Bourdieu, P. (1979) *La Distinction*, Paris: Les Editions de Minuit.

Cairns, A.C. (1975) 'Political science in Canada and the Americanization issue', *Canadian Journal of Political Science* 13: 191-234.

Collini, Stefan, Winch, Donald, and Burrow, John (1983), *That Noble Science of Politics: A Study in Nineteenth-century Intellectual History*, Cambridge: Cambridge University Press.

Crick, B. (1959) *The American Science of Politics: Its Origins and Conditions*, London: Routledge & Kegan Paul.

— (1980) 'The British way', *Government and Opposition* 15: 297-307.

Derrida, Jacques (1981) *Positions*, Chicago: University of Chicago Press.

Dogan, M. and Pelassy, D. (1984) *How to Compare Nations: Strategies in Comparative Politics*, Chatham, N.J.: Chatham House Publishers Inc.

Easton, D. (1971) *The Political System: An Inquiry into the State of Political Science*, 2nd edition, New York: Knopf.

Eco, U. (1981) *The Role of the Reader: Explorations in the Semiotics of Texts*, London: Hutchinson.

Elzinga, A. (ed.) (1971) *Vetenskapen i samhället*, Institutiionen för Vetenskapsteori, Göteborgs Universitet, Rapport 23.

Faris, R.E.L. (1970) *Chicago Sociology, 1920-32*, Chicago: University of Chicago Press.

Favre, P. (1982) 'France', in W.G. Andrews (ed.) *International Handbook of Political Science* pp. 154-68, Westport, CT: Greenwood Press.

Feyerabend, P.K. (1975) *Against Method: Outline of an Anarchistic Theory of Knowledge*, London: New Left Books.

Finifter, A.W. (ed.) (1983) *Political Science: The State of the Discipline*, Washington, D.C.: American Political Science Association.

Foucault, M. (1973) *The Order of Things: An Archaeology of the Human Sciences*, New York: Vintage Books.

— (1974) *The Archaeology of Knowledge*, London: Tavistock Publications.

Friedrich, C.J. (1947) 'Political science in the United States in wartime', *American Political Science Review* 41:978-89.

Galtung, J. (1981) 'Structure, culture, and intellectual style: an essay comparing Saxonic, Teutonic, Gallic and Nipponic approaches', *Social Science Information* 20: 817-56.

Graziano, L. (1987) 'The development and institutionalization of political science in Italy', *International Political Science Review* 8:41-57.

Gulijew, W.J., Löwe, B.P., and Röder, K.-H. (1978) *Bürgerliches politisches System und Systemtheorie: Widerspruche und Tendenzen*, Berlin (DDR): Akademie-Verlag.

Gunnell, J. (1987) 'The historiography of American political science', Paper presented at the ICSDPS conference of Cortona, Italy, which also appears in modified form as Chapter 1 in this book.

— (1988) 'American political science, liberalism, and the invention of political theory, 1940-50,' in D. Anckar and E. Berndtson (eds) *Political Science Between the Past and the Future* pp. 34-60, Jyväskylä: Finnish Political Science Association.

Haddow, A. (1939) *Political Science in American Colleges and Universities, 1636-1900*, Edited, with an introduction and concluding chapter, by William Anderson, New York: Appleton-Century.

Hayward, J. (1982) 'United Kingdom', in W.G. Andrews (ed) *International Handbook of Political Science* pp. 355-63, Westport, CT: Greenwood Press.

Heiskanen, I. (1988) 'On the role of meta-analysis in political science: from legitimation, illusions and sous-realism to transrealism, disillusionism and delegitimation,' in D. Anckar and E. Berndtson (eds), *Political Science Between the Past and the Future* pp. 119-32, Jyväskylä: Finnish Political Science Association.

Hoogerwerf, A. (1982) 'The Netherlands', in W.G. Andrews (ed.) *International Handbook of Political Science* pp. 227-45, Westport, CT: Greenwood Press.

Huntington, Samuel P. (1988) 'One soul at a time: political science and political reform', *The American Political Science Review* 82: 3-10.

Jansson, J.-M. (1966) 'Defining political science: some basic reflections', *Scandinavian Political Studies* 1:13-24.

Jensen, R. (1969a) 'American election analysis: a case history of methodological innovation and diffusion', in S.M. Lipset (ed.) *Politics and the Social Sciences* pp. 226-43, New York: Oxford University Press.

— (1969b) 'History and the political scientist', in S.M. Lipset (ed.) *Politics and the Social Sciences* pp. 1-28, New York: Oxford University Press.

Jinadu, L.A. (1987) 'The institutional development of political science in Nigeria: trends, problems, and prospects', *International Political Science Review* 8:59-72.

Jones, R.A. (1983) 'On Merton's "history" and "systematics" of sociological theory', in L. Graham, W. Lepenies, and P. Weingart (eds) *Functions and Uses of Disciplinary Histories* pp. 121-42, Sociology of the Sciences Yearbook VII, Dordrecht: Reidel.

Kanerva, J. and Palonen, K. (1987) 'Introduction', in J. Kanerva and K. Palonen (eds) *Transformation of Ideas on a Periphery: Political Studies in Finnish Intellectual History* pp. 7-15, Ilmajoki: Finnish Political Science Association.

Karl, B.D. (1974) *Charles E. Merriam and the Study of Politics*, Chicago: University of Chicago Press.

Kastendiek, H. (1987) 'Political development and political science in West Germany', *International Political Science Review* 8: 25-40, which also appears as Chapter 5 in this book.

Kuhn, T.S. (1962) *The Structure of Scientific Revolutions*, Chicago: University of Chicago Press.

Laponce, J.A. (1988) '"Canadian" political science between the relevant and the irrelevant, the rational and the irrational, the macro and the micro, the core and the peripheries: its growth and diversification in the last thirty years', in D. Anckar and E. Berndtson (eds) *Political Science Between the Past and the Future* pp. 61-73, Jyväskylä: Finnish Political Science Association.

Lepenies, W. (1977) 'Problems of a historical study of science', in E. Mendelsohn, P. Weingart, and R. Whitley (eds) *The Social Production of Scientific Knowledge* pp. 55-67, Sociology of the Sciences Yearbook I, Dordrecht: Reidel.

Lepenies, W. and Weingart, W. (1983) 'Introduction', in L. Graham, W. Lepenies, and P. Weingart (eds) *Functions and Uses of Disciplinary Histories* pp. ix-xx, Sociology of the Sciences Yearbook VII, Dordrecht: Reidel.

Lovenduski, Joni (1981) 'Toward the emasculation of political science: the impact of feminism', in D. Spender (ed.) *Men's Studies Modified: The Impact of Feminism on the Academic Disciplines* pp. 83-97, Exeter: Pergamon Press.

Lyotard, J.-F. (1984) *The Postmodern Condition: A Report on Knowledge*, Manchester: Manchester University Press.

Mannheim, K. (1960) *Ideology and Utopia: An Introduction to the Sociology of Knowledge*, London: Routledge & Kegan Paul.

Merriam, C.E. (1903) *A History of American Political Theories*, New York: Macmillan.

Merriam, C.E. and Gosnell, H.F. (1924) *Non-Voting: Causes and Methods of Control*, Chicago: University of Chicago Press.

Merton, R.K. (1968) *Social Theory and Social Structure*, enlarged edition, New York: The Free Press.

Nielsen, K.A. (1975) 'Samfundsvidenskabens samfundsmaessige rolle og fagkritik', *Nordisk Forum* 5: 51-67.

Paakkunainen, K. (1988) 'A periphery in search of a centre: the early years of the Finnish Political Science Association', in D. Anckar and E. Berndtson (eds) *Political Science Between the Past and the Future* pp. 25-33, Jyväskylä: Finnish Political Science Association.

Palonen, K. (1978) *Politiikan tutkimuksen esteet ja mahdollisuudet valtio-opissa. Tulkintaa suomalaisen valtio-opin tieteen-ja yhteiskuntakäsityksen muutoksista väitöskirjojen taustaa vasten*, Institute of Political Science, University of Helsinki, Research Reports, Series A, 48.

— (1985) *Politik als Handlungsbegriff: Horizontwandel des Politikbegriffs in Deutschland 1890-1933*, Commentationes Scientiarum Socialium 28, Helsinki: Societas Scientiarum Fennica.

Parsons, T. (1937) *The Structure of Social Action: A Study in Social Theory with Special Reference to a Group of Recent European Writers*, New York: McGraw-Hill.

Petras, J. (1967) 'Ideology and United States political scientists', in C.A. McCoy and J. Playford (eds) *Apolitical politics: A critique of behavioralism* pp. 76-98, New York: Crowell.

Popper, K. (1968) *The Logic of Scientific Discovery*, revised edition, London: Hutchinson.

Ricci, D.M. (1984) *The Tragedy of Political Science: Politics, Scholarship, and Democracy*, New Haven CT: Yale University Press.

— (1988) 'Reflections on "The Tragedy of Political Science"', in D. Anckar and E. Berndtson (eds) *Political Science Between the Past and the Future* pp. 77-97, Jyväskylä: Finnish Political Science Association.

Ricoeur, P. (1981) *Hermeneutics and the Human Sciences: Essays on Language, Action, and Interpretation*, Cambridge: Cambridge University Press.

— (1983) 'On interpretation', in A. Montefiore (ed.) *Philosophy in France Today* pp. 175-97, Cambridge: Cambridge University Press.

Rogow, A.A., (ed.) (1969) *Politics, Personality, and Social Science in the Twentieth Century: Essays in Honour of Harold D. Lasswell*, Chicago: University of Chicago Press.

Ruin, O. (1982) 'Sweden: Research', in W.G. Andrews (ed.) *International Handbook of Political Science* pp. 227-45. Westport, CT: Greenwood Press.

Seidelman, R. (with the assistance of E.J. Harpham) (1985) *Disenchanted Realists: Political Science and the American Crisis, 1884-1984* Albany N.Y.: State University of New York Press.

Skinner, Q. (1969) 'Meaning and understanding in the history of ideas', *History and Theory* 8:3-53.

— (1971-2) 'Motives, intentions and the interpretation of texts', *New Literary History* 3: 394-408.

Somit, A. and Tanenhaus, J. (1967) *The Development of American Political Science: From Burgess to Behavioralism*, Boston: Allyn and Bacon.

Stinchcombe, A.L. (1984) 'The origins of sociology as a discipline', *Acta Sociologica* 27: 51-61.

Stolte-Heiskanen, V. and Heiskanen, I. (1985) 'Intellectual styles and paradigmatic changes in Finnish sociology and political science', in R. Alapuro, M. Alestalo, E. Haavio-Mannila, and R. Väyrynen (eds) *Small States in Comparative Perspective: Essays for Erik Allardt* pp. 165-87, Oslo: Norwegian University Press.

Storing, H.J. (ed.) (1962) *Essays on the Scientific Study of Politics*, New York: Holt, Rinehart & Winston.

Therborn, G. (1974) *Science, Class and Society: On the Formation of Sociology and Historical Materialism*, Göteborg: Dissertation, Lund.

de Tocqueville, A. (1966) *Democracy in America* (J.P. Mayer and M. Lerner, eds), New York: Harper & Row.

Törnebohm, H. (1973) *A Systems Approach to Inquiring Systems, Department of Theory of Science*, University of Göteborg, Report 54.

Trent, J.E. (1987) 'Factors influencing the development of political science in Canada: a case and a model', *International Political Science Review* 8:9-24.

Truman, D.B. (1965) 'Disillusion and regeneration: the quest for a discipline', *The American Political Science Review* 59:865-73.

UNESCO (1950) *Contemporary Political Science*, Liège: UNESCO.

Veysey, L.R. (1965) *The Emergence of the American University*, Chicago: University of Chicago Press.

Vidich, A.J. and Lyman, S.M. (1985) *American Sociology: Wordly Rejections of Religion and Their Directions*, New Haven CT: Yale University Press.

Waldo, D. (1975) 'Political science: tradition, discipline, profession, science, enterprise', in F.I. Greenstein and N.W. Polsby (eds) *Handbook of Political Science*, vol. 1 pp. 1-130, Reading, Mass: Addison-Wesley.

Weber, M. (1969) *The Methodology of the Social Sciences* (translated and edited by E.A. Shils and H.A. Finch), New York: The Free Press.

Wemegah, M. (with the collaboration of Daniel Frei) (1982) 'Switzerland', in W.G. Andrews (ed.) *International Handbook of Political Science* pp. 327-35, Westport,

CT: Greenwood Press.

Whitaker, R. (1982) 'Hermeneutics and the social sciences. Some implications of Paul Ricoeur's interpretive theory for the study of politics', Paper presented at the IPSA World Congress of Rio de Janeiro.

Whyte, W.H. (1956) *The Organization Man*, Harmondsworth: Penguin Books.

Wiatr, J.J. (1978) '"The Civic Culture" – a Marxist reassessment', *Polish Round Table* VIII:5-15.

Wiener, M.J. (1971) *Between Two Worlds: The Political Thought of Graham Wallas*, Oxford: Clarendon Press.

Wilson, W. (1911) 'The law and the facts', *The American Political Science Review* 6:1-11.

Wright, Q. (1949a) 'Letter to Harvey Walker, 6 October 1949', *Quincy Wright Papers*, Joseph Regenstein Library, Department of Special Collections, University of Chicago.

— (1949b) 'Letter to Roy F. Nichols, 9 November 1949, *Quincy Wright Papers*, Joseph Regenstein Library, Department of Special Collections, University of Chicago.

3 The interaction of the state and political science in Canada

A preliminary mapping

John E. Trent and Michael Stein[1]

What we need are studies that go beyond non-historical analyses of knowledge utilization, without becoming grand overviews of the joint evolution of social science and the state . . . Historical and comparative studies of three to six advanced industrial liberal democracies could trace out the ways in which governments and their activities have profoundly affected the emergence and social organization of social science activities and disciplinary configurations, as well as their intellectual orientations. Then, in turn, particular areas of welfare-state policy-making could be probed in depth to reveal how variously organized and oriented social sciences have influenced the overall shape and content of governmental interventions. (Peter Evans, Dietrich Rueschemeyer and Theda Skocpol 1985:359)

The relationship between the state and political science[2] has been considered an important topic of analysis, in one form or another, since earliest times. For example, in the *Republic* Plato proposed that states be governed by philosopher kings, the political scientists of his day. Auguste Comte introduced the notion of social engineering based on sociological findings in his *Politique Positive*. Max Weber discussed the appropriate 'political' roles of social scientists and intellectuals in his '*Politics as a Vocation*'. More recently, a number of well-known social scientists have written essays on this topic ranging from personal reflections (Aron 1965), to a series of empirical case studies (Lipset 1969), to a macro analysis of the 'politicization' of the discipline (Lowi 1973).

Yet despite the importance of the topic, as noted in the quotation from Evans et al. above, there have been few systematic efforts undertaken thus far that examine the broad spectrum of relationships between political science and its principal subject matter, the state or polity. The only recent Canadian article that specifically addresses this subject is a presidential address to the Canadian Political Science Association by Léon Dion. In his view:

Questions concerning political dimensions of the practice of the social sciences and humanities do not constitute a major preoccupation of the specialists in these disciplines. . . . Rare are the serious references in their studies and briefs to the social responsibilities we assume as professors and scientific researchers. ... We seem to feel that we automatically fulfil our responsibilities toward our disciplines and society as soon as we are free, as researchers and members of the academic community, to act as we see fit, without any interference from any external agent (Dion 1975).

More recently, Brooks and Gagnon (1988) have completed a book-length monograph on the impact of social scientists on politics in Canada; however, the principal focus of their study is on the role social scientists (particularly sociologists and economists) have played in influencing state policy and policy-making in Canada, rather than the reverse relationship involving the impact of the state on the development of political and social science. In fact, only a handful of publications of Canadian political scientists are concerned even with the broader question of the state of the discipline in Canada, a finding corroborated quantitatively for francophone Quebec political scientists by Leclerc (1985).

Yet the topic is surely significant, and our failure to explore it more diligently may reflect the underdeveloped nature of our thinking about the current state of the discipline. The political system forms an important part of the environment within which political science is practised. What constraints and opportunities does this environment pose for the development of the discipline? What direct impact have state funding and policy interventions had on the evolution of political science? Reciprocally, what influence have the contributions of political science had on the evolving Canadian society and state? The answers to these questions are particularly important for political science, because it is the discipline which is probably most directly and heavily influenced by its subject matter. The primary objective of this chapter is to provide some tentative answers to these questions.

Our intention is to conduct a 'mapping exercise': that is, to use the Canadian historical experience to isolate some of the variables that we believe are most central to the relationship between the state and political science, particularly in the era of the modern liberal democratic state. In section 1 we trace some of the more indirect relationships between the 'late liberal state'[3] and political science in Canada, covering the period from 1888 to 1950. In section 2 we focus on two types of direct relationships between the 'modern interventionist welfare state'[4] and political science in Canada, during the period 1950 to the present: first, direct government funding of independent academic political science research, contract and survey research, and professional associational activities; and second, direct participation in or impact on government by political scientists by means of part-time contract or royal commission research, direct full-time employment in government, or the dissemination of policy-relevant ideas. We then examine the long-term consequences of these direct relationships for the discipline.

In the conclusions (section 3), we summarize our findings for Canada, compare them with parallel findings in other Western countries, and offer broad recommendations concerning future relationships between the state and political science. Much of our analysis is based on information drawn from existing surveys and writings on the history and current state of the social sciences in Canada.

1 POLITICS AND POLITICAL SCIENCE IN CANADA DURING THE 'LATE LIBERAL STATE', 1888-1950: INDIRECT RELATIONSHIPS

Although the 'late liberal state' was more active economically in Canada than in many other Western societies,[5] it still involved a limited role for itself in most social and cultural spheres, including that of higher education.[6] In the late nineteenth century several of the oldest secular English-speaking colleges and universities in Canada, such as the University of Toronto, Queen's, McGill, Dalhousie, and the University of Manitoba, were already well established; they depended heavily on private economic benefactors for their existence.[7] The state played only a marginal role in their existence, and in the establishment of their faculty and curriculum, including the political and social sciences.[8]

At the time of the founding of political science in Canada in 1888, Canada was still a sparsely-populated, self-governing colony within the British Empire, and the country's institutions, including those of higher education, were largely colonial and imitative, and dependent on imported personnel. This was a desired as well as accepted fact of colonial life. The English Canadian universities sought eminent foreign, particularly British, professors and books, and modelled their curricula and programmes of study largely on British examples. Thus the original chairs in political science (i.e. political economy), established at the University of Toronto and Queen's University in 1888 and 1889 respectively, were inspired by positive experiments with those subjects at Oxford and Cambridge (Stein and Trent 1982).

Political science in Canada was initially understood in its broadest sense, following the British example, as encompassing political, economic, social, moral-philosophical, constitutional-legal, and political-historical studies. A strong tradition of British political economy had already been developed out of the writings of the liberal classicists, including Adam Smith, David Ricardo, and the Mills, and it was quickly imported into Canada. The influence of A.V. Dicey and Sir Henry Maine on constitutional-legal and political-historical scholarship was also widely felt in this country. The part of the university curriculum devoted specifically to studies of government and politics was small, and it had a decidedly constitutional-legal or political-historical orientation, or involved rather general and abstract writings on the state. Many of the early holders of Canadian chairs of political science were economic theorists or historians, who left the teaching of constitutional-legal and political-historical subjects to part-time specialists (Drummond 1983).

The close proximity of Canada to the United States also gave an early boost to the development of Canadian political science. The first political science programme and departments in the United States were founded at Cornell, Johns Hopkins, and Columbia universities between 1868 and 1880 (Somit and Tanenhaus 1967; Ricci 1984). The content of these American programmes was often echoed in the course topics and readings assigned by the early Canadian specialists in government and constitutional law, who frequently received their training at universities south of the border (Stein and Trent 1982; Drummond 1983).[9]

The early patterns of professionalization and disciplinary institutionalization of political science in the United States were also copied in Canada. Thus the idea of a Canadian Political Science Association was originally conceived in 1912 by a group of twelve Canadian professors visiting a meeting of the newly-formed (in 1903) American Political Science Association (Trent 1987). The first annual meeting of the Association was held the following year in Ottawa from 4-6 September (Canadian Political Science Association Proceedings 1913). However, unlike in the United States, it had a distinct interdisciplinary orientation, and included economists, lawyers, historians, and political scientists among its members. Although the Canadian state had no direct role in the establishment of this Association, the opening address was delivered by then Prime Minister of Canada, the Right Hon. Robert L. Borden. He noted

> the great desirability of an organized, thorough, and impartial study of the problems with which this Association proposes to deal [since] we have in Canada no such large leisure class as is found in England, whose members can afford to devote much of their time to the study of the science of politics. (CPSA Proceedings 1913:7)

The reliance on foreign models in the hiring, curriculum, and professional associational activities of the political and social sciences in Canada continued until well after World War Two, and paralleled a very slow but steady growth in English Canada of political science departments and personnel. However, the number of full-time political scientists teaching in Canadian universities during this period never exceeded thirty, despite the rapid growth in university faculty in other disciplines, including the other social sciences.

Political science in French-speaking Canada, along with its sister social sciences, lagged even more in development during most of this period. This was due largely to the continued dominance until after World War Two of the neo-Thomist social philosophic tradition fostered by the Roman Catholic Church, which controlled higher education in Quebec and elsewhere in French Canada. In the French-Canadian social thought of the time, the late liberal democratic state was accorded limited functions in the economic, social and cultural spheres; this perspective was consistent with Catholic social thought elsewhere, as laid down in the papal encyclicals of 1891 and 1931. Thus the first full-time programme in modern social science in French Canada was established at Laval University only in 1936, and the first Political Science Department was founded at the same university in 1954 (Leclerc 1982).

The era of the late liberal non-interventionist state came to an abrupt end with the experience of worldwide economic depression in the 1930s. The teachings of the classical political economists were subjected to severe criticism and questioning, and challenging new theories advocating a more activist role for the state in economic and social matters were advanced, notably that of the Cambridge economist John Maynard Keynes. These new developments profoundly affected the Canadian social sciences, as well as those in other Western countries.

In 1929 the Canadian Political Science Association, which had become defunct after the outbreak of World War One, was established for a second time, now on a much stronger footing. Its main promoter was the internationally renowned economic historian and (later) communications theorist Harold Adams Innis. Innis and several of his colleagues at the University of Toronto played a leading role in advancing the development of the social sciences in Canada (particularly economic history and the 'political economy school' in political science), and in establishing essential institutional supports such as the Association, the *Canadian Journal of Economics and Political Science* (subsidized by the University of Toronto Press), and the Social Science Research Council of Canada (then entirely funded by private research foundations in the United States such as Rockefeller and Carnegie) (Stein and Trent 1982; Drummond 1983). It should be noted here that most of these initiatives were taken without direct government funding or involvement, although 'Ottawa officials were involved in the relaunch [of the Association]' (Drummond 1983:74). What is also notable about the intellectual contributions of these early political economists is that they did not borrow heavily from writings in the United Kingdom or the United States. For example, Innis's approach to economics was largely inductive, in reaction to the largely deductive orientation of the British classical political economists. He was influenced primarily by economic historians and dissident economic theorists such as Veblen, Turner, Hobson, and Schumpeter. The indigenous school of political economy which he pioneered included a number of different and competing perspectives, both liberal and radical; but they were all marked by their emphasis on the more unique historical, geographical, and particularly political, economic, and social factors in Canada's development (Clement and Drache 1978). However, most of these writings were familiar only to Canadian scholars.

Many of those who were associated with the indigenous 'political economy' school of the 1930s followed Innis's example and refrained from active participation in politics or government. For Innis this was a matter of professional principle. However, beginning with the first occupant of a political science chair at Queen's University, Adam Shortt, some of the leading political scientists and political economists, such as O.D. Skelton, Escott Reid, and R.A. MacKay, had been drawn into permanent public service appointments with the federal government. Their subsequent contributions to the development of the rapidly expanding federal public service were immense. In the early 1930s a number of the more radical political and social scientists, including Frank Underhill, Eugene Forsey, and Frank Scott, played leading roles in founding Canada's first democratic socialist party, the Cooperative Commonwealth Federation (CCF). Perhaps the largest direct impact by Canadian political scientists on government and politics came with the establishment of the Rowell-Sirois Commission on Dominion-Provincial Relations in the late 1930s, which dealt with some of the serious intergovernmental economic and political problems arising out of the depression. Several leading political scientists, including Henry Angus, R.A. MacKay, J.A. Corry, Alexander Brady, and Norman McLeod Rogers served as Commissioners or researchers on that body, and helped to signal the growing importance of the interventionist welfare state for managing post war economic problems.[10] At the same time their Commission work provided new impetus to scholarly writings on federal-provincial relations.

But this period of indigenous intellectual flowering, early disciplinary institutionalization, and active political involvement in government and politics by many of the leading political scientists,[11] without concomitant direct influence by government on political science, did not last long. By the end of World War Two, the 'political economy' school had been largely supplanted by the so-called 'institutional' school associated with Robert MacGregor Dawson, a senior University of Toronto political scientist trained at Oxford. Its adherents drew heavily on the constitutional-legal and institutional writings of such noted British scholars as A.V. Dicey and Sir Ivor Jennings. They produced a number of detailed, informative but rather dry descriptions of the structure of formal governmental institutions at both the federal (central) and provincial (regional) governmental levels. These institutionally-oriented scholars failed to have the impact on government that their predecessors of the 'political economy' school had, although Dawson himself did serve on a provincial government commission concerned with public service reform.

These developments in English Canadian political science had little or no impact on the emerging social sciences in French Canada. There had been isolated but largely ineffective efforts to promote the development of political science in Quebec since the nineteenth century, notably those of two eminent Quebec academics, Edouard Montpetit and Edras Minville. They were frustrated largely by the tenacious opposition of both the Roman Catholic Church and provincial governmental authorities in Quebec (Leclerc 1982:66-72). By the late 1930s a positivist reaction to Catholic social philosophy had occurred, but it was largely confined to economics and sociology. Laval's modern-oriented School of Social Sciences, founded by a progressive-minded Roman Catholic cleric, Père R.P. Lévesque, in 1938, did not initially include a course in political studies until the advanced (doctoral) level. By 1943, when the Lavel School was transformed into a separate Faculty of Social Sciences, the curriculum was altered sufficiently to provide the necessary technical base for the training of future public servants. Political science, however, remained a subordinate and marginal subject of study within its core social science programme (Leclerc, 1982:62, 77). Père Lévesque, like earlier academic reformers, frequently encountered strong resistance from both church and state in Quebec in his efforts to promote the development of the social sciences in that province.[12] Although Roman Catholic Church and provincial governmental authorities still feared that secular political and social science studies would threaten their positions of political dominance, his efforts finally came to fruition in 1954, with the establishment of the first full-time Department of Political Science at Laval University. At this point the traditional political and social order in Quebec was on the threshold of a radical transformation, which had a dramatic impact on the development of all the social sciences in French Canada, including political science, (some of these developments in Quebec political science are discussed in section 2).

As we have noted above, the character of Canadian political science, both English and French, remained largely derivative throughout most of this initial sixty-year period (with the exception of the interwar years in English Canada), and the profession remained miniscule in numbers. There are several reasons for this, such as the relatively small total population of the country and the resultant slow growth of its higher educational institutions, particularly prior to the post-World War Two period; the slow, evolutionary pattern adopted by Canadians in achieving full political independence from the United Kingdom and the concomitant tardiness in developing a distinctive national consciousness; the structural similarities which Canada's polity shared both with the United Kingdom (for example, its constitution, constitutional monarchy, Parliament, Prime Minister and Cabinet, and merit-based public service) and the United States (such as its non-ideological, centrist political parties, its pluralistic interest group structure, its regional, ethnic and economic diversity); and perhaps most important, the overpowering impact of American social, economic, and cultural institutions.

Throughout most of this early period (1888 to 1950), the Canadian state had little or no direct role in the development of the discipline. Virtually no government funds, federal or provincial, were allocated directly for political science research, and no direct government assistance was provided for the development of a professional association, professional journals, or individual or collective research projects. Of course, much of the funding for the early professional activities of this sort was provided indirectly by the state, especially provincial governments, through its increasingly predominant role in subsidizing the universities and other post-secondary institutions. But this funding was provided primarily for large capital expenditures, or for the hiring of teaching personnel in relation to the rise or fall of the student population. In general, the state kept the universities on a very tight financial leash, even in this respect (Bladen 1965; Hodgetts 1966). Moreover, educational priorities of the state during this period did not favour the social sciences.

At the same time, however, the state generally allowed the universities, including its political and social scientists, a wide area of academic freedom. Although in the earliest appointments to chairs in political science in the late nineteenth century, provincial premiers or ministers often exercised a ratifying authority, in later years this direct control was relinquished. In the few instances in which academics engaged in teaching, writing, and active organization in political matters incurred the displeasure of provincial government representatives, no effective action was taken to remove them from their positions (Stein and Trent 1982:117).

Despite this official distance between the state and political science community, close informal ties and relationships between individual politicians and officials and leading political and social science personalities did develop, particularly after World War One. As John Porter has pointed out, the intellectual community in Canada prior to World War Two, including its university professors, was a highly elitist community, which often shared similar social backgrounds, school and club ties, and friendships with the country's economic and political elites. The political and social science university community was no exception in this regard (Porter 1965; Brooks and Gagnon 1988). It is not surprising, therefore, that at several important moments during this historical period, the federal government directly recruited to top positions in its rapidly expanding public service some of the ablest of the small group of political economists and political scientists. This may have had the effect of weakening the overall strength of the discipline, thereby impeding its development. Another more positive indirect government influence on political science, also mentioned previously, was the recruitment of political scientists in the late 1930s to the Rowell-Sirois Commission on Dominion-Provincial Relations. Although these political scientists may have shared similar social and educational backgrounds and close intellectual ties with political and bureaucratic elites, they often served as strong critics of existing governmental structures, processes and policies, and sometimes even performed the role of an intellectual or bureaucratic vanguard within the state, by promoting major institutional and policy reforms. In our view, their characterization by Porter (1965:16) and by Brooks and Gagnon (1988:5) as a 'clerisy', intellectual defenders of the political status quo, is not justified.

By the end of World War Two, some prominent Canadian political scientists had already begun to call for greater government support for the social sciences. However it was not until the very end of this historical period (1949) that the federal government in Canada finally accepted responsibility for what had always been a strong, autonomous academic tradition in the arts, letters, and sciences. In that year it established the Massey Commission with a mandate to examine the state of Canadian cultural life at the time and determine what national culture existed independently of American influences (Park 1975). The Commission sponsored several studies on the state of the social sciences, including political science. All of them produced strong recommendations for a much more active and direct state role, both federal and provincial, in developing the social sciences. Five years after the publication of the Commission's report in 1951 recommending the creation of a government-funded agency for the arts,[13] the Canadian Government established the Canada Council, with a mandate to foster research in the humanities and social sciences, and with an initial annual budget for these disciplines of $1.4 million.[14] Until the Council was organized, funding for the most important research studies on political, economic, and social topics during this latter period (1940-58), such as the pioneering series on the origins of the Western Social Credit Movement, had come from American-based private foundations such as the Carnegie, Ford, and Rockefeller Foundations, through the intermediary of the Social Science Research Council of Canada (SSRCC).[15]

Throughout our discussion of this early phase in the development of Canadian political science, we have drawn attention to the uninstitutionalized and derivative nature of the discipline, and the reliance of the profession almost entirely on its own resources to make whatever contributions it could to national and international scholarship. But we have also argued elsewhere that those original and distinctive features of Canadian political science that do emerge during this period may be attributed primarily to indirect influences emanating from the political and cultural environment of the country. Thus disciplinary characteristics such as eclecticism, ideological tolerance, emphasis on cumulative research, and preference for partial rather than holistic studies are identifiable in early Canadian political science encompassing the legal-formal, political-economy, and institutional schools. They may be linked to the political, economic and social needs of a young, geographically immense, sparsely populated country tenuously united by a highly fragmented, bilingual, multicultural, and ideologically pluralistic state (Stein and Trent 1982).

The political institutions and political culture were also highly elitist, which may have been necessary in order to bind the young society at this early stage in its development. It is not surprising, then, that many early Canadian political and social science writings also reflected an elitist, conservative bias. The virtues of a British-style constitutional monarchy, a cabinet form of parliamentary government, a strong central government, strong prime-ministerial leadership, pragmatic, brokerage-style political parties, corporate-dominated, patronage-style politics, an elitist, merit-based professional public service, and a majoritarian electoral system were widely extolled in the political and social science studies of the time.

Finally, the slow involvement of government in the development of the political and social sciences in Canada should not be attributed primarily to ideological factors such as the limited role assigned to the 'late liberal state' in higher education and similar social, economic and cultural concerns. In Canada, unlike in the United States and several other Western capitalist democracies, state actors did not traditionally hesitate to intervene in the private sector when strong government action seemed necessary. For example, in their building of a national rail system, their nationalization of public utilities such as hydro-electricity, their establishment of a publicly directed banking system, their creation of a public broadcasting system, and in their institution of agricultural subsidies and marketing boards, successive Canadian governments at both the federal and provincial levels resorted to strong state action at different times during the late nineteenth and first half of the twentieth century. Even in the social welfare field, the federal government had instituted unemployment insurance and old age pensions well before most other Western countries. The importance to public welfare of higher education in general, and the social sciences in particular, was recognized much more slowly and much later by these state actors and the socio-economic elites which supported them. This was particularly true during periods of economic recession and retrenchment, or of conservative reaction, such as the immediate post-World War Two period, when higher educational institutions were virtually starved of funds, and scholars were burdened with heavy teaching loads, low salaries, and poor prospects for permanent employment. These conditions, largely a consequence of state inaction or insufficient indirect support, considerably retarded the development of the discipline in Canada prior to the 1950s.

2 THE STATE AND POLITICAL SCIENCE IN THE 'MODERN INTERVENTIONIST WELFARE STATE' ERA, 1950-PRESENT: DIRECT INFLUENCES AND INTERACTIONS

Impact of the state on political science

With the coming of the modern interventionist welfare state after World War Two, the virtues of a highly trained and technologically competent workforce became part of the accepted ethos of Western society and its elites. Moreover, the impact of demographic changes such as the postwar baby boom was soon felt politically, leading to calls for strong government action designed to channel the additional population into socially productive employment. As in other countries, by the late 1950s, the Canadian federal government, still riding the crest of a post-World War Two wave of economic prosperity, sought rapidly to expand its post-secondary academic institutions to accommodate these changes. Because education falls within provincial jurisdiction under Canada's federal constitution, the major responsibility for the institutional development of post-secondary education lay with the provincial governments. However, it fell largely to the federal government, with its primary economic resources and tax revenues, to provide the funds for this development.

In the late 1950s the central government met the challenge by channelling large sums of money to the provinces for the expansion of their post-secondary educational systems. The relatively small university system which existed up to that time was rapidly enlarged. For example, the number of universities in the country, which had remained virtually unchanged since the early part of the century, doubled from thirty to sixty in just over two decades (1950-73) (Trent 1984). The proportion of university-age students which actually attended university in Canada more than tripled, from about 6 per cent or 113,900 (in 1960), to 20 per cent or 382,600 (in 1980). By 1980, 80 per cent of total university budgets were covered by provincial governments, with approximately half the funds being transferred from Ottawa (Leslie, 1980). In addition, the federal government bore the major responsibility for funding university research.

The most obvious immediate disciplinary effect of this expanded funding was on the number of political science practitioners. In 1959 there were still only about thirty full-time political scientists in Canada in a small number of separate departments. By 1980 they had increased to 775 full-time political scientists in about forty-five independent departments, an increment of about twenty-five times in only twenty years. This trend paralleled a general increase in the number of social scientists from 1,117 in 1956-7 to 13,562 in 1979-80 holding full-time university positions in Canada (Trent 1984). This growth in personnel provided the nucleus for a flourishing professional political science community, involving much more vigorous interchange of ideas and collaborative research efforts, a self-sustaining journal devoted exclusively to political science articles, a strong, energetic disciplinary association, and well-staffed, active and independent departments composed entirely of trained political scientists. There was even a strong basis in this core of professional personnel for expansion of political science and the role of political scientists outside the university, in structures such as private or government-funded research institutes, government agencies, commissions and advisory bodies, and all levels of the federal and provincial public services.

At the same time direct federal government funding of research in the social sciences and humanities increased from $0 in 1955, to $1.4 million in 1965, to $19.7 million in 1972, and to $70 million in 1986, or an average increment of about $2 million annually over thirty years (Stein, Trent and Donneur 1982:12). Political science research assistance improved significantly as a result of this overall increase, although not in continuously larger increments or in proportion to the relative size of the professional political science community.[16] Fuller documentation on the sums of money allocated by government to political science research during part of the period from 1957 to the present may be found in two unpublished studies which appeared in 1983.[17]

A second major beneficiary of direct governmental financial support to political science was professional associational activity, including academic journals and related scholarly projects. The Canada Council first began to subsidize the administrative costs of the newly established Canadian Political Science Association, whose membership was comprised almost entirely of full-time academic political scientists, in 1968. In the same year it provided the first state subsidy for its new official academic journal, the *Canadian Journal of Political Science*. Similar assistance was extended to other social science associations. Although the initial amounts of these subsidies were small, they enabled political science and the other social science disciplines to sustain separate professional associations and associated journals.[18]

Statistics on government funding through the Canada Council and the SSHRCC of the day-to-day activities and administration of the Canadian Political Science Association since 1968 have been collated for only part of that period. They indicate that the annual subsidy to the CPSA by these government funding bodies remained virtually unchanged at about $20,000 between 1975-6 and 1980-1 (Thorburn, 1983:Table 1). It has declined slightly in recent years (CPSA Secretary-Treasurer's Report 1988). It is also well known that most of the numerous new publications and projects undertaken by the Association in the 1960s and 1970s, such as the *Directory of Canadian Political Scientists, Theses in Canadian Political Science, Papers Presented at the Annual Meeting of the Canadian Political Science*

Association, the Parliamentary and Legislative Internship Programmes, and the programme of Twinned Workshops with political scientists in other parts of the world received at least some federal government financial support through the Canada Council and SSHRCC.[19] Moreover, the federal government has recently also provided support through the SSHRCC for a French-speaking political science association based in Quebec, the Société Québécoise de Science Politique (initially the Société Canadienne de Science Politique) with its own journal, *Politique*. It has also helped to sustain the Atlantic Association of Political Studies. Finally it has funded numerous other specialized interdisciplinary associations of interest to Canadian political scientists in areas such as African studies, Asian studies, Latin American studies, Central and East-European studies, interdisciplinary Canadian studies, socialist studies, and peace research (Stein, Trent and Donneur 1983). In providing this funding, it has always been careful to maintain an arms-length relationship with these associations.

Government support to professional journals in political and social science has also increased considerably since the late 1950s. The *Canadian Journal of Political Science* has received an annual subsidy since its 1968 inception, which seems to have increased somewhat until the late 1970s, and to have declined since (Thorburn 1983: Table 1).[20] At least two other professional journals of interest to many political scientists have also received annual support from the SSHRCC in recent years, *Canadian Public Policy* and *Canadian Public Administration*. Other political science journals have obtained Canada Council or SSHRCC grants at different times to help cover part of their operating expenses; according to one estimate, there are now no fewer than nineteen Canadian journals partially or entirely dedicated to political science which owe their existence in part to government largesse (Stein, Trent and Donneur 1983).

A third area of government assistance to political and social science since the late 1960s was the Aid-to-Scholarly Publication Programme of the Social Science Federation of Canada. Under this programme, the government covered the deficit incurred by scholarly books which received favourable peer reviews but could not recover their costs of publication through normal sales in the commercial market. In the thirty years prior to 1972, only a handful of political science books were subsidized in this way. Between 1972 and 1982, about a hundred political science books, most of them in the field of Canadian politics, were supported by the government through this programme (Stein, Trent and Donneur 1983).

A final area of direct government funding of political and social science in many countries is contract and survey research. Unfortunately, statistics on government contract research in the social sciences in Canada have not yet been collated for the period prior to 1981; it is generally acknowledged, however, that government spending in this area increased substantially for the social sciences as a whole over the preceding twenty-year period. However, results of a recent questionnaire sent to relevant federal government departments and agencies on this matter revealed that only about $3.6 million was allocated to political science contract research between 1981 and 1983. Most of it, about $2.2 million, was devoted to highly specialized concerns, such as the endowment of a para-government policy research institute or for strategic studies research for the Department of National Defence. This constituted a very small proportion, about 0.025 per cent, of all federal governmental expenditures on research and development in the social sciences during the same period (Trent 1987). Similarly, in an analysis of survey research used by line departments and central agencies in Ottawa between 1974 and 1980, it was found that this research tool developed particularly by social scientists was extremely underutilized in Canadian government. Most of the government surveys were conducted on non-political topics, despite the pervasive atmosphere of political crisis on issues such as national unity during this period (Robbins 1981). Obvious exceptions, in this respect, are the highly politicized polls commissioned for the government on an *ad hoc* basis by the central agencies, especially the Prime Minister's Office. It appears, then, that in these last two areas, namely traditional state funding of contract and survey research in the social sciences, political science in Canada has benefited considerably less than other social sciences since the late 1950s. Overall, however, the new direct financial input by government in political and social science research and education in Canada since the advent of the 'interventionist welfare state' is impressive.[21]

These huge new financial increments provided by the Canadian state over the last thirty years vastly increased the research output of Canadian political scientists, as measured by their book and journal publications, their conference papers, and their unpublished research reports and contract work (Stein, Trent and Donneur 1983). It did not lead, however, to a radical change in the intellectual content of the discipline, except indirectly in certain subdisciplinary areas, and often on a temporary basis. This was the case with the so-called 'behavioral school', imported from the United States, which began to supplant the earlier 'institutional school' promoted by R. MacGregor Dawson in the early 1960s. This school emphasized studies of the social bases of political behaviour, including such informal political structures as political parties, interest groups, elections and voting structures, and processes of political socialization and communication. It also placed a premium on quantitative methods used to study these and other structures.

This trend resulted in part from the rapid growth in the number of universities in the 1960s, directed by federal and provincial governments. In order to fill the new university positions created by this expansion, university administrators imported many scholars from other countries, particularly the United States. They also sought to encourage more talented young Canadians to enter the academic profession after they had attained the requisite disciplinary training at the graduate level, generally in a foreign country (since such programmes were then often unavailable or inadequate in Canada). Not surprisingly, in political and other social sciences, these new recruits brought to Canada a somewhat critical view of the prevailing intellectual approaches to the study of politics. The reaction that set in against institutional approaches, then, was a partial byproduct of state efforts to expand the social sciences.

However, within a few years, even as the great expansion in social science personnel accelerated, this 'behavioural mood' in Canadian political science triggered a strong reaction by exponents of three new schools in Canadian political science, the neo-institutionalists (who reasserted the primacy of state structures in shaping politics), the neo-Marxists (who promoted a revised Marxist class and ideological perspective which recognized the relative autonomy of state and ideological 'superstructures'), and the public policy analysts (who called for a refocusing on the content of public policy and the process of public policy-making). There was simultaneously a strong protest from nationalist academics, including political scientists, against the Americanization of the social sciences and a call for a return to earlier, more indigenous approaches to the study of politics (MacKinnon and Brown 1969; Wood and Wood 1970; Smith 1971; Smiley 1974).

As the number of new academic positions began to decline in the mid-1970s with the onset of a general economic recession, pressure was exerted on the federal Department of Employment and Immigration to limit recruitment of foreign scholars, and to establish rules giving priority to the hiring of qualified Canadians for academic positions. This led eventually to a partial reversal of the earlier trend to Americanization, at least in the hiring of political science personnel in the universities (Stein, Trent and Donneur 1983).

The expansive pattern of the discipline and the strong support accorded it by the state also began to change in the mid-1970s, as the international economic recession set in and government began to criticize the lack of 'social relevance' of the university-based social sciences. Since that time, there has been a relative decline in state funding of academic social science research. To meet its more technical, policy-related needs, Ottawa has turned increasingly to the funding of independent, para-public and private research institutes. It has also expanded its use of private pollsters for political purposes. Notable in this respect are the new 'political gurus', the owners of private polling companies, many of them trained in political science, who analyse public opinion for parties and government, and provide advice on the content and interpretation of these polls (Graham, 1986). More recently, the federal government has attempted to heighten its visibility as the major source of academic research and development funding by identifying specific research priorities for the social sciences and adding government-defined 'strategic' research programmes to its funding agency concerns. It has also reduced the proportionate amounts of its transfer payments to the provinces for university needs, and established special funding programmes for Canadian Studies and other areas of specialization of interest to federal authorities. Finally, there has been a shift in the targets of government funding in the social sciences from individual to team research projects and to centres of specialized research; this, however, can be attributed less to the priorities of government politicians and bureaucrats than to the preferences for different research styles of academics who control the review panels of the social science funding agencies (Adair and Davidson 1983).

In the general environment of austerity, deficit reduction, and rationalization of government expenditures which emerged in the late 1970s and early 1980s (a trend common to all Western countries experiencing the so-called 'fiscal crisis of the state', according to Rose and Peters 1979), much government bureaucratic infighting occurred, with detrimental effects on the social sciences. Large powerful ministries such as Finance or Treasury Board tended to win out in the battle for revenues over smaller departments such as the Department of the Secretary of State, which was responsible for social science research funding.

Finally, the pre-1950s pattern of government recruitment of able political scientists to professional public service, noted in section 1 above, accelerated until the mid-1980s, as governments and universities competed for scarce research talent.[22] A pattern of active recruitment of social science specialists operated at all levels of the government bureaucracy. At the top echelons, it may have had an adverse effect on the quantity and quality of basic research in the discipline, since some political science practitioners placed their research on the 'backburner' in favour of government contracts, work on task forces and commissions, etc. On the other hand, there may also have been spillover benefits for political scientists, since such work often stimulated subsequent research and writing of both a basic and applied nature in fields related to the initial governmental commission. A good example of this kind of positive stimulation came from the Macdonald Commission on Economic Union and Development Prospects for Canada (1985), which in addition to its three-volume *Report*, produced no fewer than 72 full-length research volumes written largely by academic social scientists. They were subsequently published under a special arrangement by the University of Toronto Press. Many of these volumes contained original ideas and research findings of political scientists who have since continued to pursue these lines of inquiry in academic journals and monographs.

At the lower echelons of the public service, some talented, aspiring young political scientists may also have been diverted from the discipline by the attractions of immediate employment by the state. Evidence from a recent survey suggests, however, that there is little likelihood that this has seriously weakened the profession. Most of the 685 officials in the federal public service who were identified in 1982 as having received political science training indicated that they had only a BA degree. Only 25 per cent had acquired some graduate training in the discipline; of these, only a small proportion had reached the highest echelons of the federal bureaucracy (Robbins 1982). Perhaps the process of competitive public service recruitment of political science graduates has been retarded by the fact that political science is still not classified as a distinct occupational category by the Civil Service Commission; nor is it regarded, like economics and law, as a priority academic subject for such recruitment. On the other hand, this pattern may also reflect a sceptical and even critical attitude prevalent among many Ottawa bureaucrats towards the discipline and the type of training it offers to potential public servants (Robbins 1982).

Impact of political scientists on the state

As we have just pointed out, prior to 1960 English-speaking political scientists formed part of a tiny, elitist social science community whose direct relations with top Ottawa and provincial bureaucrats were sometimes close, although intermittent. When recruited to commissions or to the public service, they were often influential. During the same period the impact of their francophone counterparts was still marginal.

From 1960 on, the nature of the relationship between political and social scientists on the state began to change markedly both in English and French Canada. One important byproduct of the decision by the state in the late 1950s to assist the social sciences financially, as we noted above, was that it could henceforth draw on a much larger pool of academic social scientists for its own commission studies, contract research, and public service and political party positions. This was immediately reflected in the substantially larger number of political scientists of both language communities who have played leading roles in important federal government commissions since 1960. Political scientists were leading actors on the Glassco Commission on Government Reorganization (1962), the Laurendeau-Dunton Commission on Bilingualism and Biculturalism (1967), the Pepin-Robarts Task Force on National Unity (1978), and the Macdonald Commission on Canada's Economic Union and Development Prospects (1985), as well as some important smaller commissions or committees dealing with federal language districts, administrative reform, and legislative reform. As in the pre-1960 period, a number of political scientists have played active roles since 1960 in left-wing parties and nationalist movements such as the NDP, the University League for Social Reform, and the Committee for an Independent Canada. A few have even held senior positions in the federal or provincial public service, headed regulatory agencies and task forces, or served in the federal cabinet. Political scientists have also broadened their contacts with political practitioners in some important policy-oriented subfields of the discipline, such as public administration, municipal politics, intergovernmental relations, and foreign policy, particularly under the aegis of influential associations like the Canadian Institute of International Affairs and the Institute of Public Administration in Canada, which encompass individuals from both communities.

This does not, however, confirm Brooks and Gagnon's characterization of the post-1960 English-speaking political and social science community as a continuing 'clerisy', defending the political status quo (Brooks and Gagnon 1988: chs 6-7). It is true that with the exception of the few critics and reformers who joined left-wing parties and nationalist movements, many of the political scientists who assumed these policy-making roles shared the broad political values of state actors with whom they worked or came into contact. However, most of them did not view themselves as partisans or apologists for the prevailing regime and policy line. Most, such as those who were active on the Macdonald Commission, were careful to maintain their political independence. In other words, while they have been upholders of general regime values (such as liberal democracy, parliamentary-cabinet government, a mixed enterprise system), they were often opponents or critics of the political status quo, including the government's organization, political methods, and policy line. Moreover, they did not constitute a large proportion of the political science community in the post-1960 welfare-state era. The vast majority of the academic political scientists who have been employed by our universities in the last twenty-five years have tended to follow the philosophy of Max Weber in '*Politics as a Vocation*' or Harold Innis in the Canadian context — they have maintained an 'arms-length' relationship with the state. For the most part, they have justified this on the grounds that they can best serve their profession and society at large by pursuing their own research questions and engaging in their own independent analyses, rather than involving themselves in policy questions defined by the state. Some even cite this independence as essential to their academic roles as critics.

On the other hand, there are strong opponents of this 'objective', 'arms-length' position not only among policy-oriented researchers involved with government, but also among radical critics of the system. The latter (the radical critics) view this stance as a convenient rationalization by social scientists who use 'objective science' as an excuse for upholding the values of the dominant elites. In their view social scientists performing as policy actors or government researchers by definition constitute a 'clerisy'; they also charge the vast majority of social scientists with sustaining conservative values under the guise of academic independence. Thus the debate among 'policy activists', 'independent analysts' and 'radical critics' in political science in Canada continues to be joined, as it is in so many other countries. It is not an issue which, in our view, can be easily resolved. It does, nevertheless, deserve somewhat fuller discussion within the context of this paper. We shall expand on our observations in the next section (Consequences) and in the Conclusions below.

If the recent impact of English-speaking political scientists on the state is essentially marginal since the 1950s, can the same be said of French-speaking political scientists during this same period? Brooks and Gagnon have described the central role played by many Quebec economists and sociologists as an intellectual vanguard during the 1950s for the subsequent Quiet Revolution of the 1960s. They note that many of these economists and sociologists formed alliances with political opponents of the conservative Duplessis regime in Quebec and became socially active in anti-governmental structures or movements such as the Insitut Canadien d'Affaires Publiques, the journal *Cité Libre*, and Radio Canada (Brooks and Gagnon 1988: ch. 2). But as Leclerc points out, political scientists during this period were just beginning to acquire some institutional status with the establishment of separate political science departments for the first time at Laval University (1954) and University of Montreal (1958). The initial full-time political scientists at those institutions, with some exceptions (such as Léon Dion and Gérard Bergeron), were too few in number and too marginal in status to play a prominent role beside the other social scientists in the early political struggle for the new Quebec. In fact, there were very few francophone political scientists who even participated in the prominent government commissions of the decade, such as the Massey Commission and the Quebec-based Tremblay Commission (1956), which examined the cultural and economic bases of federalism from a French-Canadian autonomist standpoint (Leclerc 1982: ch. 3).

Beginning in the early 1960s, however, there were some changes in the relationship between francophone political scientists and the state, corresponding to what Leclerc calls the 'institutionalization' phase of Quebec political science (Leclerc 1982: ch. 3). In the 1960s at least one French-speaking political scientist, Léon Dion, served as an informal advisor to Quebec premier Jean Lesage, and several, including Léon Dion and Vincent Lemieux, were involved in senior consulting and research work for the federal Laurendeau-Dunton Commission on Bilingualism and Biculturalism (1967). In the 1970s francophone political scientists continued to serve as informal advisors to Quebec premiers Bourassa and Lévesque, or attach themselves to Quebec political bodies such as the Parti Québécois political executive, the Quebec Prime Minister's Office, the Société Saint-Jean Baptiste, and the 'Yes' Committee on the Quebec referendum. Still others served as commissioners or consultants to Quebec National Assembly committees investigating questions of legislative, administrative, and electoral system reform. A third group, notably from the more Marxist-oriented Political Science Department of the newly-created (1969) University of Quebec in Montreal, became active in the trade union movement. But as Leclerc points out, most of these were individual initiatives which were quite independent of dominant institutional interests and were not in conflict with the norm of 'social distance' from the state by then strongly embraced by all the Quebec universities (Leclerc 1982:188). Thus Quebec political scientists were clearly not a political vanguard; by the 1970s most had become part of a social scientific community generally accepting the basic values, policies, and structures of the post-1960s Quebec interventionist welfare state. The experience of Quebec political scientists seems to suggest that the relationship between social scientists and the state depends more on the process of institutionalization of higher education and its various social science disciplines, and on the level of modernization of the society as a whole, than on differences in ethnic-linguistic and cultural traits of national or sub-national communities.

Consequences: 'institutionalization' and 'professionalization' of the discipline and its isolation from the state

Despite the considerable expansion of direct influences and relationships between political scientists and interventionist welfare state actors in Canada since the late 1950s, the overall impact has not been one of encouraging a close and mutually beneficial relationship between the two communities. In fact, with rapid growth and concomitant institutionalization and professionalization have come increasing insulation and isolation of political scientists from those who are politically active in state or para-state structures. This has not been so much a result of conscious effort by political scientists to keep the state at 'arms length' in order to preserve Weberian scientific and critical norms. Rather, the institutionalization and professionalization of the discipline, and the funding support provided by government and its agencies, have made political scientists professionally and financially more secure. Provided they can meet the norms established by the academic world for permanent appointment, tenure, and promotion, Canadian political scientists no longer need struggle, in the way they once did prior to the late 1950s, to secure a livelihood or to meet the daily demands that increased university enrolments generate for all academics. They now have a financially and numerically strong professional association, a large number of professional journals, numerous commercial and university press and publication outlets, and well-established norms regulating teaching loads, theses, and other supervisory responsibilities and administrative duties. They have also continued to develop their technical skills and a specialized professional jargon which is not readily comprehensible to other academics and to the non-academic community. They therefore believe that they can proceed with a minimum of criticism to advance their research programmes and produce their research products even if these outputs are increasingly considered to be arcane, technically abstruse and irrelevant by the state and economic actors who ultimately subsidize them.

There is a danger, however, in the continued evolution of state-political science relations along these parallel and separate lines. There are recent indications that state and business elites are unaware of or do not recognize the accomplishments of academic political science, and are therefore increasingly unresponsive when called upon to provide additional resources for the survival and continued growth of the discipline. There is, in short, a widening gulf of mutual ignorance and isolation between these two institutional solitudes, which may well be detrimental to the long-run development of political science in Canada, and the utilization of its findings by the state and society.

The original purpose of the discipline, as defined in 1913 by its founding professional association, was to study 'political problems'; in recent years it has been redefined by the CPSA as that of 'developing political science'. Moreover, the changing composition of the Association may be a reflection of this change in orientation. Whereas the CPSA once included a large number of politicians and academics from other disciplines, its membership is now composed almost entirely of academic political scientists. This may well signify that as the discipline has become more professional and specialized, it has become less relevant and important to non-practitioners with political interests or involvements.

Indeed, some of the adverse effects of this trend may already be beginning to emerge. First, as we have already noted above, recent financial statements for the CPSA reveal a gradual reduction in government support for the Association and the discipline since the early 1980s. Secondly, despite the continued growth in overall government support for academic research and development, including the other social sciences, there has been virtually no growth in recent government spending on political science research and development, as also noted above. Thirdly, there is a widespread view among government officials that:

> Political scientists, especially those with advanced academic degrees, do not make very good public servants. They are quarrelsome and difficult to train. Anyway, we don't really need them. When you get down to it, all we really need is economists and lawyers. (Robbins 1981:11)

The problem appears to lie in the failure of political scientists 'to have mastered any particular set of useful or marketable skills" (Robbins 1981:9). On the one hand, the discipline is viewed as a 'soft science', without the kind of emphasis on numbers and models that has helped to make economists an attractive source of public service recruitment. On the other hand, government bureaucrats do not find the expert policy advice of political scientists very valuable, since 'policy is almost never explicitly addressed to any given "problem in society". . . . What is useful is what senior players find useful', (Robbins 1981:10).

It appears, then, that Canadian political scientists are increasingly found wanting as consultants or aides to state actors. And as the discipline becomes more institutionalized and technically sophisticated, its practitioners become more and more marginal and ineffective as objective analysts and critics of the state, at least from the perspective of those outside its narrow institutional milieu. This is as much true of radical neo-Marxist as of liberal positivist political scientists. We are, in short, in danger of becoming irrelevant to all except those initiated into the specialized norms and esoteric writings of our profession.

CONCLUSIONS: LESSONS FROM THE CANADIAN POLITICAL SCIENCE EXPERIENCE FOR OTHER WESTERN STATES

In the historical past, the fate of political thinkers and analysts who developed some relationship with state authorities was often at risk; they could lose not only their jobs or positions, but even their liberty or their lives. Today these relationships between state authorities and political scientists are much more benign. We have found, for example, in the Canadian case, that:

1 For the first seventy years after the founding of political science, during the period of the 'late liberal' state, the state and the political science profession and discipline as a whole had largely indirect influences on each other. Some individual political scientists, however, had a significant impact on parties, reform movements, royal commissions, the public service, and elite political culture. Since the late 1950s, during the period of the 'interventionist welfare state', this reciprocal relationship has become much more direct, but also less significant in its impact on state policy and institutions. The influences are now more intermittent, diffuse and long-term rather than continuous, well-defined and immediate. Rarely do political scientists working either within or outside the government have an impact on leading individual state actors, major policies or budgetary expenditures; they tend, rather, to influence broad political groupings, public orientations, and general funding objectives.

2 The state and political science have gradually developed into two distinct, relatively self-sufficient, and increasingly isolated communities.

3 In response to the questions posed in our introductory quotation from Peter Evans et al. (1985), the state in Canada has profoundly affected the emergence, social organization, and activities of the political science profession. It did so indirectly in the early period of the 'late liberal state' largely by its benign indifference, and in

the later period under the 'interventionist welfare state' by its considerable support and recognition. At the same time, the state influenced only marginally, if at all, the paradigms, orientations, and policy perspectives of the political science discipline. Canada's broader socio-economic environment and political culture, on the other hand, appear to have had a close, mutually interacting relationship with both the discipline and profession (Stein and Trent, 1982).

4 In one sense the Canadian case may be relatively unique. The creation of multiple 'arms-length' institutional relationships between the state and political science at both federal and provincial levels, through funding agencies like the Canada Council and the SSHRCC, has permitted the discipline to enjoy support from government without in any way developing a sense of dependence on it. This relationship, however, requires careful and continuous vigilance, redefinition, and balance on both sides.

5 With regard to the influence of political science on the overall direction and content of governmental interventions and policies, in the earlier pre-1950s period this was sometimes significant, although very sporadic, due to the small size of the overall community. In the current period we find no clear or well-developed pattern in this respect. Overall, the influence by political scientists is certainly not strong. But there is both close professional and policy interaction and profoundly critical thinking, sometimes coming from the same political science practitioners. This may occur both in the classroom and in a public or government forum.[23]

This trend does not appear to be confined to political science in Canada. Some recent commentators on the state of the discipline in the United States have deplored its growing lack of policy or practical relevance concomitant with its increasing institutionalization (Ricci 1984). In the United Kingdom, both Jack Hayward and James Sharpe have noted the strong suspicion which political practitioners feel toward political scientists in their country (Hayward 1982, 1987; Sharpe 1975).

In France, West Germany, and Italy, recent historical experience appears to have been somewhat different. According to Peter Wagner and his collaborators, social scientists in these three West European countries, including political scientists, established close personal and political ties with state policy-makers and actors in the late 1950s and early 1960s in order to advance their mutual goals of academic and political reform. These 'discourse coalitions', as the authors label them, 'led to a restructuring of discourse in both social science and politics, and provided a discursive foundation for institutional change in science and society' (Wagner 1988:16). Although these political alliances did not last long, their ultimate success in achieving their reformist goals had the adverse consequence of weakening the social sciences institutionally in the three countries. The policy-oriented practitioners of these disciplines duplicated the perspective of state policy-makers and abandoned their traditional function of challenging prevailing political views. This led to a fragmentation within each social science discipline between 'objective', 'critical' and 'policy-oriented' social scientists and the ultimate devaluation of the scientific legitimacy of these disciplines (Wagner 1988:25). Recently, a new and much less politically involved phase has emerged in which 'intense alliances involving the merging of political and scientific goals no longer attract large groups of social scientists' (Wagner 1987:297).

Clearly, the experience in continental Western Europe between social scientists and state policy-makers is very different from that in the largely Anglo-Saxon liberal democratic countries such as Canada, the United States and the United Kingdom. It would seem to suggest that close relationships between political scientists and state actors can have rather adverse consequences for the development of the discipline. We must therefore raise the following familiar questions concerning the relationship between political scientists and the state in Western countries: are there appropriate limits that should be applied to welfare state intervention and financial assistance for the political science discipline and profession? Conversely, is there an appropriate political participant and/or policy advisory role for the political scientists in these countries, consistent with the norms and long-term objectives of the discipline?

With respect to the first question, our own observations, based on a preliminary mapping of recent Canadian experience in this area, may be suggestive for more general, cross-national comparative analysis. We found that increased welfare state funding and steering of political science research and development in Canada has had the contradictory effect of simultaneously encouraging both the institutionalization and isolation of the political science profession from political and state actors, while increasing its overall financial dependence on the state.[24] The long-term consequences of this trend are, in our view, not salutary for the discipline. But some of the detrimental effects may be overcome by a careful balancing of state roles — expanding state involvement in disciplinary development in some areas and contracting it in others. For example, in our view:

1 Financial allocations by state funding agencies to professional political and other social science associations should be made using a more permanent, objective, mathematically-based formula, so as to be insulated from the changing whims of different parties in office, fluctuating financial and economic conditions, and uninformed assessments and prejudices of public servants.

2 There should be more efforts made by professional associations of political and other social sciences to establish their professional journals and other associational activities on a more self-sustaining, debt-free basis. This would involve more reliance on commercial advertisements and philanthropic donations from private

organizations representing business, labour and other major economic and social groups.

3 Direct state financial assistance to academically-based political science research should be offered entirely without 'strings', apart from the normal expectations concerning acknowledgement of funding sources and reporting of research findings.

4 State encouragement of and financial support for more policy-orientated political science research should be increased, but it should be done primarily through the establishment and further development of independent policy-oriented research institutes rather than through academic institutions. These research institutes might be funded in part by government and in part by the private sector. They might employ political and other social scientists on a full-time basis to conduct this research, on the model developed by a number of countries in Western Europe. Such institutes should also include career public servants temporarily seconded to help the full-time researchers carry out their policy-oriented investigations. They might eventually form the basis of a 'third community' of researchers, neither government-based nor academically-based, whose primary objective might be to foster closer state-academic exchanges and shared research activities (Lindquist 1988).

5 More government contract and survey work should be provided for policy-oriented political scientists, commensurate with that already available for other social scientists such as economists and sociologists. It should be provided in particular in areas in which political scientists have clear expertise, such as constitutional renewal, intergovernmental relations, legislative, executive, administrative, and electoral system procedures and reforms, and election finances. Political scientists should make these areas of their expertise more clearly known to government. They should also be careful to uphold the same scientific and professional standards with regard to their research work within government as they establish outside of government.

With respect to the second question, namely, is there an appropriate political participant and policy advisory role for political scientists, we do not believe that a strictly separate relationship must be established by political scientists from the state in order to maintain their professional norms and critical roles. Nevertheless, political independence in carrying out research activities must be carefully preserved. It seem to us that a middle way, which gradually reduces the communications barriers between political scientists and state actors, can still be found. For example:

1 The political science discipline should avoid close political alliances with highly partisan groups, particularly on a group or associational basis. However, individual political scientists should feel free and even be encouraged to become active and offer their expertise in

non-partisan or multipartisan political causes or movements. In the Canadian context, these would include such bodies as committees for or against a free trade agreement with the United States, committees for or against the independence of Quebec, committees for or against major constitutional amendment proposals such as the Meech Lake Accord, etc.

2 Political scientists should be communicating their strong support for or criticisms of various regime institutions and government policies not merely in their professional journals, but also in semi-professional and lay periodicals, and in the electronic and print media. The areas of expertise of various members of the national political science community should be made known to the editors and directors of these non-academic communications structures or bodies.

3 Political scientists should encourage as wide a range of personal and institutional roles for themselves as possible, *vis-à-vis* the state, since exposure to the many facets of government and political practice provides a valuable educational experience for political scientists, and has many useful spillover benefits for their research.

4 On a collective basis, representatives of the political science profession should be interacting with leading state actors to break down the institutional and attitudinal barriers between them, and to foster more joint government-academic political science activities and institutions.

5 The teaching function of political scientists in relation to the state should be expanded. For example, special courses, programmes, and workshops for professional public servants should be established or expanded, and the expert knowledge of political scientists should be conveyed to these officials in concepts and language which are readily understandable by them, using familiar cases and examples from Canadian and other national experiences.

In conclusion, what is clearly needed to understand and delimit an appropriate relationship between political scientists and the state in modern liberal-democratic societies (and also non-Western societies) is more comparative information and analysis of the experience in this area in different cultural contexts. Hopefully, this chapter will have made some modest preliminary contribution to this type of analysis.

NOTES

1 This chapter is partially based on John Trent 'Politics and political science: mapping the relationship', unpublished paper presented to the International Round Table on the Comparative Study of the Development of the Discipline of Political Science: Cortona, Italy, 21-26 September 1987.

2 We define 'the state' in the Weberian sense as a 'compulsory association claiming control over territories and the people within them' (Evans et al. 1985:7). The

Canadian state encompasses all formal governmental structures and para-governmental bodies such as governmental agencies, boards, commissions, and publicly-owned enterprises at the federal, provincial and municipal levels.

By 'political science' we mean both the study of the 'discipline' (that is, the system of academic instruction in politics and its output in research and ideas) and the practice of the 'profession' (that is, the occupation of professor and researcher in the field of politics, and related associational and administrative support structures).

3 By 'late liberal state' we have in mind the last stages of the classic nineteenth century liberal state in the West, in which the scope of state action continued to be restricted in the economic, social, and cultural spheres. Private enterprise, churches, and philanthropic and charitable institutions were still dominant in many of these areas, but the state was growing in strength and importance, and was sometimes preeminent. This period extended from about 1875 until just after World War Two in most countries of the West. See also Wittrock et al (1988:12).

4 By 'modern interventionist welfare state' we are referring to the most recent period in the evolution of Western nation-states, in which state action has expanded enormously and now permeates all areas of economic, social, and cultural life. This trend has evolved largely in response to popular demands for greater political, economic, and social equality and more comprehensive welfare benefits for all citizens. In most Western countries this period extends from about the 1950s until the present. See also Wittrock et al. (1988:26).

5 In Canada, the 'late liberal state' was a federal state, which reflected a pattern of strong competition between the two levels of government almost from its inception in 1867. The federal and provincial governments vied for larger shares of available revenues and for the opportunity to provide wider economic benefits for citizens falling within their respective jurisdictions. This had the effect of promoting greater state interventionism than in other Western countries. Moreover, it was necessary for state actors to intervene in the economy in order to provide essential economic, transportation, and communication infrastructure, protect infant industries, and exploit the natural resources of a sparsely populated young country extending over a huge geographic expanse.

6 Under the federal constitution of Canada established in 1867, education at all levels, including post-secondary training in colleges and universities, fell clearly within provincial jurisdiction. But prior to World War Two, provincial governments had much less revenue than the federal government available for such expenditures, and they did not receive any transfer payments in these areas from the central authorities. This situation changed after World War Two.

7 In addition to the secular universities, which still had very small enrolments during this period, there were a number of even smaller clerical colleges and universities throughout English-speaking Canada, then consisting of the Maritime Provinces, the two central provinces of Quebec and Ontario, Manitoba, and British Columbia. In French-speaking Canada the Roman Catholic Church funded and directed all post-secondary educational institutions (Murray 1922, cited in Goodwin 1961; Brunet 1960).

8 Drummond (1983:18-19) notes, however, that 'Professors in the Provincial University [the University of Toronto] were appointed by Order in Council, and this involvement of the Provincial Government was anything but a formality. It is said that the Ontario Cabinet was determined that whoever [sic] they might

appoint to the new chair, they would not have a freetrader who might criticize the National Policy, then a matter of burning political controversy both for the provincial authorities and for the Dominion. Before his appointment was confirmed . . . Ashley was interviewed both by Premier Mowat and by [former Ontario Premier and federal Liberal Party Leader] Edward Blake, Chancellor of the University. . . . The President of the University, Sir Daniel Wilson, played a secondary role in these discussions . . . work[ing] closely with George Ross, the Education Minister.' This pattern of direct political involvement in academic appointments became more and more exceptional in subsequent years.

9 There is an interesting inversion of this imitative pattern in the academic career of Stephen Leacock, the celebrated Canadian economist and humourist. Leacock was chairman of the Political Science Department of McGill University from 1901 until his retirement in 1936. While trained primarily in economics, he also included large quantities of what we may loosely label 'political science and government' in his lectures and courses. His basic textbook *Elements of Political Science*, first published in 1901, contained much abstract thought on the nature of the state and government. It was widely used in American colleges and universities in the first decades of the twentieth century.

10 For a lucid discussion of the significant impact of this Commission on postwar economic and political developments in Canada, see Smiley (1962).

11 By their active involvement in government and politics, these English-speaking political scientists of the pre-World War Two period were not transformed into a 'clerisy', or apologists of the political status quo, as John Porter (1965:16) and Brooks and Gagnon (1988: chapter 5) argue. Several of them were strong critics of the 'government line', and others strongly influenced pre-and post-World War Two government policy in bold new directions. For further elaboration of this point, see p.66-7.

12 Leclerc (1982) notes that in the face of this opposition, the Laval University authorities showed some ambivalence in their efforts to support the academic independence of their faculty at the School (Faculty) of Social Sciences. For example, the Principal (recteur), Mgr Vandry, apologized to Quebec Premier Duplessis for the political interventions and course materials of Père Lévesque and Maurice Lamontagne, but resisted Duplessis's request that they must be dismissed from their academic positions. Funds were therefore provided by the provincial legislature, 'subject to the changing mood of those in political power' (p.86). From 1944 until 1949, during the conservative Duplessis regime, special grants of $50,000 were provided to the Faculty for professorial salaries; this sum was reduced to $25,000 over the next two years, and finally discontinued. The capriciousness of this financial support undoubtedly influenced Père Lévesque to support federal funding of higher education in Quebec, against prevailing elite and nationalist opinion, while serving as a Commissioner on the Massey Commission in 1951.

13 This was due largely to a windfall of $100 million in succession duties the federal government had received from the Killam and Dunn estates, (see Ostry 1978:67-8).

14 Throughout this chapter, all dollar references are to the Canadian dollar.

15 The Social Science Research Council of Canada (SSRCC) was established in 1940 by the various national associations of social scientists to provide assistance for social science research. Its programmes included research and publishing grants,

leave fellowships, pre-doctoral fellowships, travel grants, and money for cooperative research grants and research planning. Its total budget for the 1940-58 period amounted to only $650,000, most of which came from American foundations in the form of block grants. By using the SSRCC in this manner, Canadian academic social scientists were able to maintain an 'arms length' relationship with American philanthropies. No government money was accepted for academic social science research until 1957 (Trent 1984:48).

16 For example, according to statistics collated by Robert Davidson of the Social Science Federation of Canada in 1982 (Stein, Trent, and Donneur 1983:19-Table 5), between the years 1967-8 and 1980-1, the number of research projects in political science supported by the Canada Council and its successor body, the Social Sciences and Humanities Research Council of Canada (SSHRCC) ranged from a high of 69 in 1969-70 to a low of 31 in 1976-7 and 1977-8, with the average considerably higher in the early 1970s than in the late 1970s. The annual sums granted for this research during the same period ranged from a low of $209,000 in 1968-9 to a high of $616,600 in 1979-80, but this included sudden drops in funding in successive years during the late 1970s of close to 100 per cent. It also fails to provide an adjustment for the deflated value of the dollar over that period. The political science proportion of the total amounts awarded to research in the social sciences and humanities during this period fluctuated between a low of 4.6 per cent in 1974-75 and a high of 10.9 per cent in 1967-8.

17 Stein, Trent and Donneur (1983), especially pages 18 (Table 4) and 19 (Table 5), based on statistics collated by Robert Davidson of the Social Science Federation of Canada in 1982; and Thorburn (1983), Appendix, Tables I, III, IV.

18 Prior to 1968, Canadian political scientists generally belonged to the interdisciplinary Canadian Political Science Association, which included economists, political scientists, sociologists, and anthropologists. The sociologists and anthropologists separated from the Association in the early 1960s, and established their own journal, *The Canadian Journal of Sociology and Anthropology*. The *Canadian Journal of Economics and Political Science*, which was launched in 1935 by Harold Innis and several colleagues at the University of Toronto, served as the official journal for both economists and political scientists in Canada until 1968. It received a small annual subsidy from the University of Toronto Press, but never obtained direct government support.

19 See various Annual Reports presented at the Annual General meeting of the Canadian Political Science Association, 1968 to 1988.

20 The precise amount of this subsidy to the *Canadian Journal of Political Science* (CJPS) cannot be provided from this table, since Aid to Publications includes two journals (in 1975-6) or three (in 1976-7 to 1980-1). The amounts ranged from a low of $74,920 in 1975-6 (for *CJPS* and *Canadian Public Policy*) to a high of $94,820 (for three journals, now including *Canadian Public Administration*), in 1976-7. The combined subsidy was gradually reduced in subsequent years (Thorburn 1983:Table 1).

21 One area of political science education which remains woefully weak, despite these trends toward increased government funding and the institutionalization of the discipline, is that of general political education of the mass public in Canada. According to recent studies, the average Canadian is still extremely ignorant of most political issues, institutions, and even public personalities and political leaders. This is due, in large part, to an almost complete absence of political education at

the elementary and secondary levels of schooling, and to a general refusal by political scientists in post-secondary colleges and universities to conduct courses in 'civics'. What little political education exists is generally elitist, and tends to encourage students to be passive spectators rather than active participants. On these points, see Jon H. Pammett and Jean-Luc Pépin (1988).

22 It has since ground to a virtual halt, as a result of a general hiring freeze in the federal public service in the current period of government fiscal austerity.

23 In an effort to facilitate comparative analysis, we present our finding in more schematic form in Figure 1, Mapping the Dominant Variables in the Historical Relationship between the State and Political Science in Canada).

24 It must be acknowledged, however, that unlike their American counterparts, many Canadian political and social scientists do not appear to be concerned about the growing financial dependence of their profession on the state, so long as their disciplinary institutions maintain an 'arms-length' relationship with it.

REFERENCES

Adair, John and Davidson, Robert (1983), *Research Activity in the Social Sciences: Funding, Productivity and Attitudes of University-Based Social Scientists*, Ottawa: Social Sciences and Humanities Research Council of Canada.

Aron, Raymond (1985) 'Réflexions sur la politique et al science politique française', *Revue française de Science Politique*, 5(1):55:22.

Bladen, Vincent W. (1965) *Financing Higher Education in Canada*, Toronto: University of Toronto Press.

Brooks, Stephen and Gagnon, Alain (1988) *Between Clerisy and Vanguard: Social Scientists and Politics in Canada*, Montreal: McGill-Queen's University Press.

Brunet, Michel (1960) 'The university as a public institution in French Canada from Louis XIII to the electoral campaign of 1960' *Canadian Public Administration*, 3(4):344.

Canadian Political Science Association (1913) *Proceedings*, Kingston: Jackson Press.

— (1988) *Report of the Secretary-Treasurer*.

Clement, Wallace and Drache, Daniel (1978) *A Practical Guide to Canadian Political Economy*, Toronto: Lorimer.

Dawson, Robert MacGregor (1950) 'Political science teaching in Canada', a report to the Social Science Research Council; reprinted in *Newsletter of the Canadian Political Science Association* vol. 2, 2, March 1973.

Dion, Léon (1975) 'Politique et science politique', *Canadian Journal of Political Science*, 8(3):367-80.

Drummond, Ian M. (1983) *Political Economy at the University of Toronto: A History of the Department, 1888-1982*, Toronto: University of Toronto Faculty of Arts and Science.

Evans, Peter, Rueschemeyer, Dietrich, and Skocpol, Theda (1985) 'On the road to a more adequate understanding of the state', in Peter Evans *et al.* (eds), *Bringing the State Back In*, Cambridge: Cambridge University Press.

Goodwin, Crauford D. (1961) *Canadian Economic Thought*, Durham, N.C.: Duke University Press.

Graham, Ron (1986) *One-eyed Kings*, Toronto: Totem.

Hayward, Jack (1982) 'United Kingdom', in William G. Andrews (ed.) *International*

Handbook of Political Science, Westport, CT: Greenwood Press.
— (1987) 'Cultural and contextual constraints upon the development of political science in Britain', paper presented at the ICSDPS conference of Cortona, Italy, which also appears as Chapter 4 in this book.
Hodgetts, J.E. (1966) in J.E. Hodgetts (ed.), *Higher Education in a Changing Canada*, Toronto: University of Toronto Press.
Leclerc, Michel (1982) *La Science Politique au Quebec*, Montreal: L'Hexagone.
— (1985) 'Pour une sociologie critique de la science politique québécoise: une impossible hagiographie', *Les Cahiers de l'ACFAS* 32.
Leslie, Peter (1980) *Canadian Universities, 1980 and Beyond*, Association of Universities and Colleges of Canada, Ottawa.
Lindquist, Evert (1988) 'Third community, policy, inquiry, and social scientists', paper presented to the Annual Meeting of the Canadian Political Science Association, Learned Societies Conference, University of Windsor, Ontario, 9-11 June 1988.
Lipset, S.M. (1969) *Politics and the Social Sciences*, New York: Oxford University Press.
Lowi, T.J. (1973) 'The politicization of political science', *American Political Quarterly*, 1(1):43-71.
MacKinnon, James and Brown, David (1969) 'Political science in the Canadian university, 1969', in Robin Matthews and James Steele, (eds), *The Struggle for Canadian Universities*, Toronto: New Press
Ostry, Bernard (1978), *The Cultural Connection*, Toronto: McClelland and Stewart.
Pammett, Jon H. and Pépin, Jean-Luc (1988) 'Preface', in Jon H. Pammett and Jean-Luc Pépin (eds) *Political Education in Canada*, Halifax, Nova Scotia: Institute for Research on Public Policy.
Park, Julian (1957) 'Preface', in Julian Park (ed.) *The Culture of Contemporary Canada*, Toronto: Ryerson Press.
Porter, John (1965) *The Vertical Mosaic*, Toronto: University of Toronto Press.
Ricci, David (1984) *The Tragedy of Political Science*, New Haven, CT and London: Yale University Press.
Robbins, Allan (1981) 'Some observations on survey research and the Federal Government', paper presented at the Sixth Annual Meeting of the Canadian Association of Applied Social Research, Learned Societies Conference, Dalhousie University, Halifax, Nova Scotia.
— (1982) 'Policy making and social science survey research: a perspective from government', paper presented at the Annual Meeting of the Canadian Political Science Association, Learned Societies Conference.
Rose, Richard and Peters, B. Guy (1978) *Can Government Go Bankrupt*? New York: Basic Books.
Sharpe, L.J. (1975) The social scientist and policy-making: some cautionary thoughts and transatlantic reflections', *Policy Politics*, 4(2):11-12.
Smiley, Donald V. (1962) 'The Rowell-Sirois Report, provincial autonomy and post-war Canadian federalism, *Canadian Journal of Economic and Political Science* 27(1):54-69.
— (1974) 'Must Canadian political science be a miniature replica?' *Journal of Canadian Studies*, 9(1):31-41.
Smith, Denis (1971) 'What are we teaching: the nationalization of Canadian political science', *Canadian Forum*, 5:4-5.
Somit, Albert and Tanenhaus, Joseph (1967), *The Development of American Political*

Science: From Burgess to Behavioralism, Boston: Allyn and Bacon.

Stein, Michael and Trent, John E. (1982) 'Canada', in William G. Andrews (ed.) *International Handbook of Political Science*, Westport, CT: Greenwood Press.

Stein, Michael, Trent, John E, and Donneur, André (1982) Political science in Canada in the 1980s: achievement and challenge, paper presented at the IPSA World Congress, Rio de Janeiro, Brazil, July, 1982.

— (1983) 'The state of the discipline in Canada in the mid 1980s: achievement and challenge, revised (mimeo).

Thorburn, Hugh (1983) 'The value of political science for Canada', unpublished paper presented to a meeting of chairmen, Canadian Political Science Association, Ottawa (mimeo).

Trent, John (1984) 'The social sciences in Canada in the eighties: the unloved middle brother syndrome', in John Trent and Paul Lamy (eds), *Global Crises and the Social Sciences: North American Perspectives*, Ottawa: University of Ottawa Press.

— (1987) 'Politics and political science: mapping the relationship', paper presented at the ICSDPS conference of Cortona, Italy.

Wagner, Peter (1987) 'Social sciences and political projects: reform coalitions between social scientists and policy-makers in France, Italy, and West Germany', in S. Blume *et al.* (eds), *The Social Direction of the Social Sciences, Sociology of the Sciences Yearbook*, XI: 277-306.

— (1988) 'Discourse coalitions and state formations: the interaction between social scientists and policy-makers in France, Italy, and West Germany', paper presented to the Annual Meeting of the Canadian Political Science Association, Windsor, University of Ontario, 9-11 June 1988.

Wittrock, Bjorn, Wagner, Peter and Wollman, Helmut (1988), 'Social science and the modern state: knowledge, institutions, and societal transformations', papers Wissenshaftszentrum für Sozialforschung, Berlin #P87-3.

Wood, Ellen and Wood, Neil (1970) 'Canada and the American science of politics', in Ian Lumsden, (ed.), *Close the 49th Parallel: The Americanization of Canada*, Toronto: University of Toronto Press.

Figure 1 Mapping the dominant variables in the relationship between the state and political science in Canada 1888-1988

	Government/political regime
Direct*	Party platforms: research and policy input Elections: polling and commentary Political leaders: advisors and critics Public service: structure and function Advisory committees Pressure groups: advisors, participants
Indirect**	Royal Commissions Electoral regimes Social movements and reform groups Support and structure for R&D Clerisy/vanguard roles of political science Interventionist/laissez-faire role of government

	Political culture
Direct*	Political science output: description, explanation prognostication, prescription Socio-economic needs and trends Central/local jurisdiction over education and R&D Participant/spectator political education
Indirect**	Liberalism, Conservatism, Socialism Political change/status quo orientation Theory of the role of the state Dissemination, circulation of political ideas and knowledge

	Political science discipline
Direct*	State, influence on discipline's configuration and orientation Institutionalization and structures Policy-oriented publications Choice of subject matter
Indirect**	Methods, theories and concepts Teaching: descriptive *vs* ideological Structure and function of graduate training Research findings

* Direct influences refer to specific individual or professional relationships with the state
** Indirect influence means relationships that stimulate basic trends and orientations.

Figure 1 continued

	Political authorities and policies
Direct*	Professional political science advice: participation, commentary Political advice, participation, critique Policy oriented sub-fields of political science University funding: levels and linkages Research support: emergence, sustaining
Indirect**	Mandate, structure and funding of research granting bodies Locale of research: academic, private, government Analysis of policy making and delivery

	Political education
Direct*	Discipline recognition Personnel and personnel policies Funding levels and orientation Curriculum Levels of political education
Indirect**	Funding and control: public, private, church Reference sources: local/imported Theory of the function of education Theory of the function of political education

	Political science profession
Direct*	Association's professional activities and lobbying Definition of career rewards for professors Government employment, internships, exchanges Personal influence and participation of political scientists
Indirect**	Political Science departments: Structures and funding Associations: Journals: Meetings and conferences: Career outlets for students (labour market)

Note: *Major issue areas in the relationship* Autonomy/politicization; Academic freedom/Government influence; Scholarly objectivity and impartiality/Scholarly relevance and involvement; Professional, scientific development/Socio-Political responsibility; Degrees and means of government support/Private and student financing; Descriptive, empirical analysis/Critical evaluation; Government-Discipline isolation/Interaction and exchange; Relations with government: corporate (profession-discipline)/Individual; Relations with government: 'Clerisy'/'Vanguard'/Professional/Teaching; Scholarly independence/Professionalization-Institutionalization.

4 Cultural and contextual constraints upon the development of political science in Great Britain

Jack Hayward[1]

The British style of political education and investigation has traditionally been Socratic in style. The stress has been upon critically questioning key concepts and assumptions, rather than building up a comprehensive and systematic science. Reflected in the tutorial style of teaching, which spread from the universities of Oxford and Cambridge, the emphasis is upon dialogue as a training of the mind not as a more specifically utilitarian exercise. In practice, the critical function has often assumed such destructive forms that what is left of political science may have no higher ambition than to 'muddle through', in ways that are familiar to the practitioner of politics. Scepticism about the possibility of political science is deeply rooted in the British intellectual tradition, represented notably by the University of Oxford. Writing in 1932, R.B. McCallum accurately conveyed both the prevailing attitudes and the state of affairs when he described the study of politics in Oxford in these disenchanted terms: 'The subject is taught by a very few specialists and a large number of philosophers and historians who approach it with varying degrees of enthusiasm or disgust'.[2] The belief that a liberal elite education could best be acquired through an acquaintance with the political philosophies of Plato and Aristotle, coupled with a knowledge of the history of the political systems of Athens and Rome, survived the Second World War. It is captured by Alfred North Whitehead (a once celebrated philosopher who had moved from England to America) in his rearguard assertion 'based upon no confusing research, that as a training in political imagination, the Harvard School of Politics and of Government cannot hold a candle to the old-fashioned English classical education' (Whitehead 1948:33).

Such defensive complacency, prompted by the emerging challenge of American political science, reflected a tradition going back to Aristotle's conception of politics as the master science, in which 'science' was conceived as synonymous with philosophy or systematically ordered knowledge. By the eighteenth century knowledge about politics was conceived as being either psychological or historical. Human nature provided the enduring element while history provided the element of change; together they were the sources of the statics and dynamics of politics. On the basis of such knowledge, in which 'facts' and 'values' were inextricably intermingled, educated citizens would be able to take part in deciding the affairs of their society, armed with the insight provided by the integrating discipline of the applied master science of politics. 'The ultimate purpose of any science of politics remained that of its earliest cultivators, namely to furnish prudential maxims, draw practical inferences, and formulate clear criteria for judging the fitness of laws and institutions which could guide the conduct of wise legislators' (Collini *et al.* 1983:14-15).

This entrenched historico-philosophical tradition successfully resisted the nineteenth century attempts, made apparently with more success in economics and sociology, to develop politics into a rigorous science with a pretence to formulating experimentally tested axioms. In politics, the Whig interpretation of British political history as a struggle to achieve parliamentary government defeated the scientific claims of Benthamite utilitarianism, which had more success in political economy. The imperial claim to order all knowledge within the social sciences became impossible to sustain once the master's servants acquired their independence. Those academics who taught and wrote about politics had belatedly and reluctantly to seek through specialization to sustain a professional authority to which they laid a contested claim.

In Britain, the most striking manifestation of this utilitarian urge to break with the gentleman-amateur Oxford tradition at the end of the nineteenth century occurred with the creation of the London School of Economics and Political Science in 1895. Graham Wallas, its first Professor of Political Science, testified that its founders — Sidney and Beatrice Webb — had adopted the Paris Ecole Libre des Sciences Politiques as their model. However, 'political science' was something of an afterthought and its use in the singular a significant misnomer.

After all, the Ecole Libre had used the customary plural 'political sciences', with its interdisciplinary and eclectic connotations. The real institutional affinity lay in the desire to train leaders for a democratic society who would have a command of relevant knowledge. The prime motivation of the Webbs as Fabian socialists (while sharing the meritocratic inspiration of their French predecessors) was to develop research because 'reforming society is no light matter, and must be undertaken by experts specially trained for the purpose' (Webb 1948:86). But how was the London School to train experts without people who were themselves masters of a science capable of application?

Beatrice Webb confided her frustration to her diary in 1896: 'Advertised for a political science lecturer — and yesterday interviewed candidates — a nondescript set of university men. All hopeless from our point of view — all imagined that political science consisted of a knowledge of Aristotle and modern(!) writers such as De Tocqueville — wanted to put the students through a course of Utopias from More downwards . . . one of them wanted to construct a 'Political Man', from whose imaginary qualities all things might be deduced . . . Finally, we determined to do without our lecturer — to my mind a blessed consummation. It struck me always as a trifle difficult to teach a science which does not yet exist.' (Webb 1948:94). Graham Wallas, whose pioneering book *Human Nature in Politics* (1908) was still endeavouring to base political science on the 'facts' of human nature, thought his successor Harold Laski's *Grammar of Politics* (1925) was a great advance upon Henry Sidgwick's *Elements of Politics* (1891), no general British textbook on political science having been published in the interim. Wallas pilloried Sidgwick for declaring: 'My deep conviction is that it [political science] can yield as yet little fruit of practical utility. . . . Still, man must work and a professor must write books.'[3] Whilst some might praise Sidgwick for his becoming humility and think that little has changed in a hundred years, the Fabians were understandably impatient with those who did not do the useful comparative research into electoral and taxation systems on the basis of which reforms they desired could be proposed and implemented.

With the failure to create in the London School a true replica of Sciences Po in Paris, with its practical concern to train an elite to serve the state (albeit endowed with a radical zeal) the next attempt came with the 1930s creation of Nuffield College in Oxford. The inspiration here was Sandie Lindsay, Master of Balliol College from 1924-49 and the mind behind the creation of the innovative University of Keele in 1950. A teacher of politics in the traditional, classicist manner, Lindsay was concerned to overcome the separation between theory and practice by creating not a Brookings-style institute but a postgraduate college in which there would be a meeting of minds between social scientists and men of action — central and local government officials, politicians, and businessmen. Lindsay was convinced that if the traditional separation of political actors and political analysts were breached, this 'could revolutionize the study of contemporary society in England, not only through the high standard of applicable knowledge which it would produce, but even more by the effect it would have in making the theorist and the practical man accustomed to helping and consulting one another' (Scott 1971:235; cf. 233-4; Chester 1986:68-77).

Although another political scientist, G.D.H. Cole, tried in the early 1940s to develop Nuffield College as a centre for research into the problems of postwar reconstruction, he was frustrated in particular by the British disease of official secrecy, which prevented senior civil servants playing any part in this work (Chester 1986:111-13). We meet here one of the bottlenecks preventing the development of an empirical British political science — lack of access to essential inform-ation and the segregation of those who know but do not write from those who write but do not know. (We shall return to this later.) So the Oxford socialist reformists, Lindsay and Cole, like their London predecessors, the Webbs, failed to institutionalize an applied political science, partly because the acknowledged expertise did not exist on the basis of which they could overcome entrenched official and academic hostility. Not even the upheaval of a world war, in which some of the few teachers of politics acquired first-hand experience in government, was able to destroy the barrier between those whose vocations were the activities of public administration and political service and those whose vocation was the study of politics and administration. As so often happens in Britain, it was a response to external — in this case primarily American — pressure that changes occurred within the academic sphere.

THE MUTED IMPACT OF AMERICAN POLITICAL SCIENCE

In 1962 former US Secretary of State Dean Acheson declared that 'Great Britain has lost an Empire and has not yet found a role'. British political science seemed to be acquiring an empire but remained uncertain about its purpose. It could be argued that during the 1960s, when the teaching and study of politics was to commence an unprecedented expansion in British universities, the full brunt of developments in a self-confident American political science was felt at a time when there was uncertainty about what to teach and how to study the subject. With the increasing introversion of philosophy in linguistic preoccupations, while logical positivism pronounced a metaphysical political philosophy as clinically dead, the traditional concern with the history of political ideas was left in a residual and debilitated state. The description of political institutions had not fundamentally changed since Bagehot (of the *English Constitution*, not the would-be scientistic *Physics and Politics*). This meant that academic specialists in politics had rather dubious claims to a professional monopoly of a particular branch of knowledge, while not possessing Bagehot's gift for penetrating aphorism.

Before considering the cool reception afforded the methodological and substantive advances made by American political scientists, mention should be made of the emergence of an organized profession under the stimulus of UNESCO. The creation of a Political Studies Association in 1950, after the (relatively) high tide of official interest in the social sciences during the Second World War from which the economists principally profited, meant that there was at least an institutional umbrella under which a variety of allied subjects could shelter. (The avoidance of the title Political Science by the Association's founders was deliberate and significant.) They were loosely enumerated as: 'Political Theory and Institutions, Government and Public Administration, Constitutional and Administrative Law, International Relations, International Law and similar subjects' (Chester 1975:152). The product of an uneasy compromise between the founders — with William Robson from the London School and Norman Chester of Nuffield College, Oxford, playing the leading roles — these categories of potential members partly overlapped. In some cases, notably in the instance of the administrative, constitutional, and international lawyers, they were — unlike Continental Europe — never to become part of the political studies community. Furthermore public administration and international relations were in an ambiguous situation, partly subsections of a broad-based political studies community and partly autonomous, specialist communities of their own, often with better links to practitioners. The diffident approach of the founders was evident from the recruiting circular sent out in 1949: 'It is not suggested that the Association should immediately embark on any ambitious functions or projects' (Chester 1975:152; Hayward 1982). Members were reassured that they would not be expected to do very much: an annual meeting 'ought to be possible' and 'publication . . . perhaps even of a journal' would be considered, the latter coming into existence in 1953. It was this rather relaxed community of about a hundred scholars, who formed the membership of the Political Studies Association in 1950, which largely ignored transatlantic developments as long as it could. By the end of the decade, this was becoming increasingly difficult and the negative response in the shape of Bernard Crick's *The American Science of Politics* appeared in 1959. It has not really been improved upon since then.

To understand Crick's negative response — a more articulate and thought out repudiation but representative of the majority allergy to the abstract scientism of the methodologies propounded — it is necessary to read his subsequent tract *In Defence of Politics*, with its vehement reassertion of a liberalized version of the Aristotelian conception of the study of politics. In it he protested against the fact that 'In recent years the growing tendency in the university study of politics has been to make the criteria for research and study not political importance, but various notions of methodological impeccability (Crick 1964a:190; cf. 23, 171). Ironically, given our earlier quotation from Beatrice Webb on the reasons for the London School's failure to appoint to a lectureship in political science in 1896, it was as a lecturer at the London School that Crick championed Aristotle and Tocqueville against those who wished to substitute predictive scientific laws for understanding (Crick, 1959:224-6). However, to demonstrate some of the weaknesses of American political science was not to vindicate the strength of British 'political studies' and by 1975 Crick was to confess 'I am a bit fed up with political science', and suggested that it was time to accept the interdisciplinary implications of being parasitic upon history and philosophy (Crick 1975:180).[4]

However, despite this sweeping call to turn away from a behaviouralism that was already in partial retreat in the USA, British political studies had meanwhile begun to adopt in a piecemeal and incremental fashion many of the theoretical, quantitative, and substantive concerns of American political scientists but without their concomitant theoretical self-consciousness. 'New perspectives may have had to burst through the more established interpretations, but this does not mean that they burst them apart. Quite the reverse. New approaches and perspectives were slowly absorbed and accepted precisely because they could be integrated so as to sustain the credibility of the core assumptions integral to the earlier accounts and to the tradition of understanding as a whole' (Dearlove 1982:438). The British response to American political science has thus been a classic case of dynamic conservatism: changing enough so as to keep things basically the same.

In terms of the context of what has been taught to students of politics, despite Crick's clarion call there has been a decline in the importance of both history and philosophy, whether in the study of political thought or of political institutions. This has been especially marked in the polytechnics, where there has been more innovation and experimentation in teaching, partly because there has been less pressure to undertake research than in the universities. Particularly when it was associated with a roseate view of the working of the British political system — a view encouraged by much American political science writing into the 1960s — the emphasis upon how successful the pragmatic British capacity for gradualist compromise was in ensuring that 'the more things change, the more they remain the same', gave way by the end of the 1960s to attacks on 'pluralist stagnation' (Kavanagh, 1974:264). The pervasive 'What's wrong with Britain' syndrome, based upon its relative economic decline and its loss of great-power status internationally, meant that a certain style of teaching that exuded a sense of political legitimation rather than critical political analysis, ceased to be fashionable first in higher education and then in the schools. Comparative studies first of political sociology, then political development, later of political economy, were clearly less concerned with celebrating consensus and instead highlighted social divisiveness, stagnation, and poor economic performance.

Before the establishment of the Social Science Research Council in 1965, British political science research was essentially artisan-like, usually done by an individual on a diminutive budget. (Its name was significantly changed in 1983 when the Conservative Government, having failed to abolish the SSRC, altered its name to Economic and Social Research Council, deliberately omitting the word 'science'.) Until the squeeze upon its capacity to offer financial support from the late 1970s, the SSRC encouraged the development of both the number of research students and of team work on 'big budget' projects. This resulted in a massive increase in political science publications, both in the form of articles and in the new general and specialist journals that were established. This phenomenon was also reflected in the number of books on political science, attested by the inflation in the size of bibliographies provided for the increasing number of undergraduates who were their major market. (Kavanagh and Rose 1977: 19-20) However, one of the most remarkable growth areas has been work that can be done on low or no budgets in political theory. Ironically it was an Englishman, T.D. Weldon, who had seemed to sentence political theory to death in his *Vocabulary of Politics* (1953), while it was an American John Rawls, who seemed to revive it with his *A Theory of Justice* (1971). The problem had not been so much the positivist rejection of normative theory as the fact that so little political theorizing had been taking place, other than critical commentary upon old theories, with a few conspicuous exceptions such as Brian Barry's *Political Argument* (1965). (Freeman and Robertson 1980: 3-6, 11, 14; Barry 1980:276-88). It should also be borne in mind that the 1960s were the hey day of the 'end of ideology' intellectual fashion.[5] Setting aside the scientistic exhortations of behaviouralism, the revival of empirical theory was actually encouraged by the behavioural emphasis upon the need for explicit theoretical frameworks to guide research by pinpointing the problems to be investigated and the kinds of data whose collection would be required. While such normative and empirical theorizing has reinvigorated the study of political theory, it has nevertheless not displaced traditional work on the history of political thought, both as a field for scholarly work and as part of the undergraduate curriculum.

THE OUTSIDER POLITICAL SCIENTIST AND THE INSIDER WORLD OF POLITICS

In many political systems, where it is not the liberal separation of state from society but the domination of society by the state that is the political scientist's predicament, the remarks that follow may seem surprising. Where the contact between government and political science is both excessive and oppressive, the indifference of government may seem highly attractive. Nevertheless where the contacts are largely non-existent, the result is the impotence of political science outsiders to penetrate the insider world of the administrators and politicians. Despite the *de facto* separation of the academic study of politics from its active practitioners, which is particularly marked in Britain, its failure to acquire acknowledged scientific status has meant a certain failure to distinguish politicians and political scientists, amounting to 'confusing the denizens of the zoo with the zoologists' (Hayward, 1986:18). However, because of the obsessive addiction to official secrecy which in Britain denies the academic access to much of the basic information — especially as it relates to government decision-making — political scientists are dependent upon the spasmodic insights afforded by the revelations of investigative journalism or the open conspiracy against official confidentiality launched by a self-styled 'lifelong political scientist' such as Richard Crossman in *The Diaries of a Cabinet Minister* (Crossman 1975:13). If we are to understand the constrained context within which British political science has had to work, we must examine the secretive Whitehall culture that made possible and seeks to perpetuate an institutionalized conspiracy of silence.

It is especially through the eyes of American political scientists, coming from a political culture where norms of openness rather than secrecy prevail, that we can best appreciate the abnormality of a British preoccupation with preserving the system of reciprocal trust among decision-makers from inquisitive outsiders such as political scientists. In comparing 'White House and Whitehall' in 1965, Richard Neustadt wrote: 'Those who govern Britain mostly keep their secrets to themselves. . . . Least of all are they inclined to satisfy curiosities of academics, especially not English academics . . . kept at bay by those three magic words, 'Official Secrets Act'. Why not? Nothing in the British constitution says that anyone outside of Whitehall needs an inside view. Quite the reverse. If academics knew, then journalists might learn, and even the backbenchers might find out. God forbid! That could destroy the constitution. Government is meant to be a mystery' (King 1969:131-2). A decade later, two more leading American political scientists, Hugh Heclo and Aaron Wildavsky, showed that it was possible to break through the barriers surrounding the administrative holy of holies (the Treasury) but commented: 'That political administrators find secrecy useful is understandable; that citizens and social scientists should acquiesce is less so. Academic reservations are clearly marked out — voting, parties, interest groups, parliament — but the Executive fortress is proclaimed sacrosanct. Those inside who do not wish to be seen make common cause with those outside who could try to see but do not. *The Constitution* is their common pretence' (Heclo and Wildavsky 1974:341). It was entry into the Cabinet in 1964 of Richard Crossman, committed to the role of participant-observer, combining his skills as journalist and political scientist with access to the 'Inside View' — the title of his Godkin Lectures of 1972[6] (Crossman 1972) — that challenged the key constitutional fiction of collective ministerial responsibility. This was to answer Neustadt's ironic remark quoted earlier that those outside Whitehall did not need the 'inside view'. In the process, Crossman stirred up an instructive public controversy.

In contrast to the self-serving writers of most political memoirs, upon which political scientists were usually condemned to rely, Crossman's detailed diaries of the day-to-day doings of British executive government were meant as a deliberate challenge to another of Neustadt's quoted remarks — that 'Government is meant to be a mystery'. In his introduction to a new edition of Bagehot's *The English Constitution*, Crossman had in advance clearly indicated his demystifying intentions: 'The decline of the Cabinet had been concealed from the public eye even more successfully than its rise to power in Bagehot's era. Here was a secret of our modern English Constitution which no one directly concerned with government — whether minister, shadow minister, or civil servant — was anxious to reveal. Yet, despite the thick protective covering of prerogative and constitutional convention under which our government is still conducted, there must come occasions on which the drapery is whisked aside and the reality of power is revealed' (Crossman 1963:64). Anticipating his future role, Crossman noted 'how little is normally revealed of what goes on in the modern Cabinet, and how much information is available about these secret proceedings, if only someone who knows the truth can be stimulated to divulge it' (Crossman, 1963: footnote 55). He was to be that person himself from 1964–70.

Lord Gordon-Walker, a former teacher of history and politics at Oxford, recalling a letter sent in 1880 by one future Conservative Prime Minister to another on the doctrine of ministerial collective responsibility being a 'constitutional fiction', argued that 'An element of concealment was inherent in the very concept of collective responsibility. The doctrine that the Cabinet must appear to be united presupposed Cabinet divisions that had not been reconciled. Ministers must in the nature of things have differences but they must outwardly appear to have none. Collective responsibility must therefore to some extent be a mask worn by the cabinet' (Gordon-Walker 1972:27–8).[7] However, whereas Gordon-Walker subscribed to the view that the fiction was constitutionally indispensable, Crossman was determined to unmask the illusion of governmental unity. Crossman wanted to show that the reality of fragmented decision-making meant that the function of the Cabinet was to give a spuriously collective constitutional legitimacy to piecemeal departmental, interdepartmental, Cabinet committee or Prime Ministerial decisions. 'Unattributable leaks' of inside information had become an increasing feature of government life for a century but Crossman wanted this selective revelation, aimed to deliberately mislead, to be corrected by general access to as full information as possible. As Gordon-Walker had shown, 'The doctrine of collective responsibility and the unattributable leak grew up side by side as an inevitable feature of the Cabinet' the leak being 'paradoxically necessary to the preservation of the doctrine of collective responsibility. It is the mechanism by which the doctrine of collective responsibility is reconciled with political reality. The unattributable leak is itself a recognition and acceptance of the doctrine that members of a Cabinet do not disagree in public' (Gordon-Walker 1972:32).

Nevertheless, a Labour Attorney General in 1975 sought to obtain an injunction to prevent publication of Crossman's *Diaries*, the report of his opening statement (*Times* 23 July 1975) containing the kernel of the traditional argument for secrecy. 'The present proceedings had been brought primarily to protect the public interest in good government, of which collective responsibility was a major pillar. . . . Intercourse in government between minister and minister and Cabinet and departments was intercourse between officers of the Crown in the affairs of the Crown. If such occasions understood to be confidential were not confidential, good government was not possible.' Despite the failure of such arguments to prevent the publication of *The Diaries of a Cabinet Minister*, nothing has changed fundamentally in Whitehall attitudes. This is evidenced by the subsequent court cases in which British governments have sought to conceal partisan or mendacious accounts of public affairs — the Cabinet Secretary's phrase about 'economizing on truth' in 1986 deserves immortality — in the name of serving the national or public interest.

It continues to be extremely difficult if not impossible for 'outsider' political scientists to acquire the 'insider' information, without which much academic 'research' ceases to be meaningful. The way in which the Law Lords, who constitute the highest court in Britain, make their decisions was studied but the results cannot be published because the access to the evidence was conditional upon a promise to maintain confidentiality. The untimely death in 1978 of John Mackintosh, who promised to provide more political scientist participant-observation of the House of Commons in the Crossman tradition, was a serious blow. A self-inflicted blow was the forced resignation of Dr Bernard Donoughue from the London School on the ground that his unpaid leave of absence to head the Prime Minister's Policy Unit could not be extended![8] This demonstrates that the separation of the world of politics and administration on the one hand and political science on the other is not attributable only to the exclusiveness of the former; it is also to be blamed on the universities' refusal to accept a *pantouflage* that has been practised with benefit in many other countries.

Despite the efforts of bodies like the Royal Institute of Public Administration and the Royal Institute of International Affairs (Chatham House) to develop mutually useful links between the academic world and the home civil service and the diplomatic service, domestic and foreign policy-makers, one has to admit that the impact of each on the other has usually been fairly modest. On the relatively rare occasions when there appears to have been some influence of academic debate upon public administration practice, it has been argued that 'one is more likely to find evidence of American managerial thought in many of the initiatives adopted since the 1960s than of British academic public administration' (Page 1986:139). A survey of five British academic journals which publish articles dealing with the senior civil service over the quarter century 1961-86 shows that 39 per cent were written by non-academic authors. They were much more willing to offer prescriptive advice (25 per cent of their output as against 7 per cent for academics). They were also, obviously, in a far better position to offer 'inside dope' than are academic political scientists, although the latter devoted over half their articles (53 per cent) to narrating a story which 'insiders' would have been in a far better position to recount, if they had been allowed to do it. (Page 1986:142-3). They eschewed theory altogether and in this they remained loyal to the view that public administration is 'an esoteric and flexible task which proceeds in mysterious ways (the anonymity convention) and which can hardly be taught because its content is always shifting and because ultimately only ministers can decide —

and no one can foretell what their decisions will be. There is thus no theory or even discussion within the Civil Service of the role and purpose of central government. Indeed this question is generally regarded by civil servants as improper and useless (Self 1977:20). Hence the impact of the 1968, partly political science-inspired, Fulton Report on the reform of the Civil Service and its offspring the Civil Service College, was predictably limited in a system in which muddling through was the height of official ambition. At the more modest level of local government, there has been a much greater involvement of the Birmingham University Institute of Local Government Studies (created in 1963) in promoting corporate management and planning as part of the reform of local government in the 1970s, as well as the greater tendency for political scientists to serve on local councils than in Parliament. Political scientists were less effective in shaping the proposals for Scottish and Welsh devolution that developed in the 1970s but which failed to secure sufficient public support in the referenda of 1979.

Because of their greater openness, Parliament and the political parties provide, within the field of national politics, opportunities for political science that are largely absent in the case of central government. The tendency towards self-adulatory praise of the 'Mother of Parliaments' went into steep decline in the 1960s, partly as a consequence of the sense that in Britain, as in most countries other than the USA, representative assemblies were being bypassed in favour of extra-parliamentary forms of representation. The Study of Parliament Group built a bridge between official insiders and academic outsiders. Following in the wake of earlier reformist campaigns by Harold Laski and others, a book by a leading member of the Group, Bernard Crick's *The Reform of Parliament* (1964b), helped put the establishment of specialist committees on the agenda and it was Leaders of the House of Commons Richard Crossman and Norman St John Stevas — both commentators on Bagehot — who played the major part in their creation despite conspicuous government reluctance. The use of foreign parliamentary experience in the best style of comparative politics was a useful antidote to the traditional insularity that had hitherto predominated.

As far as political parties and elections are concerned, the major academic impact of political science has been achieved through the work of a Canadian Robert McKenzie in *British Political Parties* (1955), of Sammy Finer in *Adversary Politics and Electoral Reform* (1974), as well as in the part played by political scientists in designing and interpreting public opinion polls, which have become an increasingly popular way of testing and disseminating some of the basic hypotheses of political sociology. More recently, Richard Rose's *Do Parties Make a Difference?* (1980) challenged another piece of conventional wisdom and like the books by McKenzie and Finer has had an impact beyond the academic audience upon the understanding and behaviour of those involved in the political process (Kavanagh

1986:98–100). It is a mark of the propensity of homegrown political scientists not to question the fundamental assumptions of the British political process that two out of these three iconoclasts started their academic careers in North America.

With only a modest impact upon those in power — although there is plenty of consultation of academic experts on foreign countries by insular, ill-informed ministers, senior civil servants and parliamentary committees — and with only a few academics being invited for comments on current affairs on the mass media, some attention has been paid to political education in the schools. There has never in Britain been the connection with civic education for democracy which played such an important part in the early development of American political science, or to some extent in Third Republic France (though in the latter it was secondary in importance to the connection with elite education). The foundation of the Politics Association in 1969 by school teachers of politics has had to overcome two traditional objections to the political education of teenagers. Firstly, there is the fear of indoctrination. Secondly, characteristic of British culture, there is the 'long-held assumption that appropriate political knowledge, skills, and attitudes are somehow absorbed by the pupil in the course of the traditional school curriculum' (Sutton 1978:248; cf. 246–7). In an attempt to reassure objectors, 'political literacy' has been defined to incorporate a generous infusion of rationalist and pluralist liberal values: 'The knowledge, skills and attitudes needed to make a man or woman informed about politics, able to participate in public life and groups of all kinds, both occupational and voluntary, and to recognize and tolerate diversities of political and social values.' Despite the support of political scientists such as Bernard Crick and Fred Ridley, the Politics Association has made only modest headway, so that political science lacks the mass audience socialized at school to think in politically literate terms, as well as not enjoying the sympathetic ear of the political and administrative elites.

CONCLUSION

Despite the endeavours of the International Political Science Association and the European Consortium for Political Research, insularity has continued to be a feature of British political science, apart from the homeopathic doses of American political science it has absorbed. As Trevor Smith has pointed out: 'It is common enough for disciplines to split into opposing camps from time to time but such divisions are rarely polarized on national lines'. Because of the split between American, British and Continental European approaches to the study of politics, 'British political science was largely bereft of any strong feeling of being part of an internationally cohesive discipline of the kind most other academic vocations enjoy' (Smith 1986:425). While this assessment may exaggerate the degree of cohesion enjoyed in its sister social sciences of economics and sociology, nevertheless it is correct to point to the culture-bound character of much political science, except where the weakness or non-existence of an indigenous tradition has meant that there has been little resistance to the absorption of a foreign methodology and set of assumptions. This may be due in part to the fact that the subject has been conceived as a nation-building, sustaining, and celebrating subject. Problems arise because of the political scientist's propensity to engage in criticism of the parent society and state. The difficulties become acute when politics ceases to be a nation-state centred discipline under the pressure of changing international society. Increasing academic specialization, furthermore, means that the discipline loses its initial focus and becomes prone to disintegration into subdisciplines. It also ceases to enjoy the societal legitimacy that its integrative role ensured.

Tocqueville, addressing the French Academy of Moral and Political Sciences in 1852, justified the role of the academic in developing and refining the conceptual language in which political discourse is conducted as helping to shape the nature of practical political debates. He circumspectly but magniloquently set out an agenda for political science as distinct but inseparable from politics: 'Among all civilized peoples, the political sciences give birth or at least form to those general concepts whence emerge the facts with which politicians have to deal and the laws of which they believe themselves to be the inventors. They form a kind of atmosphere surrounding each society in which both rulers and governed have to draw intellectual breath, and whence — often without realizing it — both groups derive the principles of action. Only among barbarians does the practical side of politics exist alone' (Mayer 1960:90). How will political scientists be able to persuade their elite and mass opinion that it is time to emerge from barbarism? How can political scientists go beyond the practical activity of politics yet remain sufficiently in touch to understand and influence it? Tocqueville's own scepticism led him to state, in a part of the speech he did not deliver, that 'actual practice avoids the sciences, and politics ends by being only a game of chance where, moreover, the dice are often loaded' (Gargan 1955:237). Such pessimism has inhibited the development of political science in Britain even more than in France. As long as it is the general view in Britain that practical men of affairs have little if anything useful to learn from academics in political matters, paralyzing self-doubt will prevail among its practitioners. A culturally induced intellectual inertia and a contextually crippling denial of access to indispensable information have seriously constrained the twentieth century development of British political science.

NOTES

1 This is a revision of a paper presented at Cortona, Italy, September 1987.
2 *Oxford Magazine*, 1931-2, L:360-1, quoted by Chester (1986:480).
3 *Manchester Guardian* 10 August 1925, quoted in Collini *et al.* (1983: 369; cf. 370). On Sidgwick, see Collini *et al.* ch. 9.
4 Ironically, it was Oakeshott, Crick's *bête noire* who has been the most eloquent champion of the view that 'the study of politics should be a historical study' based on 'traditions of behaviour' and 'the pursuit of intimations'. Michael Oakeshott, 'Political education' (1951 inaugural lecture at the London School of Economics in his *Rationalism in Politics and Other Essays* (1962: 130, 123, 125), London. See also Crick's 'The world of Michael Oakeshott', first published in *Encounter*, June 1963 and republished in *Political Theory and Practice* (1972) London, especially 123-34.
5 One can follow the fascinating process of self-questioning debate among British political philosophers in the early 1960s in the volumes of *Politics, Philosophy and Society* edited by Peter Laslett *et al.*
6 The first draft of these lectures was prepared by John Mackintosh, former Professor of Politics and then Labour Member of Parliament.
7 The reference in the text is to an 1880 letter from Lord Salisbury to Arthur Balfour (quoted from Balfour 1930:131).
8 In 1987 Lord Donoughue published a book based upon his experience in government (Donoughue 1987).

REFERENCES

Balfour, A.J. (1930) *Chapters of Autobiography*, London: Cassell.
Barry, B. (1965) *Political Argument*, London, Routledge & Kegan Paul.
— (1980) 'The strange death of political philosophy', *Government and Opposition*, XV 3-4: 276-88.
Chester, N. (1975) 'Political studies in Britain: recollections and comments', Twenty-fifth anniversary issue of *Political Studies*, XXIII June-Sept.: 151-64.
— (1986) *Economics, Politics and Social Studies in Oxford, 1900-85*, Basingstoke: Macmillan.
Collini, S., Winch, D. and Burrow, J. (1983) *That Noble Science of Politics: A Study in Nineteenth-century Intellectual History*, Cambridge: Cambridge University Press.
Crick, B. (1959) *The American Science of Politics*, London: Routledge & Kegan Paul.
— (1964a) *In Defence of Politics*, Harmondsworth: Pelican.
— (1964b) *The Reform of Parliament*, London: Weidenfeld and Nicholson.
— (1975) 'Chalk-dust, punch-card and the polity', *Political Studies*, XXIII June-Sept.: 165-82.
Crossman, R.H.S. (1963) 'Introduction' to Walter Bagehot's *The English Constitution*, 1867, London: Fontana.
— (1972) *Inside View: Three Lectures on Prime Ministerial Government*, London: Cape.
— (1975) *The Diaries of a Cabinet Minister*, I, London: Hamilton & Cape.
Dearlove, J. (1982) 'The political science of British Politics', *Parliamentary Affairs*, XXC/4; 436-54.

Donoughue, B. (1987) *Prime Minister: The Conduct of Policy under Harold Wilson and James Callaghan*, London: Cape.

Finer, S. (1974) *Adversary Politics and Electoral Reform*, London: A. Wigram.

Freeman, M. and Robertson, R. (eds) (1980) *The Frontiers of Political Theory: Essays in a Revitalised Discipline*, Brighton: Harvester.

Gargan, E.T. (1955) *Alexis de Tocqueville: The Critical Years, 1848-51*, Washington D.C.: Catholic University of America Press.

Gordon-Walker, P. (1970, 1972 ed.) *The Cabinet*, London: Fontana.

Hayward, J. (1982) 'United Kingdom', in W.G. Andrews (ed.) *International Handbook of Political Science*, pp 355-63, Westport, CT: Greenwood Press.

— (1986) 'The political science of muddling through: the *de facto* paradigm?' in Jack Hayward and Philip Norton (eds) *The Political Science of British Politics*, Brighton: Wheatsheaf.

Heclo, H. and Wildavsky, A. (1974) *The Private Government of Public Money: Community and Policy inside British Politics*, London: Macmillan.

Kavanagh, D. (1974) 'An American science of British politics', *Political Studies*, XXII/3:251-70.

— (1986) 'Changes in the party system', in Jack Hayward and Philip Norton (eds), *The Political Science of British Politics*, Brighton: Wheatsheaf.

Kavanagh, D. and Rose, R. (1977) *New Trends in British Politics: Issues for Research*, London: Sage.

King, A. (ed.) (1969) *The British Prime Minister: A Reader*, London: Macmillan.

Laslett, P. (1956) *Philosophy, Politics and Society*, Oxford: Basil Blackwell.

Laslett, P. and Runciman, W.G. (eds) (1962) *Philosophy, Politics and Society*, Oxford: Basil Blackwell.

Laslett, P. and Runciman, W.G. (eds) (1967) *Philosophy, Politics and Society*, Oxford: Basil Blackwell.

Mayer, J.P. (1939, 1960 ed.) *Alexis de Tocqueville: A biographical study in Political Science*, New York: Harper.

McKenzie, R. (1955) *British Political Parties*, Melbourne: Heineman.

Page, E.C. (1986) 'Ministers, ministries and civil servants', in Jack Hayward and Philip Norton (eds), *The Political Science of British Politics*, Brighton: Wheatsheaf.

Rose, R. (1980) *Do Parties Make a Difference?* London: Macmillan.

Scott, D. (1971) *A.D. Lindsay: A Biography*, Oxford: Blackwell.

Self, P. (1977) 'The purposes of Civil Service training', in R.A.W. Rhodes (ed.) *Training in the Civil Service*, London: Joint University Council for Social and Public Administration.

Smith, T. (1986) 'Political science and modern British society', *Government and Opposition*, XXI/4, autumn: 420-36.

Sutton, J. (1978) 'Parliament, the public and political education', Appendix 5 of Bernard Crick and Alex Porter (eds), *Political Education and Political Literacy*, London: Longman.

Webb, B. (1948) *Our Partnership*, London: Longmans.

Whitehead, A.N. (1948) *Essays in Science and Philosophy*, London: Rider.

5 Political development and political science in West Germany

Hans Kastendiek[1]

POLITICAL SCIENCE IN WEST GERMANY: SOME BASIC INFORMATION

As a distinct academic discipline, political science in Germany has a relatively short history. Although during the Weimar Republic (1919–33) there were precursory and tentative developments towards a theoretical foundation and even institutionalization, the discipline did not obtain 'academic citizenship' before the 1950s. In the Federal Republic (West Germany) the establishment of political science took about 20 years, from the foundation of new chairs for politics in 1948 until the spread of full study schemes to most universities in the 1960s. In the German Democratic Republic (East Germany), a directly comparable discipline did not emerge. Inclusion of, or even references to, political research and academic teaching in East Germany would require additional analysis beyond the scope of this article; general differences of societal structures and socio-political developments give rise to different patterns of topical and institutional organization of the academic field in the GDR.

The late emergence of the discipline seems surprising as there had been a long tradition of political analysis in Germany that had some influence or even notable impact on political science elsewhere, for example, in the United States. But it was exactly this tradition which helped to prevent an early genesis of a distinct 'science of politics' in Germany. Established political sciences, like law and history, claimed to offer adequate analyses. Because of the structure of politics in the nineteenth century and the political power relations which characterized the Weimar Republic and were mirrored in the academic system, conditions for a distinct political science simply did not exist. But when and as the form of politics and the political system changed in the late nineteenth century, new requirements in political research as well as in academic training and education developed. There was some impact on the academic system as a whole and on currents within traditional political sciences. In addition, there were new institutional arrangements for the study of politics outside the realm and below the level of the university system. Some of these changes in political research and teaching within and outside the universities can be interpreted as preparatory steps towards a distinct political science. This development was interrupted drastically when the republic was destroyed by the Third Reich in 1933 (although new research (Weyher 1985) indicates that significant steps were taken towards a distinct discipline of political science in Nazi Germany). Many social scientists had to leave the country. But what seemed to be a break also proved to be a transition stage for the emergence of the discipline. Emigration secured some continuity of socio-political analysis developed until 1933 and, at the same time, stimulated conceptual changes and innovations which should contribute to arguments for a distinct science of politics.

Compared to the situation before 1933, the foundation of a special political science in West Germany after 1945 was a speedy process although, as mentioned, the full institutionalization was not completed before the 1960s. There was still considerable resistance from within the universities, but the traditional political sciences had to cease opposition. The emergence of the discipline after 1945 was due to specific political constellations: the failure of the Weimar Republic, the experience of National Socialism and World War Two, the collapse of the German State, and political development in a divided country which became involved in a worldwide competition between antagonistic systems of societal organization. These experiences and, in particular, the political maxim 'to build up democracy', however differently it was motivated and substantiated, required new approaches to political analysis and new concepts of academic teaching. For many political supporters of the discipline and for most West German political scientists of the first generation 'to build up democracy' and to install a distinct political science were needs directly connected to each other. In retrospect, this general connection turned out to be the starting point for a somewhat uncritical identification with the course and patterns of West German society and politics; and obviously there was a coincidence of the performance of political science and its final establishment in the 1960s when it was included in the canon of disciplines for training schoolteachers.

The political role of political science was a prominent theme in the late 1960s and in the 1970s when the discipline became the subject of disputes. But the considerable unrest of that time cannot be explained in these terms alone. The eruption of internal and external controversies marked a development stage in which the analytical concepts of West German political science, which had resulted from specific political constellations, lost their power of persuasion. This was not just a result of academic development but of socio-political changes (in West Germany and elsewhere). The controversies themselves have indicated this correlation as it is neither simple nor sufficient to separate the analytical and the political arguments.

This chapter is not an attempt to present a 'concise history' of political science in West Germany. Rather, I discuss the general thesis, already implicitly introduced: academic systems in general and academic disciplines in particular are highly dependent on socio-political developments and to a large extent determined by internal politics. It would be artificial and sterile to consider the emergence and performance of a discipline as a matter of academic development as such, even more so if the analysis were limited to theoretical achievements or deficiencies and institutional progress or shortcomings.

STATE-DOMINATED POLITICS AND THE DOMINANCE OF STAATSWISSENSCHAFTEN

The long tradition of academic political analysis in Germany has tempted some political scientists to draw up an imposing genealogical tree of political analysis and thought, to which the propagation and the theoretical foundation of a West German science of politics could refer (apart from general Western and European traditions). Unfortunately, this tradition ended in the nineteenth century because, in Germany, the political sciences had become dominated by formalism and positivism. Law, history, and economics had become depoliticized because they excluded 'the political' from scientific analysis, while at the same time they had become politicized because they combined a restricted analysis with direct political argument. Thus, the bleak performance of political sciences in the Weimar period and especially during the Third Reich was seen as a result of 'faulty development'.

But it is misleading to construct a line of tradition, dissolved or not, without examining each stage of political analysis in an historically specific way. My argument is that former political sciences, however faulty their development, were quite adequate to the form of German politics in the last century. Analytic formalism and positivism mirrored a type of societal organization which was characterized by state domination because a genuine civil society did not exist. There was certainly no absence of 'politics'; on the contrary, there was a legally and administratively dominated structure of 'politics'. Corresponding to this constellation, political sciences were *Staatswissenschaften*, disciplines concerned with the state and its role in society. As the state performed predominantly in a formal and legal-bureaucratic way, *Staatsrechtslehre* (public law) became the core discipline of *Staatswissenschaften*. Surely, these disciplines, and the public law in particular, differed from political science of the present kind but, for Germany in the nineteenth century, they were adequate political sciences.

Another interpretation can be added by reversing the former one: although, because of the power relations in the political and academic systems, *Staatswissenschaften* and *Staatsrechtslehre* maintained their status as leading political sciences until 1933–45, they came more and more inadequate when the form of politics itself changed. The formal and legal-bureaucratic role of the state and its agencies, however persistent in Germany, was increasingly supplemented by an active and substantial involvement in economic and social development. This was a form of growth rather than a change of state functions as the previous functions did not vanish but had to be adapted to new ones. But the process of societal restructuring, which had accelerated beginning in the last decades of the nineteenth century, almost necessarily led to, and was associated with, significant changes in the political system: mass production, mass society, mass politics, and finally through the gradual adoption of parliamentary practices and World War One — mass democracy. Politics characteristic of the nineteenth century were followed by 'modern politics', a combination of heterogeneous principles, and a network of differentiated institutions of social, economic, and political representation and organization.

These structural alterations responded to concrete changes of class composition and class politics: the rise of labour as a social and political force; the attempts of the bourgeois classes to develop a kind of symbiosis with the state to contain labour and to secure imperial competitiveness; the experiences of World War One and of German defeat; the political turmoil of 1918-19 and the social, economic, and political crises which marked the development of the Weimar Republic. All these turbulences and ruptures shook the academic system and its disciplines.

With the advent of modern politics, the political became a matter of some concern within the faculties of law. The subdiscipline responsible for general analyses of the state in particular experienced a notable upswing after the turn of the century (see the works on *Allgemeine Staatslehre* by G. Jellinek, Berlin, 1900; R. Schmidt, Leipzig, 1901, 1903; H. Kelsen, Berlin, 1925). Occasionally the subdiscipline was urged to extend itself to *Allgemeine Staatslehre und Politik*; for example, Schmidt thought politics should become a branch of the scientific analysis of the state. But for the majority within the science of law, an empirically based and theoretically accomplished analysis of politics would not be possible because of the 'nature' of the subject matter. By contrast, H. Heller developed a concept of *Staatslehre* (Leiden 1934) which aimed at a general theory of politics. Heller was responsible for the article on political science published in volume 13 of the *Encyclopaedia of the Social Sciences* (New York 1933), but in Germany he was rejected by the academic profession. Attempts like Heller's had a limited impact on academic research. Even more, the political ruptures seemed to have favoured analyses which persistently stuck to formal and legalistic approaches. On the whole, faculties of law acted as strongholds of political restoration, trying to contain modern politics by means of academic argument.

But below the level of theory building, political sciences turned towards a wide range of political issues. To some extent, this trend was quickened by new academies or colleges (e.g. for economics and commerce) which often were able to gain the reputation and then the status of universities within a short period of time. New universities, like Hamburg, soon started to engage in political studies. Also, within or connected to universities, institutes were founded or promoted which specialized in certain fields of research, like international politics and commerce or the study of regions like Eastern Europe, oriental Asia or Latin America. Mostly, these institutes reflected the imperial race in which Germany was involved until the end of World War One. They worked to obtain factual knowledge of social, economic, and political constellations in special countries or regions. But, in general, the performance of these new institutions and this form of studying facts did not lead to discussion of the need for a special discipline to pilot a theoretically guided study of politics.

With the exception of Heller's *Staatslehre*, I have discussed patterns and conditions of academic political analysis which obstructed the development of a special political science. But, in a certain way, these patterns and conditions contributed to the emergence of the discipline, as they provoked developments which later favoured the genesis of a distinct science of politics. When tracing its institutional precursors we have to consider developments *outside* universities.

PRECURSORY DEVELOPMENTS TOWARDS A SPECIAL DISCIPLINE OF POLITICAL SCIENCE BETWEEN 1920 AND 1945

In the late nineteenth century, mass political education became a prominent topic for academics and politicians. As most of the 'German mandarins' (Ringer's famous phrase for the academic establishment of that time) kept aloof from this concern, and as the academic community as a whole seemed to be quite incapable of managing a broader political education, extramural activities prevailed. The demands for political education stemmed from different concerns, which included: 1 ideological warfare against trade unionism and the Social Democratic party; 2 pragmatic reactions to meet new requirements for the training of civil servants, schoolteachers, etc., as a result of modern politics; 3 chauvinist claims that, to obtain and secure world power, Germany had to develop its internal resources by means of political education; and 4 progressive objectives to improve conditions for further democratization. By 1919, these demands had led to several initiatives committed to the organization of courses in politics on a regular basis. Although they were — by and large — of limited importance, they are relevant to our topic because some of them prepared the ground for the Deutsche Hochschule für Politik (German Academy for Politics) which was founded in Berlin in 1920. It became a major institution of political teaching until it was taken over and finally dissolved by National Socialism. In 1948, it was refounded in West Berlin, and was — as an institute — integrated into the Free University of Berlin in 1959.

Later, when the university was reorganized, it became one of its largest departments. Formal changes notwithstanding, the academy/institute/department became a main centre and major promoter of West German political science.

After 1920, the academy combined pragmatic and democratic concerns for political education. There was still concern, however restrained, to contain political forces from the left. The chauvinist argument persisted in the form of a nationalistic one. For most of its proponents and supporters, the academy had two objectives: to contribute to a rebirth of Germany after its military and political defeat, and to promote political conditions that would stabilize the new republic. For the political constellation of that time, dominated by disputes on the question of which groups within society had been responsible for the 'German catastrophy' and antagonistic controversies on the future order of German society, this twofold concept was a precarious starting point for the academy. From its very beginning it was involved in the course of German politics.

The Deutsche Hochschule had been founded and supported by a coalition of political forces which largely mirrored the so-called Weimar coalition of Social Democrats, Liberals and the Catholic Centre party, an alliance which had promoted the new constitution and supported the first republican governments between 1919 and 1923. The academy was financed by the central government, by the government of Prussia (also formed by the Weimar parties and occasionally based on larger coalitions), and by some industrialists who were supporters and sponsors of the Liberals. The political origins of the new institution were reflected in its academic staff, although later some members were recruited from the extreme right. The Communist party was minimally represented. From today's perspective, the politically shaped staff composition might seem irritating, but we have to take into account that some of the political strata to be found in this institution were denied any development within, or access to, the established academic community, even in the Weimar Republic. Thus, the foundation of the academy and its personnel policy should be seen as countermeasures.

In spite of its political character, the Deutsche Hochschule was conceived as a truly academic institution, below the level of universities but clearly above that of extramural education. Initially, courses were offered to civil servants, schoolteachers and other professionals in need of additional training on political matters. There were no special requirements for registration. In the first years few formal patterns of teaching and studying were employed. Soon, the academy learned that this relaxed approach generated problems for lecturers and students as interests and objectives within both groups diverged. Access to courses became regulated, some of the part-time lecturers became employed on a full-time basis, and in 1922-3 four chairs were founded. By stages, the academy became like a university, and finally claimed to offer a scientific study of politics, a claim which was emphasized by the installation of a research department in 1932. Two years earlier, the Prussian ministry for cultural affairs had authorized regulations for the conduct of diploma examinations.

From the late 1920s, the academy characterized its intentions and achievements by using terms like 'politics as science' or 'political science'. Obviously, these did not represent the emergence of a new *discipline* to complement existing subjects. Politics as science claimed politics was a necessary and possible *topic* of academic analysis; the term was directed against notions in the established *Staatswissenschaften* which still rejected this necessity and possibility. But compared to many institutions of political science in West Germany, and compared to institutions in other countries, we may conclude that this academy, within ten years, had almost achieved the patterns and standards of a distinct political science — a development which had to be achieved, and could be attained, only outside the German university system. This development, however, was halted in 1933.

Although the academy declared its own dissolution, it was taken over by the National Socialists. In 1937, it became a state institution and was strengthened in its research capacity. Finally, in 1940, its merger with the Academy for Foreign Studies led to the creation of the Faculty for Foreign Studies at the University of Berlin. To the best of my knowledge, reports and studies of the development of political research and teaching published since 1945 have interpreted this development as counteracting former attempts to promote scientific political analysis. This view is challenged by new research presented by Johannes Weyher, who argues that, from 1933 onwards, the academy developed from an institution of pedagogical concern (following the patterns of the former academy) to a promoter of a genuine scientific analysis of politics which was able to emancipate itself, at least partly, from fascist politics, especially in 1943 and 1944 (Weyher 1985).

Weyher may be right to criticize former studies (including my publication of 1977) which neglect political science in fascism, the 'forgotten twelve years' as Weyher says. But his criticism of those analyses which stress the importance of emigration both for the decline of political analysis after 1933 and for the foundation of West German political science from 1948 onwards is not very convincing — especially as Weyher does not comment on the impact the existence of a political science in fascism might have had on the emergence of the discipline after World War Two. Already, in 1933, the staff of the Academy for Politics had changed almost completely. Some members switched to other professions but, sooner or later, many had to emigrate for 'racial' and/or political reasons — A. Brecht, H. Heller, R. Hilferding, E. Jaeckh, F. Neumann, S. Neumann, H. Simons, and A. Wolfers, to name just a few. It would take one or two pages to list only the most famous social scientists and it would take a booklet to list the names of all academics and intellectuals who had to leave

Germany (numbers were estimated at more than 3,000; almost one-third of the professors and *Privatdozenten* of 1931 were driven into exile; cf. Pross 1966). The social and political sciences in particular became, actively or passively, instrumentalized in Germany. Already fairly remote from major analytical developments in other countries up until 1933, they came almost totally isolated until 1945. For academic development in general and for socio-political analysis in particular, emigration meant heavy permanent losses. Many emigrants dropped out of their profession because they did not find posts; others who did preferred not to return to Germany. At the same time, however, emigration was also a chance to continue efforts toward a reconceptualization of socio-political analysis. These efforts, especially stimulated by experiences with American political science, would contribute to demands for a distinct political science to be established in postwar Germany.

THE EMERGENCE OF POLITICAL SCIENCE IN WEST GERMANY

In West Germany after 1945, in contrast to the Weimar period, the objectives and demands for a special science of politics were clearly stated. Its foundation was propagated as a necessary contribution to making up for the disastrous developments of German politics and to a reform of an academic system which, in many aspects, had shown analytical incompetence and political irresponsibility. That a political science was possible had been demonstrated by academic systems in other countries, but also by the performance of the German Academy for Politics until 1933 and by the achievements of scholars within the traditional German political sciences, however isolated in their professions. Rebuilding the discipline would not be just an adaptation to alien traditions shaped by different political cultures, but rather a reform which could close the gap between political research and teaching in Germany and abroad. The impact of those German scholars who emigrated after 1933 on American political science, for example, was seen as further evidence that the discipline could be staffed adequately, especially because of the possibility that some scholars would return. At least, they should be encouraged to once more transfer their knowledge and analytical skills, and thus support further progress within the field of political analysis.

To argue in favour of an intensified political analysis and to demand a new discipline were, of course, quite different undertakings. The course of German politics until 1945 and the political problems after the war so obviously required new efforts in political studies that their promotion could not be questioned. But arguments which transformed this need into one for a distinct political science still aroused strong suspicions among representatives of traditional political sciences and among the academic community as a whole. As the universities in West Germany had not been reformed (in the academic field, 'denazification' and 'democratization' had been limited), there were, for the time being, only restricted opportunities for significant changes within this sector of society. Thus, the discipline could be reestablished at the universities only step by step, and nearly every step had to be initiated and implemented by political intervention.

When looking at institutional developments which finally led to the emergence of a distinct political science, we can trace two lines: the foundation of single chairs in politics to improve political education at universities, and the introduction of full study schemes for political studies outside the universities. In the immediate postwar period, the occupation authorities, but also the German political parties, interest groups, churches, etc., referred to former failure of the academic system and stressed the need for special arrangements which should guarantee the acquisition of a basic knowledge of politics by all students, whatever their subject. Proposals ranged from special lectures within a voluntary *studium generale* to obligatory courses on socio-political topics which might be included in the examination regulations of certain disciplines. To secure these arrangements new chairs for politics should be added to existing faculties. This was not such a daunting problem as, in Germany, new chairs can be established relatively easily by state authorities without the full cooperation of a university. But to introduce a new study scheme requires the participation and active commitment of existing disciplines and faculty bodies. Neither of these happened in the 1940s and early 1950s because, within a few years, the universities had been able to restore the patterns of the Weimar period. Thus, again, initiatives to build up new institutional patterns had to start with academies outside the universities. The most significant foundation was the new Deutsche Hochschule für Politik — the decision by the parliamentary body of West Berlin was taken in March 1948, and the Academy opened early in 1949. At about the same time, a whole set of colleges for social and political studies were founded. Some were organized as institutions for extramural education, some developed new degree-level curricula — although the degrees did not carry full university status. Thus, political science as a university discipline had not emerged in the 1940s, but the new chairs and especially the new academy proved to be effective starting points for its development.

From 1949-50 onwards, the proponents of the discipline combined forces and started new initiatives. Plans to develop a special science of politics were made outside the established universities by a coalition of academics and politicians which was supported by occupation authorities, mainly by Americans and their German advisers, most of whom, having been forced to leave Germany before 1945, returned temporarily or re-emigrated. These plans were shaped, and publicized, in a series of conferences. The first one, in autumn 1949, was stimulated by the Americans and convened by the government of Hessen (in the Federal Republic, the federal states are responsible for cultural, educational, and academic affairs; a partial shift towards an overall competence of the central state did not occur until the 1970s). Discussions and resolutions concentrated on demands to establish new chairs for 'political sciences': world politics, political sociology, comparative state analysis, contemporary universal history, political theories, and so on. But there were no common conclusions on whether these chairs should be seen as steps towards a new discipline or whether they should be added to law, history, economics, etc. Thus the Hochschule für Politik in Berlin took the initiative and called another conference which, in March 1950, stated:

> There is a distinct science of politics. In keeping with the specific situation in Germany it has to be developed in research and teaching. . . . For the purposes of political science present German reality demands the foundation of special research centres, chairs, and working groups within all institutions of academic education and also the development of a science of politics at special academies. (For the full quotation, see Kastendiek 1977:178-9).

Only a few months later, another conference, again organized by the government of Hessen, referred to successful steps towards an introduction of political science, and demanded further initiatives. To advance activities, this conference prepared for an association for the science of politics, which was founded in early 1951 and later renamed the German Association for Political Science.

At that time, the conditions for a new discipline were met only in West Berlin. Within the Free University (founded in 1948 because the traditional University of Berlin was in the eastern part of the city) a research institute for political science was set up in the summer of 1950. Two years later, the Freie Universität and the Deutsche Hochschule reached formal agreement on a joint effort to promote the discipline of political science (new university chairs for politics, and access to doctoral examinations for students-graduated by the German Academy). The academy itself — as in the Weimar period — started with extramural courses, and again developed a full study scheme which step by step was extended to four years. In 1959, the academy was integrated into the university, in the form of an 'inter-faculty institute': in other words, its ten and then eleven chairs were linked to traditional faculties (philosophy, economics and social sciences, law). Thus, the former academy avoided subordination to established political sciences and could demonstrate its obligation to a distinct discipline of political science. Full equality status was reached in the 1970s when the university changed from faculty to department structures: the institute became the Department for Political Science. What had started as an extramural institution had developed into the largest department within West German political science, and one of the largest departments of the Free University.

On the national level, this was an early and exceptional

development. Until the mid-1950s, only a few universities were equipped with new chairs for politics, and their holders found themselves in a fairly isolated position. The distribution of single chairs mostly followed the notion of *studium generale* as described above. In 1954, the conference of university rectors recommended the foundation of new chairs *if* there was a chance to appoint qualified scholars. Protected by academic self-government and independent of daily politics, they should be in a position to study political power processes and to develop political theory by scientific means. These reservations were formulated as implicit criticism, and demonstrated suspicions about the political process which had led to earlier foundations of chairs and academies. When the universities declared their readiness to share responsibilities they also wanted to share decision-making powers. Eventually, nearly all of them got chairs in politics, and sometimes sets of chairs were granted to build up new institutes. Thus, a multi-centre structure of West German political science developed; West Berlin would retain its dominant position but had to share reputation and influence with Freiburg, Munich, Marburg, Frankfurt, Heidelberg, and Hamburg. By the early 1960s, the discipline had completed its constitution process.

The emergence of West German political science does not fit the theory that new disciplines result, or should result, from autonomous changes within the academic system favouring theoretical progress and analytical diversification of established disciplines. Many arguments against the foundation of political science invoked these ideas. Occasionally, it was described as an imported discipline forced upon the academic system by Americans and their German advisers, and its introduction was characterized as an adaptation to foreign traditions shaped by different political cultures and academic structures. Allegations of this kind ignored the limits of autonomous academic development and helped to disguise the real performance of the German academic community until 1945. They also did not correspond to the facts in the postwar period. In academic matters, interference by Western occupation authorities in the 1940s had been, by and large, limited, and was of no significance in the 1950s. Clearly, West German political science was stimulated but not imposed from abroad. American policy and American money, for example from the Ford Foundation, supported the emergence of the discipline but did not direct it. The suspicious failed to see the preponderance of German initiatives and they could not explain why the discipline became accepted in the 1950s and early 1960s.

Presumably, references to the political introduction of political science were not so much aimed at the role of the Americans but that of Social Democrat scientists and politicians who were the most active proponents and promoters of a science of politics, occasionally supported by politicians from other parties. Adequate analyses of the disastrous course of German politics until 1945 and contributions to an overdue democratization could not be expected from disciplines which had demonstrated complicity in conservativism, nationalism, chauvinism, and fascism. For many Social Democrats, political science was to be 'oppositional discipline' to existing ones. From 1949 onwards, after the failure of the Social Democrat party and the Social Democrat-dominated trade unions to determine the future patterns of West German society and politics, and after the electoral defeats in 1949 and 1953 (followed by defeats in 1957, 1961 and 1965), Social Democrats defined a further task of political science: it should guarantee independent analysis of the Federal Republic's political development and be a 'control discipline' to ensure democratic development. Though in opposition on the national level, the Social Democrat party had direct access to political decision-making because of the federal structure of West Germany. Some of the federal states were maintained as Social Democrat strongholds. Thus it was no accident that, in its early years, the discipline achieved its most spectacular progress in such federal states as West Berlin or Hessen. It was also no accident that for some time there was a Social Democrat bias in the composition of staff. In abstract or ahistorical terms, this may be a matter of serious concern. But it is important to remember that, until 1945, Social Democrats, or academics with Social Democrat leanings, not to speak of those to the left of the movement, had almost no chance of being appointed to a university chair. Eventual access depended on access to political and administrative decision-making.

We may safely assume that steps toward the introduction and expansion of political science, stimulated in particular by Social Democrats, forced other federal states and their universities to act and to secure influence in the further development of the discipline. This activity was more than a matter of party politics. Studies on the policies and politics of its foundation and implementation only partially explain why the discipline developed so rapidly. The content of West German political science itself should contribute to its recognition. Again, this was not just a result of academic development. West German political science, which had been seen as a precondition for political and academic change, became caught up in political conditions and restraints.

POLITICAL CONDITIONS AND RESTRAINTS: EMERGING PATTERNS OF WEST GERMAN POLITICAL SCIENCE

Initiatives for a science of politics started when the future of West German politics seemed still to be a matter of fundamental decisions not yet taken. In 1949, the main parties had agreed on the basic constitutional law (for a long time seen as a preliminary constitution) and on the foundation of the Federal Republic, but the Social Democrats hoped to become the governing party and to implement far-reaching economic and social changes blocked by the occupation authorities and/or the German opponents of social democracy. But this hope underestimated certain socio-political conditions of the postwar period and proved false. Capitalism was fully restored and, from 1949 until 1966, the Federal Republic was politically dominated by the Christian Democrats. West German politics complemented the antagonism of the superpowers and their economic, political, and military competition, and the 'economic miracle' (a result of modern equipment installed by the war economy, of low wages and the availability of skilled labour, and of a quick reintegration into the world market, favoured by the 'Korea boom') added much to the stabilization of the socio-political structures that developed after 1947.

In political practice, the spectrum for political analysis narrowed. The labour movement abandoned many of its political and theoretical traditions, which it saw as 'burdens', and so did political scientists. Throughout the 1950s and the 1960s, socialism was avoided in politics and academic analysis. The most significant and well-known consequence, for political argument and for academic analysis, was the spectre of 'totalitarianism versus liberal democracy'. Until the late 1940s, many Socialists, Communists, and others believed that a critique of and change in German politics required a critique of capitalism as a social form that could be transformed into fascism, in Germany and elsewhere. The need to approach political theory within analytical concepts of social organization and authority was regarded as one of the major lessons of German history, whether these concepts were Marxist or not. But the catch-phrase 'totalitarianism versus liberal democracy' prevailed. Political opposition to and theoretical criticism of capitalism vanished. Even the term became something of a foreign word and, for some time, nearly disappeared from the literature of West German political science. Concentrating on political forms of authority and decision-making, West German political science became a discipline concerned with politics in a narrow way, and failed to explore many proposals for socio-political analysis that had been essential to the proponents and founders of the discipline.

Caught up in these developments, the discipline took a general line compatible with practical politics, one which did not interfere with the basic doctrines of traditional political science. As it did not engage in the analysis of 'totalitarian systems' and 'liberal democracies', political science gained responsibility for a wide range of themes. The supposedly 'oppositional' discipline became an addition to the field of political analysis. Except for persistent hardliners, traditional political science could coexist with the new one; so could practical politics. Many observers of different political and analytical backgrounds have stated that West German political science in the 1950s and 1960s did not perform as a 'control discipline'. Those of its members who attempted the task remained a small minority.

Political and social pressures induced political science to refrain from political interference and even more so from non-conformist statements on the actual course of politics. Suspected as representatives of a 'political' discipline, political scientists may have feared to confirm such suspicions. This did not prevent preoccupation with actual developments, especially by the cold war. But a more general feature of 'early' West German political science should provide more insight into the discipline's development: its main concern was with institutional and normative analyses of democracy which often converged into normative approaches to the analysis of political institutions. This concern was a product of 1 the failure of the Weimar Republic, because of deep-rooted anti-democratic patterns of political thought and behaviour, to stabilize as a parliamentary system and a bulwark against National Socialism; 2 the obvious superiority of 'Western democracies' *vis à vis* authoritarian and fascist types of political organization; and 3 the emergence of a Communist regime in East Germany. Social Democrat political scientists reflected other experiences: the inability of the labour movement during the Weimar period either to develop genuine concepts for institutionally transforming socio-economic objectives into political action or to secure civil rights in general, and organizational and political rights for the labour movement in particular; the factual exclusion of Social Democracy in East Germany; political developments in many European countries where parties of the left lost their dominant position of the immediate postwar years and were excluded from government in the 1950s; signs of political and academic reinterpretations of the principles of party government and interest intermediation in West Germany which could endanger the position of Social Democracy and trade unions and lead to further restoration. If we consider these experiences we may understand why early West German political science primarily concentrated on attempts to explain basic principles of Western democracy and to promote knowledge of formal processes and institutions of parliamentarism, democratic party government, and pluralistic interest intermediation.

FROM CONSOLIDATION TO FRAGMENTATION: WEST GERMAN POLITICAL SCIENCE SINCE THE LATE 1960s

By the mid-1960s, the discipline was on firm ground in terms of internal formation and external recognition. Political science could now aim to expand as a new generation of scholars had been trained on the basis of widely accepted notions on central topics, analytical approaches, theoretical foundations, and political-pedagogical objectives. Expansion would cover those topics and themes neglected because of institutional and personnel shortcomings. In particular, political science strove to obtain responsibility for the academic training of student teachers, and finally succeeded in the late 1960s. At about the same time, West Germany experienced a lively debate on the need for academic training and education to catch up with larger proportions of university students in other countries, and the number of students increased to such an extent that universities, including institutes and departments of political science, became mass institutions. As a result, the number of staff grew, especially on the level of assistants and lecturers. Later, there were also more professors, mainly because of the university-wide creation of new categories of professorships below the level of chairs. Today, compared to other countries, the profession of political science is well represented in West Germany; its membership is one of the largest within the International Political Science Association.

But this record, however notable, contrasted with internal ruptures and fragmentation. Since the late 1960s, the performance of the discipline and its prospects for further development have become issues of heavy dispute. In particular, scientific and Marxist approaches to socio-political analysis challenged the basic concepts of early West German political science. I would argue that the analytical and pedagogical orientation of former West German political science which had resulted from specific constellations in postwar Germany had become, at least partially, inadequate in the 1960s when and because these constellations had changed. The discipline was shaken not only by the emergence of new approaches but by new requirements for political research and teaching which could not be met in the former way. These requirements, however, flowed from problems which were topics of general dispute in the political arena — a situation which has been mirrored within political science.

We confine ourselves to some highlights of socio-political change. By the 1960s, many of the specific competitive advantages of the West German economy had vanished. The economic miracle came to an obvious end when, in 1966, there was no economic growth for the first time since 1950. Governments increasingly turned to Keynesian concepts of active political involvement in economic development which meant increased state intervention in industrial relations and in interest intermediation. In public debate, socio-economic issues became repoliticized. 'Social justice' became a topic of increasing concern. Even the principles and patterns of the economic and social order, as reconstructed after 1945 and taken for granted at the end of the 1950s, were questioned as results of specific political constellations and power relations. The economic and political bases of legitimation were no longer self-evident. Another main source of legitimation vanished: with the emergence of détente, 'totalitarian versus democratic systems' no longer sufficed to organize consent. The Federal Republic would have to be legitimated by its own ability to cope with socio-economic and political changes, in addition to contrasting 'Western democracy' with 'Eastern totalitarianism'. Comparisons of this kind became precarious when the United States tried to secure its world hegemony by a brutal military intervention in Vietnam. In political terms, this action led to a massive loss of US hegemony. For many German intellectuals and students, and eventually for much of the public, the United States, which had been praised by normative West German political scientists as an outstanding 'piece of political art' (Fränkel 1960), had discredited Western democracy. Vietnam and the tradition of intervention became a topic in West German politics, as the main parties and the mass media supported American policies for a long time. The student movement of the late 1960s and early 1970s probably would not have spread to other strata of society without these experiences. West German politics had changed considerably since the mid-1960s. Political science began to be judged by its ability and capacity to cope with these developments.

In the early 1960s its analytical concerns still seemed to develop along straight lines. There were two tendencies which seemed to complement each other: on the one hand, because of the consolidation of West German politics at that time, the normative approach gathered momentum; on the other hand, there were many efforts towards neglected empirical studies on West German politics. The first line strove for a philosophical foundation for previous normative analyses and was influenced by the Freiburg School of Bergsträsser, which concentrated on an ontological foundation of 'practical politics' to reconstruct traditions of political thought extinguished in Germany since the nineteenth century. The second line also followed previous analyses but concentrated on attempts to display and describe institutions and processes of democratic party government and pluralistic interest intermediation. Very soon, and for different reasons, both approaches exposed a need for new efforts in the theoretical study of politics. The normative-ontological approach showed a strong bias towards conservative thought and, as it tended to equate political theory with political philosophy, it was not very helpful in guiding and organizing empirical studies and in systematizing their results. This experience heavily contributed to the 'Americanization' (von Beyme 1982) of West German political science.

Compared to its American counterpart, West German political science was characterized as theoretically backward. Thus, ironically, a massive import of conceptual approaches and analytical methods took place two decades after alarmed denunciations of the 'imported discipline'. At the same time, for many younger political scientists, the highly differentiated debate on positivism and critical rationalism between Popper *et al.* and Adorno *et al.* demonstrated a 'methodological innocence' in their own discipline. But the appeal of modern social science which resulted from this confrontation with achievements in other disciplines was not just an intellectual event. Popper's piecemeal engineering and American conceptualizations seemed to offer analytical instruments for political studies engaged in the promotion of political reforms. 'Reform policy' was a guiding motto of German politics from 1966 onwards when, due to socio-political changes, the Social Democrats entered the national government for the first time since 1949. In 1972, 'policies of internal reform', in addition to earlier changes in foreign policy, were proclaimed by Willy Brandt when he introduced the policy of the second Social Democrat-Liberal government. These slogans expressed, more than others, the changes in the political climate of that time. For some years, until the crisis of the mid-1970s and the subsequent shifts first to austerity and then to neo-liberalism and neo-conservatism, they also promoted changes within West German political science.

Although there were bitter disputes between 'traditionalists' and 'modernists', the most controversial change within West German political science has been the re-emergence of Marxist political analysis. In the early 1970s, the discipline was blamed by politicians and the mass media for having encouraged this change, but Marxist political analysis was primarily stimulated from outside the discipline. For a long time, Marxist theory had been or become an anathema for most West German social sciences. Marxist analysis had survived only outside the academic system (in trade union and political circles) or at its margins (in academic niches and in student circles). In the mid-1960s, these circles were able to provide the student movement with analytically trained activists. That so many students (and also trade unionists and Social Democrats) rediscovered Marxist theory was, however, not a master stroke by activists, but followed from the socio-economic and political changes in West Germany highlighted above. Practical politics itself had changed to an extent which was quite remarkable. Industrial disputes increased when the economy experienced its first backlash and when workers experienced the mechanisms of recession, and social democratic policies, however progressive compared to former Christian Democrat policies, led to critical discussions on the political objectives of labour.

For many students, however, the hard facts of industrial relations and economic policy were not a principal concern. Rather, they engaged in the themes developed and promoted by the critical theory of the Frankfurt school of social science. The combination of political discourse expressed in protest movements and socio-political interpretations offered by the critical theory provided the student campaigns with some of their most influential arguments. As in other social sciences, students and younger lecturers in West German political science saw the analyses of the Frankfurt school as prominent starting points in attempts to overcome analytical and political shortcomings in their discipline. This, in turn, favoured the dissemination of the critical theory. On the one hand, the contributions of the Frankfurt school to the *Positivismusstreit* had limited the appeal of modern social science; on the other hand, critical theory had transported notions of Marxist theory which now experienced a new upswing. These developments coincided with the expansion of the academic system in the early 1970s. Thus many who were appointed as lecturers had been shaped by the student movement. In addition, there were organizational changes within the universities: institutes and departments, formerly directed by professors, were now governed by councils which included representatives of students and lecturers. Both factors facilitated 'new blood' appointments and an increase in Marxist-oriented lecturers and, occasionally, professors.

Although the three-cornered configuration of disputes (and of partial coalitions) between traditionalists, modernists, and neo-Marxists has not vanished, the situation has calmed down. In his discussion of political and academic changes since the 1970s, von Beyme noted 'Polarization decreases, but pluralism is preserved to a greater extent than in most other West European countries' (von Beyme 1982:175). I want to refrain from comparative statements but to point out further some of the mechanisms by which, I would argue, *limited* pluralism has been restored since the early 1970s. Although (perhaps with one exception) no political science department or institute became dominated by Marxists, the partial change in personnel policies led to bitter conflicts and public discussions, often initiated by members of the profession, on the nature of political science, which was now considered by many to have become 'red'. A main cause for alarm was that the discipline had been entrusted with the training of student teachers. Thus, not only political science, but the education system were declared to be at stake (the same was said of other disciplines in charge of teacher training). Against these dangers, counter measures were implemented with gave new cause for dispute and turbulence: applicants for jobs were vetted politically; final examinations for student teachers, which are conducted by special state agencies, were designed to control study schemes, examination theses, and academic examiners; councils of departments were changed in their composition to reduce the participation rights of lecturers and students; and so on. These measures were accomplished 'by a combination of informal changes within the institutes and departments, and within the discipline as a whole. In addition, appointment policies of some federal states were tightened. (In West Germany professors are appointed by federal state ministries; the minister considers a list of three candidates chosen by a university and may appoint one, or none). Meanwhile, most of the Marxist lecturers of the 1970s had to leave their jobs, as the lower categories of West German university teachers (assistants, assistant professors) are appointed for a five- or six-year period only and extension of contracts is legally prohibited, even if formal qualification for a professorship is obtained.

Because of these limitations of pluralism, West German political science no longer hangs in the balance of events.

NOTES

1 This is a revised version of a paper originally presented to the Joint Symposium of the Finnish Political Science Association and the International Political Science Association on 'Development and Institutionalization of Political Science' at Espoo, Helsinki, 2-6 October 1985 and subsequently published in the *International*

Political Science Review (1987).

REFERENCES

Arndt, H.-J. (1978) *Die Besiegten von 1945: Versuch einer Politologie für Deutsche samt Würdigung der Politikwissenschaft in der Bundesrepublik Deutschland*, Berlin: Duncker and Humblot.

von Beyme, K. (1982) '(Political science in the) Federal Republic of Germany' in W.G. Andrews (ed.), *International Handbook of Political Science* pp. 169-76, Westport, CT/London: Greenwood Press.

Blanke, B., Jürgens, U., and Kastendiek, H. (1975) *Kritik der Politischen Wissenschaft: Analysen von Politik und Ökonomie in der bürgerlichen Gesellschaft*, 2 vols, Frankfurt am Main/New York: Campus.

Böhret, C. (1985) 'Zum Stand und zur Orientierung der Politikwissenschaft in der Bundesrepublik Deutschland', in H.-H. Hartwich (ed.) *Policy-Forschung in der Bundesrepublik Deutschland*, pp. 216-330, Opladen: Westdeutscher Verlag.

Faul, E. (1979) 'Politikwissenschaft im westlichen Deutschland', *Politische Vierteljahresschrift* 20(1):71-103.

Fränkel, E. (1960) *Das amerikanische Regierungssystem*, Cologne/Opladen: Westdeutscher Verlag.

Gantzel-Kress, G. and Gantzel, K.J. (1980) 'The development of international relations studies in West Germany', in E. Krippendorff and V. Rittberger (eds) *The Foreign Policy of West Germany: Formation and Contents*, vol. 4 of *German Political Studies*, pp. 197-269, London/Beverly Hills: Sage.

Günther, K. (1985) *Politisch-soziale Analyse im Schatten von Weimar*, Frankfurt am Main/Bern/New York: Verlag Peter Lang.

Kastendiek, H. (1977) *Die Entwicklung der westdeutschen Politikwissenschaft*, Frankfurt am Main/New York: Campus.

Mohr, A. (1985) Politikwissenschaft als Alternative – Stationen einer Disziplin auf dem Wege zu ihrer Selbständigkeit in der Bundesrepublik Deutschland 1945-65, Doctoral dissertation, University of Heidelberg.

von Örtzen, P. (1974) *Die soziale Funktion des staatsrechtlichen Positivismus: Eine wissenssoziologische Studie über die Entstehung des formalistischen Positivismus in der deutschen Staatsrechtswissenschaft*, Frankfurt am Main: Suhrkamp.

Pross, H. (1966) 'Die geistige Enthauptung Deutschlands: Verluste durch Emigration', in *Universitätstage 1966 der Freien Universität Berlin: Nationalsozialismus und die deutsche Universität*, pp. 143-55, Berlin: Walter de Gruyter.

Ringer, F.K. (1969) *The Decline of the German Mandarins: The German Academic Community, 1890-1933*, Cambridge, Mass.: Harvard University Press.

Weyher, J. (1985) 'Politikwissenschaft im Faschismus (1933-45): Die vergessenen zwölf Jahre', *Politische Vierteljahresschrift* 26(4): 423-37.

6 The development and institutionalization of political science in Italy

Luigi Graziano[1]

INTRODUCTION

The present mood in Italian political science may be best described as one of measured satisfaction. Not that there is a lack of awareness of persistent shortcomings or the need — felt by practitioners in a number of countries — for new directions and paradigms. Despite this awareness, there is a recognition, as one authoritative observer put it, that 'Italian political science has accomplished remarkable steps' (von Beyme 1986:97) and that the road travelled in the last twenty to thirty years has been 'very great and fruitful' (Sartori 1986:108).

The signs of this growth and the grounds for such qualified optimism are many. For one thing, the discipline which, in the 1960s and early 1970s, was barely present as a form of academic study, had few positions and hardly any chair, is now firmly grounded in the Italian university structure. The organization of the profession has been put on firmer ground with the foundation in 1981 of the Società italiana di scienza politica, a much more professional body than the previous association.[2] Also, the scientific output, as we see in greater detail later on, has grown immensely over the last twenty years, both in quantity and quality. The presence and visibility of Italian scholars in international organizations and meetings have much increased. Finally, and perhaps most significantly, the discipline has achieved social recognition, and there is a distinct feeling that the contributions of its practitioners may help to cope with major problems in state and society — from institutional reform to labour relations and other drastic changes which are confronting the country.

This optimism must be tempered by the recognition that the child looks so healthy mainly because it is so young. To be understood, the present feeling of accomplishment must be put in context and in a proper historical perspective. We need to explain both this remarkable growth and the fact that it happened so comparatively late, later than, say, in Germany, Britain or France (Leca 1982) not to mention the United States. Why has this growth come about? Which barriers, cultural and institutional, had to be overcome? And which conditions have favoured the discipline's coming of age? These are some of the questions to be answered in any reconstruction of the development of political science as a learned profession in Italy.

The growth of Italian political science can best be seen, I believe, as the result of the interaction of four factors, which all manifested themselves around the same time, the late 1950s and the 1960s.[3] The first factor was a conscious effort by a few authoritative scholars to rescue political science from academic oblivion and reestablish it as a distinct field of study, methodologically and substantively autonomous from such older disciplines as public law, history, and political philosophy. Prominent among these scholars were Norberto Bobbio, Giovanni Sartori, and Bruno Leoni. The second factor has to do with the social and economic development of Italian society, which by the 1960s had changed beyond recognition, and the democratic context which made it possible. The underlying philosophy of positive political science was 'scientific realism', and such realism was seen by many as instrumental in bringing about both reform (Bobbio 1969a:10) and the political modernization of the newly established Italian democracy (Sartori 1970:24). The problem was to bring the political system into line with a fast-moving society.

The third factor was the push from the outside, especially the impact of American political science and behaviouralism. Through the funding of research and other forms of institutional cooperation, American institutions — both government agencies and private foundations — played a decisive role in introducing new methods and themes of investigation, as well as helping a weak corporation to find a place in the Italian academic structure. The fourth and last factor has to do with changes in the university system, changes which allowed for the development of the Facoltà di Scienze Politiche and of teaching positions in political science within such departments.

THE SEARCH FOR AUTONOMY AND PURPOSE

Whoever wanted to reintroduce political science in postwar Italy had to start practically from scratch. Mosca and Pareto, the founders of the Italian school of political science, had no real followers,[4] and paradoxically their work was to become influential again among Italian scholars in part via American sociology and the rediscovery in the US between World War One and World War Two of elite theory. The Fascist regime, while founding a number of *Facoltà di scienze politiche* (Pavia, Padua, Perugia, and Rome), suppressed the teaching of political science in the only department in which it already existed, the Istituto Cesare Alfieri in Florence (Spreafico, 1964:205).[5] Nor was much progress made in the first decade after the war.

It is no wonder then that when, in 1960, Bruno Leoni of the University of Pavia commented on the state of the discipline in an article that was to become well-known — which is also a perceptive statement of what a science of politics should be by scope and method — he bitterly concluded that 'the balance sheet of . . . [Italian] political science over the last forty years is lamentable' (Leoni 1960:41).

Of course there were many 'political studies' in the older tradition. The subject matter of political science was, so to speak, farmed out and hegemonized by older disciplines — especially history, public law, and political philosophy — which tended to cover and exhaust the whole field. There was no 'political science' but, as in the French and other traditions, *scienze politiche*, in the plural. Nor was the question simply one of name since, as Jean Meynaud (1963:81), reporting on an interdisciplinary conference held in Turin in 1962 noted: 'The political sciences do not correspond to a specific category of knowledge; rather, they are simply a collection of subjects'. The official label (political science in the plural) thus tended to imply more than the idea that things political were susceptible of being studied from a variety of disciplinary perspectives, which is a perfectly legitimate view; it also tended to deny the need for and legitimacy of a specific point of view which purported to study politics 'scientifically'.

It may be interesting to review some of the arguments put forward at the time in the course of the discussion with neighbouring disciplines. The arguments were probably not much different from the ones advanced in other European countries with cultural traditions similar to Italy's. Distinctive Italian characteristics were, first, the cultural barriers to overcome, especially idealistic preconceptions against the social sciences and a deep-rooted tradition of anti-empiricism; and, second, the social functions assigned political science as they emerged in the course of the debate.

The 'battle' was fought in two successive stages. The first stage consisted of an attempt to establish the scientific status of the social sciences, and of political science within such sciences, *vis-à-vis* history, philosophy, and law. This was masterfully done, mainly by Bobbio, in the late 1950s and 1960s. The second stage was to argue for the autonomy of political science *vis-à-vis* both sociology as the fastest-growing social science, and the anti-empiricist tradition of Italian philosophy. This work was essentially that of Sartori (1970, 1971), especially in his influential introduction to the *Antologia di scienza politica* (Sartori 1970), the first systematic presentation of mainstream (mainly American) political science to the Italian public.

According to Bobbio (1969), traditional historiography, especially idealistic historiography, was premised on a view of social reality which precluded the possibility of a science of society. History and the social sciences also fundamentally differed in method. Historians typically saw history as a sequence of individual, unique, and unrepeatable events, a view which was 'typical of Croce and *crocianesimo* and was generally accepted by [Italian] professional historians'. It resulted in an irrational conception of history which made the development of social science either impossible or unnecessary. Instead, the development of the social sciences, Bobbio added, 'has always been accompanied by the tendency to acknowledge the "place of reason" in history' (Bobbio 1969:20). It is such a belief which makes plausible the search for 'probabilistic lines of development in social life', as well as (cautiously) corrective interventions based on the knowledge of such regularities.

Difference in method followed from such divergent views of history. The basic, often repeated (and I should add not always unjustified) criticism levelled by historians against social scientists is that of *schematismo*, that is, of having recourse to general concepts and schemes of interpretation while disregarding historical specifics. Bobbio's rebuttal was, first, that historians too make abundant use of general concepts and ideal types, often without fully realizing it, and second, that contemporary societies as *mass* societies based on increasingly mass phenomena (elections, mass parties, etc.) make a science of society both necessary and possible.

While history and political science differed in method, political science and public law differed fundamentally in the perspective from which each looks at an overlapping subject-matter (the study of the 'state'). Here the familiar opposition was formalism *vs* realism. Jurists study social behaviour inasmuch as it is regulated by norms, and behaviour which is not so regulated 'lies beyond the jurist's scope of interest' (Bobbio 1969:21). Political scientists are characteristically interested instead in the motivations and consequences of social behaviour, in substantive differentiations (in social status, power, etc.) which may manifest themselves even among people of formally equal status (party members, citizens, etc.) and the like. We need not elaborate on a line of reasoning which has been typical of political science at least since Bentley, except to note that Bobbio's defence of realism, made by a man who was himself a trained philosopher of law, was especially important in a country as thoroughly dominated by juridical formalism as Italy, in its culture no less than in many of its institutions.

In arguing for the plausibility of a science of politics, Bobbio was led to explore the scientific foundations of the discipline as part of his effort to convince a recalcitrant milieu. Here the main inspiration came from Mosca and Pareto, the early theorists of Italian political science to whose work Bobbio (1969a) devoted many important studies, convinced as he was that their joint contribution had laid the 'ground for the empirical study of politics' (Bobbio, 1961:215; cf. Bobbio 1969a). A brief reference to Pareto, the most interesting writer of the two, illustrates Bobbio's method of argument.[6]

Pareto, like Mosca, had been predominantly read as an elite theorist, that is, as a writer whose main contribution was thought to be more substantive than theoretical or methodological, and essentially linked to the idea of the role of organized minorities in history. Bobbio thought that such a reading did not begin to do justice to the complexity of his work. In Bobbio's view, a more adequate interpretation was one which saw in Pareto's writings a general theory centred on a theory of ideology, as the rationalization of man's basic social impulses. In a number of essays devoted to the sociologist, he could easily show, texts in hand, that 'the most substantial part of the

Trattato . . . refers to neither the elites nor to social equilibrium', adding that 'the core of the book lies in the analysis of man as an ideological animal' (Bobbio, 1969a).

Not only had Pareto set out to unmask man's ideological practice, much as Marx had done before him; more important as an operational canon for empirical research was the fact that he had indicated a method to separate objective truth from ideology, facts from their symbolic representation. Relevant here was the distinction, drawn by Pareto and stressed by Bobbio, between 'objective' and 'subjective' phenomena; namely the idea — central to Pareto's theory of action — according to which any verbalized human activity is best understood in terms of (1) whether a statement corresponds to the actor's actual motivations; (2) whether it is persuasive and has practical social efficacy and (3) in terms of social utility for the equilibrium of the system. Here was, if not a model, a theory of social life which opened the way to the empirical study of society, as the new science purported to do.

When Sartori (1970) published the *Antologia di scienza politica*, the problem had in part changed. For one thing, the cause of the social sciences had made some progress, except that the discipline which was profiting most from the new situation was sociology, not political science. The introduction, in 1963, of three university chairs in sociology, at a time when political science had none, was enough to raise the spectre, in the words of one careful observer, of sociology's 'intellectual imperialism' (Meynaud, 1963:86). Also, Sartori was even more concerned than Bobbio with empirical political science in the behavioural tradition, and here the prime 'enemy' was the anti-empiricist orientation of much of Italian political philosophy and culture.

Sartori viewed the distinction between sociology and *scienza politica* as one of the division of labour. To put it crudely, while sociology wished to study the impact of society on the 'state', political science was specifically concerned with the influence of the state on society (how the various political parties may affect local government, how elites are organized, exercise power, etc.). In terms of conceptualization and empirical research, this meant essentially a concern for different sets of variables. Sartori (1970:15) writes: 'To a large extent the independent variables . . . of the sociologist *are not* the independent variables of the political scientist [and] in any case the *independent* variables of the one are changed into the *dependent* variables of the other'. Furthermore, problems of institutional engineering, which are a prime concern for political science, were largely alien to the sociologist's scope of interest.

The theme of institutional engineering and applied science was also central to Sartori's critique of political philosophy as meta-empirical knowledge. Science and philosophy have recourse to sharply different types of language and concepts, and perform two distinct heuristic functions. Philosophic discourse is not meant to describe or represent empirical reality, but rather to grasp the essence or meaning of things (the essence and ultimate *raison d'être* of the state, etc.). In Croce's terms, its concepts are 'ultra-representative', in that they transcend all specific manifestation of the objects to which they refer. By contrast, empirical political science employs a language which is observational and descriptive, one in which 'words register observations and "stand for" what they represent' (Sartori 1970:20). Only the latter type of language makes possible the framing of propositions in a falsifiable form — the hallmark of any science *qua* science (cf. Sartori 1979).[7]

Philosophic knowledge not only cannot be, and is not meant to be, tested according to the canons of science; it is also not meant to be treated as applied science. Philosophy cannot be applied to social reality without further elaboration because the philosopher's main concern is with the problem of *why* rather than *how*. Lacking operational knowledge, the philosopher cannot produce (immediately) operational prescriptions. In particular, for Sartori, philosophical prescriptions for change and revolution (and here the primary target was Marxism and the Marxist orientation of large sectors of Italian culture) were both unscientific and potentially dangerously misleading, since they were unsupported by specific knowledge of the real functioning of institutions. Furthermore, and perhaps more importantly, confusion about the proper role of philosophy prevented political science from performing its practical function as a potentially corrective mechanism — as a tool for effectively improving the functioning of the system and the quality of institutions, which Sartori viewed as a prime responsibility of the discipline.

In order to understand fully Sartori's strictures on political philosophy and their general implications, a word should be said about the anti-empirical tradition in Italy, to which I have already alluded. That tradition, much reinforced under Croce's influence, ran deep in both the official culture of the elite and mass culture as shaped by the school system (Recuperati 1973:1714), for complex reasons which are probably connected with Italy's late, problematic and uneven encounter with modernization and industrialization (Bollati 1972). As Bobbio wrote in a masterful portrait of Italian ideology since 1900:

> If we understand by ideology a dominant orientation . . . which makes appear heretical any manifestation of thought which does not conform to it, such an orientation has consisted in Italy of a sometime speculative, sometime rhetorical and pedagogical spiritualism, which rules out . . . positivism, empiricism, materialism, and utilitarianism as vulgar, narrow-minded, mercantile and impure philosophies (Bobbio 1969b; cf. Dal Pra 1984)

A final point has to do with the extra-scientific responsibilities of scholars. The fact that political science re-emerged in the midst, and partially as a result, of great transformations in Italian society squarely posed the problem of the social functions of the discipline. The general problem, to whose solution social scientists could make an important contribution, was political modernization. As Sartori put it:

There is in Italy a very large gap between socio-economic modernization on one hand, and political archaism on the other. A socio-economic dynamic which poses . . . very serious problems of political modernization uneasily coexists with a political culture which is very backward, stagnant and incapable of 'knowledgeable responses' (Sartori 1970:26).

There were a number of intermediate steps for the profession, which need to be very briefly recalled. In Sartori's view, political scientists were to contribute to the 'common good' of the country, which he rather sceptically defined as a need to remedy 'that "common evil" which consists in being badly governed'. Freeing Italy of a political class made up of 'incapable and incompetent politicians' was the most urgent task in Italian politics, one to which political scientists could make an important contribution (Sartori 1970:23).

The practical task was to influence and reshape the culture of those 'men of culture' (presumably journalists, intellectuals, teachers, experts of various kinds) whose views carried much weight with members of the political class, and to instill in the outlook of the former (and by implication in the outlook of the political personnel) a more realistic and competent knowledge of the political process. The goal was to introduce into the political culture of the elite 'a parameter of seriousness and competence by which to measure the actions of politicians', instead of the old view of politics as a mixture of art and ideology (Sartori 1970:26).[8]

It is debatable whether Italian political scientists, assuming they would agree on such a 'mission', will ever have the strength to carry out such a programme. In any case, both the two-step approach (that is, the idea of reaching the political class through the cultivated strata of 'public opinion') and the elitist element in Sartori's prescription, perhaps a reflection of the highly stratified nature of Italian society and the traditional role played in it by intellectuals, are interesting. Be that as it may, it is a far cry from the function of civic and democratic training for the population at large which, together with the training of government personnel, has been the main responsibility of political science in such countries as the United States (Somit and Tanenhaus 1967; Ricci 1985), post-war Germany and others.

DEPENDENCE AND INTERDEPENDENCE: THE IMPACT OF AMERICAN SOCIAL SCIENCE

The scientific effort meant to provide an autonomous status for the discipline, briefly analysed in the previous section of this chapter, was part of a broader picture in which other influences and factors were at work, except on a much larger scale. In fact, when one looks at the overall development of political science in Italy, particularly at the early stage of the process, one is struck by the disproportion between indigenous forces and external influences. I refer in particular to the impact of American social science, arguably the most important factor in setting the pace and shaping the course of social science in postwar Italy.

This is not the place to review the general factors — cultural, political, institutional — which made Italy an environment very receptive to American influence. But one general observation is in order. In the process of the interaction with the United States, there has been at work a push factor which was typically American and affected many other European countries besides Italy, and a pull factor peculiar to the Italian situation. The push factor has to do with the heightened status of American social science after World War Two, particularly as a result of the involvement of many American scholars in government matters during the war, and the role social science came to play in American expansion abroad. As LaPalombara (1986: 74) has reminded us, 'Postwar America launched a wide variety of activities designed to increase American influence abroad, and the social sciences were accorded a prominent place in this strategy'. This was a decisive element in bringing about the sort of lopsidedness which was to characterize the relationship between American and West European social science since the war.

What I have called the pull factor was mainly due to Italian bureaucratic inaction and lack of concern with the development of the social sciences, as part of the scientific infrastructure of any modern country. Governmental insensitivity, coupled with academic hostility, deprived Italian scholars of institutional support at home (through lack of research funds, openings at universities, etc.), making a number of them eager to accept the support which might come from other patrons.

Institutional cooperation and exchange between Italy and the United States may be conveniently grouped under three broad headings: research and training; exchange of personnel; and translations.[9]

Research and training

Among collaborative research projects, undoubtedly the most important has been the series of studies on political participation in Italy carried out at the Carlo Cattaneo Institute in Bologna between 1963 and 1965. Financed by the Twentieth Century Fund and executed by a team of Italian researchers outside the formal university structure, the study constitutes the most thorough investigation so far of the two major parties, the PCI and the Christian Democrats. Topics covered in the six volumes which resulted from the project (Istituto Carlo Cattaneo 1967, 1968a, b, c, d; Prandi 1968) range from electoral behaviour to party structure, party membership and elite; party militants; linkages with supporting organizations, such as the Church, unions, etc.; and the record of the two parties in parliament and in local government.[10]

The overall interpretation which emerged from the study, and which may be called the subcultural model of Italian politics — centred on the primacy of ideology and subcultural fragmentation — quickly became a dominant theme in any discussion on the nature of the Italian political system and the problems to be confronted for its modernization (Galli 1966). In summary, by the methodology employed, research design, and range of topics covered, the Cattaneo study may be said to have given great impetus to behavioural research in Italy and a new awareness to the discipline, constituting a true turning-point in the development of postwar political science in Italy.[11]

An earlier collaborative project centred on public administration. Co-sponsored by the University of California at Berkeley and the University of Bologna, the project led to the establishment in the 1950s of a postgraduate school in Bologna, the only one of its kind then in Italy (Scuola di perfezionamento in scienze amministrative dell'Università di Bologna), and the publication of a journal — *Problemi della pubblica amministrazione*. The fact that Bologna has since become one of the most important centres in administrative studies is not unconnected with this earlier input. One overspill effect of the Bologna-Berkeley connection has been the opportunity for a number of scholars to complete their postgraduate education at Berkeley — Di Palma, Freddi, Poggi, and Sani, among others.

In the field of training one should also mention the Bologna Centre of the Johns Hopkins, which is partially subsidized by the US government and the Ford Foundation, and grants a master's degree in international relations. Of special note in the context of our discussion is the fact that until recently, the Bologna Centre was authorized to run courses for future Italian diplomats. Italians are regularly present both on the teaching staff and as students, and the centre has provided an arena through which American approaches to the study of international relations have gained wide currency in the Italian university milieu.

Even more central to the building of the profession has been COSPOS (Comitato per le scienze politiche e sociali), a cooperative enterprise for postgraduate training set up in the mid-1960s with the financial assistance of the Ford and Olivetti Foundations and the support of the Social Science Research Council in New York. The general aim was described by one of its co-founders as an attempt to involve, alongside the founding organizations, 'leading Italian scholars, the Italian universities and, eventually, the CNR (the Italian National Research Council) in the promotion of graduate-level training in the social sciences' (LaPalombara 1986:80). In the area of political science, COSPOS set up postgraduate centres in Florence, Turin, and Catania, under the directorship of Sartori, Bobbio and Spreafico, respectively (Bobbio was later succeeded by Paolo Farneti in Turin). COSPOS played a very important role in institutional innovation, acting as an authoritative pressure group with the Italian authorities for the institutionalization of the social sciences within the academic structure, and as an arena within which a core of young Italian scholars could receive appropriate advanced training.

Exchange Programmes

The structure of dependency is equally clear if we look at exchange programmes, the most important of which has been the Fulbright Program. Between 1949 and 1982 some 8,315 Americans and Italians took part in the programme (see Table 1). Through the years, an increasing number of these came from the social sciences, although presumably social science was only a small element of the overall exchange.

Table 1 Fulbright Program: Italy and the United States, 1949-82 by category

Category	Italians to United States	Americans to Italy
University study	2,194	2,143
Advanced research	1,277	529
University lecturers	233	521
Practical experience	90	
Teaching, educational seminars	579	749
Total	4,373	3,942

Source: Board of Foreign Scholarships, *Fulbright Program Exchanges*, 1982 (Washington, DC, December 1982: 30-1); from LaPalombara (1986:76)

As LaPalombara commenting on these figures has remarked, the motivations behind exchanges labelled 'university study' have been generally quite different among Americans and Italians. While most Americans were coming to Italy to complete their own research, generally in the context of PhD programmes, Italians went to the USA to study rather than practice political science as students formally enrolled in advanced university programmes (MA or PhD) and perhaps more often for shorter periods of time. In the case of 'advanced research' the imbalance is quite clear, with many more Italians going to the States for research than American scholars coming to Italy, just as it is in the case of university lecturers, again with many more American lecturers coming to Italy than Italians being invited to the United States.

Translations

A final important indicator of dependency is the number of translations. An enormous number of books and other materials are translated each year in Italy. Although the phenomenon is difficult to measure precisely, this general trend seems to be present in a magnified form in the social sciences. Here again spontaneous trends in the book market have been powerfully encouraged by the explicit policy of a number of American institutions. LaPalombara recalls past agreements between the United States Information Agency (USIA) and Il Mulino, a publishing house which has been very active and successful in making American social science literature available to the Italian reader. Another publisher to be mentioned in this connection is Comunità, the publishing house of the Olivetti Foundation. USIA used to run its own bookshops in a number of Italian cities (Rome, Florence, Naples, etc.). Needless to say, the number of Italian social science works accessible to the English-speaking public is negligible.

The thrust of my comments about interaction with the US is not, of course, to 'regret' such a broad *brassage*, from which Italian political science has emerged much enriched, diversified, and methodologically sophisticated. If the discipline has experienced the growth which I mentioned earlier, and to which I return later, to an important degree it has been due to exposure to more advanced traditions of research and training. Furthermore, as I have argued elsewhere (Graziano 1986:39-40), reception of American political science has been quite selective and anything but acritical. The point is rather that exchange is no substitute for a national government policy in the field of university teaching and research. Exchange left largely to itself produces one kind of result; when guided by a conscious policy towards science and a view of the teaching needs of the country, it produces quite different effects.

It is no mere coincidence, for instance, that while American-Italian cooperation has produced a sizeable amount of American Italianists now grouped in the Conference Group on Italian Politics and Society (CONGRIPS), it has produced very few Italian experts on the American political system. Italians, as we shall see, study almost exclusively Italy, despite the broad exposure I have described. The same applies to the 'brain drain' which has seriously affected Italy, some of the best scholars having left for the US or (more rarely) other countries. (One has only to think of such academics as Sartori, Pizzorno, Sani, Poggi, Di Palma, and others, some of whom have returned to Italy).

OUTPUT

It is difficult to summarize the output of a discipline, all the more so since until quite recently there were no surveys of the discipline as a whole. Italy was not, for instance, among the countries included in Andrews' *International Handbook of Political Science* (1982). Previous attempts at delineating the 'state of the art' were either partial and limited to a few years or predated the expansion of Italian political science in the last 10 to 15 years (Spreafico, 1964).[12]

In 1983-4 the Centro di Scienza Politica Feltrinelli in Milan organized a series of seminars in which experts were asked to review output and trends in the various subfields of the discipline over the last twenty years or so — from international relations to administrative studies, political parties, elections, government institutions and other areas.[13] The seminars provided documentary material for an international conference held in Milan, Italy, in May 1984 under the general title 'Political Science in Italy: Retrospect and Prospects', the first of its kind.[14] On the basis of this material a few general observations may be made on the present state of the discipline and some of its emerging trends.

The first striking fact is simply the physical growth of scientific output. In 1970, when Sartori coined the term *analfabetismo politologico* to characterize the paucity of works in the field, there were perhaps thirty-to-fifty books in political science as currently defined. A rough count of titles listed in the various chapters of *La scienza politica in Italia* (Quaderni Fondazione Feltrinelli 1984) indicates about 500 titles. A second general trait is that Italian scholars have explored the input side of the political process much more systematically than the output side — a trait well in keeping with the general orientation of early behavioural studies. Research has focused mainly on such areas as political parties (Belligni 1984), elections and electoral behaviour (Mannheimer 1984), and studies on political attitudes and values (Marradi and Arculeo 1984; Sani 1984).

Much less has been done in the field of international relations (Bonanate 1984), in the area of government institutions and that of public policy (Dente 1984a, b). In the realm of administrative studies, empirical research has focused especially on the judiciary, and the whole field is still somewhat the object of 'contending approaches' from different perspectives. So far a satisfactory integration between the various disciplines interested in the field (history, law, organizational studies) has not emerged.

Another general characteristic of political science in Italy, already mentioned, has to do with the fact that Italian scholars study mainly Italy, and pay very little attention to other countries. Studies on France, Germany, the Soviet Union, the United States, and Third World countries are extremely rare and mainly the work of historians, with consequent shortcomings in substantive knowledge of things non-Italian, and in the conceptual richness which might come from

Table 2 Research in Italy, by topic, 1983

Subject areas	No.	Per cent[a]
Local representative assemblies	3	4.5
National representative assemblies	6	9.0
Political attitudes and orientations	9	13.4
Institutions of local government	1	1.5
European Community	4	6.0
Conflict, violence, war	4	6.0
Civil rights	0	0.0
Women and women's movements	1	1.5
Elections	13	19.4
Elites and leadership	9	13.4
Armed forces, army, police	1	1.5
Youth and youth movements	2	3.0
Justice and judicial system	3	4.5
Central government	9	13.4
Local government	14	20.9
Pressure groups	3	4.5
Political identification	1	1.5
International organizations	1	1.5
Electoral and political participation	7	10.4
Political parties	6	9.0
Ethnic problems	2	3.0
Decision-making processes	8	11.9
Public administration	10	14.9
Public opinion	2	3.0
Representation	5	7.5
International relations	7	10.4
Unions and labour movement	7	10.4
Italian political system	5	7.5
Legal system	1	1.5
Public expenditure	2	3.0
Administrative studies	1	1.5
Constitutional studies	1	1.5
Community studies	1	1.5
Regional studies	0	0.0
Organizational studies	2	3.0
Religious studies	0	0.0
Historical studies	4	6.0
Theory of the State	0	0.0
Political communication	1	1.5
Total	156	

Source: Repertory of Empirical Research Projects and Files in Italy (1984:6)
Note: [a] Percentage of each option over the whole of research reported (n = 67). The total is higher than 100, as it was possible to indicate more than one research area.

Table 3 Techniques of Data Collection 1983

	No	Per cent
Not mentioned	1	1.5
Survey	23	34.3
Analysis of institutional and statistical data	19	28.4
Survey *and* analysis of statistical data	3	4.4
Analysis of documents or other non-statistical sources	15	22.4
Content analysis	6	9.0
Total	67	100.0

Source: Repertory of Empirical Research Projects and Files in Italy (1984:7)

comparative studies and a comparative perspective.

A somewhat more precise and systematic picture may be gathered from a survey of current research and files conducted in 1982-3 by the Feltrinelli Centre, and repeated in 1984-5 (Repertorio delle ricerche empiriche e dei files in Italia 1984, 1986). A questionnaire was sent to all professional political scientists and major research centres in the country, asking questions on research topic, methods of investigation employed, access to data and other items. The number of questionnaires returned — 79 in 1983 and 58 in 1985 — makes the surveys quite representative of empirical research being conducted in Italy, or at least of the majority of research and certainly its most significant portion.

In 1983 two areas — electoral studies and local government — comprised almost 50 per cent of reported research. Other major areas of concentration were, in decreasing order, public administration, central government institutions, elites and decision-making processes. Other topics, by contrast, are little studied or not studied at all. Pressure groups score very low (although 10 per cent of reported research centres on unions), while such central topics as mass media and public policy are hardly present or not even mentioned (see Table 2). In terms of research techniques, survey methods come first (34.3 per cent), followed by institutional and statistical sources (28.4 per cent), and documentary and other non-statistical data (22.4 per cent) (see Tables 3 and 4).

A final point has to do with access to data files. For more than 80 per cent of research projects reported in 1983, the authors stated their willingness to disclose data and research material, either immediately (25.4 per cent) or in the near future (58.2 per cent). The figure is even higher in the 1985 survey (86.5 per cent). Access to data opens up interesting possibilities for secondary analyses and other collaborative efforts.

Table 4 Techniques of Data Collection by Selected Subject Areas, 1983

Subject areas	Not mentioned %	Survey %	Statistical sources %	Survey and statistical sources %	Non-statistical sources %	Content analysis %	Total %
Political attitudes and orientations	0	7 (77.8)	0	0	1 (11.1)	1 (11.1)	9 (100.0)
Elections	0	3 (23.1)	8 (61.5)	1 (7.7)	1 (7.7)	0	13 (100.0)
Elites and leadership	0	7 (77.6)	1 (11.1)	0	0	1 (11.1)	9 (100.0)
Central government	0	2 (22.2)	4 (44.4)	1 (11.1)	2 (22.2)	0	9 (100.0)
Local government	0	5 (35.7)	4 (28.6)	1 (7.1)	4 (28.6)	0	14 (100.0)
Decision-making processes	0	4 (50.0)	2 (25.0)	0	2 (25.0)	0	8 (100.0)
Public administration	0	2 (20.0)	3 (30.0)	2 (20.0)	3 (30.0)	0	10 (100.0)
International relations	0	2 (28.6)	0	0	5 (71.4)	0	7 (100.0)
Unions and labour movement	1 (14.3)	2 (28.6)	3 (41.9)	0	1 (14.3)	0	7 (100.0)
Others	1 (1.5)	24 (35.8)	13 (19.4)	4 (6.0)	18 (26.9)	7 (10.4)	67 (100.0)

Source: Repertory of Empirical Research Projects and Files in Italy (1984:9)

Table 5 Distribution of research by location, 1983

Locations	No.	Per cent
Berlino[a]	1	1.5
Bologna	7	10.4
Catania	11	16.4
Cosenza	1	1.5
Florence	3	4.5
Messina	2	3.0
Milan	13	19.4
Padua	1	1.5
Pavia	5	7.5
Rome	7	10.4
Salerno	1	1.5
Turin	7	10.4
Trento	1	1.5
European University (Florence)	7	10.5
Total	67	100.0

Source: Repertory of Empirical Research Projects and Files in Italy (1984:11)
Note: [a] Refers to one scholar active in Italy for the last few years.

The 1985 survey basically confirms the picture, but with some significant changes. Political parties emerge as the single most important research area, but local government and elite studies remain important. A second change has to do with a better integration of different research techniques. In almost 15 per cent of research reported, scholars make use of *both* survey and statistical data (as against 4.4 per cent in 1983). As in 1983, research is mainly concentrated in the major universities (Bologna, Milan, Florence, Rome, Pavia, Turin, Padua and Catania) (See Table 5).

THE PROFESSION TODAY

It seems appropriate to conclude our discussion by briefly commenting on the institutionalization of Italian political science as both an academic discipline and as a profession.

There are today 19 Facoltà di Scienze Politiche (some may have slightly different names), which are relatively evenly distributed throughout the country: seven in the north (Turin, Pavia, Genoa, Padua, Trieste, and two departments in Milan); seven in central Italy (Bologna, Florence, Pisa, Siena, Perugia, and two departments in Rome); and five in the south (Catania, University of Calabria,

Table 6 Official teaching positions in political science and related subjects in Italian universities 1985[a]

Departments	No. of positions
Bologna	13
Florence	11
Roma LUISS[b]	7
Turin	6
Catania	6
Padua	5
Università della Calabria	4
Pavia	3
Milano Statale	3
Genoa	2
Milano Cattolica	2
Trento	1
Trieste	1
Milano Bocconi	1
Modena	1
Pisa	1
Siena	1
Perugia	1
Roma Scienze Politiche	1
Roma Magistero	1
Salerno	1
Messina	1
Palermo	1

Notes: [a]Besides the Facoltà di scienze politiche, the list includes other departments with at least one teaching position in political science
[b]Libera Università Internazionale di Scienze Sociali, Rome

Messina, Palermo, and Salerno). Under current government policy, a few more departments are being planned or have been recently instituted as dependencies of existing universities, to be eventually turned into full-fledged, autonomous faculties (this is the case for instance of Alessandria).

The number of teaching positions in political science varies greatly among the various departments. Many have just one position; other faculties have ten or more (see Table 6). Listed under 'positions' are official courses which, in the Italian system, fall within political science. This does not mean, however, that all the positions listed in Table 6 are currently filled by political scientists. In a few cases, the courses may be taught by jurists, historians, etc., reflecting past assignments. The second observation is that not only the number but the type of course offered may vary greatly from one university to another. Under the Italian system in which each position is assigned an official label (Professor of Comparative Politics, Professor of Italian Political System, etc.), it is quite possible for one department to offer a course, say, in public opinion studies but not in political science (this is the case in Perugia, one of the oldest faculties in Italy). The State University in Milan, with one of the largest departments of political science in the country, had no chair in political science for years and only recently the position was filled.

This does not diminish the fact that political science as a teaching profession has grown enormously. In 1971, the year in which the *Rivista italiana di scienza politica* (Italian Political Science Review) was founded under Sartori's directorship, there was only one chair in political science — Sartori's in Florence. In 1980 there were about fifteen full professors, and there are at present some thirty-five — an exponential increase in twenty years. In addition, there are about forty associate professors and approximately as many scholars with the official status of researcher.

The Società italiana di scienza politica, founded in 1981, currently has some 150 members. The membership is comparatively small, but it should be remembered that unlike similar associations in other countries, for instance in France and the US, the Italian Association includes noone (or virtually noone) outside the academic profession. The Società holds regular annual meetings and performs all the functions of a fully institutionalized professional organization.

One final very important development has been the launching in the mid-1980s of the two PhD programmes, on in political science and one in international relations. The PhD in political science, in which about 15-20 students are currently enrolled, is run through a consortium of five departments (Florence, Turin, Pavia, Bologna, Catania). It has a special arrangement with Yale and Columbia and the Institute for Political Studies in Paris for regular exchange of teachers.

NOTES

1 This is a revision of a paper presented at Cortona, Italy, September 1987.
2 Before 1981 political scientists were part of a broader and more loosely organized association – Associazione italiana di scienze politiche e sociali (AISPS) – which included, besides political scientists, historians, students of political thought, etc.
3 For a more extensive discussion of these developments, see Graziano (1986, 'Introduction':13-43).
4 One exception is Maranini (1983), whose important study on the structure of power in Italy, first published in 1967, was explicitly inspired by Mosca.
5 Because of their association with the Fascist regime, the Facoltà di Scienze Politiche were looked upon with suspicion after the fall of the regime and long afterward.
6 On Bobbio's interpretation of Mosca, cf. Bobbio (1969a, 1986).
7 Writing about the 1960s, Morlino (1989:15) notes that 'Italian political science could not be considered completely "reborn" until it had made the "great leap" (*il*

grande salto) in the direction of empirical research'.
8 For a discussion of Sartori's more substantive contributions to the discipline, especially in conceptual and methodological matters, cf. Graziano (1986, 'Introduction':30-38).
9 The following section draws heavily on LaPalombara (1986).
10 A summary in English by the two directors of the Cattaneo study is in Galli and Prandi (1970).
11 Two earlier important research projects benefited from American support: Sartori *et al.* (1963); Spreafico and LaPalombara (1963).
12 Spreafico's (1964) survey covered works published between 1961 and 1963. To my knowledge no other systematic survey was conducted before the Feltrinelli surveys in 1983-5.
13 See Quaderni (1984).
14 See Graziano (1986) for a general presentation of the meeting and some of the papers delivered at the conference.

REFERENCES

Andrews, W.G. (ed.) (1982) *International Handbook of Political Science*, Westport, CT: Greenwood Press.
Belligni, S. (1984) 'Italia: il puzzle del "sistema partitico": Cosa dicono i politologi', *Quaderni Fondazione Feltrinelli* 28/29: 155-97, Milan: F. Angeli.
von Beyme, K. (1986) 'La scienza politica in Italia: uno sguardo dall'esterno' in L. Graziano (ed.) *La scienza politica in Italia: bilancio e prospettive* pp. 90-97, Milan: F. Angeli.
Bobbio, N. (1969a) *Saggi sulla scienza politica in Italia*, Bari: Laterza.
— (1969b) 'Profilo ideologico del Novecento italiano', *Storia della letteratura italiana*, vol. IX, Milan: Garzanti.
— (1986) 'La scienza politica e la tradizione di studi politici in Italia' in L. Graziano (ed.) *La scienza politica in Italia: bilancio e prospettive* pp. 46-60, Milan: F. Angeli.
Bollati, G. (1972) 'L'italiano', *Storia d'Italia Einaudi*, pp. 951-1022, Turin: Einaudi.
Bonanate, L. (1984) 'Gli studi di relazioni internazionali in Italia: la sindrome del "brutto anatroccolo"', *Quaderni Fondazione Feltrinelli* 28/29: 49-76, Milan: F. Angeli.
Dal Pra, M. (1984) *Studi sul pragmatismo italiano*, Napoli: Bibliopolis.
Dente, B. (1984a) 'Gli studi di scienza politica sulle istituzioni di governo: una rassegna problematica,' *Quaderni Fondazione Feltrinelli* 28/29: 351-75, Milan: F. Angeli.
— (1984b). 'Gli studi sull'attuazione delle politiche pubbliche', paper presented at the Conference on Political Science in Italy, Retrospect and Prospects, Milan, Italy held in May, Centro di Scienza Politica Feltrinelli.
Galli, G. (1966) *Il bipartitismo imperfetto*, Bologna: Il Mulino.
Galli, G. and Prandi, A. (1970) *Patterns of Political Participation in Italy*, New Haven and London: Yale University Press.
Graziano, L. (ed.) (1986) *La scienza politica in Italia: bilancio e prospettive*, Milan: F. Angeli.
Istituto Carlo Cattaneo (1967) *L'attivista di partito*, Bologna: Il Mulino.
— (1968a) *Il comportamento elettorale in Italia*, Bologna: Il Mulino.

— (1968b) *L'organizzazione partitica del PCI e della DC*, Bologna: Il Mulino.

— (1968c) *La presenza sociale del PCI e della DC*, Bologna: Il Mulino.

— (1968d) *Il PCI e la DC nelle amministrazioni locali e in Parlamento*, Bologna: Il Mulino.

LaPalombara, J. (1986) 'Dipendenze e interdipendenze nello sviluppo della scienza politica italiana' in L. Graziano (ed.) *La scienza politica in Italia: bilancio e prospettive*, pp. 61-89, Milan: F. Angeli.

Leca, J. (1982) 'La science politique dans le champ intellectuel français', *Revue française de science politique* 32(4-5): 653-78.

Leoni, B. (1960) 'Un bilancio lamentevole: il sottosviluppo della scienza politica in Italia', *Il Politico* 25: 31-41.

Mannheimer, R. (1984) 'Gli studi sul comportamento elettorale', *Quaderni Fondazione Feltrinelli* 28/29: 263-89, Milan: F. Angeli.

Maranini, G. (1983) *Storia del potere in Italia*, Florence: Nuova Guaraldi Editore.

Marradi, A. and Arculeo, A. (1984) 'Rassegna dei sondaggi sui valori degli italiani', *Quaderni Fondazione Feltrinelli* 28/29: 291-332, Milan: F. Angeli.

Meynaud, J. (1963) 'La scienza politica in Italia: un convegno del Centro studi metodologici', *Tempi moderni* 11:80-7.

Morlino, L. (1989) *Guide agli studi di scienze sociali in Italia. Scienza politica*, Turin: Edizioni della Fondazione Giovanni Agnelli.

Prandi, A. (1968) *Chiesa e politica*, Bologna: Il Mulino.

Quaderni Fondazione Feltrinelli (1984) *La scienza politica in Italia: materiali per un bilancio*, 28/29, Milan: F. Angeli.

Recuperati, G. (1973) 'La scuola nell'Italia unita', *Storia d'Italia Einaudi*, 5: 1695-736, Turin: Einaudi.

Repertory of Empirical Research Projects and Files in Italy (1984) *European Political Data Newsletter*, 51:4-16, Centro di Scienza Politica Feltrinelli.

Repertorio delle ricerche empiriche e dei files in Italia (1986) *Rivista Italiana di Scienza Politica* 15(1): 153-64.

Ricci, D.M. (1985) *The Tragedy of Political Science: Politics, Scholarship, and Democracy*, New Haven and London: Yale University Press.

Sani, G. (1984) 'Gli studi sugli attegiamenti politici di massa: bilanci e prospettive', *Quaderni Fondazione Feltninelli* 28/9, Milan, F. Angeli.

Sartori, G. (1970) 'Per una definizione della scienza politica', in *Antologia di scienza politica*, pp. 11-28, Bologna: Il Mulino.

— (1971) 'La politica comparata: premesse e problemi', in *Rivista italiana di scienza politica*, 1(1): 7-37.

— (1979) *La politica: logica e metodo in scienza sociali*, Milan: Sugarco.

— (1986) 'Dove va la szienza politica?' in *La scienza politica in Italia: bilancio e prospettive* (L. Graziano, ed.), pp. 98-114, Milan: F. Angeli.

Sartori, G., *et al.* (1963) *Il parlamento italiano*, Naples: ESI.

Somit, A. and Tanenhaus, J. (1967) *The Development of American Political Science: From Burgess to Behavioralism*, Boston: Allyn and Bacon. Enlarged edition (1982) New York: Irvington.

Spreafico, A. (1964) Studi politici e scienza politica in Italia, *Annuario politico italiano*, pp.202-30, Milan: Comunità.

Spreafico, A. and LaPalombara, J., (eds) (1963) *Elezioni e compartamento politico in Italia*, Milan: Comunità.

7 French political science and its 'subfields'

Some reflections on the intellectual organization of the discipline in relation to its historical and social situation

Jean Leca[1]

The guiding hypothesis of this chapter is that the way in which a scientific discipline organizes and controls its subfields is determined to a large extent by its social situation, and more specifically by its relation to the other relevant social fields, above all the intellectual field.

'Subfield' is sometimes used in this article as an equivalent for 'subdiscipline', for example micro-politics or political philosophy. But the notion has a broader scope: it may apply to research domains within a subdiscipline (for example French 'géographie électorale' was long a part of voting behaviour studies, themselves a part of political sociology); it may also cover several subdisciplines ('area studies' are a nice illustration). From an epistemological point of view, these different varieties are clearly not homogeneous: the objects and approaches of formal political theory have nothing to do with, say, the study of Southern Asian States which combines history, geography, anthropology, and sociology in order to characterize the form and nature of their political systems. But sociologically speaking a subfield always comprises the four following features: 1 a communication network linking its members as producers and consumers of a certain kind of product; 2 a common mechanism to set the price of the product; 3 a reproductive system endowing the network and the price mechanism with a sufficient durability throughout a long time span; 4 a measure of submission to the whole field's dominant rules. This characteristic is by far the most problematic.

'Field' (in French *champ*) means here a set of interactions and of social positions related to a specific type of activity, with specific goods at stake. A field is usually enclosed within relatively precise, if not always airtight boundaries. A field may be represented as a space where various influences interact, so causing motion or changes in motion (a kinetic field), according to specific rules of the game (in this respect a field is both a playground and a baseball stadium); and as a battleground where various contenders use different strategies to gain decisive advantage.[2] Like every other field, the intellectual field is regulated by economics (a system of production and exchange, Boudon 1981) and politics (a system of power and domination, Lemert 1981).[3] The intellectual field goes beyond the scientific field since it also covers producers and consumers of ideas (from columnists to members of various agencies), essays, and even novels. It interferes with the political field, but in France, as in most of the pluralist democracies, the politics of the various fields are not dependent on 'politics' (that is the politics of the specialized political field).[4] The comprehensive study of a discipline's social situation would require us to take into account all the relations between the three fields (scientific, intellectual, political) and the historical genesis of their construction. I will limit myself here to the intellectual and scientific fields, sometimes introducing the political one as a contextual element. The examples will be drawn from the economics of each field rather than from their politics. I will deal at some length with the genesis of political science as a scientific (more accurately a professional) field without lingering on the two others.

A few more points have to be made by way of introduction. The relation of a field to its subfields is ideally crystal-clear: either the so-called subfields merge or ally to constitute a new discipline, or they spring from the process of differentiation going on within an already constituted discipline. In each case, the subfields, once constituted communicate (or do not), cooperate (or do not), but they are clearly recognized as dependent on the whole 'field': the control exerted by the discipline is a necessary condition of its autonomy *vis-à-vis* the other fields.

Admittedly, things are never as simple as that, and a subfield may be also a part of another field, or even a field of its own (Gunnell 1983). Moreover, whether it is a process of aggregation or differentiation, the development of a discipline is seldom a purely endogenous process dependent on some would-be laws of evolution governed by the logic of reason, in a Comteian or Hegelian fashion. It is not at all certain that contemporary political science (supposing it is an autonomous and unified discipline endowed with the same basic characteristics throughout the whole world, which I feel inclined to doubt) is the 'natural' offspring of the 'noble science of politics' pictured by careful practitioners in intellectual history (Collini, Winch, Burrow 1983). The mere existence and organization of a discipline depends on complex socio-historical processes (Favre 1989) and so does its eventual decay or withering away. Nobody will deny the fact that a scientific development is a social development, but with due respect to this triviality, nobody will question, either, the simple fact that a discipline (whatever the arbitrary bases of its constitution) cannot exist as a social organization unless its members, regardless of their specific subfields, feel compelled to acknowledge their belonging to the same all-encompassing community. It is not necessary that they share the same paradigm, nor even the same concerns, but they should at any rate recognize the relevance of the topics and issues considered as the common good of the whole community. A discipline can afford mavericks and dual citizens whose presence is always a good remedy against routine and sclerosis, but if it ceases to maintain a minimal control over the various subfields, each becomes dependent on outsiders' appeals and the progress of knowledge is more likely to be put in jeopardy than by an excess of routinized control.

The two first parts of this text delineate the social historical processes which have made French political science a profession but not yet a socially legitimate discipline.[5] Political science is not perceived as autonomous *vis-à-vis* the 'political knowledge' that any well informed citizen (members of the media, high civil servants, novelists, members of other academic disciplines) is supposed to be able to display. There are no sharp nor even loose boundaries between political science and political discourse (or more precisely any discourse about politics and society at large). The process is perverse since knowledgeable people deduce that a political scientist does not need specific training. In this respect, French political science is not yet a *Wissenschaft*, if a *Wissenchaft*'s basic character consists in being transmitted through specific training processes. Maybe such a situation is due to good epistemological reasons: if political science is a 'crossroad science' ('*science carrefour*'), no core of knowledge is needed; all one has to do is master one of the roads leading to the crossroad. But that raises a tricky epistemological question: how are we going to recognize that we have reached the crossroad?[6]

A discipline lacking sufficient autonomy is unlikely to be able to recognize or control autonomous subfields. This is a hindrance to the students, who cannot get a complete training; and to the young scholars, who have still to work out by themselves some viable way of using and combining the resources provided by the various subfields to achieve their specific research. But there may be more serious consequences. I will mention just one: the only subfields not likely to be questioned are the research areas which are imposed on scholars from the outside: Latin American politics, Eastern European politics, Arab politics, French politics, international politics, etc. The result is that we are always on the verge of forgetting what comparative political analysis is about, and that we run the risk of taking for granted the practical paradigms imposed on us by the 'indigenous actors'.[7] There is no sound scientific reason to legitimize such subfields just because they need specific cultural and linguistic prerequisite (international politics being the only possible exception).

Finally, a more specific consequence will be underlined. A small and frail discipline has a natural tendency to close ranks: to avoid a process of segmentation it will pretend to ignore the divisions that separate the different possible subfields. So we do not recognize that political philosophy is not the history of ideas, that the history of a specific sequence of events is not the same thing as a production of a comparative analytical framework of explanation (a 'Skocpol-like' endeavour),[8] that the comparison of political regimes does not belong exactly to the same parish as the study of Indonesian politics (for a reason beyond my understanding the study of foreign regimes is considered as a part of comparative politics, even if the scholars dealing with them do not do any comparative analysis, whereas 'French politics' stands alone, whether it is comparative or not; most of the time, it is not). The result is that any possibly interesting and attractive subfield is liable to be 'swallowed' up by another professional (or more broadly 'cultural') field which can impose its own rules of the game. In itself, this is neither good nor bad: after all it is quite possible that professional political science is a hindrance to the noble science of politics (it sometimes occurs to me when attending the American Political Science Association that Leo Strauss was not completely wrong in his attack against the 'new science of politics'). Specifically, I intend to show how the situation I have outlined induces (or may induce) specific biases in the study of politics, making political science less accessible than it should be to the intellectual debates of our time.

ORGANIZATION OF POLITICAL SCIENCE IN FRANCE: HISTORICAL OVERVIEW

Although political science appeared historically as a concept before sociology, it hasn't given birth to a strong scientific community and has little (or poorly) imposed its object in the intellectual field. This general vision, however, obscures the essential fact that the material organization of the discipline has not evolved in the same way as the representations that constitute it in the intellectual field. To a large extent, two evolutions cut across one another: materially, the community has evolved a growing self identity; symbolically, its object has evolved towards ubiquity and dilution. The turning point was at the end of the 1960s, which allows us to divide our story roughly into two periods.

1870-1960

The academic community had little professional identity of its own due to the conjunction of the four following features:

1 Political science was a science practised by 'crossroad men' who instead of using this manifold position to make a new paradigm emerge upon which to found a school,[9] used it to maintain a pluralist debate between people from diverse horizons in the intellectual and political field of liberalism. The originality of the founder of the Ecole libre des sciences politiques, Emile Boutmy, with respect to Durkheim for example was not the concern to maintain an 'empire of the mind' and 'government by the best', nor to base the hold of a 'political hegemony' of the 'upper classes' on the 'rule of the fittest' (Boutmy 1871), but rather the means of pursuing this enterprise: not by taking the high ground of

'constituted science', but by offering a 'liberal higher education . . . varied and almost encyclopedic . . . (that stays) just within the limits of constituted science and (that) moves within these limits'. Ample evidence of this is provided in the list of courses projected by Boutmy for what the Ecole libre des sciences politiques should become.

2 Within the constellation of disciplines, two modes of analysis dominated: history, and a 'formal-legal' analysis of the state that insisted strongly on organizations studied from a public law point of view.[10]

3 The goal of political science was to contribute to the education of the citizen through the coexistence of history, law, economics, philosophy, and normative theory: the 'middle class of intelligence that is the strength and bond of a society' didn't exist in France. It was thus necessary to create 'the enlightened citizen, a competent judge of political questions, capable of discussing them soundly and directing opinion' (Boutmy 1871:7).[11]

4 This 'science' admitted the voice of politicians and civil servants as legitimate members of the scientific community, provided that when they spoke they analysed their actions instead of indicating what in practice was to be done. Let Boutmy speak:

My first concern was to reduce the immense gap that separates the society man from the well-read, the citizen from the politician. The scholar and the well-read man form a group at the summit of a hill from which they survey the ever-widening plains of science. The society man struggles up a single incline, the classical one, and he stops at the first slopes. The politician worthy of his name has a vast experimental knowledge that serves as a check for his abstract principles; the citizen lives on a few commonplaces and the relatively poor empiricism that he gleans from the daily chronicle of facts, such as the newspaper provides. (Boutmy 1871:8-9)

Boutmy thus distinguishes two classes of individual: the society man and the citizen; and the scholar and the politician. Within each class, each subgroup is the homologue of the other without confusion, since each covers a different domain: that of speculative knowledge, and that of experimental knowledge.

		Class	
		Non-specialist	Specialist
Domain	Speculative knkowledge	Society man	Scholar
	Experimental knowledge	Citizen	Politician

It follows that the politician, the possessor of political knowledge, participates to all intents and purposes in political science, which in turn further extends the frontiers of the scientific community.

On the other hand, the boundaries of the object studied were relatively precise and were hardly the object of discussion: the state, government and public institutions were clearly the object of political science. Each one would have readily adopted Sheldon Wolin's classic formulation:

> Although one could multiply the ways in which human activities become 'political', the main point lies in the 'relating' function performed by political institutions. Through the decisions taken and enforced by public officials, scattered activities are brought together, endowed with a new coherence and their future course shaped according to 'public' considerations. (Wolin 1960:7)

Let us make it clear that this object was seen particularly from 'above', from the decision-maker's point of view: it comes under *Staatswissenschaft* more than political science. Moreover, the study was directed in a practical perspective. As Pierre Favre notes:

> The political sciences of the 1880s had three characteristics:
> 1 They were divided, split between irreconcilable currents which hadn't conserved, even in their designation, the formal unity of their beginnings and whose incumbents were from the most diverse origins.
> 2 They were more sciences of the state than a political science. Aimed essentially at the training of senior civil servants, they united the 'political, administrative, diplomatic, economic, and financial knowledge' necessary to these practitioners and demanded teachers 'of an overly practical and professional nature' (Boutmy 1876, 1881).
> 3 They were to be embodied in the 'debate of ideas', talks, topical conferences, the joining of discussion. (Favre 1981a:461-2)

The general deficiency of the social sciences *vis-à-vis* politics has been denounced by Pierre Bourdieu as one of the traps that reality lays for knowledge. In his analysis of 'modes of domination', Bourdieu characterizes the modern mode of domination as an objectified domination, that is to say, produced by self-regulated mechanisms that dress the arbitrary in social necessity. Extending Karl Polanyi's notion of a self-regulated economic market, he conceptualizes modern politics thus:

> It is the existence of relatively autonomous fields, functioning according to strict mechanisms capable of imposing their necessity on agents. That means that those who possess the means of mastering these mechanisms and of appropriating the material

and/or symbolic profits produced by their functioning can do without strategies that are oriented expressly (which doesn't mean, to the contrary, manifestly) and directly (that is to say, without passing by the mediation of mechanisms) towards the domination of people. (Bourdieu 1976b:122)

The existence of these objective mechanisms has allowed the belief in determinism to be mentally imposed on people. Bourdieu continues:

But social reality had a last trap in store for science. The existence (of these mechanisms) allows for the recognition as political only those practices which tacitly exclude, from the legitimate competition for power, the mastery of the mechanisms of reproduction. Thus in giving itself as a principal object (what is today called political science), the sphere of legitimate politics, science has long made use of the preconstructed object imposed by reality. (Bourdieu 1976b:126)

It is necessary, without discussing its interpretation, to clarify Bourdieu's terminology: the 'social science' targeted is not sociology but political and moral sciences. Indeed, post-Durkheimian French Sociology is a long way from reducing politics to the sphere of legitimate politics. Marcel Mauss in his important article in the *Année sociologique* of 1927, wrote: 'The political art and the science of this art have therefore, like sociology itself, to take account of all the social facts. In particular, in our modern societies, economic and morphologic (demographic) phenomena come under its jurisdiction. Especially, since important things that don't fit under our rubrics — tradition, education, upbringing — are essential parts of it' (Mauss 1927, 1971:73). Mauss didn't as such neglect legitimate politics. If he explicitly excluded 'politics' from the *Année sociologique*, it was because he didn't want to confuse the science with the art: 'Looking for applications has neither to be the object nor the goal of a science; this would be to distort it. And the art can't wait for the science: the latter has no priority' (Ibid:68). He didn't exclude politics from sociology as such; he excluded it only because it hadn't (yet) been the object of scientific research, whence his lofty condemnation of 'what is called in certain parts political and moral sciences, financial science, diplomatic science, etc. . . . so-called sciences . . . crude mnemonics, collections of circulars and laws, less well-digested than the old codes . . . catalogues of precepts and actions, manuals of formulae . . . teachings of pure apprenticeship' (Ibid: 71). But 'positive politics' (at this time people were not yet ashamed to refer to Comte) 'had the same origins as sociology, both being born from the 'great movement that had rationalized social action at the start of the nineteenth century'. Mauss therefore developed an elaborate programme of the sociology of politics using the resources of legal theory, systematically classified case law, and social research. This science wouldn't be for the use of decision-makers; on the contrary, it would avoid leaving politics to 'politician-theorists and bureaucrat-theorists', widen the knowledge of decision-makers, make them more modest about their failings, and might just reach 'this assurance in diagnostic and prudence in therapy, in the *propédeutique*, in teaching above all'. Mauss concludes: 'The principal goal will be to see the day when, separate from it but inspired by it, it will be possible to put into practice a positive politics on the basis of a complete and concrete sociology' (Ibid:78-9).

One sees in these quotations the distance that separates Mauss from Boutmy, though both have the highest concern for an improvement in the government of societies through the seeding of knowledge. For Mauss, practical preoccupations can't be transcribed directly in a scientific process, even if they are to be found at its beginning, and are eventually to benefit from its development. In this sense, he is closer to present conceptions of political science, whatever our scepticism about the dream of a 'positive politics'.

We should not, however, lose sight of the wood for the trees: Mauss's project never turned into fact. Globally, French sociology has kept, before and after him, politics (legitimate or not) outside its field of study (Favre 1982).[12] The work of Bouglé and Davy[13] should not be considered as such. Mauss doesn't even mention authors that he is nevertheless well placed to know. He fails to quote Siegfried, probably because he didn't like the study of parties and elections to the detriment of 'morals, especially those of sub-groups' (Mauss 1927, 1971:77). On the other hand, he quotes with praise, next to Merriam and Park, jurists such as Pound and the efforts of Hauriou and Duguit 'to derive the principles of public law' (Ibid:71). He criticizes them only for having considered no more than 'forms and constitutions' and he expected sociology to 'give them an important impetus'. This did not come[14] and it was the Faculties of Law that took over much of political study.

The eminent French jurists of public law,[15] in developing the autonomy of law with respect to sociology,[15] but refusing to base it on specific features of a science of law exclusive of all sociology, prepared the ground for occupation by the professors of constitutional law.[16] It was in this way that the 'political sciences' of the 1880s — those of the Ecole libre des sciences politiques — were juxtaposed against the 'Political Science' of the 1930s, expressed for example, in the lectures of professor Rolland, and, above all, admirably systematized by the first edition in 1949 of George Burdeau's *Traité de science politique*, where we read 'Political science is only a method for one of the most fruitful studies of constitutional law, a widened angle of vision that frames the traditional problems of public law' (Burdeau 1949). The only way that political science, once abandoned by the sociologists, could escape the superficiality of the 'debate of ideas', consisted, for the jurists, in linking it solidly to the 'traditional discipline of constitutional law'.[17]

The unexpected result was that political sociology, even though separated from the principles of legal theory, was also developed by professors of law (see the two chapters on the 'sociology of political regimes' by Maurice Duverger,[18] in George Gurvitch's *Traité de sociologie*). At the same time, more or less on his own, Raymond Aron represented the political sociology of the Faculté des lettres. In the company of Pierre Renouvin (writing on international relations), he was one of the two sole French contributors to the UNESCO volume on *La science politique contemporaine* to come from the humanities. The others came from the law faculties (M. Duverger, C. Eisenmann, A. Mathiot, J. Rivero) and from the Institute of Political Sciences (F. Goguel) (UNESCO 1950).

The two currents, the 'political sciences' of the Ecole libre and the 'constitutional law and political science' of the law faculties, each contributed in their own way, and to a certain extent, against their original project, to encouraging the birth at the end of the 1950s of a new community which was more autonomous if less heterogeneous. This was foreshadowed from 1949 onwards by the creation of the French Association of Political Science, and the creation of courses in political science in the law faculties in 1955.[19] It is true that these courses were not named as such, except for 'Methods in Political Science'. Political science pursued *vis-à-vis* constitutional law a path homologous to that of sociology *vis-à-vis* morals.

1960-1989

From the 1960s onwards, political science has sought to become a community, aspiring to specialization and an identity. This finds expression among other things in the capture of specialists breaking (peacefully, with their discipline of origin (jurists, to a lesser extent historians, as well as sociologists and economists on occasion), by the appearance of specific training (*maîtrise* and doctorates of political science). This is accompanied by a certain freedom in the way in which rewards are distributed and intellectual status accorded to the producers and their products (we will see later that this system is neither very precise nor particularly legitimate). Finally, groups of specialists previously more or less unknown except as regards electoral studies, have arisen: specialists on behaviour, socialization, discourse, communication, and political culture (Favre 1981a and b). One can even distinguish within French political science different *'problematiques'* (empirical, macro-sociological, institutionalist, Marxist, psychoanalytical) (Favre 1980). The fact that these classifications please noone (above all those concerned) shows perhaps that these taxnomies are premature, if not useless, but it does establish the existence of something to classify.

Nonetheless it would be impossible to say of political science what Charles Lemert says of sociology:

Having avoided the Scylla of mimicking American empiricism and the Charybdis of philosophical devolution, French sociology stands as a small but coherent body of research, the quality of which is frequently very high. Stylistically, its example of theoretical inventiveness and scope is well worth our while. Substantively, its consideration of such topics as inequality, critique, practice, structural analysis, social change, control and the state, among others, deserves international attention. (Lemert 1981:666).

There is good reason to take advantage of the advances that French sociology has made, notably in the study of the state, provided that two cumulative phenomena are not forgotten: the non-political tradition of French sociology on the one hand, the growing vagueness of the object of political analysis on the other. This second point merits attention.

A small mystery must be pointed out: political science's most classic problems occupy in France, as elsewhere, a part of the intellectual field — democracy, totalitarianism, freedom, authoritarianism, the paradoxes of collective action, the crisis of the welfare state, etc. — but these problems are rarely dealt with in the scientific field of political science, due to the fact that the political scene, constructed as an object of study, has vastly expanded . There is now a politics without limits in which not only all determinants of relationships, behaviour and political structures, are scrutinized but above all in which these relationships, are considerably extended. Every form of social domination would come under the socio-political system of which official politics would only form a small part, studied too often to mask 'the real mechanisms of domination'. At the very moment when, on the one hand, it appears less and less possible to exclude from the political field the mastery of the social reproduction which contributes to the inclusion of culture, the family (baptised 'ideological apparatus of the State'), work relations, daily life, cultural action (baptised 'the equipment of power'), etc., it appears, on the other, that these mechanisms are becoming more and more objectified, that is to say, out of reach of political actors' choice: the further the political field extends, the more it seems to lose its autonomy in favour of the macro-structures of domination.[20]

It would be tempting to explain the crisis of identity of political science by the 'identity crisis of politics' (to use G. Sartori's expression) (Sartori 1973, 1974), and this by the crisis of regulation of post-industrial societies, however one explains it (the explosion of needs; demand-push, supply-pull; the final avatar of mass society; the internationalization of economic and cultural domination; the weakening of the community and the development of specialized organizations that straddle public and private sectors, etc.). This line of reasoning, satisfying because it is global, is probably not entirely wrong. However, a problem remains: why, in France, doesn't the crisis excite the scientific field's productivity and stir up the intellectual field?[21] The crisis of politics will not explain the fact that French political science has no monopoly and that even cultivated opinion doesn't detect the difference between an editorial in *Le Monde* and a piece of political science research,[22] nor that many elements of the intellectual field invest themselves with competence in political analysis, while others, equally numerous in scientific fields, ask, with some semblance of reason, what political science consists of. It is thus necessary to make a detour into the economy of each field.

ORGANIZATION OF AREAS OF RESEARCH: MARKETS OF THE DISCIPLINE

The economy of fields can be expressed in the notion of market, a place of exchange and fixing of prices. Nothing prevents us from maintaining, with R. Boudon amongst others, that 'intellectuals (that is to say intellectual producers), following the example of other categories of producers, are more or less well informed about the nature and the structure of the demand coming from this or these market(s)' (Boudon 1981:466). My presentation differs slightly from that of Boudon to the extent that I don't classify the markets in the same way and that I integrate not only the supply of production to a 'public' into the market, but equally a supply addressed to a specialized organ (a committee of academics for example). Five markets can be distinguished.

1 The national market

This is the classic market of the 'judgment by peers', characteristic of positive sciences having attained in Kuhn's terms a high degree of 'normality' — what Clark calls 'institutionalization'. Here, the expectations of the 'public' are in principal strongly structured. Outside periods of crisis, it is a tightly centralized market. In fact, the political science market is for the most part loose and decentralized. This is seen in the extreme variation in the level of work presented in postgraduate diplomas and theses of the *Doctorat d'Etat*. Supervisors and 'patrons' preoccupy themselves little with the integrated production and promotion of a product (for example, in the form of 'clustered' thesis subjects attached to the same research programme). They have several excuses for this: their uncertain legitimacy[23] forbids them from being excessively directive. Above all, the existence of few professional openings, reflecting the small number of social demands addressed to scientists[24] make teachers and pupils sceptical about producing papers that neither interest anyone nor guarantee a job.

The rules of the game of the national market are uncertain to the extent that 'peers' can vary considerably in number, even to the point of being entirely submerged by specialists of other disciplines or by unexpected groups (journalists, civil servants) who take over the market for a particular product. Pluralism in itself is excellent, but it makes the forms of price fixing so badly known to the producers that it appears to be pure chance . . . or the machinations of an evil political genius! This is not always a disadvantage: the multiplicity of criteria of evaluation allows floating resources not previously allocated to be concentrated on such or such product, thus encouraging 'surprises' and the advancement of underdogs. For a change, counterproductive mechanisms are more or less bound to have productive effects.

However, the negative effects are more important: a loose market and insufficient openings are at the same time cause and consequence of an often criticized institutional mechanism. The function of teaching is changed; the political academic, knowing that his students 'won't enter the profession' and will hardly use political science in the careers open to them (openings in secondary education are kept for historians with the participation of economists), has to adapt his teaching, in particular to the exams of *culture générale* of the entrance competitions for administration, while avoiding giving it a character that is too technical or critical. In doing this, 'he further nourishes the all too fixed idea that political science is no different from the informed political ideas that everyone should have' (Favre 1980:20). There follows a disassociation between teaching and research, difficulty in stabilizing the functioning of the market, and loss of confidence.

2 The international market

This market is tighter and more encouraging but its relationship with the French national market causes problems: not that the French as individual producers are absent, but that the communication between markets works in such a way that in many respects the French market gives the impression of being isolated and dominated by the international market, which immediately calls to mind the 'dual society' of colonization. This manifests itself in the fact that entire sectors can function without reference to the international market; that a French political academic participating in the international market as a 'native' crosses into the camp on the colonizing society, with the problems that he encounters on both sides; that the initiative for programmes comes from the international market, and the French are required only to bring information on France as case study material. Furthermore, the reluctance of researchers to work on countries in the 'centre' (the United States, Great Britain, Germany) and their willingness to work on the history of their village or neighbourhood and naturally on the former Empire (above all African) awakes troubling thoughts in the specialist of culturally unequal relationships.

3 The market of the national system of research in social science

This market, active if not always very tight, collects the 'calls for bids' sent out by the *ex-Délégation générale* for scientific and technical research on programme set up by the administration that are often interdisciplinary. These programme touch themes as varied as the consequences of social change, scientific policy, the management of local communities, transport policy, etc. It is a market in which judgement by peers is combined with the judgement of decision-makers. Without its always being very clear who dominates whom, the two classic models of the 'colonized administration' or the 'clientelized researcher' are both possible, without excluding tit for tat bargaining.

Only two comments will be made: in political science, the players in this market are quite frequently in contact with market 2, much more rarely so with market 1, which adds further to the segmentation and isolation of the latter. Moreover, in this market largely dedicated to public policy, the political academics are not as present as in the United States or Germany: there is no equivalent here of a Wildavsky, a Lowi or a Heclo. This can be explained by the early training of French political academics involved in this area. Often influenced by a legal background, they are more comfortable with the description of the formal functioning of institutions that make public policy than by an analysis of the substance of policy. Often excellent commentators on the basis of a *problematique* that they don't construct themselves but which is already furnished in law sources, at times excellent advisers and reformers (even actors when they leave their profession), jurists and political writers who have become political academics, divest themselves with difficulty of practical preoccupations in order to elaborate a 'scientific' *problematique* (even roughly) for the study of public policy. This is why they do not venture onto territory of which they are suspicious.

This hypothesis is insufficient. The French administration which has developed these methods, notably in the area of evaluation, is more sensitive to technical and sociological evaluation, leaving 'political evaluation' to the representatives of the people. (I understand by 'political evaluation' the value judgment itself and the bringing to light of the cognitive and normative mechanisms that precede this judgment). Now, in the French institutional tradition, the representative does not have the means (or perhaps the desire) to control an autonomous system of research. It is possible that political academics suffer on account of this.

4 The market of general cultural goods

This corresponds to Boudon's markets 2 and 3. It is the important market of the intellectual field, all the more for political science, due to the weakness of market 1 and the relative isolation of market 2. In this market, the product is not explicitly submitted to the community of peers, even if, employing the technique of the 'bat'[25] the producer presents himself as a scientific political academic to the gaze of the public, thus making sure of an additional resource, while at the same time whispering to his peers that this work, after all, mustn't be judged by the norms of market 1. A symmetrical technique is that of the short circuit, in which an author gains recognition of the scientific value of his work in market 4 and imposes it on market 1 before the latter can intervene autonomously.

These two techniques, the most sophisticated, don't exhaust the ways in which this market is used: it is equally open to the expert-prince's-adviser, to the value-creator, to the popularizer, to the scholar-who-reflects-on-his-activity (frequent in natural sciences), even to the producer in market 1, dragged to his surprise into market 4. All these cases are a lot healthier, to use prophylactic language, than the first two (the bat and the short circuit). Only these two are directly imputable to the weakness of market 1; it is too unattractive and its system of remuneration leads to 'push-effect' towards market 4; at the same time, it is sufficiently loose for it to be manipulated so that a minimal benefit be drawn.[26]

Other general causes are put forward by Boudon to explain the growth in demand and attraction of market 4 for scientists. The intellectualization of private life provokes the demand for knowledge of the social, biological, and psychological conditions of education, health, family relationships, etc. The intellectualization of political life (Shils 1968) emphasizes the political conditions of social situations considered as 'natural' in former times, at least by those benefiting from them, whence the demand for information, full of good intentions and guilty consciences, on inequality, the situation of immigrants, the implementation of capital punishment. The desire for a clear conscience in a society experiencing an identity crisis (a vague term that refers to a muted and confused uneasiness, above all in the middle classes) favours the success of more conservative attempts that emphasize the positive results of the established order, threatened by the undermining criticism of left-wing intellectuals: the debates about sociology or law and order are a case in point. Finally, the absence of automatic transmission of values and roles from generation to generation, that means that society has something to reinvent each decade, poses in a crucial way the problems of individual and collective identity: if 'everything' is in everything and if 'everything is to be done', the attraction of big questions becomes very strong in market 4, and except in the case of extremely strict asceticism it is almost impossible for a French intellectual to resist the pull-effect of market 4 in combination with the push-effect of market 1.

5 The political market

Market 5 remains, the specifically political market upon which we touch only lightly. This ticklish subject lends itself less to rigorous analysis than to the note of humour that produces a memorable image (thus the famous 'cultural Yalta' that, from 1958 to 1981, would have handed over the domination of market 4 to the left and the domination of market 5 to the right). It shows neither other worldliness nor a blind faith in the autonomy of scientific research to make the hypothesis of a relative airtightness between markets 1 and 5.

The physical interpenetration of the two markets turns out to be limited. As Daniel Gaxie has noted, 'the frictions most associated with the intellectual field (artists, researchers) are practically absent from political competition (Gaxie 1980:30), that is to say from the competition for professional positions in politics. It is different for teachers, not only in secondary teaching (lycées and colleges), whose position in the Communist and socialist parties has often been underlined, but equally in the university (Gaxie 1980, Guédé and Rosenblum 1981). The interpenetration grows further as one passes from the category of professional politician (representative, party leader) to that of the prince's adviser (official or unofficial ministerial cabinet members, members of the innumerable working groups put together to aid decision-making, etc.). Let me emphasize, however, that political science's position in this respect is not exceptional. The exiguity of its own market invites all the errors of erroneous quantitative estimation: one could insist on the large number of political academics involved in the political field (an illusion facilitated by the small size of the market for political academics) as well as underline the small number of protagonists from market 1 engaged in market 5. Does this prove a great deal?

More interesting is the question of the reciprocal evaluation of the products of each market. Does a good rating in the discipline's market favour the valorization of the product in the political market? Commonsense suggests answers both positive (the attraction competence exerts on the professionals of politics) and negative (the position of the politician is not that of the scholar; successful political careers are failed university careers, etc.) — that is to say, no response at all. Anyway, the number of concrete examples is possibly too small to allow evaluation. It is difficult to see how, with perhaps a dozen cases, one can deal with technically stated questions of the sort: Would political academics who succeed in the discipline's market succeed better in the political market than the political academics who don't succeed in their discipline's market?

One can answer the opposite question better: does a good rating in the political market favour the valorization of the product in the discipline's market? Evidence is obtained only from commonsense, and is not specific to France: for example, the professional highly rated by the political market has, by definition, abandoned a good part of his scientific activity; he can only have, at best, the status of a fallen star; but, the eminent trade unionist, a former minister, even the representative beaten in elections are frequently warmly welcomed as associate professors in universities (but have difficulty in building a career as an ordinary academic). One should, however, mention several institutional particularities of the French system of managing university staff in teaching and research. Part of the national committees that judge the quality of work done (the Conseil supérieur des Corps universitaires and the Comité du Centre national de la recherche scientifique) are named by the responsible minister, which enhances the suspicion that the political market has a hold on the discipline. The management of market 3 (the market of the national system of research) can often go the same way. It is often the political authorities, through the mediation of senior administrative staff and of some 'eminent academics', that evaluate the usefulness of results produced, if not their validity, which leads to the tendency of excluding certain types of research (and certain researchers) that can return in force when political change takes place. But these movements are always cushioned by the particular inertia of markets 1 and 3 in which constituted networks of contacts work together to uphold an autonomous valuation, eventually strengthened by the ideology of necessary pluralism and by the effect of the example of market 2 (the international market).

Can the combination of these five markets contribute to valorizing a group of products that, although not belonging to the same class (scientific, cultural, political), are combined in an ideological whole that determines the classification of these products as well as their value? Does there exist between members of different groups (eminent academics, senior administrators, national political figures, enlightened employers, etc.) this sense of affinity comprising a sizable dose of mutual consideration due to a common relation to the central value system? (Shils 1975:12).[27] Is political science present in those neutral areas, one of whose functions is to favour what one commonly calls the exchange of views, that is to say reciprocal information on the vision created of the future by agents who have, at the same time, more information on the future and more power over the future, (Bourdieu and Boltanski 1976:54). One cannot answer, without being exposed to the suspicion of ideological bias and self-justifying discourse. Let us hazard, however, that the Boutmy model outlined earlier responds to these questions in a marvellously positive way and for good reason: it was exactly what Boutmy wanted. This is why kindly spirits see in the functioning of the Institute of Political Sciences in Paris the paradigm example of the 'production of a dominant ideology'.[28] In a vigorous text Pierre Bourdieu theorizes what had been the practical effort of the founder of the école libre (without referring to it explicitly):

The correlative dispossession of the concentration of the means of production of the instruments of the production of discourse or acts socially recognized as political has not ceased to grow in proportion to the gains in autonomy of the field of ideological production with the appearance of political bureaucracies of full time professionals and appearance of institutions (as, in France, the Institute of Political Sciences and the National School of Administration) charged with selecting and training professional producers of schemes of thought and expression of the social world, politicians, political journalists, senior administrators etc., at the same time as codifying the rules of the functioning of the field of ideological production and the corpus of knowledge and savoir-faire essential to conforming there. The political science that is taught in these institutions, in its inception directed to this end, is the rationalization of the competence demanded by the political universe and that is possessed by professionals in practice: it aims at raising the efficiency of this practical mastery by putting in its service rational techniques such as the opinion poll, public relations or political marketing, while at the same time aiming to legitimate it by giving it a scientific appearance and by instituting, as the business of specialists, political questions that it is the concern of specialists to decide in the name of knowledge and not in the interests of class'. (Bourdieu 1981:6)

This text merits in depth discussion.[29] For our purposes, it is enough to indicate that the empirical examples furnished refer little to the academic specialists and a great deal to administrators and journalists. They are therefore more relevant to the situation before 1960 than to market 1 outlined earlier. The fact that political science is still considered as the 'political sciences' associated with the Ecole nationale d'administration and television programmes is 'proof more of the weakness of market 1 than of its connection with market 5. A different interpretation is that, because current political science is doubly dominated, in the academic field and in the intellectual field, its producers, disenchanted, withdraw into the scientific market and are little present in the political market, or at least, being dominated themselves in their field, are sensitive to those who are dominated in the political field.

The clearest conclusion to be drawn from this brief examination of our five markets concerns therefore the effect of attraction exercised by market 4: that it keeps Tocqueville's famous thesis up to date; that French intellectuals have a taste for abstract generalities, the grandiose hypotheses that fashion our vision of the world, and the 'literary spirit'; and that it puts ideological production a step ahead of cognitive production. This is not entirely bad: we do not share, in this respect, the puritan discourse on the corruption (in Aristotle's sense) of the French intellectual field (we would be sensitive rather to its incorrigible parochialism and ethnocentricity); but to the extent to which this further weakens market 1 and gives fresh life to the Boutmy model of a crossroads of ideas extended from the well-to-do classes to the whole state, and from whole state to intellectual or politically aware society,[30] we feel worried for both political science as a modest but autonomous discipline, and for the government of our societies, because we cannot manage to believe in social regulation by science, even experimental, even when it is nourished by the best of intentions.

INDUCED BIAS IN FRENCH POLITICAL SCIENCE

French political science appears to have trouble in asserting its identify (as a part of the intellectual world) and being recognized by others. As usual, when a group is not strong enough to maintain a coherent image, it is subjected to certain biases (I would not go as far as to say debasements) caused by the social pressures put on it both from inside and outside.

I am not saying that the biases I am going to present are entirely despicable. Far from it. Properly mastered, they might serve to rejuvenate our discipline. I am not going to discuss the most usual biases, either; everybody knows that French political science is subject to two oft commented upon biases, the 'institutional' and the 'journalistic'. I do not think it is true any longer. On the contrary most of the professional political scientists (with important exceptions such as Jean-Louis Quermonne, François d'Arcy, Pierre Avril, Evelyne Pisier, Alfred Grosser) do not take public law seriously enough, and it is high time to take a fresh look at legal processes and outcomes as an autonomous topic of research.[31] As for the journalistic bias, it has been fought off so adamantly that it is hardly possible to find a book written by a French political scientist which displays the usual characteristics of the category: elegant style, flippant opinions, interesting little anecdotes, collected from the horse's mouth, etc. In a way, it is a pity since we are accused of yielding up ponderous books, full of jargon and useless empirical documentation, addressing irrelevant issues and so on. Fair enough; we cannot have it both ways, to be both scientific and attractive. The real issue is that political scientists cannot master the channels through which their concerns (and possibly their findings) are popularized (the only significant exceptions being the studies of voting behaviour and the endless debates about the 'correct' interpretation of a few articles of the constitution of 1958). The consequence is that very few political scientists can be considered influential members of the intelligentsia at large (Maurice Duverger and to a lesser extent Alfred Grosser are towering exceptions). Hence the temptation to borrow from the disciplines which seem to have succeeded in addressing larger audiences: history, philosophy, economics.

Historical bias

It has repeatedly become fashionable to insist on the necessity of 'returning to history'. In the late 1960s the point was made by Marxist scholars eager to take issue with the structural-functional (or developmentalist) perspective, to emphasize that all the concepts were historical concepts, and to dissociate themselves from a specific breed of structuralist Marxism exemplified by the works of Louis Althusser, Etienne Balibar, and Nikos Poulantzas. Some Marxists, whether or not espousing historicist views, have turned to detailed studies of forgotten historical processes: for example what did nineteenth century French manual workers or small entrepreneurs actually think (Cottereau 1980, Rancière 1981)? What did the planners have in mind from 1945 to 1970 (Fourquet 1980)? This movement did not give rise to any specific French school of historical sociology. The most interesting works came from non-Marxists such as Pierre Birnbaum, Bertrand Badie, and Guy Hermet (Badie and Birnbaum 1979, Hermet 1982 and 1986, Badie 1987).[32] But in spite of their efforts (and mine), the influence of Theda Skocpol, Perry Anderson, Charles Tilly, Eric Hobsbawm, not to mention Stein Rokkan, Reinhard Bendix, or Barrington Moore Jr does not go very far, even though several of their books have been translated into French.[33]

The movement toward history came from elsewhere, namely from the stronghold of French economic history, the *Annales* school. At first glance, that seems logical, but let's be careful to note that this movement coincided with deep transformations in the orientation and outlook of this school. The original impulse given by Lucien Fèbvre, Fernand Braudel, then Ernest Labrousse, was oriented towards a kind of motionless history (*l'histoire immobile* to quote Braudel): this should be a history of basic economic structures the rhythm of which was supposed to be slower (and in any case basically different) than the rhythm of political history. So the *Annales* courteously ignored (and secretly despised) the history taught at the *Ecole des sciences politiques* and in particular political and diplomatic history. Even Alexis de Tocqueville was not held in high regard given his interests in cultural and political factors. Ironically, Braudel's legacy has been enhanced in political sociology by Immanuel Wallerstein, while most of the members of the former *Annales* (Georges Duby, J. le Goff, E. Leroy Ladurie) have been moving toward cultural and political history. A case in point is François Furet whose book *Penser la revolution française* (Furet 1978) played a decisive role not only in renewing the endless arguments about the historical meaning of the Great Revolution, but in giving new lustre to the study of political interactions seen as part of a new casual network and not as the mere reflection of underlying socio-economic processes. F. Goguel, R. Remond, J. Touchard, R. Girardet were in some sense retrospectively praised (they did not need it, having their own audience and scholarly network: cf. Remond 1988). Even diplomatic history (rechristened history of international relations) was granted full citizenship, and biography (long time the subject of contempt)[34] began to be recognized as true scholarly endeavour and not just entertainment for the public.

Such a greening of cultural and political history, as testified by the success of Claude Nicolet's *L'idée républicaine en France* (Nicolet 1982) and of the volumes edited by Pierre Nora *Les lieux de mémoire* (Nora 1984 and 1986), had various consequences: a few political scientists have been strengthened in their belief that the only political science is political history; historians have begun to deal with political science issues (for example how did political representation evolve? What changes have taken place in the processes of political recruitment?), while retaining their basic interests and methods as historians, and in particular maintaining that any sequence of events (the plot, to quote Paul Veyne) is unique and must be studied in itself without any reference to an overall framework of explanation drawn from sociological generalizations. To be more specific, historical generalizations are accepted as necessary hypotheses (for example Tocqueville's providential trend towards democracy and individualism) but not the sociological ones (for example Durkheim's or Parson's hypotheses on division of labour, social differentiation, or individualization).[35]

The problem is that history has to tell stories about something unique which cannot be replicated or used as a crucial experiment carried on to test a tentative generalization (I wish to avoid the terribly loaded term 'law'). Almost everybody agrees on the logical impossibility of 'laws of history', while holding that 'history is the great teacher', but the lessons of history are construed as lessons of wisdom, reliable as far as prudence and art are concerned, but not to be used for the sake of science. So far so good, but why should such a view (sensible enough in my opinion) keep us from using comparative history, first, to elicit and elucidate tricky and vague concepts such as elite, ideology, dictatorship, empire, nationalism, civil society, intellectuals, civil religion etc. . . (I am mixing up on purpose historical and ahistorical concepts)[36] and second, to test particular and partial 'laws' bearing on micro-behaviour or macro-structures?[37] Admittedly, concrete societies are not systems but combinations of various processes the overall outcome of which cannot be forecast (even though probabilistic predictions should not be forbidden), but this is not sufficient reason to renounce any attempt to build up a science of comparative politics.

Two footnotes will conclude my remarks on this topic:

1 Some younger scholars or advanced students are tempted to turn towards the social history of tiny areas (for example a village, usually 'their' village in the 1860s, or voting behaviour in small neighbourhoods in the early twentieth century). This is not entirely new, of course (nor fruitless: after all the anthropologists learn a

great deal from a Balinese cockfight, or from patron–client relations in small villages in Jordan or Malta) but I suspect the infatuation may be caused by the success of Leroy-Ladurie's *Montaillou* (Leroy-Ladurie 1976) (not to mention a discreet nostalgia for the long-lost *Gemeinschaft*). Once again, nothing wrong with that, at first sight. But, as the German social historian Jürgen Kocka has put it:

A price . . . has generally to be paid for this kind of micro history: the renunciation of a recognition of connections, the ignoring of the 'big questions' of state and class formation, of religion and churches, of industrialization and capitalism. . . . Most of our politics, and with it the setting of the trends that affect individual persons and the smallest groups, necessarily take place above the local and regional level. . . . Partiality in historical understanding . . . an identification with the little space by means of blacking out the connections, is not intellectually satisfying and in the long run is politically problematical.[38]

Such a trend should not be encouraged since it is conducive to a subtle kind of parochialism if the scholars are not very well trained, in particular in anthropology. Using as a framework the native cultural framework of the period and the area they are studying, they lose sight not only of the big issues but also of the general questions raised in the scientific international community; henceforth either they'll go on doing research nobody cares about or they'll be utilized by a clever international entrepreneur who will provide the theoretical and methodological hypotheses and will ask the local scholar to fill in the blanks by supplying a bit of fresh information. This may not be so bad if the young scholar is able to learn something from this unequal exchange — which I am inclined to doubt.

2 The history of ideas (as distinguished from political theory and political philosophy) has not benefited to the same extent from the new trend of history. Most of the political scientists are more interested in commenting upon great thinkers than in reconstituting the intricate social network that makes up the context of a 'political thought'. The methodological issues raised by Weber, Lovejoy, Elias, and Oakeshott, among others, are not taken really seriously, though most are known. Only Pocock seems to exert some influence though the scattered articles of Miguel Abensour and Skinner begin to be recognized. Most surprisingly, the Marxist persuasion (Gramsci, Lukacs, Goldman, Althusser) seems provisionally in decline.[39] When it survives, it is through the works of Jürgen Habermas (a kind of star for part of the intelligentsia, which comes as a mystery since I guess that less than fifty persons have ever been able to go over everything this outstanding scholar has written so far), but Habermas is more appreciated as a social philosopher

than as a scholar who has shed some light on the history of ideas (*L'espace public* is less often used than *Connaissance et intérêt* or *Théorie et pratique*).[40]

The same could be said regarding Hannah Arendt's legacy. When her works are discussed, it is almost invariably for their contribution to political philosophy and seldom as an example of historical interpretation (about the comparison of French and American revolutions, or the evolution of imperialist and nationalist ideas). Likewise Leo Strauss is seldom commented upon for the questionable history of ideas he had put forth in his criticism of 'the new science of politics', or for his interesting comparison between ancient and modern liberalism, but he is praised (or criticized) as the representative of classical political philosophy. Even though the problem of interpretation is far from being ignored (Gadamer is frequently cited), it is not part of a coherent programme of research in the history of ideas. Likewise the social explanation of the emergence of a given constellation of ideas is not dealt with adequately. The situation may not be better elsewhere (Manuel 1987); besides, there are significant exceptions with good (albeit hardly comparable) works on a specific thinker (Lacroix 1981), a discourse (Jaume 1989), or more ambitiously an ideological schema (Taguieff 1988).[41] But one cannot say yet that the history of ideas has found its contemporary Siegfried or even its Elie Halévy. I suggest that the situation has something to do with a second, induced bias, the philosophical one.

Philosophical bias

Social interests and specific strategies do not explain everything. However, it is useful not to ignore them. A specific state of affairs makes the treatment of the philosophical bias difficult and almost impossible; the swords and guns are always at hand and as during the Dreyfus affair, when the best friends have 'talked about it' (*ils en ont parlé*) they are likely to be angry at each other for a long time. A number of young philosophers, disappointed by the limited job opportunities offered by the Aggrégation de philosophie (usually teaching philosophy twenty-four hours a week, in an obscure provincial lycée to teenagers who do not give a damn about Plato, Hegel, Heidegger), and conscious that the university departments of philosophy are overcrowded with people working twenty years on a thesis on a tiny point of interpretation of Kant or Descartes, have made a move towards political science, considered as more open to new talents. Ironically, political philosophy has never been an important subfield of French philosophy (Montefiore 1983) nor was political sociology within the school of sociology: there are good books written by scrupulous philosophers, about, say, *Descartes et l'ordre politique* (Guenancia 1983), but they do not address specific issues of political philosophy (Guenancia considers that Descartes negates any kind of political philosophy); there are also philosophers either involved in politics or thinking that their work carries out important political consequences (Sartre's legacy); and finally there are philosophers who fancy that, as 'everything is political', it is enough to talk about a hospital, a spanking, or the way people take care of their body, to make a significant breakthrough in the understanding of politics (Foucault's legacy).

For all that there are few political philosophers in the French tradition (the late Eric Weil was almost the only outstanding exception).[32] Hence the intellectual importance of this new mood. But it makes it more difficult for things to evolve in a sensible way: as there is no specific tradition of political philosophy or political theory, a majority of political scientists feels threatened by new and more attractive competitors; by the same token it is also very difficult to voice criticism against a philosophical bias without appearing to some as simply jealous and mean. Several real intellectual debates are smeared by this underlying resentment.

There are many philosophical biases. To be quite clear I would like to discard at least one (unfortunately it is precisely the one which is most commonly mentioned): I do not think that political philosophy has nothing to do with political knowledge and should be considered as a fancy, the topics of which should be studied as ideologies, so becoming a part of the social history of ideas.[43] Philosophical works should of course be scrutinized as ideological rationalizations, but so should 'scientific' works and empirical findings, and in both cases there is more than that in their respective endeavours. Admittedly, some philosophers come very close to deserving this kind of sweeping rebuke. Nobody has made the point more clearly than Hegel himself: stating at the outset that, 'The task of a writer, especially a writer in philosophy may be said to lie in the discovery of truth . . . the dissemination of truth and sound concepts'.[44] He goes on to mock many philosophers of his time, 'Busybodies (who) talk as if the world had wanted for nothing except their energetic dissemination of truths, or as if their *rechauffe* were productive of new and unheard of truths and was to be specially taken to heart before everything else today and every day'. Hence in Hegel's opinion, the widespread contempt for philosophy: 'Everyone is convinced that his mere birthright puts him in a position to pass judgment on philosophy in general and to condemn it. No other art or science is subjected to this degree of scorn, to the assumption that we are masters of it without ado'. Without going into any detailed argument about the Hegelian theory of knowledge (I myself happen to feel much more Kantian than Hegelian and I do not go for the scattered critiques levelled by Hegel against Kant in the preface), it should be recognized that Hegel's quotations vividly remind us of the endless quarrels opposing a few current philosophers to their scientist critics. Besides these on going (and not really serious although sometimes bitter) quarrels, there are more serious issues at stake. From the more pedestrian to the more sophisticated ones, let's sort out three.

1 Philosophy as a commentary on previous philosophers: I do not know whether or not this is a French national sporting game (I guess not) but it may be worrying to see so many books commenting upon say, Hegel, Arendt, Weber, Fichte, etc. I am not in the least claiming that such works are useless; it is always fruitful to have fresh accounts and interpretations of great or even minor thinkers, either put within their contextual historical framework or studied in and for themselves. But it is only a small part of political science and even of political theory. It is time to recall Hobbes's admonitions: 'For words are wise mens counters, they do but reckon by them; but they are the money of fooles, that value them by the authority of an Aristotle, a Cicero or a Thomas, or any Doctor whatsoever, if but a man.'[45] Political science (and political theory as well) is about first hand issues imposed by real historical life and constructed by the scientist and the theorist, and not primarily about second hand issues already mediated by a covering work. I am quite aware of all the relevant debates about 'normal science' and I fully acknowledge that any intellectual activity must start somewhere and build upon a foundation paradigm. I would even go so far as to admit Kuhn's observation (in *The Copernican Revolution*) that seemingly endless, scholastic and sterile commentaries may help to bring a given paradigm to exhaustion (but I strongly doubt it can be so with great philosophical works). In any case, commentaries though useful in themselves, cannot substitute for hard thinking about what is (or has been) going on. I would like more people to work like Michael Walzer (for example), to think seriously (with the help of relevant empirical findings, and keeping in mind the relevance of politics and the shortcomings of philosophical conversation) about such issues as racial justice, ethnic conflicts, corporations or whatever. To be sure, there is the risk of being accused of preaching (paradoxically a deadly sin in the country of Boussuet, Rousseau, Saint-Just, Comte, Michelet and Sartre, all prominent preachers). But as Albert Hirschman has put it, it may be permitted to dream of a social science in which we could alternatively shift from preaching to proving, and vice versa, provided we do it consciously and in the open (Hirschman 1983).

2 But is it not precisely the case? Are not French philosophers politically committed (*engagés*)? After all, the two old buddies, Sartre and Aron are, in this respect, still very much alive. Is not philosophy a commentary on reality? There is certainly nothing wrong with that. Merleau-Ponty and Foucault are cases in point, not to mention the whole Frankfurt School. But we ought to keep in mind that detailed and sophisticated social scientific knowledge, backed when possible by numbers, can deepen the way we address

philosophical questions. If philosophy is divorced from empirical knowledge, unintended consequences ensue: not only, as Robert Dahl pointed out long ago (Dahl 1958), modern political philosophy (or a part of it) is no longer able to entail any empirical knowledge (after all, this is not an unintended consequence since many philosophers ridicule empiricism as an unwarrantable knowledge) but, above all, when talking about something 'going on' (even the most sophisticated abstract philosopher has to address common sense issues) some philosophers take things (an historical event, a social movement, a cultural trend) for granted and start interpreting them without making sure that this reality may be relied upon.[46] There is something of a paradox in that attitude; the data produced by empirical political science are sometimes (not always) neglected or looked down upon (as ideological, irrelevant, etc.); but unchecked data (provided by what the newspapers report, or what the intellectual has experienced at a specific moment) take revenge and impose themselves on the philosopher (and his readers) seemingly unaware of his own previous epistemological caveats.

This statement is by no means a rejoinder to the philosophical criticisms of empirical sciences (whose usefulness is beyond question). Nor do I mean to imply that philosophy should from now on be the servant of the social sciences, waiting humbly for the sunset before spreading diffidently its wings. I am not even sure that 'philosophy is . . . the servant of history' as Marx would have it.[47] Finally as Charles Péguy used to remind us with his usual pungency, (in his polemics against 'scientific' history in the 1900s), the philosopher is quite at liberty to use his memory, regardless of historical records: to keep a vivid account of what occurred to a living person may trigger philosophical reflections, whereas to be surrounded by documents may be just a factor of sterility. For all that, is it unfair to ask the philosophers not to forget or spurn the help that they themselves can get from the existential statements (and hopefully the empirical generalizations and tentative sociological 'laws') issued by social sciences?

3 The last bias worth mentioning consists of using philosophy as a denial of politics. I do not mean the familiar search for a prepolitical stage from which the basic components of a political society should be deduced (e.g. a part of the contractualist tradition) nor the classic Marxist distinction between the state and the political state, (although there may be some remnants of Marxist thinking in this). What I have in mind is the propensity to consider everything as political, whether or not this 'political' should be construed as a gigantic system of domination or just as scattered and uncoordinated power machines. Four distinct intellectual sources may be spotted. First, a Nietzschean influence (coming from *The Genealogy of Morals*) pervades the works of Gilles Deleuze and Félix Guattari, combined with a peculiar interpretation of Freud. Second, Erving Goffman may also be cited; even though

Goffman is by no means a philosopher, his books *Asylums* and *Stigma* have been quoted and interpreted far beyond their original intent and actual contents; third, the later Wittgenstein and his language games are making their way among certain philosophers; and, last but by no means the least, Michel Foucault (and particularly *l'Archéologie du savoir* and *Surveiller et punir*) has fascinated philosophers, historians, and even a significant number of political scientists in such a way that there was a time (the late seventies) in certain university departments when it was as impossible to escape his spell as it was not to revere Althusser in the late 1960s.[48]

The only feature common to all these influences is the tendency to neglect or demean politics proper. By dint of insisting on the social, cultural, or symbolic dimension of political domination, those currents end up emphasizing the political dimension of any kind of social interaction. For example linguistics (or the sheer study of literature) have been used, and rightly so, to stress the manipulation of linguistic codes involved in totalitarianism (e.g. Jean-Pierre Faye's *Languages totalitaires*) (Faye 1972), and then any kind of linguistic code has been labelled totalitarian. The basic problem is not that there is sophistry there (Charles Lindblom played the same kind of trick when he referred to 'the market as a prison'): after all it is just a matter of conventional language games.[49] The main trouble is that the real political issues may be neglected, by dint of calling every issue political. The issues involving the use of coercive power (and physical violence, and the struggles to control it), the authoritative allocation of resources, the institutional constraints imposed on these processes, the ways in which collective actions are managed and collective choices made, are downgraded, and too much emphasis may be put on impersonal or structural processes (or systems) of domination.

I do not pretend to ignore Marx's warning: the principle of politics is will, and the essence of 'political mind' is to be blind to the will's material and moral limits. This is common scholarly knowledge by now. Likewise, I am quite aware of the familiar Weber-Bourdieu thesis on the 'modern mode of domination': impersonal, objective routinized and machine-like; and finally we should not forget that one of the most interesting Tocqueville intuitions was to construe democracy not as a political regime but as a societal process encompassing many different spheres of life. For those reasons, I do not mean to deny the connection between the public world of citizenship and the private sphere present in the very theories which aim at keeping them apart (Pateman 1988a: 237, cf. Pateman 1988b). But all this is not sufficient reason for overlooking the political object by immersing it in the whole societal process. This approach is crippled by two methodological drawbacks.[50] First, a kind of 'sublimation of politics', to quote Sheldon Wolin (out of his context since his critique was levelled at the behaviouralist revolution and organizational theories). Instead of analysing, say, political language as a specific class of language derived from natural language,[51] the philosopher intoxicated by Roland Barthes will decree that any natural language is political, which is quite plausible when Louis Marin studies *La logique de Port Royal* (Marin 1975) but a bit farfetched should the same attempt be made with Mallarmé's poetry or impressionist painters.[52] Citizenship and government no longer have autonomous meaning since they are confused with any kind of membership and directiveness. 'Conformity' and 'power' are everywhere, and so are 'politics' without any useful distinction between various kinds of politics.[53] Second, is the near impossibility of making sense of comparative politics: either, nothing is comparable since each historical society has its own way of articulating knowledge, power, language and behaviour (and at the very end you cannot talk about British social policy if you do not know in great detail how Wimbledon's lawn is mown and kept in its glorious shape); or everything is comparable since everything is the same, from the point of view of the philosophical 'concept'.[54] As, in most of the countries we usually deal with, there are overlapping processes linking family, corporations, bureaucracy, police, welfare, art, science, whatever, making up something in which it is very difficult to tell the public from the private, the economic from the cultural. It may sound attractive to declare that there is no significant difference between such political regimes as pluralist democracies, socialist states, military regimes, nor between more specific political structures and processes (elite recruitment, legislative behaviour, judicial behaviour, etc.).

Economic bias

I will not expand in great detail on the third bias. First, it is most familiar to the political scientists of the Anglo-Saxon persuasion and almost everything has been said about this issue. Furthermore the overwhelming majority of French political scientists, lacking an adequate training in micro-economics and formal theory, do not go for the sophisticated exercises familiar to certain among their European and American colleagues: the 'prisoner's dilemma', the 'tragedy of the commons', the Arrow theorem of impossibility, the cooperation games, and many other jewels are known, taught, sometimes discussed, but I have difficulty in citing any one work as a significant follow up. The same could be said regarding policy or strategic studies. The leading works have been written in various fields, by professional economists (for example Xavier Greffe, Guy Terny, Alain Wolfelsperger, Serge-Christophe Kolm) but practically none of them is interested in what the French political scientists have to say (if they have anything to say). On the other hand, the only economic works really popular in French political science are Olson's *Logic of Collective Action* and Hirschman's *Exit, Voice and Loyalty*, but I suspect that the latter is popular precisely because it is supposed to be free of economic bias and also because it can be easily understood in a non-technical fashion. Let us recall, too, that Olson's book has been translated into French thanks to the efforts of the sociologist Raymond Boudon. Some political scientists are willing to use economic analogies, following Weber and Schumpeter (it is apposite to speak of political 'entrepreneurs', political 'markets', political 'goods' and so on) e.g. Gaxie (1985) but they are keen on emphasizing that this economic analysis is a remote cousin of the economics of politics practised by the neo-classic economists. The reason why Hirschman is appreciated is that he is supposed to deviate from the basic standards of economic analysis.

Unlike the philosophers, none of the young scholars trained in economics have moved into professional political science: at the Concours d'agrégation de science politique no candidate has made formal models and theories a first choice. Economists have enough job opportunities not to need to get entangled with a group of scholars whose status and wealth are unpromising. There is, however, something akin to an economic bias: it affects less the professional political scientists than a fraction of the intellectual world, and it has a distinct ideological flavour, namely an 'ultra liberal' one. Any kind of political process can allegedly be explained and assessed by using the categories and concepts of the Virginia School, such is the creed of the 'new economists' (why new? because of the 'new' philosophers, of course; and maybe because of the huge success of *La nouvelle cuisine*).[55] In their opinion, actual political history is interesting and even amusing as a fairy tale but it should be discarded as long as it cannot be used to work out abstract processes which can be subject to models and tests leading to deductions, predictions, and advice for a systematic set of policies. Political sociology, on the other hand, is useless, since it is neither scientific nor individualist enough. It is worth noting that the individual and his absolute autonomy have become almost the only ideological flag of the conservative camp in France: no wonder that the Front National and the far right attract new supporters! They are able to mobilize the old political repertory — community, tradition, authority — abandoned by the moderate right. But nothing is simple; a few new economists belong or are close to the Front National, and help to cook a new ideological recipe, combining traditional community political values with individualistic economic values.

The problem is not the existence of this science, which is neither new nor scientific (or at least no more scientific than, say, the Marxist political economy which flourished in the 1970s after the Althusserian revolution', when some Marxist — or even non-Marxist economists saw the light reading *Lire le Capital*) (Althusser *et al.* 1968). The real problem is that political scientists are not equipped to use their own knowledge to confront the views exposed by the new economists. For example we are not able to assess correctly what Buchanan really means.[56] We do not know the economics of institutions, we lack the usable knowledge which would enable us to make significant connections between institutions, behaviour, and policy outcomes. French political science has focused so far on the study of institutions (from a legal-formal standpoint), behaviour, and social structures. It is powerless when challenged by people holding that specific institutions are liable to produce specific policy outcomes. We have good reasons to be sceptical about this kind of construction; apart from certain overall statements (for example, a monolithic institution is more likely to tell than to ask; a pluralistic one is likely to do the opposite, etc.), we hold that political institutions are more grown than designed and, as they have not a single end and do not perform a unique function, they can produce quite unintended outcomes. But we cannot argue on the ground imposed by the economists: for the moment we have to reconcile ourselves to telling stories, ie. laying out specific historical sequences and processes to prove that in certain circumstances the economic theory was not upheld. But it is not enough: as everybody knows, facts never disprove a theory. In this respect the challenge of the new economists has not been met satisfactorily. It is a pity that France, once considered as the stronghold of constitutional studies, has not been the source of any significant comment on Buchanan's 'constitutional level' of analysis: several political scientists would agree on what Vincent Ostrom calls 'a key element in Buchanan's heuristic . . . taking the perspective of hypothetical individuals as the motors that drive human societies, those individuals being conceived as acting in relation to structures of incentives established by the way that rules and material conditions are interrelated to create opportunities and constraints in what might be called the logic of situations (Ostrom 1987: 242).[57] But the job has been done so far (and very insufficiently) by a few economists devoid of constitutional literacy, and no one has filled the vacuum.

To return to my original statement, such a situation may be due to the absence of an autonomous subfield labelled 'institutional economics'. This shortcoming explains the lack of contributions by political scientists to such issues as public finance, fiscal policy, and even (in spite of some good sociological works) social and health care policies. Instead of being used to rejuvenate the discipline and open up new areas of research, the economic bias is viewed as a hindrance to the current political science. The same could be said (with proper nuances and for different reasons) of the two other biases.

To finish in optimistic mood, let's assume that this is a temporary situation: as soon as our officialdom is convinced that political science is worth a try (and if political scientists are ready to assert themselves), things may change and the prospects will look brighter. The lack of effective connections between the discipline's subfields, and the ongoing difficulty of having political science recognized as a *Wissenschaft* may be due to good epistemological (pertaining to the nature of political knowledge) and political (related to the current 'crisis' of political regulations) reasons. But it is also relevant to scrutinise, as I have done here, the intellectual field as a social field and to emphasize the domination exerted by the fourth market (the cultural goods market) over the first (the professional market). That does not tell the whole story but that is at least a significant part of it.

NOTES

1   This chapter incorporates revised and updated parts of a paper presented to the International Round Table on the Comparative Study of the Development of the Discipline of Political Science, Cortona, Italy, 21-26 September 1987; and of an article published in the *Revue française de science politique* (Leca 1981).

2   On the notion of *champ*, see Bourdieu 1969, 1971a and b, and 1976a. In Bourdieu's opinion, the scientific field is organized around a central conflict for the monopoly of scientific authority. He seems to think that a field is always structured by a central conflict pertaining to the monopoly of the most valued good in the field which is far from being evident. All Bourdieu's fields, are modelled on the modern Weberian 'State' and the struggle for the monopoly of legitimate physical coercion. In this text, I will use the notion in a much less systematic way.

3   For a nice application of the problematique to a single case in two different contexts, see Lamont 1987.

4   For some interesting insights about those interactions, see for example, Boudon 1977 and Bourricaud 1980.

5   I am not using the term 'profession' in the usual sense: 'sociology of professions'. In this context, 'profession' means that within the university some scholars are called professors of political science (or *chercheurs en science politique*) and that their recruitment and career depend on specific Political Science Committees. Even within the limits of that definition, our profession is a slender one: there are only seventy 'political scientists' of the National Centre for Scientific Research – less than half the number of sociologists; there are about eighty professors of political science, compared to three hundred-odd professors of law. Between 1972 to 1988, an additional thirty professors of political science had been recruited, compared to growth in the numbers of professors of law of more than 35 per cent. (In France, a university professor is in fact a state professor, recruited through a national competitive exam.)

There are only six institutes of political studies, most of whose courses are not about political science or even about 'government'; one department of political science; and about fifteen teams of scholars involved in research, of which five or six have a significant number of members. Admittedly, political science is taught to undergraduates in several other universities (and the teachers are not always political scientists themselves), and PhD courses are offered by about twenty universities, but most of the time the professional political scientist is isolated in a law school and seldom asked to teach in Departments of History or Sociology.

This is the perverse consequence: as there are so few research centres, most of the professors flock to the universities where the centres are located. This leads to a concentration of teachers in those departments, which then appear to the university managers and ministry bureaucrats to be overstaffed. The result is that when a professor retires, he is not always replaced, because the regulations grant the boards of universities the power (within limits) to appoint someone from another discipline, provided his candidature has been admitted by a national committee. The young professors cannot join the departments where they would find a suitable intellectual environment, and they have to make do by working on the fringes of university life, often finding themselves inferior to lawyers, and lacking both facilities and intellectual infrastructure. So the young professors usually choose to commute, which makes them look still more remote from the university where they are supposed to teach as full-time professors.

One of the most overlooked causes of this curious situation is that in France, the law schools teach both undergraduate and graduate students. The government ministries cannot develop since their potential audience is held captive by the law schools.

6 These issues are not abstract. As a member of the political science committee of the National Centre for Scientific Research, I can testify that we are constantly having to confront them every time we meet. It is sometimes difficult to convince other members that it is not enough to do a good legal, or historical, or literary analysis of a political institution and then call it a good analysis in political science. It also takes a lot of time to convince them that someone working on the internal politics of a corporation, a factory, or some other interest group, can at the same time be a political scientist. It has taken nearly ten years for 'policy studies' to be recognized as a legitimate part of political science, as distinct from that catch-all havoc called *science administrative*. 'Administration' has become a portmanteau term to include the study of officialdom, and its terms of reference are monopolized by the study of the role of top civil servants, descriptions of institutional mechanisms, the sociology of beaucracy, etc.).

7 I will return to that point in a different context when dealing with historical bias. Let's make it clear that the indigenous paradigms are of the utmost importance in understanding the working of any kind of social system. Maybe they are the only viable paradigms from the point of view of a *verstehen* science, but, at the very least, these questions should be open to discussion.

8 Skocpol's *States and Social Revolutions* has been translated into French thanks to Pierre Birnbaum's efforts, but is little studied. Neither Reinhard Bendix nor Stein Rokkan were ever translated. Barrington Moore Jr and Perry Anderson were, but that is probably because of their Marxist flavour. Barrington Moore's *Social Origins* had to wait nearly twelve years before being reprinted.

9 Cf. in general Favre 1989. See also Favre 1981a and the reference to L'Emaine, MacCleod, Weigant 1976. The crossroad perspective explains, in my opinion, why French political science hasn't known a founding work that participates in the discipline's institutionalization and in establishing its legitimacy. Montesquieu and Tocqueville are precursors, Siegfried and Duverger, genuine potential founders that the crossroad has elevated (or reduced) to the status of symbols or semaphores.

10 At this point in time, France had not the slightest monopoly of such a tendency. cf. Eckstein 1979.

11 What follows merits full quotation as much by its style and inspiration (very Tocquevillean) as by the contradictory echoes that it evokes in the contemporary reader: 'Grievous lacuna! A nation falls further each day when scholars have no other audience than special men, when the Statesman finds capable seconds only among those in place, and competent criticism only from candidates coveting his. Why, in France have great works of erudition, science and art never been possible

without the support of the State? It is that, except for special men, none is in the position to understand their value nor to be interested by them. Why does the government of opinion belong to frivolous as much as, or even more than, serious journalism? It is that the men who might appreciate an enlightened press, get it up and running, are too in small number to give it life. Amongst other necessary things, France has failed to know how to scatter every year two or three hundred highly cultured minds that, mixed in with the masses, would have maintained the respect of knowledge, the serious attitude of intelligence and the healthy attitude of finding difficult things difficult. Those who judge without study and decide everything (Alas! they were only gentlemen in the days of Molière; they are in charge nowadays) would have received a mortal blow'.

12 This doesn't take anything away, of course, from the fundamental importance of Durkheim's work for political science, stressed notably by R. Bendix, E. Allardt, S. Lukes, P. Birnbaum and B. Lacroix.

13 Bougle 1923, 1925, and 1935, Davy 1923 and 1950.

14 A possible explanation as to why this happened lies in the position of social philosophy within the arts faculties. Political philosophy was weak but moral philosophy was strong. Academic sociology developed from moral philosophy (cf. the Certificate in Moral Philosophy and Sociology). Imagine what would have happened had there been Certificates in Philosophy and Political Sociology!

15 Hauriou 1889, Duguit 1989. Though he liked to call himself a 'legal sociologist', Duguit always resisted the sociology of the Durkeimian school. Cf. Eisenmann 1930.

16 Kelsen, who best justified the epistemological incompatibility of legal science with sociology (Kelsen 1928), had only a narrow influence on the French school of public law, with the notable exception of Charles Eisenmann.

17 Recalling this first edition, Georges Burdeau, in the preface of the second edition (Paris, LGDJ, 1966) states firmly: 'Jurists, I know what (political science) is looking for. It is the why and how of that by which a society "holds"; that is to say, the institutions and the rules in which lie both the supports of political power and the instruments of its action' (p.7). This firm profession of legal faith doesn't in the least prevent G. Burdeau from constantly trying to go beyond the limits of the legitimate political scene in order to analyse 'the structure of a whole group', nor from criticizing in no uncertain terms 'the systematically anodine character of subjects on the agenda of political science conferences'.

18 Gurvitch 1960 (the other authors were F. Gouguel and G. Dupeux).

19 See Prelot 1957, Eisenmann 1957, Duverger 1959 and Meynaud 1959.

20 The work of Michel Foucault is a convincing example of this phenomenon.

21 To illustrate this point, without suggesting I have proved it, why, in the United States, has the debate on social transfers contributed, as R. Boudon remarks, to a renewal of professional political philosophy, with the work of John Rawls and R. Nozick, while the French intellectual field has been busy with the brilliant 'essay' by J. Attali and M. Guillaume (*L'anti-économique*)? Why was it necessary to wait fifteen years for a translation of *A Theory of Justice*? Just as interesting is the fact, unexplained to this day, that the first discussion of Rawls appearing in 1975 in the *Revue Française de science politique* (from the pen of Raymond Boudon) was not taken up until ten years later by the ingénieurs polytechniciens.

22 Pierre Favre notes in this respect: 'This is the reason why *Le Monde* reviews so few books on political science, compared to the number of reviews of books on

philosophy, sociology, history, or psychoanalysis). *Le Monde* being "full" of politics and reflections of politics and not being aware of political science's specificity, has no need to explain in any special particular way the work of political academics' (Favre 1980:12). Let us add that it is not a case of making a self-pitying claim (it is absolutely normal that the press chooses what it judges important for its market), but of stating simply that as far as political studies are concerned, the scientific field makes little impact on the intellectual field (which is more or less the case everywhere) and that the intellectual field considers itself to largely be the scientific field (which is encountered less frequently elsewhere).

23 The system of awarding diplomas was one of the strangest, and is likely to stay that way for the foreseeable future. In principle, because every university has autonomy, each one can create any diploma it likes. But for a diploma to receive the universally respected label of 'national diploma', it has to be authorized by the Ministry of Education. The Minister draws on the 'judgment of peers' to authorize a diploma, but it does not follow that he necessarily follows their advice. Moreover, these experts do not, in fact, like to express a preference where this has administrative consequences; they tend either to grant their benediction to everybody or to fall back on the ministry's bureaucratic criteria in order to justify a decision, and query, for example, the number of teachers, seniority, etc.

24 Scientists are, in return, the object of a large specific social demand on the part of their universities, or of civic and cultural associations. As for the general social demand it appears in the market of general cultural goods. The area of opinion polls and electoral estimations (and to a certain extent public policy), constitutes a relative exception: there is general demand directly addressed to the scientific field (of a mostly technological type).

25 The 'bat technique', freely translated, means to be all things to all men. The expression originates with the poet La Fontaine: 'Je suis oiseau, voyez mes ailes; je suis souris, vivent les rats.' It means that someone with two sides to their character, shifts from one to the other depending on the nature of the audience. When speaking to the general public or to politicians, he is a social scientist; but if he is speaking to fellow professionals, he claims he wrote his book as a concerned citizen and not as a social scientist at all.

26 Let us avoid moral judgments: these works exist, not because their authors are bad people, but because the incentive to produce them exists. Moreover, they are not necessarily insignificant and can contribute to knowledge.

27 These 'affinities' are not purely ideological. They assume that the individuals have had a similar academic career and that they also enjoy similar salary and/or prestige.

28 Bourdieu, Boltanski 1976, see in particular, 'La science royal et le fatalisme du probable: 39-55; and Les professeurs de l'Institut d'études politiques: 66-70.

29 One should look particularly carefully at the distinction made between the political questions decided in the 'name of knowledge' and those decided in the 'interests of class', as if 'the interests of class' were given and weren't constructed by a knowledge based itself on the competence of 'specialists' of another sort. But to answer in this way is to become exposed to being considered by Bourdieu as a typical product of 'political science'. The debate is circular.

30 If one tried, by referring to the categories used in the first part, to construct the Boutmy Model and adapt it cavalierly to the 1980s, the table might be something like this:

		Class	
		Non-Specialist	Specialist
	Speculative knowledge	Mass Society Man	Scholars
			Experts
Domain			Senior Administrators
	Experimental knowledge	Alienated Voter	Politician
		Grassroots Militants	Experienced Militant

31 See the interesting but debatable thesis of the philosopher, François Ewald on the socio-political interpretation of the development of social science (Ewald 1986). In other directions see the use of legal documentation made by Blandine Barret-Kriegel or Bertrand Badie (Barret-Kriegel 1979; Badie 1987).

32 I would not forgo the opportunity of mentioning the good pieces of historical sociology written by Guy Hermet on Franco's Spain, Alain Rouquie on military dictatorship in Argentina, or D. Pecaud on Colombia.

33 Only Stein Rokkan's and Reinhard Bendix's books are not available in French. Tilly's works have been widely discussed, in particular by historians but *La France Contesté* (Paris: Fayard 1987) has not been extensively reviewed so far and Tilly and Shorter's *Strikes in France* was never translated.

34 In this respect, France stands in sharp contrast to the British tradition, in spite of scholars such as Jean Favier et Jean Tulard. Sartre's *"idiot de la famille"* stands apart as a monstrous attempt to supply a total explanation and understanding of a single historical individual (Flaubert).

35 It is not entirely supporting that Marx and Weber stand in between, sometimes neglected, sometimes used as 'founding fathers' by political scientists and by historians as well. But when Paule Veyne cites Weber, he hastens to specify that Weber was a social historian and not a social scientist. See also his cursory and somewhat unfair critique of Eisenstadt's *The Political System of the Empires*.

36 Maurice Duverger has been trying for some time to bring together leading historians and political scientists to carry on ambitious projects about subjects such as empire and dictatorship, but the results do not look convincing, at least for the moment, may be owing to the lack of detailed historical knowledge displayed by the scientists, but most certainly because of the aloofness of the historians.

37 Good examples are Badie and Birnbaum among others. See also Michel Dobry's theoretical essay *Sociologie des crises politiques* (Dobry 1986), which tries to avoid the traps of a 'scientist' (in the French meaning of the term: concrete historical societies seen as the mere application of a single number of general laws which would explain any particular outcome) without giving up determinist explanations of specific processes. I am greatly indebted to the works of such different scholars as R. Bendix, Ch. Tilly, and A. Giddens, but it is too bad that French historians, given their enormous influence in the scholarly field, pay too scanty attention to them (with a few exceptions). Raymond Aron's teachings seem to be forgotten.

38 Quoted by Gordon A. Craig 'Getting along with Hitler' *New York Review of Books* XXXIV, 12 July 1987:32.

39 The debate is, fortunately, still very much alive among the historians (Chartier 1982).

40 This is an example of the French craze: The most questionable part of Habermas's work is glorified but K.O. Apel is less well known and H. Albert is almost ignored. A collection of his essays has just been translated *La sociologie critique en question* 1987 Paris: PUF.

41 It is apposite to recall Jean Touchard's great book *La Gloire de Beranger*, scandalously forgotten (Touchard 1969).

42 Significant contributions to political philosophy have been made by 'general' philosophers, such as Jacques Maritain, François Chatelet and Paul Ricoeur. Sometimes Claude Levi Strauss comes very close to being a political philosopher *en passant*, in particular when he comments off handedly on Rousseau.

43 The only philosophies to be granted some legitimacy by several tough minded scientists are the philosophy of mind and the philosophy of language (what some computer scientists call with reverence 'real technical philosophy'). Better late than never: this kind of philosophy deserves certainly better than mere lip service, but it is difficult to understand the craze that drives some people to throw out the baby with the bathwater.

44 *Philosophy of Right* (Preface; translated by T.M. Knox (1967) London: Oxford University Press (paperback) p.2). Later (on p.11) Hegel emphasizes that 'this book . . . as a work of philosophy . . . must be poles apart from an attempt to construct a state as it ought to be'. It is one of the most popular misconceptions among political scientists (and sometimes among philosophers as well) that because political philosophy has something to do with argument and values, it is a purely normative activity.

45 Leviathan ch.4 'Of speech' edited by C.B. MacPherson (1981) Penguin Books p. 106. Also ch. 5 'Of reason and science': 'To forsake his own natural judgment, and be guided by general sentences read in authors, and subject to many exceptions, is a sign of folly and generally scorned by the name of pedantry' (p.117).

46 As it is useless to get personal, since the problem has less to do with subjective qualities (honesty, fairness, good faith) than with objective intellectual biases (by no means irresistible, though), I will content myself with evoking Sartre's *Les communistes et la paix* and his 'Preface' to Fanon's *The Wretched of the Earth*, and more recently the interesting philosophical-historical 'interpretation' of the Iranian revolution supplied by Foucault in 1979 (in *Le Monde*): a completely new form of politics was allegedly emerging, and, gallantly enough, Foucault, regardless of what was actually happening – and in particular the fierce struggles within the revolutionary movement – named it 'political spirituality'. The disenchanted world has some interesting backlashes.

47 'Contribution to the critique of Hegel's *Philosophy of Right: Introduction*' in Robert Tucker (ed.) (1978) *The Marx Engels Reader*, 2nd edition, N.Y.: Norton p.54.

48 Admittedly, Foucault's influence was not limited to France and in particular certain American scholars were as spellbound as their French colleagues. But I do not know in France of any thorough critique addressed to Foucault from the standpoint of political philosophy (and not of history or sociology). Nobody has done a job comparable to Michael Walzer's or J.G. Merquior's (Walzer 1988; Merquior 1986). Luc Ferry and Alain Renaut have done something similar in *La pensée 68* (Ferry and Renaut 1986) but, in my opinion, with too much flippancy.

49 This does not imply that I approve of such a practice. What Sartori calls 'the brave new thought that words have arbitrary meanings' should be adamantly combated (Sartori 1987: IX).

50 For a more sweeping critique, see Eulau 1977: 55-59.

51 Or, more accurately, as a specific class of ideo-systems (this class could be named 'ideology') within a larger class of ideo-systems derived from natural language, (see Bon 1985).

52 This is not to deny the many linkages existing between the various networks of meaning (and power) called 'languages' (scientific, aesthetic, political, etc.) but we must start with some distinctions if we want to highlight these interlocking networks with reasonable accuracy.

53 The only distinctions to be readily admitted are based on macro-historical criteria (e.g. 'classical', 'feudal', 'patrimonial', 'modern politics'). It has seldom made use of structural criteria to sort out various politics within a single polity (eg. 'corporation', 'trade-union', 'government' politics). I am not saying that the first kind of distinction is irrelevant, which would be preposterous; but that is not a reason for blurring the other kind of distinction which has been the core of political philosophy from Aristotle to Hannah Arendt. With this respect, the 'return to Arendt' we have been noticing for some time (e.g. Enegren 1984) may be considered a way toward recovery.

54 The bizarre outcome of such an approach is that certain philosophers use the concept 'totalitarianism' as an all-encompassing notion whereas others subsume it under an even more general 'philosophical' concept (e.g. the 'state' as a philosopheme, as Jacques Derrida puts it) allegedly relevant to all the contemporary states. I do not think that by doing so they clarify any issue.

55 It would be tedious to supply a detailed list of references, all the more so as it is difficult, for a non specialist, to tell the really serious and innovative contributions from the more repetitive and sometimes nonsensical ones. We may cite a leading promoter of the new economy who summarizes and simplifies the other's findings (Lepage 1980 and 1983).

56 It is likely that many French economists (and political scientists as well) would be surprised at Vincent Ostrom's assessment: 'If Buchanan's basic conjunctures have merit, we might anticipate major shifts in the practice of doing political science, economics, sociology and related forms of inquiry. Rather than assuming that human societies can be explained by simple concepts like states and markets, an emphasis upon multiple levels and foci of analysis drives to the presupposition of ordered complexity. . . . It is possible that the work of both Buchanan and Simon will (in 2087) be seen as pioneering a new thrust in the development of both the economic and political sciences. If such a course of development were to occur, the efforts' to build a "new political science" and a "neoclassical economics" are likely to be viewed as intellectual efforts, which were marked by strong degenerative tendencies associated with a quest for excessively simplified explanatory efforts' (Ostrom 1987: 244-5).

57 This type of approach is very congenial to Raymond Boudon's analyses, but the French sociologist stays too far from political analysis proper.

REFERENCES

Althusser, Louis and Balibar Etienne, (1968) *Lire le Capital*, Paris: Maspero.

Badie, Bertrand (1987) *Les deux etats*, Paris: Fayard.

Badie Bertrand and Birnbaum Pierre (1979) *Sociologie de l'etat*, Paris: Fayard.

Barret-Kriegel, Blandine (1979) *L'Etat et les esclaves*, Paris: Calmann-Levy

Bon Frederic (1985) 'Langage et politique', in Madeleine Grawitz and Jean Leca (eds) *Traité de science politique*, Vol.3 ch.8, Paris: Presses Universitaires de France.

Boudon Raymond (1977) 'The French University since 1968', *Comparative Politics*, October: 89-118.

— (1981) 'L'intellectuel et ses publics: les singularités françaises', in Jean-Daniel Reynaud and Yves Grafmeyer (eds) *Français qui étes-vous?* pp 465-80, Paris: La Documentation Française.

Bouglé, C. (1923) *La démocratie devant la science*, Paris: Alcan

— (1925) *Les idées équalitaires*, Paris: Alcan.

— (1935) *Essai sur le régime des castes*, Paris: Alcan (reprinted, Paris: Presses Universitaires de France).

Bourdieu, Pierre (1969) 'Intellectual field and creative project', *Social Science Information* 8(2):89-119.

— (1971a) 'Genèse et structure du champ religieux', *Revue française de sociologie*: 295 ss.

— (1971b) 'Champ intellectuel, champ du pouvoir et habitus de classe', *Scolies* 1:7-26.

— (1976a) 'Le champ scientifique', *Actes de la recherche en sciences sociales*, June:89 ss.

— (1976b) 'Les modes de domination', *Actes de la recherche en sciences sociales*, June.

— (1981) 'La représentation politique: éléments pour une théorie du champ politique', *Actes de la recherche en sciences sociales* 38, February-March.

Bourdieu, Pierre and Boltanski Luc (1976) 'La production de l'idéologie dominante', *Actes de la recherche en sciences sociales* 2-3, June.

Bourricaud, Françoise (1980) *Le bricolage idéologique*, Paris: Presses Universitaires de France.

Boutmy Emile (1871) *Quelques idées sur la création d'une faculté libre d'enseignement supérieur*, Paris: Imprimerie Adolphe Lainé.

— (1876-1881) *Observations sur l'enseignement des sciences politiques et administratives présentées à l'occasion de la proposition de l'honorable M. Carnot tendant à la création d'une Ecole d'Administration*, Paris: Imprimerie Martinet, 1876. Reprinted in *Revue internationale de l'enseignement* I (1881):237-249.

Burdeau Georges (1949) *Traité de science politique* 1, Paris: Librairie Générale de Droit et de Jurisprudence.

Chartier Roger (1982) 'Intellectual History or Socio-cultural History? The French Trajectories', in Dominick La Capra and Steven Kaplan (eds), *Modern European History: Reappraisals and New Perspectives*, Ithaca: Cornell University Press:13-46.

Collini Stefan, Winch, Donald and Burrow, John (1983) *The Noble Science of Politics: A study in Nineteenth Century Intellectual History*, New York: Cambridge University Press.

Cottereau, Alain (1980) *Le sublime*, Paris: Maspero.

Dahl, Robert (1958) 'Political Theory: Truth and Consequences', *World Politics*: 89-102.

Davy G. (1923) *Des clans aux empires*, Paris: Renaissance du Livre.

— (1950) *Eléments de sociologie*, Vol. I: *Sociologie politique*, Paris: Vrin.

Dobry, Michel (1986) *Sociologie des crises politiques*, Paris: Presses de la Fondation Nationale de Sciences Politiques.

Duguit, Leon (1889) *Le droit constitutionnel et la sociologie*, Paris: A. Colin.

Duverger, Maurice (1959) *Méthodes de la science politique*, Paris: Presses Universitaires de France.

Eckstein, Harry (1979) 'On the "science" of the state', *Daedalus*:1-20.

Eisenmann, Charles (1930) 'Deux théoriciens du droit: Duguit et Hauriou', *Revue philosophique*:231 ss.

— (1957) 'Droit constitutionnel et science politique', *Revue internationale d'histoire politique et constitutionelle*:72 ss.

Enegren, André (1984) *La pensée politique de Hannah Arendt*, Paris: Presses Universitaires de France.

Eulau, Heinz (1977) 'The Politicization of Everything', in V. Van Dyke (ed.) *Teaching Political Science*, New York: Humanities Press.

Ewald, Françoise (1986) *L'etat providence*, Paris: Grasset.

Favre, Pierre (1980) *Regards sur la science politique française*, paper presented to the Association Française de Science Politique, June (mimeo).

— (1981a) 'Les sciences d'etat entre déterminisme et libéralisme: Emile Boutmy et la création de L'ecole libre de sciences politiques', *Revue française de science politique*:429-65.

— (1981b) 'La science politique en France depuis 1945', *International Political Science Review*:95-120. English version in W.G. Andrews (ed.) *International Handbook of Political Science*, New York: Greenwood Press, 1982.

— (1982) 'L'absence de la sociologie politique dans les classifications durkheimiennes des sciences sociales', *Revue française de science politique*, February; English version in Philippe Bernard (ed.) *The Durkheimian School*, Cambridge: Harvard University Press.

— (1985) 'Histoire de la science politique', in Madeleine Grawitz and Jean Leca (eds) *Traité de science politique*, vol. I, ch. 1, Paris: Presses Universitaires de France.

— (1989) *Naissances de la science politique en France, 1870-1914*, Paris: Fayard.

Faye, Jean-Pierre (1972) *Langages totalitaires*, Paris: Hermann.

Ferry, Luc and Renaut, Alain (1986) *La pensée 68*, Paris: Presses Universitaires de France.

Fourquet, Françoise (1980) *Les comptes de la puissance*, Paris: Encres.

Furet, François (1978) *Penser la révolution française*, Paris: Gallimard.

Gaxie, Daniel (1980) 'Les logiques du recrutement politique', *Revue française de science politique*, February.

— (ed.) (1985) *Explication du vote*, Paris: Presses de la Fondation nationale des sciences politiques.

Guédé, Alain and Rosenblum, Serge-Allain (1981) 'Les candidats aux élections legislatives de 1978 à 1981', *Revue française de science politique*, October-December:982-98.

Guenancia, Pierre (1983) *Descartes et l'ordre politique*, Paris: Presses Universitaires de France.

Gunnell, John (1983) 'Political Theory: The Evolution of a subfield', Ada Finifter (ed.) *Political Science: The State of the Discipline*. Washington, D.C.: American Political Science Association.

Gurvitch, Georges (ed.) (1960) *Traité de Sociologie* 2, Paris: Presses Universitaires de France.

Hauriou, Maurice (1899) 'Philosophie du droit et sciences sociales', *Revue du droit public*:462 ss.

Hermet, Guy (1982) *Aux frontières de la démocratie*, Paris: Economica.

— (1986) *Sociologie de la construction démocratique*, Paris: Economica.

Hirschman, Albert O. (1983) 'Morality and the social sciences: a durable tension', in N.Haan *et al* (eds) *Social Sciences and Moral Inquiry*, New York: Columbia University Press.

Jaume, Lucien (1989) *Le discours jacobin et la démocratie*, Paris: Fayard.

Kelsen, Hans (1928) *Der soziologische und der juridische Staatbegriff*, Tübingen.

Lacroix, Bernard (1981) *Durkheim et le politique*, Paris: Presses de la fondation nationale des sciences politiques.

Lamont, Michèle (1987) 'How to become a dominant French philosopher: The case of Jacques Derrida', *American Journal of Sociology* 53 (3), November:584-622.

Leca, Jean (1982) 'La science politique dans le champ intellectuel françoise', *Revue française de science politique* 32:4-5, August-October.

Lemaine, G. MacLeod, R. and Weigant P. (eds) (1976) *Perspectives on the Emergence of Scientific Disciplines*, Chicago: Aldine; Paris: Mouton.

Lemert, Charles (1981) 'Literary politics and the *champ* of French sociology', *Theory and Society*:645-69.

Lepage, Henri (1980) *Demain le capitalisme*, Paris: Seuil.

— (1983) *Demain le liberalisme*, Paris: Seuil.

Leroy-Ladurie, Emmanuel (1976) *Montaillou*, Paris: Gallimard.

Manuel, Frank. E. (1987) *Lojevoy revisited*, Daedalus:125-47.

Marin, Louis (1975) *La critique du discours*, Paris: Minuit.

Mauss, Marcel (1927, 1971) 'Divisions et proportions des divisions de la sociologie', *Année Sociologique*, Nouvelle série 2, 1927; reprinted in *Essais de sociologie*. Paris: Editions de Minuit (Collection Points).

Merquoir, J.G. (1986) *Foucault et le nihilisme de la chaire*, Paris: Presses Universitaires de France.

Meynaud, Jean (1959) *Introduction à la science politique*, Paris: A. Colin.

Montefiore, Alan (ed.) (1983) *Philosophy in France Today*, Cambridge: Cambridge University Press.

Nicolet, Claude (1982) *L'idée républicaine en France*, Paris: Gallimard.

Nora, Pierre (ed.) (1984) *Les lieux de mémoire: La république*, Paris: Gallimard.

— (ed.) (1986) *Les lieux de mémoire: La Nation*, 3 vols, Paris: Gallimard.

Ostrom, Vincent (1987) 'Buchanan and the constitutional bases of political decision-making', *Political Science* (APSA Newsletter), spring.

Pateman, Carole (1988a) 'The patriarchal welfare state', in Amy Gutmann (ed.) *Democracy and the Welfare State*, pp 231-60, Princeton: Princeton University Press.

— (1988b) *The Sexual Contract*, New York: Polity Press.

Prelot, Marcel (1957) 'La fin d'une extraordinaire carence', *Revue internationale d'histoire politique et constitutionnelle*: 1 ss.

Rancière, Jacques (1981) *La nuit des prolétaires*, Paris: Fayard.

Remond, René (ed.) (1988) *Pour une histoire politique*, Paris. Le Seuil.

Sartori, Giovanni (1973) 'What is Politics?', *Political Theory,* February:5-26.

— (1974) 'Philosophy, theory and the science of politics', *Political Theory*, May: 133-62.

— (1987) *The Theory of Democracy Revisited*, vol. 1, Chatham, N.J.: Chatham House Publishers.

Shils, Edward (1968) 'Ideology', *International Encyclopaedia of the Social Sciences*, vol. 7:66-76, New York/London: Macmillan.

— (1975) *Center and Periphery: Essays in Macro-Sociology*, Chicago: University of Chicago Press.

Taguieff, Pierre-André (1988) *La force du préjugé: Essai sur le racisme et l'anti-racisme*, Paris: La Decouverte.

UNESCO (1950) *La science politique contemporaine*, Paris.

Veyne, Paul (1971) *Comment on écrit l'histoire*, Paris: Seuil.

Walzer, Michael (1988) *The Company of Critics*, New York: Basic Books.

Wolin, Sheldon (1960) *Politics and Vision*, Boston: Little, Brown.

8 Political science in the Nordic countries

Dag Anckar[1]

In an essay on the growth of the political-science profession, Nils Elvander writes: 'Academic teaching in political science has a relatively long history in Sweden compared with the other Nordic countries' (1977:75). This statement is echoed by another Swedish scholar, Olof Ruin, who maintains that Swedish political science research 'is based on quite a long tradition in comparison with the other Nordic countries' (1977:157). Ruin points out that a chair in political science, the Johan Skytte Professor of Discourse and Politics, was established as early as 1622 at the University of Uppsala; however, he admits that the scholars holding this chair did not concentrate on the study of politics until the 1840s. This means that political science has a longer tradition in Finland than in any other Nordic country. At Åbo Academy, founded in 1640, a chair of politics, the holder of which was called *Professor Politices et Historiarum*, was an integral part of the university from the beginning. The first holder of this chair was Michael Olai Wexonius, one of the most productive professors at the university, who dealt mainly with political theory issues of that time and in 1647 published his most important work, *Politica* (Nurmi, 1984).

In Sweden and Finland, the academic study of politics was introduced on a broader basis at the beginning of the twentieth century. In Sweden, political science chairs were established at the universities in Lund and Gothenburg and later in Stockholm, whereas in Finland a chair was established at Åbo Academy in 1918[2] and at the University of Helsinki some years later. In both countries additional chairs were introduced during the following decades. The development of the discipline is very different in the other Nordic countries, Denmark, Norway and Iceland. In fact, it is questionable if one can talk about a tradition at all in these countries. In Denmark the first university institutes of political science were established at the end of the 1950s (Nannestad, 1977), and in Norway the first regular chair was established in 1965 (Kuhnle and Rokkan, 1977:65). In Iceland, according to one Icelandic writer, the virgin field of social science was, in the early 1970s, still 'waiting for the first plough' (Grimsson, 1977:48). By and large, political science appears to be a rather recent addition to the academic disciplines in the Nordic countries, although problems which now belong to the field of political science have been investigated for a long time within the framework of other sciences such as history, philosophy, and constitutional law.

Political science in both Sweden and Finland is partly rooted in neighbouring disciplines. In his paper on political science research in Sweden, Olof Ruin (1977) points out that the content of research was dominated by three main currents during the first half of the 1900s, each of which was oriented toward another academic discipline. One current was related to the study of the background, substance and application of written law and was thus related to constitutional law; another current was influenced by the discipline of history and focused on political events, devoting a particular interest to the development of political institutions and processes; and a third gravitated toward philosophy and the history of ideas (Ruin, 1977:157-8). The development of academic political science in Finland after World War One followed a similar pattern, although the scope of the discipline was much more restricted. During the years 1916-49, fifty-one doctoral dissertations in political science were presented in Sweden (Johansson 1980:4), but there were only five Finnish dissertations during the same period (Anckar 1973). Three of these dissertations were about the development of political institutions in Finnish political life and were historical in outlook; the remaining two were about political ideas. Influences from other disciplines can be found in other Nordic political science communities. For instance, it has recently been argued that part of the work by Stein Rokkan in Norway can be regarded as a continuation of Norwegian tradition in the study of history (Nilsson 1984).

The brief overview of Nordic political science that follows focuses on three themes. First, we discuss the place of Nordic countries in the international network of political science; second, we present a very general account of central issues, models, and concepts; and third, we focus on recent signs of disciplinary disintegration, manifest mostly in the institutional establishment of academic subfields within political science and in trends towards sector research and sectoral funding of research. This plan displays a strong emphasis on institutional and organizational matters rather than on the content and substance of Nordic research.[3]

INTERNATIONAL CONTACTS

It is probably true that in the early 1930s Germany stood out as a scientific centre for Nordic scholars. Since then the situation has changed. In a recent paper, Kari Palonen (1984) described how the political science peripheries of Sweden and Finland have turned their backs on the earlier centre. A new centre has emerged to dominate the Nordic political research culture. 'One exceedingly important area of contacts for Sweden, as well as for the other Nordic countries, is American political science,' Olof Ruin writes. He also notes that it is 'almost a general rule that young Swedish political scientists study for a period of time at a university in the US' (Ruin 1977:159). Although exceptions to this rule certainly can be found, Ruin is right to stress the importance of the American political science community for the development of political science in the Nordic countries.

The Nordic countries are not unique in this respect. American influence in the social sciences has been strong all over western Europe, especially in the first decade after World War Two when teaching and research were reestablished. The emergence of various exchange programmes, offering study scholarships in the US, was an important mechanism for conveying American influences to Europe, and served to impress major theoretical and methodological innovations on a rising generation of European political scientists. There have, however, been changes in this general pattern during later decades. The dependence on American sources has been criticized as well as counteracted, and political science in Western Europe has managed to release itself from some of the ties to American models, although the Nordic countries have not been in the forefront of this movement. The scientific climate has become more pluralistic in terms of influences and dependencies, but the reliance on American traditions and conceptions still dominates the picture.

A few figures describing the situation in Finland may be illuminating in this respect. Finland is an interesting case insofar as it has sometimes been suggested that the impact of American political science has perhaps been less marked in Finland than in the other Nordic countries. This belief, however, appears groundless. Finnish postwar social science has been strongly dependent on basic influences from the US. A survey made in 1983 indicates that 30 per cent of the Finnish professors in the social sciences made at least one trip to the US of at least two months' duration for purposes of research, teaching, or graduate study (Vuorinen and Heikkonen, 1983:24-5). In a review of the Finnish-American scholarly exchange in the field of social sciences, Erik Allardt and Krister Ståhlberg (1983:49) quote an investigation which shows that no less than 34 per cent of the citations in doctoral dissertations in political science and sociology at Finnish universities during the period 1952-78 are from US sources. When sources are classified as crucial or less important, the importance of the American references becomes even more obvious. No less than 57 per cent of the crucial references are to American sources.

The Nordic contacts with political science in Western Europe have developed during the 1970s principally because of the European Consortium for Political Research (ECPR), an organization founded in 1970 by representatives of eight political science institutions in Europe to foster communication and collaboration between European political science scholars. The organization has expanded rapidly and now covers more than 100 institutions representing most countries in western Europe, including the Nordic countries. ECPR pursues a variety of activities including, since 1973, annual joint sessions workshops, which attract a growing number of participants and have become important for the development of a sense of community within European political science. ECPR also arranges annual summer schools in the field of quantitative research, the aim of these schools being to improve the level of professionalism in political science and to ensure that younger scholars work more closely together.

The Nordic participation in ECPR activities has stabilized at a fairly high level. A Norwegian, Stein Rokkan, was the chairman of the organization during its formative years from 1970 to 1976, and approximately thirty to forty Nordic scholars now attend the joint sessions workshops. The distribution by country of participants in the summer school from 1968 to 1978 shows that Denmark was represented by 31 participants, Finland had 16, Iceland one, Norway 48 and Sweden 37 participants (ECPR 1980: 21). The differences between the countries may reflect variations in extroversion among the political science cultures, and also, to some degree, variations in the emphasis on quantitative methods and techniques. ECPR, which publishes the quarterly *European Journal of Political Research*, a highly professional publication, has entrusted one of the two co-editorships to Professor Mogens N. Pedersen from Odense University in Denmark. ECPR also supports the *European Political Data Newsletter* which is published jointly by the ECPR Data Information Service and the Norwegian Social Science Data Services. The newsletter provides systematic reviews of data being produced and stored in western Europe, and it is edited by Professor Stein Kuhnle from Bergen. Nordic scholars have also contributed as editors to the Sage Modern Politics Series which is sponsored by ECPR (e.g. Goldmann and Sjöstedt 1979).

Nordic contacts with political science groups in Eastern Europe have been sporadic and in the form of individual contacts and exchanges rather than organized collaboration. The Finnish Political Science Association has engaged in bilateral cooperation in two meetings with the Soviet Association for Political Sciences, in Helsinki in 1977 and in Moscow in 1984. A third meeting is planned for 1987, and the groups have agreed that collaboration should become regular in order to continue and develop this scientific contact. Two Finnish-Polish political science seminars have focused on the concept of political culture. The first was in Warsaw in 1981; the second in Lahti, Finland, in 1983. A third meeting took place in 1986. There is considerable room for effort to widen scholarly contacts with eastern Europe, especially because the study of socialist political systems has aroused growing interest in the Nordic countries and has produced several works of high quality (e.g. Tarschys 1971; Susiluoto 1981; Lundquist 1982; Nygren 1984).

The Nordic political science communities are affiliated with the International Political Science Association (IPSA), and this world organization of political scientists assists its members to establish connections and to widen contact networks. These possibilities have

Table 7 IPSA 13th World Congress, July 1985: Nordic representatives as leading scientific functionaries

	Total	From Nordic countries
Convenors/co-convenors for sessions under the main theme:		
Subtheme 1	16	0
Subtheme 2	16	2
Subtheme 3	18	3
Subtheme 4	15	2
Presidents/chairpersons at sessions arranged by:		
IPSA Research committees	48	3
IPSA Study groups	21	0
IPSA Special sessions	51	2
Total	185	12

not been fully explored by the Nordic region, and Nordic contributions to the IPSA community have been rather sparse in terms of administration, travel and publications, and the hosting and arranging of round tables and meetings. Furthermore, Nordic scholars do not seem to be well integrated in the scientific networks of IPSA. If we exclude the IPSA council meetings and the executive committee and programme committee meetings, we find that only twelve scholars from the Nordic countries participated in the various seminars and round tables arranged by IPSA in the years 1979–82, Norway being represented by seven participants.[4] There is active participation in the IPSA world congresses; for instance, ninety Nordic scholars attended the 11th Congress in Moscow, in 1979. However, the Nordic representation among scholars entrusted with leading and organizing congress functions is hardly striking. Some figures describing the situation in the recent IPSA 13th World Congress in Paris, July 1985, are presented in Table 7,[5] and they indicate that only 6 per cent of the leading functionaries are from the Nordic countries. Estimates of this participation depend on the criteria one uses: if the quality of research input is regarded as a criterion, then the figure obviously is on the small side. It appears that the Nordic countries are on the periphery of IPSA in more than just the geographical sense. Two remarkable exceptions to this rule must be noted: Stein Rokkan was the president of IPSA during the years 1970–3, and Francesco Kjellberg, also from Norway, was programme chairman for the congress in Paris.

RESEARCH PROBLEMS AND APPROACHES

In the late 1950s and the early 1960s, the behavioural wave swept through Nordic political science, and the behavioural mood soon came to dominate the discipline. The rapid breakthrough of the behavioural movement in Finland has been explained by Finland's lack of a firm political science tradition which could have withstood the wave or inspired attempts at resistance (Nousiainen 1983:195). This is a valid explanation, and it is also valid for the political-science communities in Denmark and Norway which, at that time, were in formative stages and therefore especially sensitive to foreign impulses. Interestingly enough, the behavioural movement made less rapid headway in Sweden, where a long and diversified tradition incorporated the American methodological and technical innovations in a more balanced manner.

Robert Dahl predicted that the behavioural mood would slowly 'decay as a distinctive mood and outlook'. Dahl believed that the behavioural approach was becoming incorporated into the main body of the discipline and that it therefore was disappearing because it had succeeded. 'As a separate, somewhat sectarian, slightly factional outlook it will be the first victim of its own triumph' (Dahl 1961:770). The prediction has come true for the Nordic countries, but with several important reservations. The behavioural triumph has been only partial, and the after-effects of the behavioural revolution do not characterize the whole discipline. It is true that research on electoral behaviour and party behaviour has flourished in the Nordic countries and still does so to a considerable extent. It is also true that attempts to gather and analyse extensive sets of mass data to reach empirical generalizations and thus to promote theory-building marks Nordic political science. But there has been much in the discipline that deviates from this pattern. There has been ample room for epistemological, methodological, and theoretical disputes which have concerned the foundations of the behavioural belief system and have drawn inspiration from many directions, such as phenomenology, hermeneutics, Marxism and structuralism. These directions have been somewhat evenly represented in the Nordic countries. Marxism was an important stream in Danish political science in the 1970s and still is, although now in a much less dogmatic form (Albaek 1984). In the other Nordic countries, Marxism has been no more than a peripheral source of inspiration. Interest in phenomenology and structuralism has perhaps been greatest in Finland and increasingly so during later years (e.g. Heiskanen and Hänninen 1983). Furthermore, there is a tradition in the Nordic countries, especially in Sweden (see Ruin 1977:164), which focuses on modern political theory issues relating to the formulation and operationalization of research problems and to the methods for drawing conclusions. The development indicated by the subtitle 'From behaviouralism to policy analysis' of an analysis of trends in Finnish political science (Anckar 1977) has not been peculiar to Finland but common to all Nordic countries. This development has implied a dissociation from the behavioural doctrine and the dogmas of behaviouralism, although not from American influences.

It is difficult to point at clear-cut differences between the political science communities in the Nordic countries. Some differences have been suggested above, others seem likely. For instance, it is probably true that the study of the problems of democracy has received special attention in Swedish political science. To take another example, a quantitative analysis of the output of Finnish political science research in 1960-72 (Anckar 1977) suggests that the study of central institutions of government and of international relations was more prominent during that period in Finland than in her Scandinavian sister countries, and a similar quantitative analysis of the political science outputs in Denmark, Norway, and Sweden in the years 1970-83 indicates noticeable differences in the emphasis put on various subfields, such as political institutions, political participation and political decision making-making. In fact, it could be argued that Sweden's strongest position has been in the subfields where Denmark and Norway are weak, and vice versa. The three countries have not frequently made simultaneous research investments in the same subfields (Eliassen and Pedersen 1984:93-5). On the whole, however, descriptions of Nordic political science stress similarities rather than dissimilarities. The political science cultures do not differ much; the features that unite quite clearly outweigh those that divide.

Political science is quite ethnocentric in all Nordic countries. This similarity accounts for others, for instance, the extensive interest that Nordic scholars have shown, since the 1970s, in research on corporatism and the interplay between government and organized interests. The interest is ethnocentric insofar as all Nordic countries have experienced the same corporatist developments and the same need to come to an understanding of how corporatism relates to the guiding principles of representative government. There are many exceptions to this rule of ethnocentricity, and political systems other than the Nordic have attracted attention, especially in connection with international politics and international relations. African politics has interested many Nordic scholars, and at least one book (Vanhanen 1984) compares all contemporary independent states over the very long period from 1850 to 1979. Still, Danish political scientists write mostly about Denmark, Finnish political scientists about Finland, etc. This rule applies to the largest political science projects launched in the Nordic countries during the 1960s and 1970s. A Danish project, still in progress, examines the political decision-making process in Denmark and the working of the Danish political system. The two largest political science projects in Finland during the 1970s both dealt with democracy and equality in Finland. A Norwegian project, recently ended, dealt with power relations in Norway. A very large Swedish project, involving all Swedish political science departments and carried out in the years 1965-74, was devoted to the study of communal politics in Sweden. This research has been followed up with a similar project on communal politics and communal problems.

A related similarity is that Nordic political science has not paid much attention to comparative research. This seems surprising as the Nordic countries should be rewarding objects for comparison: on the one hand they are similar enough to encourage comparisons from a methodological point of view; on the other they are dissimilar to an extent which guarantees variation and thus provides the basis for meaningful comparisons. There are some truly comparative works, of course (e.g. Berglund and Lindström 1978; Elvander 1980), and comparative approaches to the study of Nordic politics have lately become more frequent in the research literature, but much of the work labelled comparative is in fact ethnocentric in the form of country-specific treatments of political phenomena. Comparisons between Nordic political systems and external political systems are rare. However, Norwegian political science has taken a rather lively interest in the comparative politics movement, and some fields of inquiry, for instance international politics and peace research, are almost by nature more open than others to comparative ventures. One eminent example of Norwegian achievements in comparative politics is Stein Rokkan's effort to construct a 'conceptual map' of Europe' (Allardt 1981), and there have been various efforts in Norway to organize data files for comparative analyses.

One further characteristic of Nordic political science is that the discipline is synchronous. The time dimension is often neglected; analyses aim at present situations and conditions rather than the processes leading to them. Exceptions to this rule abound, and it has become much more common to pursue research in dynamic terms, analysing change rather than the present. Still the static profile although more vague, prevails as it has done since the time political science set itself free from history and was caught by the behavioural wave. This is in itself rather strange. The behavioural credo attempted to formulate generalizations about politics that are not bound by time or place, and therefore should have reasonably directed research attention towards the past as well as the present. This did not happen in the Nordic countries or elsewhere. The behavioural movement made the discipline contemporary in outlook. Paradoxically, as behavouralism fades, the demand for timelessness that it should have raised is beginning to be satisfied.

Towards Disintegration?

In a recent paper the Norwegian scholar Johan P. Olsen quotes a statement by V.O. Key, who in the late 1950s advocated the view that the behavioural revolution would give political science 'an intellectual unification of all its elements' (Olsen 1984:2). This integrating effect did not take place. In a paper published in 1966 the Finnish political scientist Jan–Magnus Jansson declared that there was not 'anything approaching a consensus among political scientists as to the goals and methods of their science. . . . A glance at some volumes' Jansson claimed, 'which . . . attempt to map out the field of political science shows a bewildering variety of opinions on this subject' (1966:13). That description has been echoed by, for instance, Victor Wiseman, who wrote that, 'At any conference of political scientists one might find experts in sixteenth century monarchomachism, municipal refuse disposal, public finance, international government, corrupt practices acts, American constitutional law, village life in India, regional planning, nationalism and international power politics, methodology in general political research, community power structure, and many other subjects' (1969:6). The situation remains much the same today; Olsen (1984:4) for instance, concludes that the identity of political science still appears unclear and that the fragmentation of the discipline constitutes the main problem.

The problem is accentuated by the fact that this fragmentation shows signs of becoming institutionalized. Two trends seem alarming in this respect in the Nordic countries. One is expressed in the establishment of professional chairs within subfields of the discipline; this trend is discernible, to a varying degree, in all countries. The other, especially observable in Sweden, has to do with an increased emphasis on sector-oriented research, based on short term political priorities.

It has been common in the Nordic countries to view the field of political science as divided into three: general political science, international politics, and public administration. The very rapid growth of the discipline, illustrated, for instance, by the fact that there were only three full-time staff members in Danish political science university institutes in 1960, whereas the number was about 80 in 1975 (Nannestad 1977:19), soon led to an institutionalization of this categorization in terms of professorships. In Finland, where the development has been perhaps most rapid in this respect, chairs in international politics and public administration were established in the late 1960s[6] and other countries have followed, although the discipline certainly appears more homogeneous in Denmark and Norway. (It should be noted in this respect that special institutes for foreign policy research and peace research were established in Finland, Norway, and Sweden during the late 1950s and the 1960s; however, the Swedish Institute of International Affairs was founded in 1938). This disintegration of the field was not in itself any great source of concern. The disintegration was in form rather than content and the theoretical and methodological links to the mother discipline remained, on the whole, quite strong. Political science showed tendencies to disintegrate into subfields, but these were still subfields of political science. However, the disintegration has continued and has lately taken on different forms which renounce the identity of political science.

This development is above all a consequence of the emergence of a new conception of the relation between science and society. In short, this conception sees science as an important promoter of productive capacity, and consequently sees the practical use of science as dependent on the choice of research problems. In most west European countries, as early as the 1950s, political decision-makers asserted the right to interfere with the planning of research and responsibility for the allocation of resources to and within the scientific community. This new emphasis on the technological and societal relevance of science gave birth to new schools of thought in the field of science policy (e.g. Paloheimo 1979), which we cannot dwell upon here. Suffice to say that the state activity in planning for universities and science increased in the Nordic countries in the 1960s and especially in the 1970s. The result was somewhat subversive reforms of the university and science systems, and a strong emphasis on the interaction between science and society. The emphasis was, in other words, on the problem-solving capacity of science and, consequently, on scientific ventures that were interdisciplinary in character. For political science this has meant the establishing of chairs and disciplines that are only partially rooted in the mother discipline and are oriented towards needs defined outside the scientific community. One example is the establishing of chairs in the interdisciplinary field of health administration. Another is the introduction of the discipline of communal politics in Finland and the establishing of a chair in this discipline. Attempts at defining the scope of this new discipline clearly departed from an ambition to assist and advise the political decision-makers at the communal level (Anckar 1976:16-22).

It is perhaps too early to give a definite opinion on the disintegrative effects of this new trend. One cannot, however, avoid the impression that the trend is towards isolation, insofar as the new disciplines tend to remain outside the political science community. This is not because the community is eager to expel the newcomers; other mechanisms are at work. Some are structural: the new disciplines are often placed in faculties and institutions other than those forming the traditional environs of political science. Others relate to scientific interests. Interdisciplinary ventures have a built-in incapacity to use or promote theory-building, and it is doubtful if anything constructive in this respect emerges from the efforts to bring political science closer to 'society'. Such doubts are anyhow often expressed by representatives of traditional political science, who regard the new orientation as theoretically superficial. Representatives of the new orientation obviously do not share this view.

The impact of the emphasis on social relevance in political science has been most striking in the emergence of sector research. Sector research is research which is motivated by the needs of special social problem sectors (such as, for instance, housing and labour), and which is financed by the sector in question. We have already mentioned that this phenomenon is characteristic of Sweden and does not manifest itself to the same extent in the other Nordic countries. Swedish political science has, however, become dependent on sector research and sector funding to a degree which must cause anxiety. There are today more than fifty sector research organs in Sweden, with the foremost task of fostering communication and contacts between those who conduct research and those who consume and buy research.

In their report on Swedish political science, Kjell A. Eliassen and Mogens Pedersen (1984: 62-3, 96-8) have pointed at one circumstance that accentuates the risks of this development. They emphasize the importance of the fact that political science in Sweden works under structural conditions that differ from conditions in the other Scandinavian countries. The difference is that there are comparatively few permanent research posts in Swedish political science departments, so that many Swedish researchers lack permanent appointments and therefore are dependent upon financial resources outside the university system. These resources, i.e. the sector resources, are however intended to advance applied research rather than basic research, and this condition may, in the long run, have negative consequences for the quality of research if the aspiration to promote policy relevance overshadows the ambition to advance cumulative knowledge. These goals are perhaps not always conflicting, they may be coincident. As pointed out by the Swedish political scientist Kjell Goldmann (179:258), coincidence requires that policy problems can be transformed into research problems and that an interpretation of relevance is accepted which is logically independent of who pays for research and of the motives of the author. Such interpretations are, however, rare rather than commonplace. Goldmann maintains that 'primitive and premature efforts to offer policy advice demonstrate concern with policy, but also a lack of concern with the serious business of creating cumulative knowledge'. There is every reason to fear that the present preoccupation with relevance can and will call forth such a one-sided concern with policy.

It has not been my intention to suggest that Nordic political science faces disintegration. True, Nordic political science is pluralistic in outlook. But so is political science almost everywhere the discipline is practised. However, I do intend to draw attention to the fact that trends towards disintegration are discernible, and that they have been brought about by efforts to involve political science in an ongoing battle to raise the policy relevance of science. These efforts are, to my mind, based on a misunderstanding of the task of political science. It is the task of the discipline to advance social betterment. But this must be done through mechanisms of enlightenment, not by way of engineering and problem-solving. Political science offers criticism, not advice.

NOTES

1 This is a revision of a paper originally presented at Espoo, Helsinki, October 1985 and subsequently published in the *International Political Science Review* (1987).
2 This is not a reference to the chair originally held by Wexonius nor, in fact, to the same university. Åbo Academy was destroyed in 1827 in a devastating town fire, and the university was later moved to Helsinki. In 1918, on private initiative, a new university, also called Åbo Academy, was founded in Åbo.
3 Readers interested in the achievements of Nordic political science are advised to study volume 12 of the *Scandinavian Political Studies Yearbook* (Oslo: Universitets forlaget, 1977) which contains several stocktaking reports on political science research in the Nordic countries as well as a cumulative bibliography of the research literature of 1960-75. There are only a few special monographs on the subject; Nordic political scientists have not devoted much research interest to their own intellectual history. Finland has perhaps been most active in this field: there are, for instance, two monographs by Kari Palonen (1978, 1980) dealing with the history and centre–periphery relations in Finnish political science, and there is a recent collection of essays, sponsored by the Finnish Political Science Association, dealing with the learning history of Finnish political science (Nousiainen and Anckar, 1983). These Finnish contributions are, however, available in the Finnish language only. A wealth of data on developments in Swedish political science are reported in a Swedish project on postgraduate education (Johansson 1980); however, the analysis is scanty and preliminary. There is also a recent evaluation of Swedish political science undertaken by two non-Swedish scholars (Eliassen and Pedersen 1984). The main report from this project as well as connected papers are, at least for the time being, available in Scandinavian languages only.
4 The figures are calculated from the IPSA Secretary-General's *Three Year Report 1979-82*, discussed at the IPSA council meeting in Rio de Janeiro, 8 August 1982.
5 The calculations are based on information provided in *Participation* (IPSA Newsletter), Special Issue, 1984, 8(2). The issue presents the detailed programme of the Paris Congress.
6 A personal professorship in international politics (Yrjö Ruutu) was established at the Yhteiskunnallinen Korkeakoulu (Helsinki) in 1948.

REFERENCES

Albaek, E. (1984) 'Ny-marxismen i dansk statskundskab', paper presented to the 7th Nordic Political Science Congress, Lund, 20-22 August 1984.

Allardt, E. (1981) 'Stein Rokkan om politikens makroföreteelser', *Statsvetenskaplig Tidskrift* 4; 1: 87-92.

Allardt, E. and Ståhlberg, K. (1983) 'Social sciences', in *Finnish-American Academic and Professional Exchanges: Analyses and Reminiscences*, pp. 49-53, Espoo: Foundation for Research in Higher Education and Science Policy and United States Educational Foundation in Finland.

Anckar, D. (1973) Dissertationer i finsk statskunskap: anteckningar kring en bibliografisk forteckning: Meddelanden från Institutet för samhällsforskning, Åbo Akademi, Series B: 24.

— (1976) 'Kommunalpolitik – vad det är och vad det inte är', *Kunnallistieteellinen*

Aikakauskirja 1:5-22.

— (1977) 'Political science in Finland 1960-75: from behaviouralism to policy analysis', *Scandinavian Political Studies Yearbook* 12, pp. 105-26, Oslo: Universitetsforlaget.

Berglund, S. and Lindström: (1978) *The Scandinavian Party System(s)*, Lund: Studentlitteratur.

Dahl, R.A. (1961) 'The behavioural approach in political science: epitaph for a monument to a successful protest', *The American Political Science Review* 4: 763-72.

ECPR (1980) A *Decade of International Training in the Social Sciences*, Essex Summer Schools in Social Science Data Analysis 1968-78, European Consortium for Political Research.

Eliassen, K.A. and Pedersen, M.N. (1984) *Svensk samhällsorganisation och fövaltning: En inventering av svensk forskning*, Uppsala: Humanistisk-samhällsvetenskapliga forskning srädet.

Elander, N. (1977) 'The growth of the profession 1960-75: Sweden, *Scandinavian Political Studies Yearbook* 12:75-82, Oslo: Universitetsforlaget.

— (1980) *Skandinavisk arbetarrörelse*, Stockholm: Liber Förlag.

Goldmann, K. (1979) 'Concern and cumulation: a note on research strategy', *Cooperation and Conflict* 4:255-9.

Goldmann, K. and Sjöstedt, G. (eds) (1979) *Power, Capabilities, Interdependence*, London: Sage.

Grimsson, O. (1977) 'Pioneering political science: the case of Iceland', *Scandinavian Political Studies Yearbook* 12: 47-63, Oslo: Universitetsforlaget.

Heiskanen, I. and Hänninen, S. (eds) (1983) *Exploring the Basis of Politics*, Tampere: Finnish Political Science Association.

Jansson, J.-M. (1966) 'Defining political science: some basic reflections', *Scandinavian Political Studies Yearbook* 1:13-24, New York and London: Columbia University Press.

Johansson, L. (1980) 'Forskning om politik', En studie av doktorsavhandlingarna i statskunskap 1890-1975' Delrapport 6 inom UHÄ-projektet Forskarutbildningens resultat 1890-1975.

Kuhnle, S. and Rokkan, S. (1977) 'The growth of the profession: Norway', *Scandinavian Political Studies Yearbook* 12:65-73, Oslo: Universitetsforlaget.

Lundquist, L. (1982) *The Party and the Masses: An Inter-Organizational Analysis of Lenin's Model for the Bolshevik Revolutionary Movement*, Stockholm: Almqvist and Wiksell International.

Nannestad, P. (1977) 'The growth of a profession: political science in Denmark 1960-75'; *Scandinavian Political Studies Yearbook* 12:13-27, Oslo Universitetsforlaget.

Nilsson, S.S. (1984) 'Stein Rokkans verk: Fortsettelse av en tradisjon, formidling av tradisjoner, opphav til tradisjon (er)', paper presented to the 7th Nordic Political Science Congress, Lund, 20-22 August 1984.

Nousiainen, J. (1983) 'Valtio-opillisen tutkimuksen behavioraalinen murros', In *Valtio ja yhteiskunta*, pp. 179-224, Juva: Werner Söderström Osakeyhtiö.

Nousiainen, J. and Anckar, D. (eds) (1983) *Valtio ja yhteiskunta*, Juva: Werner Söderström Osakeyhtiö.

Nurmi, H. (1984) 'Michael Olai Wexonius and sixteenth century European political thought', paper presented to the 7th Nordic Political Science Congress, Lund, 20-22 August 1984.

Nygren, B. (1984) *Fredlig samexistens: klasskamp, fred och samarbete. Sovjetunionens*

200 Dag Anckar

detente-doktrin, Swedish Institute of Affairs, Research Report 12, Stockholm.

Olsen, J.P. (1984) 'Nyinstitusjonalismen og statsvitenskapen', plenary paper presented to the 7th Nordic Political Science Congress, Lund, 20-22 August 1984.

Paloheimo, H. (1979) 'Tiedepolitiikan koulukunnat', *Turun Yliopisto, Politiikan tutkimuksen ja sosiologian laitos, Valtio-opillisia tutkimuksia*, Sarja A. 36, Turku.

Palonen, K. (1978) 'Politiikan tutkimuksen esteet ja mahdollisuudet valtio-opissa', *Helsingin Yliopiston yleisen valtio-opin laitoksen tutkimuksia*, Sarja A. 48, Helsinki.

— (1980) 'Politiikan ja valtion käsitteiden kriiseistä suomalaisen valtio-opin historiassa', *Jyväskylän Yliopisto, Valtio-opin laitos*, Julkaisuja 39, Jyväskylä.

(1984) 'Ungleichzeitigkeiten zwischen Zentrum und Peripherie', paper presented to the 7th Nordic Political Science Congress, Lund, 20-22 August 1984.

Ruin, O. (1977) 'Political science research in Sweden 1960-75: an overview', *Scandinavian Political Studies Yearbook* 12:157-84, Oslo: Universitetsforlaget.

Susiluoto, I. (1981) 'The origins and development of systems thinking in the Soviet Union', *Annales Academiae Scientiarum Fennicae: Dissertationes Humanarum Litterarum* 30, Helsinki.

Tarschys, D. (1971) *Beyond the State: The Future Polity in Classical and Soviet Marxism*, Stockholm: Läromedelsförlagen.

Vanhanen, T. (1984) *The Emergence of Democracy*, Commentationes Scientiarum Socialium 24, Ekenäs: Societas Scientiarum Fennica.

Vourinen, J. and Heikkonen, I. (1983) 'The implementation of Finnish-American academic and professional exchanges', in *Finnish-American Academic and Professional Exchanges: Analyses and Reminiscenses*, pp. 24-39, Espoo: Foundation for Research in Higher Education and Science Policy and United States Educational Foundation in Finland.

Wiseman, V. (1969) *Politics: The Master Science*, New York: Pegasus.

9 Political science in contemporary Spain

An Overview

Josep M. Vallès

INTRODUCTION

The first attempt at liberal political organization in Spain took place in the period 1810-14: contemporary Spanish politics can be said to date from that time. Since then, the history of Spanish politics has been one of rupture and discontinuity.

The instability of the model of political organization meant permanent and deep disagreement about how this model could gain legitimacy. Both the lack of continuity in Spain's political institutions and the ongoing controversy about how to justify conflicting projects had strong repercussions on the conceptual definition of politics, on the official position of political studies and, finally, on the development of political science itself.

Therefore, we will briefly trace the evolution of political studies, identifying their sociopolitical context, the main subjects examined and approaches used, and the leading authors of every stage. Four major periods of Spanish history will be analyzed. Though the dividing of history into periods is always open to discussion, it is even more arguable when attempts are made to combine events and scientific and cultural movements in specific categories. Although this approach certainly raises important problems, it is nonetheless useful in a preliminary approach to our subject here.

We have deliberately limited our scope to a description of the situation in Spain, with no attempt to make a theoretical or comparative study of the development of political science as a discipline. The current state of political science in Spain and the available bibliography are such that it is difficult to advance much beyond this descriptive stage, although inevitably there will be explanatory hypotheses and references to a more general model of the discipline.

A final remark: On many occasions, I have deliberately used the term 'political studies' and avoided reference to 'political science'. I feel that the broader term is more suitable when attempting to trace the historical evolution of the field in Spanish context. I have pinpointed the moment at which one can legitimately refer to political science as such, regardless — or in spite of — the official denominations given to these studies at the time.

The following periods will be briefly examined: 1 1810-98: political studies and the struggle to legitimize the Liberal State; 2 1898-1939: political studies and the crisis of liberal democracy; 3 1940-75: political studies under a conservative dictatorship: from 'political doctrine' to 'political science'; and 4 1975- : political studies and the new democratic regime.

Each period is relatively long and could be divided into subperiods, to which I will refer when necessary. If feel, however, that the subject will be more readily understandable at this point if we take contemporary history as divided into longer and more general periods.

1810-1898: POLITICAL STUDIES AND THE STRUGGLE TO LEGITIMIZE THE LIBERAL STATE

During the nineteenth century the Spanish Liberal State remains a fragile organization.[2] It was struggling against the diehards of the Ancien Régime, and was simultaneously under pressure from radical democrats anxious to turn liberalism into democracy. This resulted in three civil wars in less than a century.

Political studies of the time mirror the Liberal State's problems in gaining its legitimacy. This fact can explain the ambiguous position of these studies, carried out by faculties (graduate schools) of law, but not very juristic in nature or approach.

Politics were studied as part of legal philosophy or of political law. When they were a part of legal philosophy, emphasis was put on political and social theory, with a strong ethical accent. When they were examined in courses of political law, the emphasis was on the history of political institutions. It is important to remember that until quite recently political law (*Derecho Politico*) in Spain was the official name for what in most Western countries was known as 'constitutional law'.[3]

The reason for this can be traced back to the already mentioned weak position of the Spanish Liberal State of the nineteenth century, and can be interpreted as the result of a compromise between the partisans of absolutism, who refused to accept constitutional law as a typical liberal outcome, and the moderate or middle-of-the-road version of liberalism, which finally prevailed over more radical positions.[4]

Political law during these years was given nearly encyclopedic status in order to express three approaches: philosophical, historical, and legal, combined with any of the authors and schools (Portero 1980). Three relatively different tendencies can, however, be traced. The first was inspired by German-speaking legal historicism. Works by Savigny, Bluntschli, and Stahl were translated and used in university courses. Its political orientation was clearly conservative and occasionally downright anti-liberal. E. Gil Robles (d.1908),[5] a Catholic professor of political law, was its leading representative.

The second school, or tendency, was the so-called 'Krausism', which developed an organicist social theory rooted in Kantian philosophy.[6] Some of the Krausist oriented scholars showed in their analysis of political problems a partly socio-economic slant. Critical of the existing situations, the Krausist political stance was basically democratic. Among its representatives or sympathizers, we can mention G. de Azcarate (1840-1917)[7] and J. Costa (1846-1911).[8]

Finally, a third orientation — highly eclectic — paid more attention to the legal aspects of organized politics, but without a clear stance for the public law theory of positivistic orientation, whose theoretical bases were being built up in Europe. Its political orientation fitted within the framework of the moderate liberalism prevalent at that time. M. Colmeiro (1818-94),[9] as an early and influential professor of political law and, later, V. Santamaria de Paredes (1853-1924),[10] can be considered as the better known representatives of this tendency.

Thus political studies at the university level[11] were never completely appropriated by constitutional or positivistic public law as they were in other countries, where law was seen as the main ground upon which the Liberal State established its legitimacy. But neither did 'social positivism' flourish, as a viable alternative. Krausism — in which social aspects of politics were emphasized — could have been close to some kind of social positivism, if it had not been by definition openly dependent on a humanistic moral philosophy.

Some historians consider that Spain at the end of the nineteenth century was only an unfinished Liberal State in both political and economic terms, unable to shape the academic and intellectual structure that could legitimize the very existence of its political organization. This situation became increasingly more complicated when, at the turn of the century, the most powerful European countries began re-examining their liberal constitutionalism in the light of the radical changes taking place in their economies, politics, and culture.

1898-1939: POLITICAL STUDIES AND THE CRISIS OF LIBERAL DEMOCRACY

Historical background

During the final decade of the nineteenth century, a number of movements and events took place that marked the beginning of a new period in Spanish history. The Spanish-American War of 1898, which brought about the loss of the last Spanish colonies (Cuba, Puerto Rico, and the Philippines) and moved forward a deep social and cultural crisis, is taken as a conventional milestone in Spanish contemporary history. In this new period, which lasted from the beginning of the century until the Civil War of 1936-9, the Spanish political system was in a permanent state of crisis, made worse by European doubts about democratic liberalism after World War One. Political studies were influenced by this general atmosphere.

Development and orientation of political studies

The three tendencies mentioned above — conservative historicism, Krausist social organicism, and eclectic legal positivism — were still in evidence in the 1898-1939 period. But they became less clearly defined when exposed to influences of intellectual trends in other European countries, which were then facing the crisis of individualistic liberalism. Changes were introduced in the academic bylaws governing the course of studies, and a new discipline, administrative law, appeared as a distinct discipline separated from political law, a decision that would affect the development and orientation of political studies of the time. The leading representative of this new situation, when differences between tendencies or schools became less clear, is A. Posada (1860-1944).[12]

Professor of political law, prolific author and the guiding light of a number of journals and publications, Posada was far and away the most active and influential academic of the time in the social and political studies area. Though Posada had his roots in Krausism, his approach to political studies, under the traditional label of political law, was influenced by contemporary constitutionalists, sociologists and even by some of the early authors of US political science.[13]

Posada affirmed that it was impossible to analyse constitutional law without applying a Theory of the State which had a definite sociological slant. 'Theory of the State', he wrote, 'can be considered to be a political sociology' (1915:1,55). As a consequence, political law was for Posada a combination of theory of the state and constitutional law, backed by political sociology.

Latter day observers disagree about the value of Posada's approach, with its broad focus and its somewhat eclectic refusal to give a more precise definition to what in other countries were already becoming autonomous disciplines. Some feel that it is this very broad eclecticism that gives Posada's position its value because it sacrifices none of the facets which are present when politics are manifested in society (Ollero 1955). However, others feel that this broad approach is at the roots of the scientific weakness of an academic denomination — political law — which they feel is a juxtaposition of disciplines which has made it impossible to develop constitutional law and political science as clearly defined independent disciplines (Rubio Llorente 1973).

Posada's attempts to redefine the contents of political law came just as Spain began receiving the impact of the trends reflected in the legal-political studies of a Europe where the institutions and the legitimacy basis of the Liberal State were in crisis. This also was a time of cultural ferment in Spain when, after centuries of isolation, the country was wide open to the influence of scientific and cultural trends from abroad.[14] This is how G. Jellinek's revision of legal positivism,[15] M. Hauriou's neo-Thomistic-inspired institutionism,[16] H. Kelsen's normativism[17] and also H. Laski's[18] social — and social-democratic — approach to politics made their way into Spanish university circles.

Nevertheless, none of these trends had a predominant or decisive influence. They served in some way to increase the scientific perplexity of Spanish scholars, fully aware that the liberal system, which had never been solidly implanted in their country, was now in a state of general crisis. This was dramatically underscored by the military uprising of 1936 against the Republic and the subsequent Civil War of 1936-9, which led to a lengthy conservative dictatorship.

Conclusion

During the 1898-1939 period, there were no major alterations in the institutional position of political studies, which continued to be attached to the faculties of law. Emphasis on the 'non-juridical' approach increased to a certain point. And this fact underscored a paradoxical state of affairs: the institutional relationship with the faculties of law coexisted with an increasing reluctance of the so-called 'political law' to accept a strictly legal approach to the issues it entailed.

The crisis of the Liberal State and the openly declared loss of confidence in the ability of law to settle social conflicts in the interwar period in Europe probably exerted a decisive influence, when Spanish scholars of political law generally refused to assimilate their discipline to a strictly juristic one. This reluctance failed to produce a clear cut alternative, as no other global proposal was strong enough — perhaps for institutional reasons, perhaps for lack of historical opportunity, or of an outstanding personality — to relocate political studies in a different institutional stage or to view them under a new light.

1940-75: POLITICAL STUDIES UNDER A CONSERVATIVE DICTATORSHIP: FROM 'POLITICAL DOCTRINE' TO 'POLITICAL SCIENCE'

Historical background

The military victory of the conservative alliance led by General Franco had long and important effects on Spanish political and social organization. A new political cycle which lasted nearly forty years began in 1939. However, if we follow the country's social and economic evolution, we perceive that this political cycle contains the succession of two great periods. At the beginning of the 1960s, Spanish society underwent deep mutations: general industrialization, urban expansion, cultural secularization, and mass education. We could say that there is a greater distance between the Spain of 1950 and the Spain of 1970 than between the Spain of 1850 and the Spain of 1950.

It is not easy to summarize and read the evolution of this period, as we still lack historical perspective. But it can be admitted that such changes had a clear impact on scientific and cultural fields, including social and political studies.

Orientation and development of political studies

In which way did Civil War and a dictatorial system of government affect political studies? We must differentiate the two great periods which we have just referred to.

1 In the first stage of the period, which continues till the end of the 1950s, the direct impact of the new political situation on political studies is very visible.

(a)   From an institutional perspective, one must first point out the rigid control exercised by the Francoist regime over scientific and academic institutions, especially those which affected the mechanisms of social and political legitimation.

First of all and as a direct outcome of this control, many of the authors and professors active in the previous period disappeared physically or professionally, either obliged to leave the country or condemned to intellectual exile in their own country, as they suffered imprisonment, expulsion from the university, or were relegated to secondary posts.

Second, we observe an attempt to systematize and diffuse an official 'political doctrine', in the style of the Nazi or Fascist ideology. With that aim in mind, *nacionalisindicalismo* or *doctrina del Movimiento Nacional* was introduced as an academic subject in the programmes of university faculties and other education centres.

This attempt did not altogether succeed, because of the varied ideological support — conservative Catholicism, the Falange local version of Fascism, traditional monarchism, etc. — of General Franco's dictatorship and also because of the pragmatism of the dictator himself, who was not eager to adhere to any theoretical construction which tended to be too complex.

But this rather elementary ideological project was important in another aspect: the creation of new institutions primarily devoted to the elaboration and diffusion of the official doctrine, namely the Instituto de Estudios Políticos (1941) and the Facultad de Ciencias Políticas y Económicas in the University of Madrid (1943).

Outside the university system, the Instituto de Estudios Políticos was regarded as an organism devoted to research and teaching of political studies. The Instituto was directly attached to the only authorized party — Falange Española — and its minor associated groups. The function of the Instituto was to bring about doctrinal support for the new regime as a contribution to its intellectual legitimation. As I will point out further on, the Instituto has had an important role in the later evolution of political studies in Spain.

The Facultad de Ciencias Políticas y Económicas in Madrid was the first university centre which had as a direct objective the formation of graduates in politics and economics, who would act as a future elite of state servants, either through public administration or through the political apparatus of the regime.

From this moment on, studies on political subjects developed simultaneously in the law faculties and in the new faculty in Madrid, which for almost forty years was the only university centre devoted to political disciplines.[19]

Even so, the naming of the chairs and courses related to political studies still lacked explicit reference to political science. In the faculties of law, the traditional *Derecho Político* (political law) went on being used. In the new faculty of political sciences, different labels were successively employed. When special faculties of economics were created in the late 1950s, *Teoría del Estado* (state theory) was to be the official name of a course on politics. Finally in 1973, after a studies reform, a course entitled 'Introduction to Political Science' appeared in the Madrid Faculty of Political Sciences.

(b) Focusing on content, political studies after the Civil War were centred on the crisis of the liberal-democratic state, moreover of the state as political organization, both at a national level — Francoism also spoke about the need for a *Nuevo Estado* — and at an international one. But this confirmation of rupture did not lead to new paths. It led to the readoption of two already well-known approaches.

The first was a critical attitude to legal positivism, following the work of two German scholars who for different reasons had been known in Spain in the immediate years prior to the Civil War: C. Schmitt's decisionism[20] and H. Heller's sociological approach.[21] In spite of their different political stances, both authors helped to stress the view of political studies as a 'theory of the state' — or of its crisis.

The second was the reinforcement of the axiological emphasis of conservative Catholicism, inspired by the moral and political philosophy of Thomas Aquinas and the Spanish authors of the seventeenth century (Vitoria, Soto, Báñez, Suárez, Molina), whose influence was emphasized by the highly nationalistic thrust of the Franco regime.

In an official climate that refused liberal democracy and far from any positivistic legal approach (which had no object of its own in a political system without formal constitution), political studies wavered between two poles. On one side, a political theory — or state theory

— of a relatively 'sociologistic' character and often compatible with the justification of an authoritarian political system. On the other side, the moral-philosophical approximation of the Catholic natural law. Among the most representative authors of this moment, we must mention F.J. Conde,[22] I. de Lojendio[23] and E. Gomez Arboleya.[24]

We should also add — in a transition towards the next period — the names of L. Sanchez Agesta[25] and C. Ollero,[26] who would gradually import some elements of the political analysis that was being carried out in the United States and in Western Europe. Their lasting position as active professors of political law until the early 1970s gave them the chance to act as a bridge between the old tradition and the new developments that we shall observe from the middle 1960s.

(c) As I have already pointed out, a feature of continuity with the pre-Civil War period could be the mistrust for legal positivism, and — except for the Catholic iusnaturalism — this tradition gives way to the sceptical approach of 'realist political theory'.

But this permanent refusal to entertain a legal approach to politics meant an alternative approach could not be openly assumed, as it was in other Western European countries where the well-established school of US political science was received after World War Two as a substitute for the legal positivism approach to politics.

With some exceptions,[28] this general exposure to mainstream political science of the 1940s and early 1950s did not occur till a later date, when some of its dominant currents had already run into crisis. How can this fact be explained?

A first and general reason may lie in the isolation endured by the Spanish academic world, as a result of the estranged relationship that intellectual circles of Western countries had with general Franco's dictatorship after World War Two.

A second reason could be the difficulty of applying specific tools of a positive political analysis to a system that openly denied freedom for public political opinion and action, concealing its decision-making process to those who intended any kind of empirical approach.

Finally, we should not forget the traditional weakness of social positivism, be it due to a lack of research resources and organization, or to a preference for a more theoretical and philosophical approach.

2 The situation outlined above was partially modified towards the end of the 1960s, when Spanish society came under important social and economic changes. At that moment, it was important for the regime to add modernization to its military triumph of 1939 in order to legitimize its actions.

The para-Fascist and/or Catholic conservative ideologists were gradually replaced by technocrats (economists and engineers) not bothered about formal ideology, and given over to the launching so-called 'social and economic development plans'. Repercussions of these changes can be seen in different ways.

(a)   First, greater recognition of social sciences in general began from two different standpoints: because social sciences were regarded as auxiliary tools to a 'developmentalist' official policy, but also because they were seen as giving the conceptual basis for a critical opposition to the political regime. Economics and sociology stood out as 'fashionable' disciplines, producing an increase in the number of new faculties of economics, chairs of these disciplines, and public and private research centres.

(b)   Second, contacts and exchanges with the international scientific community increased, opening the door to the great trends in social sciences: logical positivism, functionalism, neo-Marxism, behavourism (which till that moment had had a marginal presence in the Spanish scientific community). This opening up also meant that greater numbers of Spanish graduates and scholars travelled abroad, especially to France and the United States, to extend their education in social sciences.

3 Specifically what happened with political studies?

(a)   First of all, political studies benefited from the global movement of attention to the processes of social and economic change: these gains refer to a relative rise on the institutional side, to a closer relationship with the international state of the discipline, and to a meaningful increase in the number of Spanish scholars with specialized political science training in foreign universities.

(b)   Concerning content, political studies began to receive the varied influence of theories and approaches currently prevailing in other Western countries,[29] which relegated the normative outlines of the previous period to marginal positions. In an attempt to group the general tendencies, we list the following orientations:
    The study of foreign political systems, with a fundamentally institutional approach and a 'realistic' kind of constitutional analysis, not applicable to the Spanish political regime of the day.[30] Two names must be mentioned because of their influence: M. Garcia Pelayo[31] and M. Jimenez de Parga.[32] A second orientation was the reception of critical theory and neo-Marxist political analysis (Gramsci, French Marxism-structuralism, Anglo-American New Left) in state and social theory studies, based upon the concept of conflict and class antagonism. In this area, one of the most well-known figures is E. Tierno Galvan,[33] among a set of younger scholars (R. Morodo, J. A. Gonzalez-Casanova, J. Sole-Tura).
    Finally, there arose a more clearly oriented political science approach, grounded upon current concepts and interpretative frameworks of American and European political science. F. Murillo Ferrol,[34] J.J. Linz[35] and P. Lucas Verdu[36] must be mentioned here, in spite of their differences of emphasis and orientation. Murillo and

Linz have also been pioneers in undertaking empirical research about social and economic aspects of the Spanish society, when politics continued to be a risky research subject.

However, these three groups cannot be considered as totally closed: the connections between one another are quite frequent, as when some of them are able to receive more than one influence and to develop more than one approach.

This diversity of tendencies fits into the official denominations of 'political law' and 'state theory'. Under these two official labels, programmes of these courses could alternatively include, for example, political theory and the history of political ideas, Marxist state theory, comparative government or Spanish social structure analysis. This enabled a well-known professor to define political law of this period as a 'hydra of many heads and a universal master card'.[37]

Conclusion

We could conclude that the 'prehistory' of political science ended sometime between 1960 and 1975, when political studies in Spain started to approach the main trends of the field in the Western scientific community.[38] Yet political science as an autonomous discipline did not manage to define clearly a scientific and institutional position that would have given it decisive legitimation within the field of social sciences.

A first reason for this relative frailty may be found in the diversity of theoretical definition of the discipline, once behaviourism ceased to be the identification signpost that, for good or bad, had existed until the early 1960s. This situation gave way to an increase of perplexity among Spanish latecomers to the discipline. This lack of self confidence was reinforced by the fact that political studies were still predominantly attached to the faculties of law and economics, where the traditional concepts of political law or state theory determined the faculty recruitment system of public competition (*concurso-oposición*).[39]

A second factor was probably dependent on the political environment. I have already pointed out that social sciences became, during the 1960s and throughout the early 1970s, instruments for socio-economic modernization, but also weapons for radical criticism and socio-political opposition. While certain economics and sociology approaches could analyse Spanish reality bordering on the fringe of the vetoed territory of political affairs, political science found greater difficulty in reaching its own object, to which it had to refer through allusions or comparisons, either with other countries' systems, or with Spanish historical past.[40] This ban on important contemporary political subjects could also explain the paradoxical fact that some of the best academic (strictly non-political) sociology was being developed by political law scholars: many of today's best known sociologists started their careers in political law or state theory departments and chairs.

A third motive could be found in the narrow field offered for professional alternatives, in other words, the lack of social legitimation of the political scientist. In other countries, two major professional fields — together with research and university teaching — have been opened to political scientists: public administration and high school teaching. In Spain, political science has not gained access to secondary education, partly because of political control reasons, partly because of the traditional position of history and geography teachers. On the other hand, political scientists have not been significantly incorporated into public administration, still under the hegemony of lawyers and, as a new and recent development, of a growing number of economists. Because of the professional orientation of Spanish university education, political studies, lacking sufficient professional impact, did not obtain a clear cut social legitimation, thus also affecting the academic situation of the discipline.

A final reason may be found in the institutional weakness of political science, regarding teaching and research. We have already mentioned the fact that only two publicly supported bodies, the Instituto and the Facultad in Madrid, have been till very recently the exclusive centres specifically devoted to political studies. The refusal of the Franco education authorities to increase the number of political studies institutions was clearly based on negative experience of these two existing centres, which paradoxically became a focal point of opposition to the regime.

The situation impaired, in my opinion, the diffusion and strengthening of both the discipline and the profession, when in dialogue with other scientific and institutional actors, within the university itself, with public administration bodies and with other social actors like the media, the non-profit making organization or the business community. In this respect, the contrast with other social disciplines like economics or sociology is remarkable.[41]

1975— : POLITICAL STUDIES AND THE DEMOCRATIC REGIME

Political background

The death of General Franco in 1975 expressed the political exhaustion of the dictatorship and forecast democratic changes demanded by three main factors: the needs of the economic and social system, the aspirations of a majority sector of the elites (economic, intellectual, working, professional) and the pressures coming from countries such as the US and Federal Germany, both with important strategic and/or economic interests in contemporary Spain.

The so-called 'political transition' resulted from an agreement between reformist sectors of the Franco regime and the leaders of democratic opposition parties, clandestine trade unions and nationalist (Catalan and Basque) movements. The 1978 Constitution legally records this transaction, carried out without political banning. But, although the state services (army, police, courts, high civil servants) have been left intact, the political class has been largely renewed by the recognition of party pluralism and open competition.

Thus, democracy has opened new perspectives for political studies, as access to opinions and decisions of political actors became relatively easier. At the same time this smooth transition from dictatorship to democracy has become an attractive subject for foreign and national political scientists.

Development and orientation of political studies

How have political studies evolved under the new political situation? We will examine the institutional and more substantial aspects of this evolution.

From an institutional point of view, I want to point out circumstances that can be interpreted as signs of a somewhat better position of the discipline. These circumstances are related to the university status of political science, the organisation of the teaching profession and the publishing activity.

With regard to the university status of political science, two facts must be mentioned, that can lead to a balanced conclusion:

In 1985, the Faculty of Madrid lost its monopoly, when two new faculties were created: at the Universitat Autònoma de Barcelona and at the UNED (Open University). The creation of a third was announced. As teaching seems to be an important factor towards the consolidation of the discipline, this greater institutional presence of political science studies at the university level can be seen as a positive step towards a stronger position.

On the other hand, a general university reform established by a University Reform Act (1983) implies the revision of programmes leading to university degrees. In this process, the presence of different disciplines in every one of the graduate studies administered by the faculties is now being discussed.

As far as political science is concerned, its old and relatively solid *de facto* position in many faculties of law is now being seriously threatened. The present trend points towards its traditional position being exclusively occupied by the expanding faculties of constitutional law. Thus, there is a risk that the institutional locus of political science might be limited to the faculties of political science and sociology. Given the minority situation of these faculties with regard to the large number of faculties of law, what may be gained in scientific coherence may mean a loss in institutional and personal resources.

Recent developments in teaching are as follows:

In 1978, an association was created that gathered all political law, political science and theory of state professors and associate professors of the Spanish universities. The name of the association — a member of IPSA — is Asociación Española de Ciencia Política y Derecho Constitucional (an expression of a still undecided borderline inside the profession). The goal of the association is scientific discussion, but this is limited to an annual conference and workshops. There are no professional formal aims, as university teachers are state civil servants, with a general and rigid recruiting system and status.

Nevertheless, one of the provisions of the University Reform Act (1983) establishes the organization of university teachers by scientific areas, whose names have been imposed by the education authorities. In our field, old labels such as Derecho Político or Teoría del Estado have been replaced by two new 'scientific areas': Derecho Constitucional and Ciencia Política y de la Administración.

The education authorities have taken the responsibility of solving, with an administrative decision, the old scientific debate about the nature of 'political law'. Professors assigned to this traditional discipline have therefore been forced to choose between the two new areas. The result of this choice has been that those choosing the option of Derecho Constitucional outnumber those who opted for Ciencia Política y de la Administración, in a proportion of about four to one.[42]

Many of those who opted for 'constitutional law' had mainly worked in the fields of political theory, comparative government, or political behaviour. Their personal decision has come about, in many cases, as a tactical answer to needs related to the recruiting processes for new teachers. Thus, the result of the dynamics opened up by this event is still to be seen.

Another important fact has been the stronger connection of Spanish political scientists with the international academic community, by means of their scientific cooperation in joint research projects with foreign scholars interested in Spanish politics or by means of their more active participation in international bodies such as IPSA or ECPR. This can help the Spanish profession reinforce its identity.

Referring to publishing, there are new journals devoted to political studies, and new book collections, which gather original works by Spanish authors, and translations of classical and recent foreign works.[43]

Concerning content, some facts and trends related to political studies must be pointed out.

The first is the push given to the legal approach to politics, due to the importance which the interpretation and implementation of the new Constitution of 1978 have received. After nearly half a century without a formal object of analysis, the legitimation of political processes grounded on legal norms acquires an outstanding importance. As a side result, the labour market has considerably increased its offer to specialists in constitutional law. This a partial explanation of the previously quoted consitutionalistic 'conversion' of some erstwhile political scientists.[44]

In the context of the historic development of political studies, it could be said that there is now a better definition of two different forms of political analysis. In this sense, I would affirm that the reappearance of constitutional law as a strong scientific discipline favours better delimitation of the political science field, relieving it of the complicated exercises of self-definition to which I referred before.

The second important fact is the intellectual and political curiosity stirred, in Spain and abroad, by the working of the new democratic institutions and the issue of continuity and change in the country's political culture and its agents and expressions: political parties, unions and interest groups, elections, local government, political attitudes, etc. And, as an important element of the Spanish political scene, the phenomenon of nationalism, its origins, forms and performance also gains special relevance. From a 'scientific division of labour' point of view, these subjects are being worked on, not only by political scientists coming from the old political law chairs and departments, but also by a sector of sociologists which regard political facts as an object of analysis without the risks or limitations suffered in the previous period.

In this way, sharing — or fighting for — the new political reality as a scientific subject can revive in Spain the old debate about the respective identities of political science and political sociology.

The strongly 'ethnocentred' focus of today's Spanish political science stands out at a first glance. The attention given to the country's political evolution in recent years has relegated other fields and subjects to a minor position. As a result, research has been mainly focused on topics such as the process of political transition, electoral system and electoral behaviour, political parties, political attitudes and opinions and nationalism, among others.[45]

The theoretical framework on which these analyses are based is often unstable. The critical theory trend, inspired by a neo-Marxist approach, which developed spectacularly in the years immediately before the democratic transition, has lost its momentum, with the exception of the work of some marginal sectors or individuals.

In the analysis of the transition process, studies of political culture and public opinion lean upon a schematic functionalism, with greater or lesser accumulation of historical explanations. Concerning data selection and research techniques, the development of quantitative techniques applied to the analysis of electoral or opinion data is impressive.[46] Contributing to this rapid development, is the swift assimilation by the new democratic regime of political mass-communication, based more on political advertising and audio-visual media than on political parties or social organizations.

Even so, the abundance of opinion studies and polls rarely give way to interesting interpretations, because of the frequent absence or weakness of a previous theoretical framework or sound subsequent exploitation. This is due to the fact that such research often responds more to well-timed reasons of the political market — pre or post electoral polls demanded by parties or media — than to research programmes. Thus, a 'vulgar positivism' prevails, and with it also the risk of identifying political science with the unhappy, and sometimes journalistic, treatment of a specific field such as the analysis of opinion and behaviour.

The 'ethnocentrism' of today's Spanish political science and the limited human and institutional resources of the profession have an immediate and negative effect: Spanish political science has neglected other important subfields, such as formal theory, local and mesogovernments, comparative politics, and policy studies.

Conclusion

The evolution of Spanish political science since 1975 defies easy characterization. In global terms, we can point out as positive aspects: first, the improved political conditions concerning the environment for its development, once a political system based on public freedom and political pluralism seems to be consolidated: second, institutional changes such as the creation of new university faculties and departments, the reorganization of a better defined political science 'profession' and the stronger relationship between Spanish political scientists and their foreign colleagues and the international scientific community.

Political science in Spain also faces some negative factors: first, less favourable general attitudes from public opinion and decision centres towards social sciences, thus largely differing from the situation in the 1950s and 1960s when political science was institutionalized in other Western European countries; second, the absence of widely accepted paradigms which, in other times, gave a feeling of security to the discipline and its followers; and, finally, with regard to political science itself, a weak legitimation in a rather limited labour market, in which it has to compete with stronger corporations such as lawyers, sociologists and even journalists.

A 'BESIEGED POLITICAL SCIENCE'? A PROVISIONAL REMARK BASED ON A COMPARATIVE APPROACH

The position of political science in contemporary Spain must be seen in contrast to the position held by the discipline in other Western societies, where political science evolved according to a relatively common pattern. This pattern may be summarized as follows.

A The emergence of political science as an autonomous discipline can be explained as an effect of two processes, whose results have differently combined under specific social and political conditions.

(a) The first process has to do with the constitution of politics as a subject of intellectual discourse, when the 'social construction of politics' gradually took place in the work of historians, moral philosophers, and lawyers. Political activity began to be intellectually distinguished from socio-economic action, and the world of power started to be shown as distinct from the world of production.

Since then, a 'science of politics' was more or less clearly affirmed, a science that did not necessarily pretend to be the immediate knowledge demanded by the requirements of practical action. So, this intellectual activity which had 'politics' as its subject tended to approach it, with either a prescriptive aim or a descriptive one.

The 'science of politics', mainly developed in Western Europe, had no specific institutional setting: traditional and well established disciplines such as history, law or moral and legal philosophy gave it, for many years, more or less permanent shelter. Its importance was based — more than on institutional grounds — upon the intellectual influence of some individual's work, which was part of a more general social knowledge. When one of these influential authors succeeded in becoming established as a classical source of reference the 'science of politics' acquired a stronger legitimation.

(b) The second process or sequence of events starts with a pragmatic political purpose, when individuals or groups related to academic circles try to influence the political conditions of a society. Their political project is based on the belief that the 'science of politics' — that scientific discourse about politics — is an essential tool for the implementation of their practical project. As a part of it, the organization of specific political studies is seen as an instrument for the advancement and diffusion of political knowledge and, consequently, for the success of their political project.

Academic institutionalization of political studies took place in Italy, France and the United States in the last quarter of the nineteenth century, and Great Britain at the beginning of the twentieth century, when some groups and individuals saw their political societies as lacking a scientific basis for political and administrative action. In this sense, Cesare Alfieri, Emile Boutmy, John Burgess, and the

Webbs appear to be the promoters of political science institutionalization in their countries, as a political answer to a given social and
political situation.

Whether this was an effective answer to these specific situations or
not, the fact is that political science — or political sciences —
gradually became an established academic reference and the identification label for a professional group.

The most successful process of this kind took place in the United
States, from whence it was partially exported after World War Two to
Western European countries. IPSA and the participation of young
European scholars in graduate programmes of US departments of
political science were the main vehicles of this influence, which
combined with local traditions and adapted to the different situations
in each country.

2 Looking now to the Spanish experience, it is not difficult to see
how both processes have historically given very scarce results.

With regard to the first process, Spain has occupied — from the
seventeenth century on — a peripheral position in the social and
cultural development of Western Europe. The social and economic
conditions that in other countries produced the construction of politics
as an object of scientific discourse were hardly present in Spain,
where a strong theological and legal tradition hindered specific
consideration of the new economic and political phenomena.

Spain was reduced to the role of a late recipient of other societies'
intellectual production. No Spanish name can be found among the
classical 'political thinkers' who appear in traditional lists, where not
only central countries — such as France, Germany or Great Britain —
but also others like Italy, have outstanding representatives.

Referring to the second process — institutionalization of political
studies based on the impulse of a political purpose — the unstable
political history of contemporary Spain shows no other formal and
lasting attempts[47] apart from the Facultad de Ciencias Políticas at the
University of Madrid and the Instituto de Estudios Políticos, which
were created by general Franco's authoritarian regime. Because of its
origin and historical timing, both institutions were, for a long period,
unable to give clear and full support to the kind of analysis carried
out by 'standard' political science in other countries.

Thus, the lasting monopolistic position exerted by those two
academic organizations made more difficult the development of the
discipline, blurred its identity among social sciences and limited the
social impact of the profession.

It can be affirmed that in both respects Spain has been a late comer
to the science of politics. And when political science has got a chance
to develop under conditions of free political activity and less traditional academic organization, some of the factors that strengthened
political science in other countries, in Spain seem to have lost their
thrust.

In the last fifteen years, political science in Spain has gradually gained a better position, but the discipline and the profession still show important weaknesses. We would be exaggerating and making a parody of a well know article,[48] to refer to political science as besieged: Spanish political science of the 1980s, has painfully succeeded in conquering a territory of its own, but a number of circumstances (historical, institutional, and scientific) still appear to be reducing its chances for easy and immediate expansion.

NOTES

1 This chapter is a revised version of the paper presented to the International Round Table on the Comparative Study of the Development of the Discipline of Political Science, Cortona, Italy 21-26 September 1987. I would like to thank participants in the Conferences and colleagues of my Department, at the Universitat Autònoma de Barcelona, for their critical comments.

2 In 1810, the traditional Cortes – or Ancien Regime Parliament – was called after centuries of political hibernation. A large part of the country was under the control of Napoleon's army. Napoleon forced the abdication of the Spanish King, Fernando VII, who renounced his rights in favour of Napoleon. But the Spanish Cortes considered this abdication void and without legal effects, declared war against Bonaparte and assumed all political powers as a representation of the free will of the country. The Cortes also decided to write and approve a liberal constitution. This first Constitution of 1812, which remained in force for only a short period is nonetheless considered the starting point of Spain as a liberal state.

3 Montesquieu (*De l'Esprit des Lois* 1, ch 3: 1748); Burlamaqui (*Principes de Droit Politique*, 1751); and Rousseau (*Le Contrat Social: Principes de Droit Politique*, 1762, had used the expression, but not always with the same meaning. They seemed to share the 'enlightened' position: that politics can be submitted to law, as against Ancien Régime political ideas.

4 This label, already used by J. Donoso Cortes (*Lecciones de Derecho Político*, Madrid 1836-7), was still uncertain in the middle forties, as we can see in the title of the textbooks of two influential professors of the time: A. Alcala Galiano (Madrid, 1845), *Veinte lecciones de Derecho Político Constitucional*, and J. F. Pacheco (Madrid, 1845), *Leccoines de Derecho Político Constitucio*,

5 *Tratado de Derecho Político según los Principos de la Filosofía y el Derecho cristiano*, (Salamanca, 1899-1902, 3rd edition).

6 K. H. Krause (1781-1832) and his disciple H. Ahrens (1808-74) were translated and introduced by J. Sanz del Rio (1814-69), philosophy professor at the University of Madrid. His interpretation of Krause's Kantism stressed an ethical approach, producing a loose intellectual system that inspired an active group of scholars and scientists of politically radical and socially reformist orientation. The Institución Libre de Enseñanza, founded in 1876 by F. Giner de los Rios (1839-1915), worked as their institutional basis and had a strong academic and political influence, until the Civil War of 1936-9.

7 Among Azcarate's works, see *El self-government y la Monarquía doctrinaria* (Madrid, 1877); *El Poder del Jefe del Estado en Francia, Inglaterra y los Estados Unidos* (Madrid, 1878); *El régimen parlamentarios en la práctica* (Madrid, 1885);

Relaciones de la política con los problemas económicos (Madrid, 1890); *Tratado de Política* (Madrid, 1897). About Azcárate's position, see Gil Cremades, V. (1967) and J.R. Torregrosa (1964) 'El pensamiento político de don Gumersindo de Azcárate': in *Revista de Estudios Políticos* 135-6: pp. 121-34.

8 Among Joaquín Costa's works, see *Colectivismo Agrario en España* (Madrid, 1898); *Crisis política de España* (Madrid 1901); *Oligarquia y Caciquismo como la actuel forma de gobierno de España* (Madrid 1901-2).

9 *Elementos de Derecho Político y Adminstrativo* (Madrid, 1857); *Derecho Político según la Historia de León y Castilla* (Madrid, 1873).

10 Curso de Derecho Político según la Filosofía Política moderna: la Historia General de España y la legislación vigente (Valencia, 1880-1). This long title is a clear expression of this author's highly eclectic approach, in which political philosophy, history and positive law are jointly considered.

11 Outside the University, political analysis was also carried out by members of scientific and debating societies (*Academias* and *Ateneos*) or in the press. In the work published by some political writers of the day, we often find an approach to political phenomena that takes account of social and economic elements. We should mention, among others, Jaime Balmes (1810-48), Andrés Borrego (1802-91), Francisco Pi y Margall (1824-1901) or Valenti Almirall (1841-1904).

12 As his most representative work, see *Tratado de Derecho Político* (Madrid, 1915, 2nd edition). See also *Principios de Sociología* (Madrid, 1908); *Evolución legislativa del régimen local de España* (Madrid, 1910); *España en crisis: La política* (Madrid 1923); *El régimen constitucional* (Madrid 1930); *La idea pura del Estado* (Madrid 1933); *La crisis del Estado y el Derecho Político* (Madrid, 1934).

13 Among the authors cited by Posada in some of his recommended bibliographies are Spencer, Marx, Durkheim, Gumplowicz, Giddins, Burgess, Wilson, Bryce and Dicey.

14 J. Ortega y Gasset (1883-55), professor of metaphysics at the University of Madrid, is a well-known and representative intellectual figure of this time. His approach to social and political subjects was influenced by contemporary authors such as Pareto, Simmel and Spengler. His *La rebellión de las masas* (1930) was widely translated and diffused in the international academic community.

15 *Teoría General del Estado* (Madrid, 1914). This translation of the *Allgemeine Staatslehere* is due to F. de los Rios, a professor of political law, bred in the Krausist tradition, who evolved towards a non-Marxist socialism. He was an active member of the Socialist Party (PSOE) and one of the writers of the Republican Constitution of 1931.

16 *Principios de Derecho Público y Constitucional* (Madrid, 1927), translated by C. Ruiz del Castillo, a conservative professor of political law.

17 *Compendio de Teoría General del Estado* (Barcelona, 1934); *Teoría General del Estado* (Madrid, 1934). Kelsen's work was introduced by L. Recasens Siches, professor of legal philosophy. Recasens was, however, a critical commentator who opposed a sociological and ethical approach to the Kelsenian 'pure theory of law' and its political consequences.

18 *El Estado moderno: Sus instituciones políticas y economicas* (Barcelona, 1932). This is the Spanish translation of Laski's *A Grammar of Politics*. The translator is T. Gonzalez, professor of political law.

19 Not until 1985 was a second Facultad de Ciencias Políticas opened at the Universidad Autónoma de Barcelona.

20 *La defensa de la Constitución* (Madrid, 1931); *Teoría de la Constitución* (Madrid, 1934); *Escritos Políticos* (translated by J. Conde, Madrid, 1941).

21 *Teoría del Estado* (Mexico, 1942) is the translation of his *Staatslehre* of 1934.

22 *Introducción al Derecho Político actual* (Madrid, 1942); *Representación política y régimen español* (Madrid, 1945). Javier Conde became director of the Instituto de Estudios Políticos (1948-56). During the 1950s, Conde and Gomez Arboleya introduced at the Instituto elements of an empirical approach to social and political studies that would partially develop in the late 1950s and early 1960s.

23 *Régimen político del Estado español* (Barcelona, 1942).

24 Gomez Arboleya, a professor of legal philosophy, is the author of *Historia de la estructura y del pensamiento social* (Madrid, 1959). See also his *Estudios de Teoría de la Sociedad y del Estado* (Madrid, 1962), a collection of essays published between 1940 and 1956, dealing – among other subjects – with Heller's *Staatslehre,* the Spanish political philosophers of the seventeenth century and positivistic sociology in Europe.

25 Lecciones de Derecho Político ('Teoría de la Política y del Estado') (Granada, 1943); *Principios de Teoría Política* (Madrid, 1970).

26 *Introducción al Derecho Político* (Barcelona, 1948); *El Derecho Constitucional de la postquerra* (Barcelona, 1949); *Estudios de Ciencia Política* (Madrid, 1955).

27 T. Fernandez Miranda, *El problema político de nuestro tiempo* (Madrid, 1950); N. Ramiro Rico, *El animal ladino y otros estudios políticos* (Madrid, 1980) is a collection of essays written between 1949 and 1974.

28 The group of scholars, led by Professor Etierno Galvan who, as early as in 1954, edited the *Boletín Informativo del Seminario de Derecho Político de la Universidad de Salamanca* (1954-64), opened a varied range of topics and approaches to political studies.

29 The new academic periodicals enlarged on the more traditional contents of the old *Revista de Estudios Políticos,* published by the Instituto de Estudios Políticos since 1941. See *Boletín Informativo de Ciencia Política* (Madrid, 1969-73), directed by Professor C. Ollero, and *Revista Española de la Opinión Pública* (Madrid, 1964), renamed as Revista Española de Investigaciones Sociologícas (Madrid, 1978).

30 Some foreign influences must be mentioned here. First, the 1954 French reform of law studies, with the inclusion of Institutions Politiques et Droit Constitutionnel and Sociologie Politique, as core or elective courses. The works by French professors of the discipline, like G. Burdeau, M. Duverger and A. Hauriou, were translated in those years. On the other hand, the approach to institutional analysis made by some German-American authors such as C. J. Friedrich and K. Lowenstein also had an influence.

31 Garcia Pelayo, who had left Spain in the early 1950s for political reasons, has been professor of political science in Latin America (México, Puerto Rico, Venezuela). But his work on political theory and comparative politics (mainly based on the study of political institutions and their constitutional frame), has been highly influential among Spanish scholars: see, for instance, *Derecho Constitucional Comparado* (Madrid 1984, 1st edition 1950); *Mitos y Símbolos políticos* (Madrid 1964); *Burocracia y Tecnocracia* (Madrid 1974); *Las transformaciones del Estado contemporaneo* (Madrid, 1977).

32 *Los regímenes políticos contemporáneos* (Madrid, 1960); *Las monarquías europeas en el horizonte español* (Madrid, 1966).

33 See *Introducción a la Sociología* (Madrid, 1961); *Razón mecánica y razón dialéctica* (Madrid, 1964); *Escritos 1950-1960* (Madrid, 1971).

34 Francisco Murillo Ferrol (1918) has been professor of political law at the Universities of Granada, Valencia and Autónoma de Madrid. Among his works, see *Las clases medias españolas* (Granada, 1959); *Estudios de Sociología Política* (Madrid, 1965); *Estructura social de Andalucía* (Alcalá, 1970).

35 Juan J. Linz (1926), in spite of his university career in the United States (Columbia, Yale), has been permanently involved with research and teaching in the Spanish social sciences community, where he has exerted an important influence.

36 *Principios de Ciencia Política* (Madrid, 1969-71, 3 vols); *Curso de Derecho Político* (Madrid 1972-6, 3 vols).

37 Ramiro Rico (1980):105.

38 It is important to stress the fact that two attempts at an appraisal of the Spanish political science of the day were published in the early 1970s: Pastor 1972 and Santamaria 1974, taking as a reference two collective works of different approach and political inspiration: *Estudios de Ciencia Política y Sociología (Libro homenaje al profesor Carlos Ollero)* (Madrid, 1972); and M. Fraga (ed.) *La España de los años setenta: El Estado y la política* (Madrid, 1974).

39 In this respect, the analysis of the reports (*memorias*) that candidates to a chair have to present shows the limits of this situation. In these reports, we find highly refined conceptual exercises in order to make compatible the traditional denominations of political law and state theory, with contents such as political systems analysis, behaviourist research, Marxist social theory, and positive constitutional law.

40 See for instance the studies on the political institutions, pressure groups, parties, and elections of the Second Republic period (1931-6) undertaken in the 1960s and 1970s by young scholars like M. Ramirez, I. Molas, and J. R. Montero, among others.

41 The evolution of the institutional position of sociology is highly significant. Even if sociology had been taught in the Faculty of Political Sciences since its foundaton in 1973, the first specific sociology degrees were given by the University of Madrid. However, sociology studies were not confined to this University as academic sociology also expanded throughout the existence of faculties of economics where a special sociology section existed. This increased the number of teaching positions for sociologists and the number of graduates as well. As a result, sociologists had a stronger feeling of identity already expressed in some 'state of the art and the profession' reports published in the early 1970s. See, for instance: CECA (Confederación Española de Cajas de Ahorros, 1971): *La sociología española de los años setenta*, Madrid: DIS (Departamento de Investigación socioreligiosa de Fomento Social 1971): *Las Ciencias Sociales en España*, Madrid; and Miguel, A. de (1972): *Sociología o Subversión*, Barcelona.

42 There are currently eight active professors (*Catedráticos*) of political science and about thirty associate professors (*Titulares*).

43 With regard to journals, the old *Revista de Estudios Políticos*, which first appeared in 1941, has now been joined by others devoted, mainly or partially to political studies: *Revista de Derecho Político* (Madrid, 1978); *Revista Española de Investigaciones Sociólogicas* (Madrid, 1978); *Revista de Política Comparada* (Madrid, 1980), and *Estudis Electorals* (Barcelona, 1978).

44 The old Instituto de Estudios Políticos which in recent years has played an active

role in supporting political science research and activities, has also been renamed the Centro de Estudios Constitucionales, as an expression of this trend.

45 A summary of recent work by Spanish scholars can be found in Gonzalez Encinar, J.J. (ed.) (1984), *Diccionario del Sistema Político Español*, Madrid.

46 One of the most active institutions in the field is the Centro de Investigaciones Sociológicas. It is attached to the Spanish government and the best equipped social research body in the country. On the commercial side, there is a wide range of more or less accredited poll and survey organizations.

47 We should mention, for the record, a short-lived project (1878-9) of the already-quoted 'Krausist' tradition, when a private Escuela de Ciencias Sociales organized in Madrid courses on topics connected with political institutions, history, political economy, and political theory. The intention, which had an ephemeral existence, was the side-effect of a political conflict at the State University in Madrid, from which a group of well-known liberal professors had been temporarily expelled. In addition, the possible influence of the then new Ecole Libre des Sciences Politiques in Paris cannot be included.

48 D. Easton (1981) The political system besieged by the state, in *Political Theory* 9, August 1981: 303-25.

REFERENCES

AAVV, (1972) Estudios de Ciencia Política y Sociología (Libro nomenaje al professor Carlos Ollero), Madrid.

— (1979) *Sociologia española de los años setenta*, Madrid.

Fraga, M. Velarde, J. and Campo, S. (eds) (1974) *La España de los años setenta: El Estado y la política*, Madrid.

Gil Cremades, J.J. (1969) *El reformismo español*, Esplugues: Barcelona.

Lopez Pintor, R. (1982) 'A ciência política na España contemporánea', in Lamounier B. (ed.), *A ciência política nos Anhos 80*, Brasilia.

Lucas Verdu, P. (1965) 'Situation de la science politique en Espagne depuis 1965', *Social Science. Information sur les Sciences Sociales* 4, Paris.

Pastor, M. (1972) 'Notas sobre la actualidad de la ciencie política en España (recensión del libro-homenaje al prof. Ollero), *Boletín Informativo de Ciencia Política* 11-12 Madrid, pp. 205-11.

Portero Molina J.A. (1978) 'La Revista de estudios políticos, 1941-5', in M. Ramirez, *Las fuentes ideológicas de un régimen* (España 1939-45), Saragossa.

— (1980) 'Algunas cuestiones en el Derecho Político Español', *Revista de Estudios Políticos* 18:71-100.

Ramiro Rico, N. (1980) *El animal ladino y otros ensayos*, Madrid.

Recasens Siches, L. (1950) 'La science politique en Espagne depuis trente ans', *La Science Politique Contemporaine*, UNESCO: Paris.

Rubio Llorente, L. (1970) 'Nota preliminar a la edición española', in E. Stein, *Derecho Político*, Madrid.

Sanchez Agesta, L. (1962) 'Las primeras cátedras españolas de Derecho constitucional', *Revista Española de Estudios Políticos* 126:157-67.

Santamaria, J. (1970) 'En torno al objeto y funcion de la Cientcia política, *Boletin Informativo de Ciencia Política*, 4:101-5.

— (1974) 'Política y ciéncia Política en la España de hoy', *Revista Española de la opinion publica* 37:189-98.

10 The sociology of political science in the People's Republic of China

Zhengyuan Fu[1]

Introduction

This paper attempts to address the issue of the development of political science in the People's Republic of China since its establishment in 1949.

A discussion of the development of political science cannot be isolated from the broader issue of the development of social sciences of which it is a part. Furthermore, the evolution of social knowledge can only be understood in the context of the social system within which it operates. Within the social system, the power structure (the political sub-system) and the all pervading political culture[2] have been the main forces that determine the progress, or rather the retardation, of the knowledge system. However, this does not deny that the knowledge system has a dynamic of its own.

As everywhere in the world, the study of social life has always been watched with deep suspicion by the state and church, which feel their authoritarian interest constantly threatened by its progress. Whether rightly or wrongly, they regard any innovation of social knowledge as undermining the established social order. As soon as the state is firmly entrenched, it does all in its power to block any advent in social speculation that challenges the core value embedded in the political culture which sustains and reproduces the political system. Wherever the state enjoys an absolute hegemony over the civil society, social knowledge will be stultified and whatever remnant is left has to play the role of handmaiden to politics.[3]

In instances where the state has less control over the civil society or when its attention is focused on other issues, social knowledge enjoys a better chance of development. In Chinese history, the Period of a Hundred Contending Schools (551-233 BC) when Chinese social philosophy was at its zenith, coincided with the late Spring and Autumn Period (722-481 BC) and the Warring States Period (403-221 BC) when the Zhou (Chou) dynasty was falling apart into hundreds of belligerent states.

This was the time when China produced Confucius, Mencius, Mo Tzu, Lao Tzu, Chuang Tzu, Hsun Tzu, and scores of others. Even the lesser stars in that galaxy would rank as the best in any country. Sun Tzu predated Clausewitz by more than two thousand years; Han Fei, who was more Machiavellian than Machiavelli, finished his work eighteen hundred years before his Western counterpart. This period is in extreme contrast with the following two thousand years of stalemate and ossification after the reunification. The parallel in the West would be the Hellenic Age in contrast with the Dark Ages.

The negative impact of the political system on social knowledge came into evidence once the dominance of the state *vis-à-vis* civil society was firmly entrenched. Ever since the establishment of the Qin (Chin) dynasty in 221 BC, the emperor and a handful of power elites had always played a major role in shaping social change. A typical example of state impingement on social knowledge happened right after the political unification of China under the Qin emperor, Qin Shi-Huang-Di. The famous incident of the imperial decree to burn all old classics and to execute heretical scholars occurred under his reign.[4] Though the 'trillion generations' of the Qin dynasty envisioned by its first emperor lasted only fourteen years, it left an indelible imprint on Chinese history.

Ever since, the Chinese state has enjoyed an absolute monopoly of ideology and authority to mandate social knowledge. What was unique in the case of China was the absence of a strong church in competition with the state. The state in ancient China was so powerful that it was able to eliminate all autonomous social forces and enjoy absolute authority. It was the state that prescribed ideological orthodoxy. Religion operated only under the tolerance of the state. In most cases, the church had to serve the interests of the state.

Since the establishment of a reconstructed version of Confucianism as the state orthodox ideology adapted for imperial rule in the Han dynasty circa 140 BC, the main function of social knowledge was to give legitimacy to the imperial authority and political structure, in order to exact compliance from the populace. Almost all writings in social philosophy were concerned with annotating, classifying and codifying the ancient Confucian classics. The hegemony of the official ideology was not only upheld by force but also guaranteed by the civil service examination system which controlled entrance to official life. This ensured that no heretics would be recruited into the bureaucracy and anyone aspiring to public career should conform to the state orthodoxy. Since this examination system was the major, if not the only, channel to upwards mobility — and in a highly politicized society the alternatives to an official career were few and unattractive — Chinese traditional scholarship in the study of social life was encased into the orthodox mould. These conditions remained almost unchanged until the middle of the nineteenth century.

The state's policy toward knowledge was determined by its usefulness as perceived by the power holder (in most cases the emperor). This fact was reflected in the differential treatment towards technology (handicrafts, engineering, agriculture, medicine, etc.) in contrast with that towards social knowledge. Since the social utility of technology was evident, it has been treated with greater toleration and enjoyed a certain measure of autonomy, although a technical career would not lead to great honours and riches. Whereas social inquiry has always existed under close state supervision and political persecution of heresy abounds in Chinese history, lavish honours have been heaped on scholars for classical Confucian learning which conformed with the official interpretation.

The study of social sciences in China received its greatest impetus in the middle of the last century as a result of the contact with the West. Beside opium, drug pushers, cannon balls, technology, and Christian missionaries, there was also importation of Western social speculation. The imperial complacency of the Manchu court was utterly shaken by the defeat of the Chinese army in the face of superior British naval ships and cannons during the Opium War in 1840. The need to meet the Western challenge with improved technical and military knowledge was apparent despite xenophobia. Self-strengthening, reform, and modernization became high priorities in the political agenda of the imperial court. The immediate need so sorely felt by the Manchu court was the importation of Western technology to combat the Western 'barbarians'. Western learnings which were thought to be useful for the renovation of the state included ship building, firearms, military tactics, and diplomacy.

Although the first Chinese graduated from a US university (Yale) in 1854, it took another decade to establish the College of Foreign Languages at Peking in 1862 and a similar school at Shanghai in 1863. From 1872 to 1881, 120 Chinese students went to the US; in 1876 another thirty went to England and France. These were the first batch of Chinese students sent officially abroad, only to be recalled and the whole project cancelled in 1882. The immediate cause for the withdrawal was because they did not perform the traditional kowtow to the superintendent for students at the Chinese embassy in Washington D.C. They were accused of having 'forgotten their original civilization and disregard their teachers and elders. . . . They could not be of any use to China'. Although there were some objections to this demand of cancellation as being too extreme, the conservatives with the support and sympathy of the court won the day. The request for the cancellation of the mission was granted by the Manchu government in 1881 (Teng and Fairbank 1979).

Despite this incident, the state eventually had to relinquish one of its main instruments of ideological control in the face of Western challenge. The need to modernize prompted the abolishment of the civil service examination system by imperial decree in 1905. This signified the breakdown of the state's monopoly over ideological orthodoxy. The significance of this event for the development of social sciences in China is best described by the words of the famous social philosopher Liang Qichao (Liang Ch'i-chao) in 1922:

The most vital turning point is the abolition of the civil service examination system. This system has had more than one thousand years' history, and can be really be regarded as deeply rooted and firmly based. Its greatest shortcoming was to make the minds of the scholars of the whole country hypocritical, traditional, and vague, and thus block all sources for the development of learning and thought. (Liang 1936)

One of the earliest Chinese students to study abroad, Yen Fu (1865–1924) returned from the Greenwich Naval Academy in England and set out a full fledged introduction of Western social sciences. In 1898 Yen published his translation into classical Chinese of T.H. Huxley's *Evolution and Ethics*, which was followed by John Stuart Mill's *On Liberty*, Spencer's *Study of Sociology*, Adam Smith's *Wealth of Nations*, Montesquieu's *Spirit of the Laws*, etc. Though limited in scope and circulation at the time, these would later exert a tremendous influence on Chinese intellectual development during the early twentieth century.

The importation of Western knowledge into China exhibits a common feature of cultural contacts, i.e. the difference between the attitude toward technological and social knowledge.[5] The former was eagerly sought after, whereas the latter was regarded with deep suspicion. The deeper underlying cause was the perception of the state which regarded technology as useful for its strength whereas innovation in social knowledge as subversive to social order, as mentioned earlier in this paper.

Thus began the famous issue of 'Chinese learning as essence, Western learning as means'[6] propounded by those Chinese scholars who felt the old social order threatened by the importation of foreign knowledge. What it boiled down to was: how to retain the traditional Chinese political culture, as 'essence', in the face of Western cultural challenge. Many Chinese still believed the superiority of their culture. Even a late nineteenth century reformist like Shao Zuozhou declared that, 'Though Chinese techniques are inferior to the West, in matters of ethics, learning, institutions, and literature China transcends far above the West'. Hence the solution: 'The employment of Western means under the guidance of the Chinese way (*tao*)' (Shao 1958).

Most elites were more interested in using Western technology as the 'means' for strengthening the traditional Chinese polity. As Wei Yuan put it in 1842, the purpose of learning about the West was 'to control the barbarians by the technology of the barbarians' (Wei 1960). Western learning which was technical in nature (such as engineering, natural sciences, medicine, military techniques, etc.) was tolerated and even sought after; yet Western social sciences were regarded as dangerous heresies that would undermine the imperial rule, which was the 'Chinese essence'.

This premonition was not unfounded. The first Chinese republican revolution led to the overthrow of the imperial dynasty in 1911. Under the leadership of Dr Sun Yat-sen, the Chinese revolutionaries gathered behind the banners of 'freedom, equality and fraternity', which were imported Western political ideas. The subversive influence of Western social knowledge is well proven.

Yet, even after the first democratic revolution in China, it took another eight years to start the May Fourth movement in 1919, whose slogan was: 'Welcome Mr D. and Mr S.' (at that time there were no Chinese terms equivalent to 'democracy' and 'science'). This movement was also responsible for the repudiation of the orthodox Confucianism which was believed to be the fountain head and defender of Chinese feudal despotism. Thus, for a time at least, the end of the Chinese imperial rule opened the gate for the untrammelled influx of Western social knowledge.

However, it should not be construed that the loss of prestige of traditional Chinese political culture means its total annihilation. A tradition which spans more than two thousand years and enjoys the longest history in the world will not depart from the stage so easily. It lies dormant. Time and again it would rouse up from its faked slumber and haunt the Chinese scene, attired in new costumes and voiced in new languages.

Despite the fact that most of the half century before 1949 China was torn by civil wars and foreign invasions, political science as a discipline was gradually institutionalized on the mainland. Chinese scholars were eager to learn from the West.

In 1903 the first course on politics was offered in the Capital Academy (the predecessor of Peking University). In 1905 and 1906, the Manchu court sent two missions abroad to investigate the politics and constitutions of Western countries. In 1908, some Chinese visiting scholars in Japan translated and edited *Shiliu Guo Xienfa Yiyuanfa Yuanjian* (A Compendium of Constitutions and Parliament Laws of Sixteen Countries, Tokyo: Jienyi She). The Manchu court did not benefit from these efforts and fell in the first Chinese democratic revolution in 1911.

In 1915 the Chinese Social and Political Science Association was established. Its quarterly journal *Chinese Social and Political Science Review* first came out in April 1916. The contributors consisted of both Chinese and Western scholars and politicians, and it was published in English. In 1932 the Chinese Political Science Association was established. By 1949 around forty political science departments had been set up in Chinese colleges and universities. Many books were written on jurisprudence and diplomacy. However, little empirical political analysis was conducted.

Some of the best known works in political science were *Bijiao Xienfa* (Comparative Constitution) by Wang Shijie (1926) and *The Government and Politics of China* by T.S. Ch'ien (Qian Duansheng) (1950), which was preceded by his *Minguo Zhengzhi Shi* (A History of the Political Institution of the Republic) (Qian *et al.* 1939). Two works also worth mentioning are Zhongguo Waijiao Xingzheng (Chinese Foreign Affairs Administration) by Chen Tiqian (1943), and *Zhongguo Zhengfu* (Chinese Government) by Chen Zhimai (1944). Aside from jurisprudence and foreign relations, other works in political science were primarily concerned with introducing Western ideas and translation of foreign books.

Yet, generally speaking this period was characterized by the flourishing of social sciences in contrast to the previous thousand years in China. The outstanding case was sociology, as noted by a Western sociologist: 'It could be argued that before the Second World War, outside North America and Western Europe, China was the seat of the most flourishing sociology in the world, at least in respect of its intellectual quality' (Freedman 1962).

Even so, whatever progress Chinese social science had made should be attributed to the fact that during the period of 1911-49 the state had neither the time nor the ability to interfere with its development, being engrossed in domestic strife and foreign invasion. In a certain sense, the revolution of 1911 had not only broken the moral legitimacy of traditional Chinese political culture but also the absolute hegemony of the state over the civil society.

THE MAO ERA

1949-66 Institution building

The establishment of the People's Republic of China in 1949 ushered in a new era for the social sciences in the mainland. The Communist parties in power have always had an overriding concern in controlling social knowledge which is believed to influence social perceptions and definitions. Ideological orthodoxy must be kept pure and untainted.

The period immediately after 1949 was a time of institution building. As with all Communist movements, victory of revolution was followed by nationalization of all aspects of social life. Political *Gleichschaltung* was in smooth operation and found fertile ground in traditional Chinese political culture. Once again the state began to enjoy absolute dominance over the civil society. The party-state directly controls education, mass media, culture and publication. It has both the will and the means to oversee the development of social knowledge. In a sense, the Chinese Communist revolution was a restoration of the traditional hegemony of the state over the civil society.

This was during the Stalin Era in the international Communist movement. With Mao's famous pronouncement of 'leaning to one side', the Soviet model was zealously emulated. The impact of the Stalinist Soviet model was, to say the least, not conducive to the development of social sciences in China. This together with the restoration of the Chinese tradition of state intervention in social inquiry and enforcement of ideological orthodoxy caused the virtual stalemate of social sciences for almost three decades.

One of the main tenets of the newly enforced official Marxist orthodoxy conceptualizes social knowledge as a superstructure erected on an economic basis. Hence the class character of all disciplines of humanities and social sciences. Partisanship was the highest principle. Objectivity in social sciences was perceived as impossible and presumably irrelevant. Both social sciences and humanities must be harnessed to the needs of party propaganda. Natural sciences fared better, though physics was still divided into bourgeois and proletarian physics and so were genetics and other disciplines.

Once again the state gave different treatment to technical and social knowledge. Since political science and sociology were abolished in the Soviet Union during the late 1920s, there did not seem to be any *raison d'être* for their presence on Chinese campuses. Political science and sociology as Western imports were now branded as bourgeois pseudo-science, whereas Russianized Marxism (Stalinism) and Sinicized Marxism (Mao Zedong thought) were regarded as an indigenous Oriental product.

After the consolidation of the new political order under the Chinese Communist Party, during the restructuring of higher education in 1952 both political science and sociology were banished as disciplines by official decree in the PRC. According to the official version, three reasons were cited for its indictment: (1) it was reactionary, anti-Marxist, and bourgeois in character; (2) it was taken for granted that under socialism there would be no political or social 'problems'; (3) since the elder brother (Soviet Union) could dispense with it, so should the Chinese.

As a result, political science department faculty members, students, and researchers were assigned to other departments or institutes, with the majority going to law. Henceforth jurisprudence and politics were regarded as identical, in the sense that these were perceived as concerned primarily with keeping social order under dictatorship of the proletariat through the Party leadership.

Generally speaking, the three major components of official Marxism (i.e. political economy, dialectical materialism and historical materialism, and scientific socialism) were deemed suitable substitutes for economics, philosophy, sociology, political science, and all other social sciences. In fact, familiarity with writings of Marx–Engels–Lenin–Stalin–Mao and experiences in revolutionary practice were regarded as sufficient and necessary conditions for a qualified social scientist.

For more than two thousand years the official version of Confucianism had been a substitute for the study of social life in China. Once again, work done under the heading of social sciences became mainly annotation, hair splitting interpretation, post hoc policy justification, and 'verification' of classical writings — this time with a major change: orthodox Marxism took the place of orthodox Confucianism. One subject that merits the attention of the political sociologist is the inherent organic compatibility between orthodox Marxism and the oriental political culture that flourished in imperial China.

During the early 1950s when the Thought Remoulding Movement was underway, political scientists along with other Chinese social scientists had to make recantations and self-criticisms in an atmosphere of medieval inquisition. They became witnesses for the reactionary and decadent character of Western bourgeois political science, which was declared by party ideologues to be not only useless but harmful for socialist construction. Today, reading the criticism of the Chinese Marxists levelled at Western social sciences and the self-critiques of those so-called 'bourgeois intellectuals' during the 1950s, one is struck by their similarity to the attacks against Western 'barbarian' learning made by the defenders of traditional Chinese imperial order around the turn of the century. Paradoxical as it may seem to our Western colleagues, contemporary Chinese Marxists had accomplished what the earlier imperial defenders had attempted but were never able to accomplish: namely, bringing Western social knowledge into total disrepute.

By 1955 when the Philosophy and Social Science Division was established within the Chinese Academy of Sciences (itself established in November 1949 and modelled after the USSR Academy of Sciences), it had the following research institutes: Institute of Economics, Institute of History, Institute of Archaeology, Institute of Linguistics, Institute of Philosophy; and later the Institute of Literature, Institute of Jurisprudence, and others. This academic division was under the jurisdiction of the Propaganda Department of the Communist Party Central Committee. As always, the natural sciences were accorded some measures of autonomy, yet social knowledge had to be supervised meticulously and directly by the party-state.

During the brief interlude of the so-called Let a Hundred Flowers Bloom campaign in 1957, which was a reverberation of the Twentieth Soviet Party Congress under Khrushchev, some Chinese political scientists had the audacity to suggest some form of rehabilitation of political science, though not voiced as explicitly as the sociologists. They were subsequently branded as rightists for their heresy during the anti-rightist movement initiated in June of 1957.[7] During that movement the president of the Chinese Academy of Science Guo Moruo announced: 'On principle, the Chinese Communist Party and all Marxists, both in past and present, can hold only a negative attitude towards modern bourgeois reactionary philosophy and reactionary 'social science', including sociology, economics, political science, jurisprudence, history etc.'; furthermore, 'our research [on it] is in order to make a better critique against it'. (Guo Moruo 1957; Xinhuashe 1957).

Later, some universities set up departments of politics in 1960. But these had nothing to do with political science *per se*. Their function was to train teachers and commissars for ideological indoctrination. Courses offered under the title of politics were mainly concerned with orthodox Marxist definitions of social situations.

By the early 1960s, with the increase of foreign diplomatic contacts, there was a demand for cadres and researchers in foreign relations. As a result, the departments of politics in Peking University, People's University and Fudan University were restructured into departments of International Politics in 1964.

Whatever remained of social sciences was still regarded with suspicion by the establishment. A resolution stating that the 'social sciences must be in the service of proletarian politics' was passed by the Third Meeting of the Social Science Division of the Chinese Academy of Sciences in 1960. During the early 1960s, when 'Mao Zedong Thought' was elevated to an official cult and became the fountainhead of all socialist achievements, it was felt that all social sciences should be overhauled. On the eve of the Cultural Revolution in 1965, the party demagogue and one-time personal secretary to Mao, Chen Bo-da, who was also the vice president of the Chinese Academy of Sciences, openly proposed the complete disbanding of all social science institutes within the Academy. Shortly after in January of 1966, the chief of secret police and a top overseer of ideology Kang Shen suggested that all social scientists should be sent to the countryside to labour for ideological purification (Li Shu 1979).

1966-76 The Great Proletarian Cultural Revolution

In the summer of 1966 Mao put his final royal seal on the initiation of the so-called Great Proletarian Cultural Revolution. This should truly be ranked as one of the greatest oddities in human history, for it was neither proletarian, nor cultural, nor revolutionary. It was not proletarian since it was initiated from the top by one man with the help of a handful of charlatans. Nor was it cultural since it was a power struggle in which culture was dismembered by political forces. Nor was it a revolution but a restoration of Chinese traditional order with the blatant revival of all the old imperial symbolism and tenets such as the identification of the ruler with the sun, with infallibility, and the ever present shout of 'live ten thousand, trillion years'.

Not long after, the normal routine of all intellectual activity in social sciences came to a standstill and research personnel in these institutes as well as faculty members were sent to the countryside to labour. Both Chen Bo-da and Kang Sheng were elevated to the status of standing members of the CCP politburo and ranked fourth and fifth in the party-state hierarchy.

The ideological justification for the Cultural Revolution rested on two basic Marxist tenets, which were also responsible for the fate of Chinese social sciences. First, the assertion that all social conflicts are basically class struggles, and the Stalin-Mao extension that class struggle will intensify under 'socialism'. Second, that all knowledge is part of the superstructure, which will inevitably be imbued with class character — and hence the impossibility of objectivity. The logical corollary deduced from the two axioms was: any academic controversy in matters concerning social knowledge and humanities must be class struggle ultimately reducible to political confrontation between the reactionary bourgeoisie and the progressive proletariat. Therefore, expressions of unofficial or unorthodox views in matters pertaining to social sciences and arts are heinous counter-revolutionary crimes punishable by both legal and administrative measures. A major function of dictatorship of the proletariat is the suppression of heresy. This was also the rationale behind all major political movements, of which the Cultural Revolution was one among many during the Mao era.

The issue of whether objective social knowledge is possible is a large one and merits a separate volume. Many eminent Western social scientists in their writings on methodology, sociology of knowledge, logic and philosophy of science have treated this issue from different perspectives. The present paper is not intended to join the debate. However, it is fitting to make the following remarks.

1 Recognition that human knowledge is limited must not be confused with the assertion that objective social knowledge is impossible.[8] Despite all the pitfalls of prejudice, bias, and value preferences, social scientists have come up with propositions that are verifiable and falsifiable. There is evidence to show that many of these propositions are reliable and have bearing on policy and action.

2 Though starting from different perspectives, some Western non-Marxists seem to arrive at the same conclusion of the Marxists about the impossibility of objective social knowledge. Cultural relativism seems to be still the fashion. It is important to realize that the same thesis will have different social consequences in different settings. In a pluralistic political system, this thesis may be used as argument for more toleration, negotiation, and conciliation among diverse interest groups; it may also propound a *laissez faire* attitude toward the social sciences. In a monistic political system, however, this would justify witch-hunting of heretics and tighter state control over social knowledge. Paradoxical though it may seem, while Western social scientists may regard 'class analysis' and cultural relativism as badges of radical progressives, when these tenets were applied to China as an official creed, they were disastrous in their social consequences. In combination they smacked of fanatical fascism.

There is consensus among Chinese intellectuals that the focus on 'class struggle' had been damaging to social sciences. Even an orthodox Communist like the present president of the Chinese Academy of Social Sciences conceded that, after the establishment of socialism, such emphasis was damaging (Hu Sheng 1986).

3 To show that an opponent's proposition is motivated by his values or self-interest does not mean it is necessarily false. This line of debate often smacks of politization of academic issues and will

ultimately backfire. In the words of Hayek: 'If whether a statement is true or false is no longer decided by logical argument and empirical tests, but by examining the social position of the person who made it . . . reason has been finally driven out'.[9] Such an incipient tendency in the Western academic community is somewhat alarming to the author of this paper who comes from a different culture and experience. Intolerance is equally unjustified even if waged under the banner of 'radicalism' or 'liberalism'.

POST MAO ERA

With the death of Mao on 9 September 1976 and the arrest of the 'Gang of Four' on 6 October in the same year, China entered a new phase in her modern history.

The last ten years of the rule of Mao had directly and adversely affected the lives of more than one hundred million Chinese according to the conservative estimate of the party. 'The national economy was on the brink of collapse', voiced the new successor Hua Guofeng. It was natural for all Chinese to probe the social causes of the Cultural Revolution. For the first time since 1949, the Chinese intellectuals and many party leaders were in agreement on their assessment of these ten years' development. At the time at least, they all felt that political movements like the Cultural Revolution should be avoided in the future. After all, most of them were the victims of this catastrophe and even shared the same cowshed during these 'unprecedented years'. They also were agreed on the necessity of modernization.

As a member of the populace who experienced the Cultural Revolution, it may seem a lack of sensibility to speak of the unintended and even beneficial consequences arising out of such an oddity and crisis in Chinese history. But this confusion which confronts Chinese social science in its aftermath also presents it with unprecedented (since 1949) opportunity for new development. However, any undue optimism must be tempered by the recognition of ever present obstacles on the path of social sciences in China. The foremost are ideological dogmatism and intervention of the state.

The establishment of the pragmatic line of Deng Xiaoping within the Party was finalized at the Third Plenum of the Eleventh CCP Central Committee in December of 1978. The transfer of focus from political struggle to economic construction and modernization (agriculture, industry, science and technology, and defence) was the result of a change of perception of the ruling elites after their experience during the Cultural Revolution. It was also felt economic progress made by other countries in the interim had created a situation which threatened the national status of China in the international community. A new set of priorities was established. It was finally realized that ceaseless political movements in the name of waging class struggle had impeded China's economic and social growth culminating in that catastrophic, farcical, and bloody hoax which lasted fully ten years from 1966 to 1976.

The more reform-oriented party leaders realized some modification of dogmatic ideological tenets was necessary for the modernization project. The first breakthrough was the 'rediscovery' that science is a part of the productive force. On 18 March 1978 Deng announced in the National Science Conference that science and technology are productive forces, and that the Chinese intellectuals are now part of the working class. The significance of this 'breakthrough' should not be underestimated. Hitherto, following the Stalinist version of orthodox Marxism, science as a part of culture was placed in the superstructure. Therefore, even natural sciences were attributed with class character. That is why there was the distinction between proletarian genetics and reactionary genetics. Targets which had undergone severe attacks, from the mid-1950s to the early 1970s, include: quantum mechanics, theory of relativity, second law of thermodynamics, genetics, symbolic logic, cybernetics, the 'black hole' theory and the origins of the universe.[10]

Since science became a part of the 'base' by proclamation of the political authority, it has lost its class character. Now, the natural scientists and engineers have some assurance that they will not be labelled as propounders of reactionary bourgeois sciences in mortal struggle against the proletariat. The natural science community henceforth enjoys greater autonomy and prestige. Party ideologues shall no longer initiate criticism against the theory of relativity.

Social science was less fortunate since it still resided in the superstructure. But some concession was made. For instance, it was conceded that some social problems have common features and the experiences of Western bourgeois social scientists are valuable in order to resolve similar problems in socialist countries, such as management science and administration. It was also realized that there still exist social problems even under socialism, such as crime, divorce, red tape, corruption, etc. This paved the way for the rehabilitation of political science and revival of other social science disciplines.

Social scientists were also called upon to provide justification for the new party line. The historic Third Plenum of the Eleventh CCP Central Committee in December of 1978 was preceded by the much publicized discussion on the issue of 'practice as the sole criterion of truth', which was propounded to break the ossified dogmatic stance connected with the Cultural Revolution and which paved the way for the ideological legitimation of the new party line.

A host of articles sprang up during this period. The titles of some reveal the general trend of the intellectual and political atmosphere at the time: e.g. 'Does truth have class character?', 'Everyone is equal before the law', 'Science and technology are also part of the productive force','aside from class struggle, productive force is also a motive force in history'. From 1979 to 1980, more than a hundred articles criticizing Chinese feudalism with reference to the Cultural

Revolution were published in the major newspapers in China. All these were intended to discredit the party line connected with the Gang of Four and the ultra conservatives in opposition to the pragmatism represented by Deng. For once the true opinions and feelings of intellectuals hitherto suspect of 'bourgeois' leaning came to the service of the establishment. Remember the post-Mao rehabilitated old party veterans were themselves the victims of the Cultural Revolution.

Unlike many Western radicals and China experts, most Chinese intellectuals looked on the Cultural Revolution as a restoration of feudalism. Even the CCP's official interpretation of this event conceded and cited traditional feudal culture as the main cause (CCP 1981).

Powers hitherto blocking the advance of social knowledge realized that it was in their interest to promote it within certain limits. Of course, it must be closely monitored and controlled, lest 'liberalization' run out of bounds. The confines within which it was permitted to develop were defined by Deng himself as the Four Basic Principles in March 1979, i.e. Marx-Leninism and Mao Thought, Dictatorship of the Proletariat, Party leadership, and Socialism (Deng Xiaoping 1983a). Shortly after, a few dissidents were arrested. By December 1979, the Democracy Wall in Beijing (Peking), which for more than a year had been the focus of attention of world media, was closed. It had served its purpose. It called for the reinstatement of Deng, criticized his opponents, demanded the rehabilitation of fallen old party veterans, supported the modernization drive, and exposed the crimes of the Gang of Four and other feudal conservatives inimical to the new party line. It had made valuable contributions for the elevation of Deng's supporters. Now that it was calling for freedom of speech and assembly and focused on human rights issues (the fifth modernization), it had gone too far. The core value of the political culture must not be threatened. Party dominance over civil society must be fully guaranteed. It should enjoy its rule of 'trillion generations'. Despite all the policy changes, the basic character of the social order must remain intact. After all, Deng's four principles of 1979 were hybrids of Mao's six principles of 1957 (Mao Zedong 1957). The latter were invoked by the late 'people's emperor' to suppress the dissenting intellectuals during the anti-rightist campaign following the Hundred Flower Bloom movement.

The crackdown on the Democracy Wall also served as a reminder to Chinese social scientists in general. Innovative thinking must not wander beyond the confines of the Four Basic Principles. Despite this incident, the general feeling was one of euphoria. After experiencing life under the imperial shadow of Mao, even such incidents would not deter Chinese intellectuals from feeling that they had not breathed so freely in the past twenty-seven years.

In May of 1977, the Chinese Academy of Social Sciences was established on the basis of the Social Science Division of the Chinese

Academy of Sciences. This provided for the institutional setting for the revival of political science and other social science disciplines.

The importance of social sciences as perceived by the establishment was also signalled by the appointment of the top party ideologue Hu Qiao-mu, who was later promoted to a full member of the party politburo, as president of the Chinese Academy of Social Sciences (CASS) in March 1978. Incidentally, this also implied the close control exerted by the party on both the humanities and social sciences.

The functions of CASS, and that of the social sciences community in general, are: 1 providing ideological justification and propaganda for policy implementation; 2 serving as a think-tank for input and social monitoring as feedback to policy formulation; 3 functioning both as import channel and shop window for international academic exchanges in the context of the post-Mao opening up; 4 storing, disseminating, mandating and developing social knowledge.

Of course, the revival of political science, as well as sociology and the further development of other social science disciplines, can only be initiated and channelled from the very top of the party-state. The first open signal for the rehabilitation of political science appeared in a speech made by Deng in early 1979. It was conceded that, 'For many years we have neglected the study of political science, jurisprudence, sociology, and world politics. . . . For many years we don't even have statistical figures' (Deng Xiaoping 1983a).

Evidently, the political leadership believed that social sciences could be harnessed to serve socialist construction, reforming the economy, restructuring certain aspects of the polity so that no calamity like the Great Cultural Revolution would again recur. We can only conjecture that this change of perspective was mainly due to their experience during the unprecedented ten years.

Under the auspices of CASS, from late 1978 to 1979 five meetings were held to discuss the revival of political science in China. In early 1980, CASS established an institute of political science. Though affixed with the label of prepatory group, it operated normally as an institute from 1980 until it was formally renamed as the Institute of Political Science on 6 July 1985.[11]

After more than two years of preparation and discussion, the Chinese Political Science Association was formally established in December 1980.

A major impetus for the rehabilitation of Chinese political science was the important talk 'Reform of the leadership system of the party and the state', given by Deng on 18 August 1980 to an extended conference of the CCP Politburo, which was subsequently passed by that body on 31 August 1980. In that much publicized talk, Deng identified the main failings of the Chinese political institution[12] since the establishment of the PRC as:

The phenomenon of red tape, the phenomenon of over concentration of power, the phenomenon of patriarchy, the phenomenon of life-long tenureship of leading positions and the phenomenon of multifarious special privileges.

He did not forget to invoke the authority of Mao for debunking the Soviet model:

Stalin had seriously destroyed the socialist legal system. Comrade Mao Zedong had said that such events could never have happened in Western countries such as England, France, and the US. Although he realized this, because the problem of the leadership system was not resolved and also due to other causes, it still led to the ten years of catastrophe of the 'Great Cultural Revolution'. (Deng Xiaoping 1983b)

Finally, the Chinese academic community was allowed to discuss issues and even failings of the existing political structure which would have incurred criminal charges of counter-revolutionary subversion just a few years before. The focus on the study of political institutions was also reflected in the six major areas of study proposed by the founding conference of the Chinese Political Science Association in the Five-Year (1981-5) National Programme of Political Science Research: (1) basic political science theory; (2) the Chinese socialist political institution; (3) the contemporary foreign political institution and political theory; (4) history of Chinese political thought and the political institution; (5) history of foreign political thought and political institutions; (6) international relations and world politics.

Since 1980, the major subject that has engrossed Chinese political scientists has been the study of the 'political institution' — which should be more appropriately termed as the study of the state (*Staatswissenschaft*). This was also in part, if not mainly, due to the call for the reform of political institutions. It was realized that the key to this reform is the reform of the leadership system of the party-state. A series of books were published introducing foreign political institutions, government organization and the civil service system. Many articles discussing the existing Chinese political structure appeared in newspapers and journals whose main theme was what had been identified by Deng in his 1980 talk.

The chief motivation behind the initiation of the discussion of political reform is to ensure the smooth functioning of the party-state. Old party veterans were also concerned that they themselves would not again be subjected to the humiliating experience of the Cultural Revolution. The first attempt of institutionalization of legal procedures and codification of the legal system since 1954 was initiated in 1979. Before that, a country of one billion was governed without a criminal code for thirty years. There was no socialist legal system for Mao to destroy simply because it was never instituted.

This discussion of the reform of political institutions, whose main themes were identified by Deng, had practical implications. With the discussion of the abolishing of life-long tenure, age limits were set for certain positions, which led to the retirement of many middle-ranking cadres, though no age limit was set for the highest positions, such as politburo members, until an informal compromise was struck among top elites in October 1987. On the other hand, there is always a limit within which academic discussion is allowed. Party members may retire but the millenum of Party Leadership should never be challenged, as stipulated by the Four Basic Principles written into the constitution of 1982.

The much publicized discussion of political reform was also prompted by the concern for economic growth. It was realized that the economic reform started in 1979 could not progress far without corresponding reform in the political sphere. As identified by Deng, one aspect that hampered the economy was the overwhelming concentration of administrative power. Centralized decision-making is not always conducive to efficiency. For example, during the first eight months of 1986, more than 180,000 occasions were recorded by the Ministry of Machinery asking for approvals, mostly from outside the capital.

Other issues identified by Chinese political scientists as fitting subjects of study were closely related to political reform. These included: the relationship between legislative, executive, and judicial powers; government structure and organization; relationship between party and government; administration; personnel management; the procedures of decision-making; and the legal aspect of civil rights. Some scholars even began to talk about checks and balances.

Some of the most influential works on political institutional reform came from outside the political science discipline. The most notable example is Su Shaozhi, director of the Institute of Marxism-Leninism of the Chinese Academy of Social Sciences. He, like most Chinese social scientists, noticed that a change of the role of the Party must be the first theme on the reform agenda. During the height of 'thawing period' in September of 1986, he wrote: 'The relationship between the party and the law must be made clear. Which one should be dominant? Party or law? Only one can be dominant over the other, not both. The constitution and the law are established by the representatives of the people, and the party is in the service of the people. Therefore, the party should, naturally, act within the confines of the law and constitution. No one should be above the constitution and the law. Hence, it is self-evident that there should be autonomy of legislature and autonomy of the judiciary. These should be the themes in any reform of political institutions'. As for the so-called 'democratic centralism', '"Democracy" under central guidance is not the rule of the people but the rule *over* the people' (Su Shaozhi 1986). Other political scientists were not as brave as Su. Soon he had to pay for his audacity.

The concept of the 'state' also underwent a major modification. With the de-emphasis of class struggle, the coercive aspect of the state solely as an organ of class suppression was downplayed. It was realized that the state had other social functions which are shared by both socialist and capitalist countries. Thus Western political science had something to offer and political scientists were allowed somewhat greater scope in their academic inquiry. During a conference held in Beijing in April of 1986, Chinese political scientists agreed that, 'A key issue of the development of political science is the handling of Western traditional political science. Western traditional political science is the theoretical summary of the experience of the building of bourgeois political regimes. Its purpose is the preservation of bougeois interests, and its class essence is most obvious. . . . It has promoted stable economic and social development. . . . This means that Western political science is still of value for us for reference and study' (Li Kejing 1986). However, Western political science must always be harnessed in the service of 'Chinese essence' embodied in the Four basic Principles.

The part of the political science that has any practical utility is, of course, administration. Interest in this area was steadily mounting. The first Conference of the Science of Leadership was convened in April 1986. In the meantime, some Party schools began to offer courses on 'science of leadership', the content of which included: structure of leadership; functions of leadership; methodology of leadership; (personal) traits of leadership (Luo et al 1985; Lu 1985).

In July 1986 a national conference on decision-making was given front page coverage on all Chinese news media. The definitive talk was the one presented by a Vice Premier and politburo member, Wan Li and called 'Democratization and scientification of decision-making are important aspects of the reform of political institutions' (Wan Li 1986). In current official Chinese vocabulary, the term 'democracy' means that decision-makers should heed the advice of experts.

Up to 1987, most work on decision theory was done by mathematicians, management scientists, and engineers. There was no article by a Chinese political scientist on public choice theory.

The focus on political institutions and administration was also mirrored in publications. From 1977 to 1986, of the ninety-eight books related to political science (not including foreign relations and world politics) which were written by Chinese authors and published during this period, twenty-four were concerned with government and political institutions, thirty-two were related to administration.[13]

For Chinese political scientists, their discipline is primarily a science concerned with the exercise of state power and its relationship to the people. For the party, the revival of political science is intended to improve the 'socialist system with Chinese character' and its smooth functioning. But no one as yet has come up with a clear definition of 'Chinese character'. However, one can safely surmise that it must conform to the Four Basic Principles which seem to the the modern version of the Chinese essence of the traditional political culture.

Though the emphasis seemed to be on administration that does not mean that Chinese political scientists have little interest in political theory, but it is safer to translate than to write. Of the fifty-six foreign works related to political science (excluding foreign relations and world politics) that were translated or republished from 1977 to 1986, twenty-nine were concerned with political theory, the rest were mainly on comparative politics.[14]

There were very few empirical political analyses by Chinese political scientists. The major themes had to be set by political leaders. Most published work dealt with explication of basic concepts, introducing Chinese political thinkers of the past, or Western political ideas and institutions. These were done under the overt purpose of serving the reform of political institutions.

During the period of 1982-6 there was a heated discussion of the role of Chinese traditional culture among the Chinese academic community and attended by some political scientists. Though the term 'culture' was never precisely defined and the term of 'political culture' was not used, their importance in shaping Chinese politics was generally recognized. From 1982 to 1986, four nationwide conferences and seminars were held to discuss the issue of culture. Some foreign scholars also attended these meetings. During the period January 1985 to June 1986, more than 200 articles on Chinese culture were published in major newspapers and journals. There was a general consensus that many aspects of present Chinese politics could be traced to traditional culture, such as the 'cult of personality', special privileges of cadres, lack of rational and legal procedure, the emphasis on class struggle to persecute people, ossification of academic activity, etc.

The debate over the relationship between Western learning and Chinese essence was again rekindled after almost a century. A few Chinese scholars even suggested that the old slogan should be reversed as 'Western learning as essence, Chinese learning as means'. This discussion came to an abrupt halt when 'Westernization' was once again condemned in January 1987, when party general secretary Hu Yaobang was ousted and the nationwide anti-liberalization struggle began. It is evident from the party decree which guides this 'struggle' that Western learning can play only the role as 'means' for the consolidation of the Chinese 'essence' — the latter being the dominance of party-state over the civil society. This seems to be the true core meaning of the term 'Chinese character'.

The 'Chinese character' expressed in scholarly work includes the idea of infallibility of the political leader whose views should be defended by social scientists. The style of scholarly inquiry on 'Chinese character' was exemplified in the 1982-4 discussion of the nature of the relationship between Deng's Four Basic Principles and the principles of the Chinese state constitution. The major three contending opinions were: (1) the principles of the constitution are identical with the Four Basic Principles; (2) the Four Basic Principles are the guiding ideas of the Constitution; (3) the principles of the Constitution are hierarchical in nature and ordered into three levels:

the highest level consists of the Four Basic Principles; next come the basic principles of the Constitution; the third level consists of the concrete principles of the Constitution (Xu and Xiao 1985).

INSTITUTIONALIZATION OF POLITICAL SCIENCE

After the establishment of the Chinese Academy of Social Sciences in 1977 its personnel expanded from around 1,800 to 5,145 by the middle of 1983 (CASS 1983). Other parts of China followed suit. By 1986 twenty-nine provincial and municipal social science academies or institutes were established with a total personnel of 4,222.

As mentioned previously, the present Chinese Political Science Association was founded in December 1980. It has now a membership of over 1,200. A dozen local associations were also set up. In 1984, after two years of negotiation CPSA joined the International Political Science Association (IPSA) and attended its 1985 Conference in Paris.

The Institute of Political Science of the Chinese Academy of Social Sciences has been in operation since 1980. By mid-1987, it had a staff of fifty-nine members, of whom thirty are research scientists and divided into three sections: political theory, administration, and political institutions. It publishes two journals: *Political Science Studies* and *Foreign Political Science*. The research priorities of the Institute included contemporary political science theories, world politics, political institutions, history of political thought, administration, political psychology. It had five graduate students by 1987.

In 1983 Fudan University in Shanghai and in 1984 Peking (Beijing) University began to enroll both graduate and undergraduate students in a political science programme, each averaging around forty undergraduate admissions per year. By 1986, more than ten Chinese universities and colleges have set up political science departments or programmes.

Since the official revival of political science in China in 1980, another source of impetus came from the international academic community, especially from the US. Many visited China and presented talks or lectures. A cursory list would include names like: Herbert A. Simon, David Easton, Gabriel Almond, Alex Inkeles, Seymour M. Lipset, Hubert Blalock, Robert Dahl, Klaus von Beyme, John Trent, Michel Oksenberg, Tang Tsou, Martin Landau, Lowell Dittmer, Robert Scalapino, just to mention a few.

From 1980, area studies began to develop which are likely to become what is termed as 'comparative politics' in the West. Since then until 1983, the Chinese Academy of Social Sciences had established the Institute of Soviet Union and East European Studies, the Institute of American Studies, the Institute of Japanese Studies, the Institute of West European Studies, the Institute of West Asian and African Studies, the Institute of Latin American Studies, and the

Institute of South Asian Studies. Recently a Centre for Taiwan Studies was set up.

ISSUES AND PROSPECT

Although political science as a discipline has by now gradually revived and become institutionalized in China, it still faces many problems both within and outside the academic community. It has yet a long and tortuous road to tread.

A number of problems pertaining to the discipline and the academic community itself can be identified. First, since political science had been abolished for more than twenty-eight years, few political scientists trained earlier are still willing to pick up their old trade; by now, most are in their sixties. Political scientists trained in the West before 1949 are very few and mostly in their seventieth or even eightieth year.

Second, even the few who could have provided guidance have been isolated from the development of the discipline for three decades. The post World War Two behavioural revolution is only now beginning to make its impact on the Chinese academic community.

Third, used to annotating official Marxist classics, providing post hoc policy justifications and making normative judgments or speculations, Chinese political scientists will take some time before focusing on more empirically orientated studies. Quantitative research methodology is only beginning to develop. Some survey research on public opinions was conducted but mostly with non-probability samples which had ill-defined target populations.

The factors that impinge from outside the discipline came mainly from the polity. The revival of political science was granted by the party-state almost as an act of grace. What had been given can at any time be taken away. Though one should not be unduly pessimistic, the unpredictability of future development was presaged by the ever shifting political winds, such as the short-lived 'anti-spiritual pollution movement' during early 1983 and the still ongoing 'anti-bourgeois liberalization struggle' started since January 1987. In the foreseeable future it is fairly certain that the scope of political science inquiry will be defined by the party and that decision will often come by *fiat* of the handful of political elites.

The feeling of uncertainty has multiple ramifications. For instance, there has been great interest in China in Western Marxism, yet when the translation of the three-volume *Main Currents of Marxism* by Leszek Kolakowski was completed in 1984 after the anti-spiritual-pollution campaign, the publisher became worried and rescinded the initial contract. One must not forget that China is one of the only two countries left today where Stalin's portrait is still on display during festive occasions and quoted in veneration — the other being Albania.

Whether rightly or wrongly, many Chinese social scientists will perceive their disciplines as somewhat precarious. This is especially true of political science and, to a lesser degree, of sociology. They often feel obliged to defend their discipline on the grounds that it has to be conducted under the guidance of official orthodox Marxism, and, at the same time stress, that the latter is no substitute for the former. Thus, even in 1985 people still felt it necessary to argue that 'scientific socialism' is no substitute for political science (Gao Fan 1985).

On the other hand, the word 'politics' itself is often associated with the idea of relentless struggle and persecution in the popular perception. For most Chinese, political science is not a very attractive profession to pursue. Politics itself is a highly sensitive field. Despite assurances from political leaders that freedom in academic discussion is to be promoted and even political issues are open to debate, most social scientists have reservations in varying degrees. The dismissal of Fang Lizhi from CCP membership and the post of vice president of the Chinese Science and Technology University in January 1987, and the removal of Su Shaozhi as director of the Institute of Marxism-Leninism of CASS six months later, proved to many that their fears were not unfounded. Fang was kicked out from the party because of his speeches on democratization. Su, an eminent Marxist theoretician whose recent work was more related to political studies, was relieved of his leading post because his writings on the democratic reform of political institutions were regarded as too liberal. Over-optimism regarding Chinese *glasnost* is ill-founded.

Generally speaking, the party-state has always placed the social sciences low on the priority list. Of the 4.11 million college graduates from 1949 to 1983, less than 10 per cent were in liberal arts and social sciences, including: humanities (6 per cent), finance and economics (3 per cent), political education and legal study (0.8 per cent) (Guojia Tongjijue 1985).

CONCLUSION

The major factors that shape the development of political science in China have been the political system, the political culture, and the internal dynamics of the discipline itself.

The political *Gleichschaltung* of all aspects of social life ensures the monopoly of the party-state on ideology, including absolute control over mass media, publication, and education. Any further development of political science depends on its utility in the eyes of the power holders.

The general attitude and behaviour of political actors is influenced by the all-pervasive political culture, which in the case of China goes back for more than two thousand years.

Despite exogenous factors, political science as a discipline seems to have a dynamic of its own. Since 1949 in China, it had repeated the pattern of its development in the West, where once it was a curriculum to educate people into becoming God-fearing and law abiding citizens (Somit and Tanenhaus 1967) and evolved into the study of the state and administration. Only recently in China has it begun to experience the behavioural revolution.

Probably it is too optimistic to speculate that the Chinese political scientists might still have a role to play in determining the future of their own discipline. Can they affect the change of the political culture which ultimately shapes the political system?

POSTSCRIPT

September 1989

Two years have passed since this paper was presented at the Cortona Conference. Much has happened in China since then. It is fitting to add some observations as a postscript.

Since the passing of Mao, the revelation of the causes of the Cultural Revolution and the influx of Western ideas brought definite changes in Chinese political culture among the intellectuals and the masses. This was the direct cause of student unrest in late 1986. Yet, the values and attitudes of the Chinese political elites remained basically unchanged. For this privileged group headed by a handful of octogenarians, economic reform and political relaxation were only means to re-enforce Chinese traditional autocracy clothed in the new Marxist garb of 'dictatorship of the proletariat'. Yet, it became evident to the people that any further economic reform is dependent on political institutional reform, which was promised but not implemented. There emerged a growing gap between the political culture of the urban mass and the holders of state power.

The crackdown on the student movement and the ousting of Hu Yaobang in 1987 seemed to have only a temporary inhibiting effect. The changes in popular political culture had evolved to the extent that the purged party dissidents in 1987 like Fang Lizhi, Liu Bingyan, Wang Ruoshuei, Su Shaozhi, etc. became heroes in the eyes of the Chinese public. Unlike previous purged dissident intellectuals, they did not make any public recantations or self-denonciations. For the first time since 1949, Chinese intellectuals had the opportunity to show that they are not devoid of backbone.

The 1987 crackdown did not deter Chinese writers and social scientists from making further criticism of their political and cultural tradition. This involved a great deal of painful introspection. The book entitled 'The Ugly Chinese' by the Taiwan writer Bai Yang was reprinted in the mainland and became an instant bestseller in 1987. Many Chinese writers and academics began similar but more moderate criticism against their cultural heritage. The indictment of the Chinese political tradition was also a national soul searching. People became increasingly aware of basic differences between the Chinese autocratic heritage and democratic institutions. The re-examination of the Chinese political heritage often turned into thinly veiled criticism of the past rule under Mao and the current rule under the living gerontocrats. The consensus of most Chinese academics, both outside and inside the party, seemed to be that in spite of 'revolutionary' Marxist rhetoric, politics under the CCP has close affinities with traditional autocracy.

The 1988 TV documentary 'Ho Shang' (Eulogy of the Yellow River) was a typical product of this intellectual self-examination. By PRC standards it was a relentless critique against Chinese cultural and political tradition. However, its instant popularity angered the party octogenarians who suddenly became defenders of the 'valuable cultural heritage of the great motherland'. Due to insistent complaints from the gerontograts, Ho Shang was officially banned after its first broadcast. Once again the Chinese state intervened because it felt its core values threatened.

Dissatisfaction with the slow pace of economic and political reform also took a new form. The sudden popularity of the so-called 'Neo-authoritarianism' among some younger generation intellectuals since 1987 is an indication of their desire for a faster pace of reform. Ironically, it is also an indication of the persistence of the Chinese political legacy even among those who should be most immune to it. Neo-authoritarianism started with the assumption that the price to be paid for economic development was authoritarian politics. The propounders of this doctrine often cited South Korea, Brazil, Taiwan, Argentina, and Singapore as examples where authoritarianism led to political stability which in turn stimulated economic growth. They believed that stagnant economic performance and the failure to create further reform were mainly due to the absence of strong political authority. They would rather see a strengthening of authoritarian politics and the appearance of a strong authoritarian leader dedicated to economic development. This was, of course, very appealing to the establishment leaders, including Deng Xiaoping. Evidently, these younger Chinese intellectuals seemed to have forgotten the lessons learned by their parents, who also longed for a strong leader to strengthen the state and at one time idolized Mao.

Paradoxical as it may seem, the discussion of neo-authoritarianism was allegedly stimulated by the publication of the Chinese translation of Samuel Huntington's *Political Order in Changing Societies* in late 1987. A few of the propounders were young scholars who had just returned after studying in the US. This is a typical case where a foreign idea may be transfigured by indigenous cultural lenses in the process of absorption.

However, neo-authoritarianism met with serious criticism from other members of the academic community, who had already fallen out of official favour. They pointed out that neo-authoritarianism is only the recurrence of nostalgia for a strong benevolent emperor under a new label.

Among Chinese intellectuals there was growing frustration with the stagnant pace of promised political reform. In the intellectual community, people became disillusioned with official ideological orthodoxy which was regarded as the main cause for the persistence of autocratic politics. The terms 'Marxism' and 'Marxist analysis' became almost dirty words in Chinese everyday vocabulary and carried the connotation of intellectual sterility, ultra conservatism, hairsplitting annotation and a medieval scholastic mentality.

During the two years since 1987, public opinion polling developed in China at a fast pace. Aside from the State Statistics Bureau, public opinion research institutes and groups were established in the Chinese Academy of Social Sciences and some major universities. Probability sampling in the PRC improved with the help of Leslie Kish of ISR at the University of Michigan. Most of the surveys showed a strong reaction by the public against official corruption, inflation, and the procrastination of political reform.

With the advantage of hindsight, one can conclude that during the two years since 1987, the growing gap between popular and elite political culture finally led to their eruptive confrontation in 1989.

Nineteen eighty-nine was a year with many celebrations. It was the fortieth anniversary of the PRC, seventieth anniversary of the May Fourth Movement, and two hundredth anniversary of the French Revolution. Then it also became a memorable year by its own right.

It started on 6 January 1989, when Fang Lizhi wrote a letter to Deng Xiaoping calling for the release of Wei Jingshen and other political prisoners. This news triggered another petition signed by 33 writers on February 13. Then followed petitions of 42 scientists on February 26 and 43 social scientists on March 14. Although such actions are perfectly normal in the West, it was the first of its kind in 40 years of the PRC. This was the first time in PRC history that Chinese people had made any independent judgment on political matters and open demands on the state in face of its disapproval. The news of the petitions by well-known academics and writers awakened student activism which had lain dormant for two years.

The death of ousted General Secretary Hu Yaobang on 15 April was the last straw that broke the dam of student demonstration. On 16 April students of Beijing came to Tiananmen Square to mourn for Hu. Then it spread to Shanghai, Nanjing, Xian and other major cities.

In the face of a stern warning in the form of an editorial in *People's Daily*, on 27 April more than 150,000 college students in Beijing staged the greatest protest demonstration since 1949. They were joined by a million Beijing residents. What is most striking was the discipline and restraint shown by the students. There had been no case in history where the gathering of one million protesters had been so peaceful. Their only demands were to have open dialogue with the government, and the implementing of basic human rights guaranteed in the Constitution: freedom of speech, of press and of assembly. That day is a watershed in Chinese modern history which showed that Chinese people have the same aspirations as any other people. This is the first time in more than two thousand years that the ordinary people of China demonstrated peacefully to the world that they are no longer content to be docile subjects of the autocratic state. Despite culture relativism, there seem to be certain universal values which appeal to all humankind.

Those youthful demonstrating Chinese students and workers may be naive and have had little experience of democratic institutions, but their aspirations for freedom, human rights, and social justice were real. On Tiananmen Square, they erected a statue of the Goddess of Democracy. They chanted Patrick Henry's call 'Give me liberty or give me death'. Some recited the Declaration of Independence. They wanted the world to know that the people of China hold the same basic values as any other self-respecting people.

China entered into a new era.

According to official public-security statistics, the crime rate of Beijing during the 'rioting period' from mid April to mid May was the lowest in the previous four years. The truth is that there was no popular riot. All violence was initiated by the government and inflicted on unarmed civilians. The Fourth of June Beijing massacre shocked the world to the reality of totalitarian politics. This was the first time in Chinese history that a government had used tanks and machine guns against unarmed civilians. No lies can whitewash the bloodstains of the mutilated bodies of hunger strikers on Tiananmen Square.

Thousands were killed, more were wounded. Many fled the country. Tens of thousands were arrested. Even now, executions and arrests, both open and secret, are still going on.

As is to be expected, in the wake of the bloody massacre of Fourth of June, the party-state once again tightened its grip upon the humanities and social science disciplines. On 21 July the Commission of Education announced that undergraduate enrolment for 1989 would be reduced by 30,000. Many social science departments in universities were ordered to stop enrolling altogether. In the summer of 1989 Beijing University was ordered not to enroll any new students in the departments of political science, international politics, sociology, or administrative management; it recruited only 800 new students instead of its previous 2,200 in 1988. All its 1989 freshmen had to undergo one year of military training and political indoctrination in the army camps before coming back as role models for students of 1990. Freshmen in other universities and colleges were ordered to undergo half a year of intensive political indoctrination. Political reliability once again became the most important criterion for college admission.

The party-state also began to impose tighter restrictions on mass media and publication. On 26 July books written by ten Chinese writers on the wanted list were decreed to be forbidden publications; another 133 titles were also banned. On 22 August 1989 the Ministry of Culture convened a National Working Conference for Rectifying the Culture Market. Coordinated action to censor publications began. According to an incomplete official estimate, some 40,000 retail book stores were under 'punitive investigation', more than 2,660,000 volumes of books were confiscated, more than 8,720,000 volumes put under seal, and more than 90,000 video tapes confiscated. In addition, radio signal-jamming of voice of America and BBC broadcasts was resumed on a regular basis.

Many writers and academics were either arrested, put on the wanted list, or placed under house arrest. Some more fortunate Chinese writers and academics either remained in foreign countries or escaped abroad. Liu Bingyan stays in the US, Fang Lizhi remains in hiding in the US embassy in Beijing, Su Shaozhi came to Europe, Yan Jiaqi (director of the Institute of Political Science of the Chinese Academy of Social Sciences) escaped to France, etc. Others were not so fortunate. Liu Xiaobo, Li Honglin (director of Fujian Province Academy of Social Sciences), Bao Zunxin, Su Xiaokang (author of *Ho Shang*) and many others were arrested.

This list of purged and demoted include the head of the Ministry of Culture Wang Meng, the editor in chief of *People's Daily* Tan Wenrui, the director of the Masses Publishing House Yu Haocheng, and many other prominent intellectuals, both inside and outside the CCP.

It is ironic that all the main figures who were responsible for launching the 1978 'practice as the sole criterion of truth', which was instrumental in providing ideological legitimacy for the ascension of Deng, were purged in one way or another.

Whatever the immediate retrogressive effects of the Fourth of June massacre, the political culture of the Chinese people had changed. This may be the first step of a protracted process of basic change in the political system. After all, are not culture, action, and structure the same elements of the social world?

NOTES

1 This chapter is based on the paper presented to the International Round Table on the Comparative Study of the Development of the Discipline of Political Science, Cortona, Italy, 21-22 September 1987.

   The views expressed are the personal views of the author and not necessarily those of the institution to which he is affiliated. The paper was prepared while the author was teaching at the university of California at Irvine and revised while he was a fellow at the Center for Advanced Study in the Behavioral Sciences. The author would like to thank these two institutions, the National Science Foundation for its financial support, and Professor Mark Petracca for his helpful comments.

2 Following Almond and Verba, in this paper the term political culture 'refers to the specifically political orientations – attitudes toward the political system and its various parts, and attitudes toward the role of the self in the system' (Almond and

Verba 1963).

3 Following David Easton, politics is defined as the authoritative allocation of values (Easton 1965).

4 The great Chinese historian Si-Ma-Qian (Ssu-ma Ch'ien, circa 145-90 BC) told us in his famous *Historical Records* that the first edicts proclaimed by the Qin emperor in late third century BC were: 'All books in the imperial archives except for the records of Qin should be burned; all persons under heaven, except learned scholars in the Academy, in possession of the Book of Odes, the Book of History and essays of the hundred school of philosophers should take them to the magistrates to be burned; those who dare to talk to each other about the Book of Odes and the Book of History should be executed and their bodies exposed in the market; those who refer to the past to criticize the present should be, with members of their family, put to death; officials who knowingly fail to report are guilty of the same crime; after thirty days from time of issuing the decree, those who have not destroyed their books are to be branded and sent to build city walls; books not to be destroyed are those on medicine, pharmacy, divination, agriculture, and horticulture; those who want to study edicts should be taught by the officials' (Sima Qian 1978).

5 Japan exhibited similar reaction in late nineteenth century, as noted by Wirth (1936).

6 This slogan was propounded in 1898 by Zhang Zhidong (1959).

7 For the case of Professor Qian, see C. Johnson (1961).

8 For some good arguments of the possibility of objective social science see E. Nagel (1961).

9 This passage from Hayek (1952) was quoted by Sartori (1962).

10 For details, see issues of *Zhongguo Keji Bao* (Chinese Science and Technology Newspaper) 3, 24 September; 1, 8, 29 October; 5, 26 November; 10, 24 December of 1986. The title of this series of articles is 'Wele Wanque De Huigu' (For remembrances that are forgotten).

11 For other accounts about the rehabilitation of political science in PRC, see T. P. Bernstein (1980) and Zhao Baoxu (1984).

12 Throughout this chapter the term institution is used to mean normative relationship among roles. It is not as inclusive as the term 'political system', which includes more than the state, nor as concrete as the term organization. The rendering of the Chinese term *zheng zhi ti zhi* as 'political system' would lead to many misunderstandings.

13 Based on the 1977 to 1981 issues of the annual *Quanguo Zon Shumu* (National General Book Catalogue) and the 1977 to 1986 issues of the monthly journal *Quanguo Xin Shumu* (National New Books Catalogue).

14 See note 13.

REFERENCES

Almond, G. and S. Verba (1963) *The Civic Culture*, Princeton: Princeton University Press.

CASS (1983) *Zhongguo Shehui Kexueyuan* (Chinese Academy of Social Sciences), Beijing.

CCP (1981) 'Resolution on certain questions in the history of our Party', *Beijing*

Review 24 (27).

Bernstein, T.P. (1980) 'Political science', in Thurston and Parker (eds) *Humanistic and Social Science Research in China*, New York: Social Science Research Council.

Chen Tiqian (1943) *Zhongguo Waijiao Xingzheng* (Chinese Foreign Affairs Administration), Chongqing: Shangwu.

Chen Zhimai (1944) *Zhongguo Zhengfu* (Chinese Governement), 2 vols, Chongqing: Shangwu; 1st vol. 1944, 2nd vol. 1945.

Ch'ien, T. S. (1950) *The Government and Politics of China*, Cambridge: Harvard University Press.

Deng Xiaoping (1983a) 'Jianchi Si Xian Jiben Yuanze' (Hold steadfast the four basic principles), 30 March 1978, in *Deng Xiaoping Wenxuan: 1975-81*, Beijing: Renmin.

— 'Dang He Guojia Lingdao Zhidu De Gaige' (The reform of the institution of leadership of the Party and the state) in *Shiyijie Sanzhong Quanhui Yilai Zhongyao Wenxien Jianbian* (Selections of Important Documents Since the Third Plenum of the Eleventh Party Central Committee), Beijing: Renmin.

Easton, D. (1965) *A Framework for Political Analysis*, Englewood Cliffs: Prentice-Hall.

Freedman, M. (1962) 'Sociology In and Of China', *British Journal of Sociology* 13 (1).

Gao Fan (1985) 'Lun Zhengzhixue Yu Kexue Shehuizhuyi' (On political and scientific socialism), *Shehui Kexue* (Gansu) (5).

Guo Moruo (1957) 'Shehui Kexuejie Fanyou Dozhen Bixu Jinyibu Shenruo' (The anti-rightist struggle in the social science community must forge deeper), *Renmin Ribao*, 19 September.

Guojia Tongjijue (State Statistics Bureau) (1985 edition) *Zhongguo Tongji Nienjian: 1984* (China Statistics Yearbook: 1984), Beijing: Zhongguo Tongji.

Hayek, F. A. (1952) *The counter-revolution of science*. New York: Glencoe.

Hu Sheng (1986) 'Guanyue Jiaqiang Shehui Kexue Yenjiu De Jige Wenti' (Certain issues concerning the consolidation of social science studies) *Hongqi* (9).

Johnson, C. (1961) 'An Intellectual Weed in the Socialist Garden' *China Quarterly* (6).

Li Shu (1979) 'Zhongguo Shehui Kexue Sanshi Nien' (Three decades of Chinese social science). *Lishi Yenjiu* (Studies in History) (11).

Li Kejing (1986), 'Woguo de Zhengzhi Tizhi Gaige Yu Zhengzhixue De Fazhan' (Reform of political institutions and the development of political science in our country), *Zhongguo Shehui Kexue* (4).

Liang Qichao (1936) 'Wushi Nien Zhongguo Jinhua Gailun' (A survey of Chinese evolution during the past fifty years), in *Yinbingshi Heji* (Collected Works of the Ice-Drinker's Studio), Shanghai: Zhonghua Shujue.

Lu, C. (1985) 'Shojie Lingdao Kexue Xueshu Taolunhui Zongshu' (Synthetic report on the First Academic Conference of the Science of Leadership) *Zhengzhixue Yenjiu* (3).

Luo, B. *et al.* (1985) 'Quanguo Shojie Lingdao Kexue Xueshu Taolunhui Zongshu' (Synthetic report on the First National Academic Conference of the Science of Leadership), *Guangmin Ribao*, 22 May.

Mao Zedong (1957) 'Guanyu Zhengque Chuli Renmin Nebu Maodun De Wenti' (On the problem of correct handling of contradiction within the people), *Renmin Ribao*, June 19.

Nagel, E. (1961) *The Structure of Science*, New York & Burlingame: Harcourt, Brace & World.

Qian Duansheng *et al.* (1939) *Minguo Zhengzhi Shi* (History of the political institution of the Republic), Zhansha: Shangwu.

Sartori, G. (1962) *Democratic Theory*, Detroit: Wayne State University Press.

Shao Zuozhou (1958) 'Shaoshi Weyen' (The admonition of Shao) in *Zhongguo Jindaishi Ziliao Zonkan* (Series of materials of Chinese modern history) (Chinese Academy of Social Sciences eds), Beijing: Zhonghua Shujue.

Sima Qian (1978) *Shi Ji* (Historical records), Beijing: Zhonghua Shujue.

Somit and Tanenhaus (1967) *The Development of American Political Science*, Boston: Allyn & Bacon.

Su Shaozhi (1986) 'Zhengzhi Tizhi Gaige Zhouyi' (Comments on the reform of political institutions, *Dushu* (9).

Teng, S. and J. K. Fairbank (1979) *China's response the West*, Cambridge: Havard University Press.

Wan Li (1986) 'Juece Minzhuhua He Kexuehua She Zhengzhi Tizhi Gaige De Zhongyao Fanmian' (Democratization and scientification of decision-making are important aspects of the reform of political institutions), *Guangnin Ribao* 15 August.

Wang Shijie (1926) *Bijiao Xienfa* (Comparative Constitution), Shanghai: Shangwu.

Wei Yuan (1960) 'Preface to the Illustrated Gazetteer of the maritime countries', in W. T. Barry, W. Chan (eds) *Sources of Chinese Tradition*, New York: Columbia University Press.

Wirth, L. (1936) 'Preface' in Karl Mannheim, *Ideology and Utopia*, New York: Harcourt.

Xinhuashe (New China News Agency) (1957) 'Zhongguo Shehui Kexueyuan Zhexue Shehui Kexuebu Fanyou Dozhen Huo Zhongda Shengli' (The anti-rightist struggle in the philosophy and social science division of the Chinese Academy of Sciences has scored a great victory), *Xinhua Banyuekan* (20).

Xu and Xiao (1985) 'Jinnienlai Woguo Xienfaxue Zhongyao Lilun Wenti Taolun Zongshu' (Synthetic report on the discussion of important theoretical issues in the study of Constitution in our country during the past few years), *Zhongguo Shehui Kexue* (5).

Zhang Zhidong (1959) 'Quengxue Pien' (Exhortion to study), in *Zhongguo Zhexueshi Ziliao Xuenji* (Selected materials from the history of Chinese philosophy) (CASS, eds), Beijing: Zhonghua Shujue.

Zhoa Baoxu (1984) 'The revival of political science in China', *Political Science*, Autumn.

11 Political science in 'Anglophone' Africa

Its context and developmental logic in
historical perspective

L. Adèle Jinadu[1]

INTRODUCTION

Objective

This chapter attempts a cartographic survey of political science as an
intellectual discipline in 'Anglophone' African universities. But I
begin with general observations on the discipline in Africa before
focusing on selected Anglophone African countries for more detailed
illustration of the general observations.

A representative sample of Anglophone African countries is
selected for detailed analysis because this category of country is vast
and heterogeneous. The countries selected for this purpose are Nigeria
in West Africa, Tanzania in East Africa, and Zimbabwe in southern
Africa. The aim is to review the current state and status of the
discipline and to identify its priority needs.

The choice of the three countries was informed by the author's
familiarity with and knowledge of the discipline in them. He has,
moreover, been engaged in a study of the social sciences and
development in Africa which has included the three countries. The
analysis in this chapter is therefore based partly on data collected
during the study (Jinadu 1977, 1984).

Problems of categorization

A basic problem in this kind of study is how political science is to
be categorized. Much of course depends on the traditions of faculty
structure and disciplinary organization in higher education in these
countries. This is partly a boundary problem. But it is also a problem
arising out of the colonial roots of education, especially of the
perceptions of political science as a discipline by colonial policy-
makers and the translation of these perceptions into faculty structure
and departmental organizations in the emergent universities in these
countries.

This, however, is also not unrelated to considerations which have
generally tended to inform disciplinary departmentalization in the
organization of higher education in metropolitan countries like Great

Britain. As a result, university structures in the metropole tended to be reproduced in the colonies.

The question, 'What is political science?' or 'What are the political sciences?' cannot therefore be answered in the abstract, without reference to conditioning historical factors such as those referred to above. Whether there are autonomous or separate political science departments in these countries will also depend on these conditioning historical factors.

The context of political science in Africa is to be situated mainly in these conditioning historical factors. This much is also true of the character of the discipline in 'Francophone' and Portuguese speaking Africa.

Problems and patterns of departmental emergence

The broad, all-inclusive scope of the 'political' has meant, however, that even in those universities in those countries where there are no specifically designated departments of politics or political science, 'politics' has inescapably been studied in one form or another. This is one reason why in those countries where there are now departments of political science, the discipline has served an apprenticeship in the humanities. And in the countries where there are no such departments, political science is nevertheless studied as part of the curriculum in faculties of letters, law, and social sciences. Here again, the practice tends to follow that of the metropolitan universities. This is generally the situation in the French and Lusophone countries.

The institutionalization of political science and the other social sciences in the universities in these countries must, in another sense, be viewed in the wider context of the global processes of socio-cultural and intellectual diffusion from the West. Part of the crisis of teaching and research in political science and the other social sciences in Africa is due precisely to the fact that the social sciences in Africa, including political science, have generally tended to mirror mainstream Western social science, which is itself but a superstructural manifestation of the hegomonic drive of Western finance capital and imperialism into Africa.

A review of the current situation of the discipline in Africa as well as the design of a political science which is relevant to the needs of the African region must necessarily take into account this cultural fact. Part of the design project that this calls for is therefore the articulation of strategic measures to facilitate meaningful and relevant dissociation from or adaptation to this mainstream social science.

Another dimension of the institutionalization of political science, and indeed of the social sciences in these countries, is the context provided by the highly statist structure of their political economies, itself a dimension of their colonial heritage. This aspect of their political economies has ensured the virtual monopoly of university

education and research by the state. The developmental logic of
political science has been very much influenced by the importance
attached to it by bureaucrats who are involved in the planning and
implementation of policies on university education in these countries.

Another dimension of the institutionalization of political science is
what was earlier referred to as its apprenticeship in the humanities
and law. By this is meant its beginnings as a unit or sub-unit of these
faculties and not as a separate independent department. This aspect of
the developmental logic of the discipline is related to a particular
philosophy of education elaborated by colonial educationalists and
later by their indigenous successors in most of these countries. This is
a humanistic conception of higher education which places a premium
on liberal arts education as a foundation for university education. The
flexibility and multidisciplinarity which this outlook encouraged in
the organization of academic programmes was no doubt an important
factor which allowed political science and the other social sciences to
enter into university curricula through the 'backdoor' initially.

The logic of multidisciplinarity was to lead in due course, especially
in Anglophone African countries, to the establishment of autonomous
departments of political science. But it was not the logic of
multidisciplinarity alone which gave rise to this development.

Departmentalization and logic of nation-building

Also contributing was the logic of colonial nationalism and the
expansion in manpower needs in the penultimate years of colonial
rule. If colonial administrations were reluctant to establish courses in
political science and related disciplines or sub-disciplines, the logic of
colonial nationalism made their establishment perhaps inevitable. In
the Anglophone countries, especially, the view was advanced that
political science and the other social sciences were relevant to national
development and nation-building; and that this was a persuasive
reason for creating autonomous departments and faculties for teaching
and research in them. There seemed to have been a meeting-point
between the need for socio-economic and political development within
the state and the creation of university education in political science.
In this sense, the discipline was expected to play a developmental role
along with the other social sciences. The argument was, moreover,
given an instrumentalist thrust in being linked to the attainment of
projected manpower needs and targets made imperative by the
planned Africanization of the public services and the need to provide
social services on a much larger scale than the colonial powers were
prepared to undertake.

This instrumentalist view has been a mixed blessing for the
development of political science. For one reason, the instrumental
value of political science was viewed as less obvious than that of
economics or sociology, for example. For this reason it has tended to

be more marginalized than the other social sciences. A development-oriented view of government as a vehicle for ensuring the material welfare of its citizens has led to much more importance being attached to economics and sociology, and even more so to the natural, physical and medical sciences, engineering and technology, and to management and business studies than to political science.

For another reason, the stigma attaching to political science as a subversive discipline which must be kept at bay has been a powerful obstacle to the growth of the discipline in most of these countries, especially in the Francophone countries. This view of the anti-status quo orientation of the discipline is itself a hangover from the colonial rule which successor regimes have inherited and which has influenced their predispositions towards the discipline.

The politics vs administration debate

Partly because of this presumed stigma and partly because of the need to appear 'relevant' in the instrumental sense, another feature of the developmental logic of political science in these countries is the tendency towards the establishment of separate departments of public administration and international relations and the offering of separate degree programmes in these cognate branches of political science.

In the Francophone countries, for example, the general trend is that 'public administration' has effectively been dissociated from political science. The various schools of administration in Francophone countries are created for the primary purpose of teaching civil servants and bureaucrats the rubrics of administrative, constitutional, public, and civil laws.

The Americanization of African political science

Another important factor in the institutionalization and developmental logic of political science in African universities is the Americanization of the discipline in the post World War Two period. The emergence of North American political science in Africa partly fed on the rising tide of African nationalism in the 1950s and 1960s. In Anglophone Africa to a greater extent than in Francophone and Lusophone Africa, the need for academic staff to match the phenonomenal expansion in university education inevitably led to recourse being had to the United States, where there were then and still are well developed and diverse graduate programmes to carry on the global task of the reproduction of university teachers.

The outward push of intellectual focus in American political science in the post-1945 period towards the developing world — part of a search for a universally valid general theory of political science — in turn fed American interest in the 'new nations' of the developing world. These 'new nations' provided opportunities of 'field' experience and fieldwork for American scholars and researchers. It was also reflected in curricula innovations in comparative politics, international relations, and area studies. Scholars and students from the 'new nations' were also deliberately recruited to the US to provide a cross-cultural dimension to graduate programmes in these disciplines in US universities.

The availability of well-developed graduate programmes in the US meant that promising African scholars and potential university staff members could be sent to the US to pursue higher degree programmes. The private philanthropic foundations such as the Rockefeller Foundation and the Ford Foundation facilitated this training objective by making available fellowships for graduate study in the US. These foundations also provided funds for the recruitment and secondment of academic staff from North American universities to teach and conduct research in African universities. In this way American political science progressively found a foothold and dug itself in Africa.

Towards a relevant African political science

These, then, are some of the important conditioning historical and materialist factors against which the present state of political science in Africa, its developmental logic, and the prospects for its improvement must be viewed.

The current crisis in development studies; the crisis of the African state; the emergent renewed faith in the capacity of African social science to chart alternative developmental paths; and the confrontation of progressive radical African intellectuals with the dominant Europo-centric social science which this faith has engendered are also factors which have called for the re-examination of the kind of African political science which is needed to serve the continent's needs.

CURRENT SITUATION

Political science in selected African countries

In this section, the current state of political science in universities in Nigeria, Tanzania, and Zimbabwe is described.

General observations

Some general observations should be made before the country-by-country description of the current situation of political science in

Africa is given. A basic concern here is with the institutional arrangements for teaching and research in the discipline in the context of the conditioning historical and materialist factors identified above.

Impact of socio-economic change

A general observation is that the rich diversity of institutional frameworks for teaching and training in political science in these countries is itself a reflection of the changing needs and priorities of African governments as they confront problems of socio-economic change. This has forced the discipline and indeed the social sciences generally to be not merely academic enterprises but also to be concretely situated among the problems of these countries. As was pointed out above, this has meant, in the case of political science, disciplinary fragmentation as sub-disciplines like public administration, local government, and international relations try to 'secede' from their parent discipline

Linkage of teaching and research

Another general observation is that in the three countries, the preoccupation with problems of development has led to the integration of teaching with research in political science and the other social sciences. This linkage of teaching with research is evident in the establishment within and outside the universities of research institutes in political science or the social sciences. It is evident, also, in faculty organization, in collaborative work between teaching and research staff, in the involvement of research staff of some of these institutes in undergraduate and post-graduate teaching, and in the linking of certain types of research to the publication of textbooks and other teaching materials for use in the universities.

Aspects of logic of departmentalization

Another general observation is the trend towards the departmentalization of the discipline and of the other social science disciplines. While each department is autonomous and is free to structure its degree programmes, overall coordination is nevertheless provided by the faculty.

But some further comments are in order with respect to the trend towards departmentalization. First, there is the increasing tendency towards specialization within the department. This is partly the result of expansion in course offerings within the department and has generally involved students choosing specialized options in their second or third year at the university. But it is also partly due to the specific manpower requirements of the public and private sectors in these countries, which demanded a shift from generalist degree programmes to specialized or career-oriented ones.

This is indeed one reason why in Nigeria, for example, the trend towards specialized degree programmes has led to the demand for and in some cases the establishment of separate departments of public administration, including local government, and international relations to be created from existing departments of political science.

A second comment about the trend towards departmentalization is that in spite of it, some multidisciplinarity is nonetheless maintained. In most cases, political science students are encouraged and even required to offer courses in other disciplines. This is generally done by the cross-listing of courses and the requirement that students offer a minimum number of courses outside of their departments before they can graduate.

Multidisciplinarity has been further facilitated in recent years by two developments. The first is the popularity and respectability which the 'new' Marxist political-economy approach to the study of African politics has enjoyed. Its focus on the interrelatedness of various aspects of social life conduces to a multidisciplinary approach to the study of politics. The second development is the increasing interest among African political scientists and other social scientists in a policy-oriented social science.

Curricular preoccupations

A further general observation concerns the general thrust or focus of teaching in political science in these countries. The curricular preoccupation is generally with development issues in their national, sub-regional, regional and extracontinental dimensions.

As was indicated above, it is inevitable, in view of the colonial inheritance of these countries and the globalization of Western political science under the hegemonic thrust of the US, that political science curricula in these countries have been influenced by developments in Europe and North America.

Generally, the state is still the main unit and focus of analysis, and it is around it that curricula in the various subfields of the discipline have been designed. The division into subfields in the three countries has been based on the traditional division in the Anglo-Saxon world into: political thought or philosophy, national and comparative politics, public administration (including local government), international relations and politics, and, in recent years, political economy.

I now turn to the analysis of the state of the discipline in each of the three countries.

POLITICAL SCIENCE IN NIGERIA

Origins

It was not until the early 1960s that autonomous departments of political science were established in Nigeria. The first such department was established at the new University of Nigeria, Nsukka and later at the University College, Ibadan (now University of Ibadan), the University of Ife, the Ahmadu Bello University and the University of Lagos. Virtually all the universities in the country now have departments of political science, the exceptions being the federal universities of technology.

Curricular focus

The teaching of political science in the country has been primarily preoccupied with the study of the state in its national and international contexts. For example, the *Handbook* of the department of political science at the University of Nigeria, Nsukka, asserts that, 'as an academic subject, political science is concerned with the study of the conditions of men as embodied in the state'.

Initially, the main thrust of the political science syllabus in the country was at formal and informal, legal and constitutional processes of government — the role of parliament and political parties, political leadership roles, and other mechanisms of institutional transfer and national integration. In much of this, Nigerian political science was influenced by the basic concerns of the modernization school in the US, in their application of pluralist theories and structural-functionalism to the study of the so-called 'new' nations. The emphasis was on order, stability and reconciliation and not on contradictions and conflict in the teaching of the discipline. By the late 1960s there had been a shift away, albeit a marginal one, from the theoretical and empirical foci of the modernization school. This shift itself resulted from the inadequacy of mainstream Western political science and social science to provide an adequate and satisfactory framework for analysing politics on a global scale. The nascent contradictions in the world capitalist system called into question the relevance of existing frameworks of analysis grounded in neo-Keynesianism.

The initial shift in Nigerian political science was reflected in new curricula concerns in the late 1960s and early 1970s with the role of the military in politics, with the incidence of violence in politics and with the inherent, structurally-induced fragility of the state in Africa.

In due course, and by the late 1970s a significant part of Nigerian political science had begun to adopt methodological and theoretical foci informed by dialectical and historical materialism. Political science syllabuses also started to reflect the interrelatedness of politics, culture, law, and socio-economic structures.

Duration of degree programmes and trends in enrolment and staff strength

The duration of an undergraduate degree course in political science varies from university to university, but it usually takes between three and four years. At the University of Ibadan and the University of Lagos, the degree programme extends over three years. At the University of Nigeria on the other hand, it extends over four years. The three-year programmes are, however, being gradually phased out in favour of the four-year ones under a new national policy on education.

Student enrolment in undergraduate degree programmes reached an all-time high in the latter half of the 1970s, reflecting a buoyant economy which enabled more subsidies to be made to the universities by the federal government. At the University of Lagos, for example, enrolment for the BSc (Hons) degree in political science has risen from two in 1964 to forty-one in 1971, to 114 in 1978 and 124 in 1979. At the Ahmadu Bell University the number of political science graduates produced rose from ten in the 1970-1 session to thirty-three in 1975-6, and 109 in 1976-7 (see Jinadu 1977). Similar increases in undergraduate enrolment were recorded in other departments of political science in other universities.

The increase in student enrolment in the mid-1970s was also accompanied by increases in the numerical strength of academic staff in political science. At Ahmadu Bello University, for example, the academic staff strength of the department of government rose from six to twenty-one during the period 1972-4.

The downturn in Nigeria's economy, induced by the current global economic crisis and declining revenue yield from oil, has brought about drastic reductions in government subsidy to the universities. This has also meant a corresponding reduction in university admissions and therefore of enrolment in undergraduate degree programmes in political science. This is because reduced support has generally meant that less instrumentally 'relevant' disciplines have tended to experience the most drastic cuts.

Structure of degree programmes

The structure of the undergraduate degree programme in the departments of political science in the country is typified by that at Nsukka where students are examined in each of the following four subfields of the discipline: political theory, government (national and comparative), public administration, and international relations. Students are, however, expected to take a number of courses from related disciplines, such as economics, sociology, psychology, history, and philosophy.

In addition to the single honours degree course in political science,

some Nigerian universities offer joint or combined honours programmes in which students combine a degree course in political science
with another degree in the social sciences or humanities.

At the University of Nsukka there are combined degree programmes in political science and sociology, and in political science and
economics. At the University of Ibadan and Ahmadu Bello University,
there is one in politics and history at each university; and at the
University of Lagos there used to be integrated BSc degree programmes in which students could offer political science in addition to two
other social science disciplines. The reduced support referred to above
was partly responsible for the phasing out of this integrated social
science degree programme at the University of Lagos.

The aim of these combined degree programmes is well expressed by
the late Billy Dudley when he observed in his inaugural lecture as
Professor of Political Science at the University of Ibadan:

> There is little doubt that in the future more varied and more
> challenging combinations of disciplines will be evolved in an
> attempt to break away from the present, cripplingly narrow
> specialization and to a better and more soundly educated type of
> graduate, of which I think our society is so much in need. (B.J.
> Dudley 1975:3)

The teaching of political science in Nigeria has therefore, in spite
of departmentalization of the discipline, been towards multidisciplinarity and integration particularly with the other social sciences and
the humanities.

Admission requirements

The basic qualification for admission to an undergraduate degree
programme in political science is usually a General Certificate of
Education or its equivalent, which shows no fewer than two subjects
passed at the advanced level and three at the ordinary level. In a
number of departments candidates seeking admission are usually
required to have ordinary-level passes in English and Mathematics.

Degree objectives

The object of undergraduate education in political science in Nigeria
has generally been defined in terms of manpower production. A
typical statement of this objective is that offered in the *Handbook* of
the department of political science at the University of Nigeria,
Nsukka for the 1983-4 academic year: 'The objectives of the degree
programme in political science are the production of high-level
management, administrative and executive manpower for services in

the public sector, industry, foreign service, teaching and research'.

Postgraduate and objectives

Most departments of political science in the country offer postgraduate programmes at the diploma, MSc, and PhD levels. An objective of postgraduate education in the discipline is to train future academic staff. But the objective is also to prepare students for higher administrative, executive, and management positions in the public and private sector.

The Master's of Public Administration (MPA) degree is particularly popular in this connection. Also popular is the MSc (international relations) degree programme. This popularity is due to the presumed marketability of advanced degrees in public administration and international relations. The increase in unemployment induced by the downturn in the country's economy has also fed the interest in postgraduate education as a stop-gap measure while fresh graduates are still looking for employment.

Research directions and research institutions

Research in political science is carried on either collectively or individually by members of the various departments. Most research is funded by a university research board or by outside national or international agencies. While much of the focus of the research is on national politics, some research in comparative politics and international relations is also carried out.

The major extra-university research institute in the country specifically devoted to the discipline is the Nigerian Institute of International Affairs (NIIA). The Nigerian Institute of Social and Economic Research (NISER) at the University of Ibadan, the Centre for Social, Economic and Cultural Studies at the University of Benin, the Economic Development Institute at the University of Nigeria, Nsukka, and the Centre for Social and Economic Research at the Ahmadu Bello University; Zaria also undertake research in areas and topics related to political science, although it is unusual to have specifically designated political science units or divisions within them.

Boundary problem: politics or administration?

Two developments in Nigerian political science must be mentioned in conclusion. The first concerns boundary or definition problems which the discipline has had to face in the country. The problems are about determining the criteria for constituting a department of political science or its sub-departments.

In some Nigerian universities, like Ahmadu Bello and Ife, departments of political science existed *ab initio*, separately from the Institutes of Administration. At issue later was whether these institutes, originally set up to offer non-degree diploma and refresher courses for public servants, should be merged with existing departments of political science in these universities or should be constituted instead into autonomous degree-awarding departments of public administration. The argument of those who wanted separate, autonomous degree-awarding departments of public administration was essentially that 'administration' was separate from and not necessarily a cognate branch of political science. Their argument is that 'administration' is much broader in connotation than 'public administration' and has closer affinity with disciplines like accounting, management, commerce, and finance. Another argument is that only a separate department of public administration can offer the professional-oriented and managerial focus lacking in a degree in political science.

This is the background to the existence of separate, autonomous degree-awarding departments of political administration at Ahmadu Bello University and the University of Ife. A sub-department of Public Administration and local Government was recently established at the University of Nigeria, Nsukka and the long-term aim is to constitute it into a full-fledged degree-awarding department.

Professionalization of the discipline

The second development is the professionalization of the discipline in the country. The Nigerian Political Science Association was founded in 1973 and now publishes its own journal *Studies in Politics and Society*. There is also the Nigerian Society of International Affairs which publishes the *Nigerian Journal of International Affairs*. Also inaugurated recently was the Nigerian Society of Public Administration. These associations provide for the exchange of information and for the discussion of national, African, and world issues for Nigerian political scientists.

POLITICAL SCIENCE IN TANZANIA

Origins

The process which led to the departmentalization of political science in university education in Tanzania dates back to the establishment of the East African Institute of Social Research in 1947 and Makerere, the University College of East Africa in 1949.

Makerere College and the Higher College for East Africa were the precursors of the University College. The Higher College had introduced a compulsory first year course in administration in 1939 and when the Institute of Social Research was established, it was hoped that it would develop close working relations with the social studies programmes which had grown out of the compulsory course in administration at the Higher College.

A Department of Social Studies was eventually created as a constituent unit of the faculty of arts at the new University College of East Africa. Political science was one of the sub-units of the department, the others being economics and sociology.

Formalized teaching in political science and the other social sciences therefore began much earlier at Makerere than at the sister University College, Ibadan. A department of political science was subsequently established in 1957 at Makerere.

The University College, Dar es Salaam was established in October 1961, with only a faculty of law. When the University of East Africa was inaugurated in 1963, the University College, Dar es Salaam and the sister university colleges at Nairobi and Makerere became constituent units of the new University. The University of East Africa was dissolved in July 1970. That same year the University of Dar es Salaam was inaugurated, replacing University College, Dar es Salaam.

When a Faculty of Arts and Social Science was established in 1964, political science was one of the eight departments in the faculty. Also established in 1964 was the Institute of Public Administration to train and organize short-term residential courses for public servants.

Degree orientation and structure

At Makerere the emphasis in the teaching of political science prior to the establishment of a faculty of social sciences there in 1963 was on a brief introduction not only to specific problems in European and African politics but also to political philosophy.

The undergraduate degree structure in political science at the new University College, Dar es Salaam and later at the University of Dar es Salaam has shown a preoccupation with the design of syllabus that is relevant to the needs of Tanzania and of African society.

This concern with relevance is part of the effort to define the mission of the university. That mission has since been defined firstly, as the transmission of knowledge; secondly, the advancement of knowledge in the context of relevance to the community and meeting the needs of the people; and thirdly, providing for the manpower needs of the country.

A major review of the undergraduate degree programme in the department was carried out in the 1970-1 academic year. This led to the introduction of a new undergraduate syllabus in the 1971-2 academic year, in which students were required to specialize in one of four streams (see Jinadu 1984 for details).

The emphasis in the new degree structure is on specialization in either public administration or international relations. The degree programme is therefore deliberately career-oriented — the specialization in public administration being intended for a career in the public sector, and that in international relations for those looking for careers in the foreign service or with international organizations. The review carried out in 1970/71 was part of a wider university curriculum review necessitated by, among other factors, the expansion of the public sector in the wake of the nationalization carried out in the late 1960s. A third area of specialization is now contemplated. This is political theory, with a focus on political thought and comparative politics.

Effect of faculty reorganization

The faculty reorganization carried out in 1971 introduced a common core of interdisciplinary courses, East African Society and Environment (EASE), spread over three years, which undergraduate students in political science and other disciplines would have to take. EASE 1 concentrated on the socio-economic and political problems of East Africa, EASE 2 focused on the application of science to development, and EASE 3 examined strategies of development.

The EASE courses were discontinued and replaced in 1978 by a two-year compulsory course in development studies serviced by the Institute of Development Studies.

Admission requirements

The requirements for admission to undergraduate degree courses in political science and other disciplines were modified in 1976 in line with the Musoma Resolution or Directive on the Implement of Education for Self-Reliance issued by the ruling party in 1974.

The implementation of the Directive meant that, from 1976, the University stopped admitting students who had just completed their Form VI education. To be qualified, candidates seeking admission, in addition to possessing the appropriate qualifications for direct entry, must have had a minimum of two but preferably several years' working experience in addition to strong letters of recommendation from their employers and local party branches.

Postgraduate and research programmes

The department of political science offers the MA degree by examination and PhD by thesis. The MA degree is divided into two major fields — development management, and international relations, in either of which students can specialize. There are, however, two compulsory or core courses: social science research methods, and socialist theories of development.

Research in political science is carried out by academic staff either as project research, funded by the university as a departmental project, or by individual academic staff. The research undertaken by academic staff is expected to be consistent with the research agenda and priorities set by the Tanzania National Research Council.

Outlets for the publication of the results of research undertaken by academic staff and students is provided by a number of journals published by the department. These are *The African Review, Taamuli*, and JIRAA (*The Journal of International Relations*). A further outlet is provided by journals like *Utafiti*, published by the Faculty of Arts and Social Science, and *The East African Law Journal*, published by the faculty of law at the university.

The department has also published a series of books and monographs: *The Cell System of the Tangayinka African National Union Building Ujamaa Villages in Tanzania, Essays on the Liberation of Southern Africa*, and *Aid and Development: Some Tanzanian Experiences*.

POLITICAL SCIENCE IN ZIMBABWE

Origins

The need for the teaching of political science at the university level has always been felt in Zimbabwe. For example, when the establishment of a university in what was then Southern Rhodesia was discussed in the territory's legislative assembly in October 1946, emphasis was placed on the need to start off with a faculty of arts in which 'administration' would be taught.

The Carr-Saunders Commission on Higher Education set up in 1952 had also recommended that the multiracial university to serve the Rhodesias (Northern and Southern) and Nyasaland that it was proposing should be established in Salisbury (now Harare), should start with a faculty of arts in which government and public administration would be taught alongside subjects in the humanities.

Although the University College of Rhodesia and Nyasaland took off in March 1957 it was not until 1960 that the first professorial appointment in government was made, with a grant from the Ford Foundation for staff development in political science.

The new department of government was one of the four departments — in the other three being economics, law, and sociology — in the faculty when a faculty of social studies was established in 1962. The name of the department was changed in 1968 from the Department of Government to the Department of Political Science, and then again to the Department of Political and Administrative Studies.

The aim of the department was primarily to offer an undergraduate degree course. Nevertheless the idea of a Diploma in Public Administration to train serving officers of the Northern Rhodesia public service was accepted in principle in 1961. The programme was terminated in 1965 but there is now a Diploma in Public Administration offered on a part-time basis by the successor Department of Political and Administrative Studies.

Courses in government were some of the options available to students when the BA general degree was begun in the 1960s. When the BSc (Hons) degree was introduced in 1960, government was one of the single subjects in which students could be examined in the Part II final examination.

Post independence structure

The achievement of independence in April 1980 raised the issue of a relevant university education in Zimbabwe and how political science and the other social sciences should restructure their undergraduate degree programme to reflect the new social order.

The new undergraduate course structure in the Department of Political and Administrative Studies has a central focus in the social sciences and offers students a wide range of options in their second and third years of study. The BSc degree in politics and administration requires students reading for the degree to study a minimum of ten courses from the department. Of this combination, four must be from courses designated as 'politics' courses and four from those designated 'administration'.

The Politics *vs* Administration Focus

While this new undergraduate structure avoids separate degrees in politics and administration, which was previously the case, it nevertheless presupposes a dichotomy between politics and administration. Debate within the department has already elicited concern among a number of academic staff about the polarization such a disciplinary division is likely to create and the tendency towards the creation of two separate departments this may engender.

Departmental growth

The department has witnessed considerable growth in student intake since 1980. This is due primarily to bureaucratic growth and proliferation in the public services since independence. In its submission to the university's Triennial Review Committee in December 1982, the department calculated that the expansion in its undergraduate admission was likely to be about 50 per cent in 1983 and 1984 and to taper thereafter to about 30 per cent in each of 1985 and 1986.

The increase in student admissions into the department has correspondingly brought about an increase in student-course numbers. The department's calculation is that in 1982 there was an increase of about 26 per cent from 578 in 1980 and 727 in 1981, to 778 in 1982 in student-course numbers. It was then projected that, assuming an annual growth rate of 20 per cent, the student-course numbers for 1984, 1985 and 1986 would be 1,120, 1,345, and 1,613 respectively (see Jinadu 1984).

When related to its academic staff strength, it is apparent that the student/staff ratio in the department is high. The estimate of the department, based on an academic staff complement of nine in 1983 was about 1:28 and 1:20 respectively.

Graduate and research programmes

Because of the Unilateral Declaration of Independence in what was then Rhodesia, graduate education in political science and other social sciences at the university suffered a setback. It did not seem, in the early years of the university, that graduate education as such was viewed as a strategic device for academic staff development. Emphasis was placed on undergraduate education, to produce manpower for the Rhodesian economy.

However, graduate education is now linked as much with academic staff development as with meeting high-level managerial and administrative positions in the public and private sectors of the country. The department offers an MSc degree in international relations, and a diploma in public administration (DPA), each on a part-time basis, to meet manpower needs in the foreign and civil service. A master's degree in public administration programme was expected to start in the 1987 academic year.

The department also offers research-based degree programmes for the M.Phil and D.Phil, each of which requires submission of a thesis after a prescribed period of research in an approved topic. Supervision is offered by academic staff in the following subfields of the discipline: political theory, political development, international relations, government and politics of Zimbabwe, and public administration.

Individual members of the department are engaged in research in comparative politics, international politics, and national politics. There has been a major concern with the politics of the Southern African region, with ethnicity, race and class in the politics of Zimbabwe, and with the constitutional issues raised by the proposed one-party state. A recent collective research project in the department studied the 1985 general elections in the country.

Other departments in the university are engaged in research in subjects that are close to political science. For example, the Department of History has conducted research into various aspects of African nationalist politics and modern African politics. The Centre for Applied Social Science (CASS), a teaching and research unit within the faculty of social studies, has carried out research on race, ethnicity and national integration, and on the role of women in development.

Outside the university, the Zimbabwe Institute of Development Studies (ZIDS) has research units/departments on Southern African studies and history and political studies in its research division. Opportunities for the publication of research work is provided by the university journal *Zambesia*.

PRIORITY NEEDS

The previous section has sought to indicate the current status and institutional framework of teaching and research in political science in three major countries in Anglophone Africa. This has necessarily involved situating the institutionalization of the discipline in the countries in the wider context of the historically-determined forces which have shaped and still shape its character. What does all this then suggest about the future of the discipline in Africa?

Indeed the current status of political science in Africa is closely linked to that of the other social sciences and it is within this context that a discussion of the priority needs of the discipline must proceed. In other words, the problems which necessitate the identification of priority needs to solve them are due to the nature of Africa's political economy and the historical patterns of the introduction of the discipline and the other social sciences to Africa.

In other words, the multinational character of political science and the other social sciences, and indeed of scholarship as such, and the processes, characterized by unequal exchange, through which they are diffused provide the background against with the character of the problems and any preferred solutions must be set.

It is also because of the global dimensions of the problems that it becomes vital to view solutions to them on a coordinated continental scale. The goal must be a political science and a social science that serve African needs, that are relevant to the continent. That they have not been able to do this adequately is itself due to the contradictions arising out of their colonial origins and the character of the international social science community as yet another superstructure for the hegemonic domination of the West.

In the ensuing discussion, the problem areas identified for priority considerations are: resource constraints, direction in teaching and research, graduate/postgraduate training within Africa, and the professionalization of the discipline. The nature of each problem area is sketched and a brief indication of the measures or strategies to combat it is then given.

Resource constraints

A major problem in teaching and research in political science in the countries studied is the endemic shortage of teaching and research resource materials. This problem can indeed be generalized for the other social sciences and disciplines in African universities.

For example, the Experts' Meeting on the Formation of Social Science Policies in Africa South of the Sahara, held in Kinshasa, Zaire in October 1979 and the Conference of the *CODESRIA* Working Group on Social Sciences and Development in Africa, held in Port Harcourt, Nigeria in July 1980, both illustrated the continental character of the problem and suggested solutions to it.

This resource material scarcity is itself a manifestation of Africa's underdevelopment and peripheralization in the global economy. It has also contributed in no small measure to the marginalization of the discipline and the other social sciences in relation to their counterparts in the West.

Concretely, this resource material scarcity has manifested itself in shortage of funds to import textbooks, journals, printing and duplicating materials, attendance at conferences, etc. The other face of this is of course the prohibititively high cost of these resource materials even when they are available, owing to imported inflation. In this respect, the problem merely reflects the wider materialist base of the current international division of labour.

Why is this, then, a problem for African political science and social science? The answer is partly that the resource scarcity impairs the access of African political scientists and other social scientists to the international social science community. Yet access is important for a well-informed, critical confrontation without which an alternative African political science and social science cannot emerge to challenge and change the unequal exchange that currently characterizes relationships between the centre and periphery of that community.

What needs to be done? First, African government should be urged, at the level of African regional organizations, to liberalize foreign exchange regulations for the import of educational resource materials. This way, something could be done about the prohibitively high cost of some of these resource materials.

Secondly, measures can be taken and pursued to encourage and generate the production of textbooks, monographs and other educational resource materials within Africa. This can help in two ways: it can contribute to self-reliance and the conservation of foreign exchange. It can also help advance African political science through the use of African data as illustrative materials in political science textbooks.

It is gratifying that in some of the countries discussed here efforts at the local production of teaching materials have been undertaken and are encouraged by the linking of teaching and research. A number of continental and regional governmental institutions and professional associations — *BREDA, CODESRIA, AAPS, OSSREA* — have also embarked on textbook publication projects.

This trend must be encouraged. But where efforts must also now be concentrated is in developing and nurturing effective and efficient distribution networks for these textbooks, so that they will not be localized or their availability and impact confined to a few countries within each region.

Directions in teaching and research

Part of the crisis of African political science is that its mainstream, insofar as it is a reflection of mainstream political science in the West, has generally failed to provide an adequate and comprehensive framework for analysing African social formations. It is therefore important to reexamine existing dominant paradigms in the teaching of political science in Africa and to redesign intellectual research agenda.

African political science has begun this process of redefinition and reexamination of its teaching and research agenda with the ultimate goal of dissociating itself from mainstream Western political science and social science. This is in fact the fundamental objective of such African social science organizations as *CODESRIA* and *AAPS*.

It is in this context that challenges have been posed, primarily from Marxist political economy perspectives, to prevailing dominant orthodoxies like structural-functionalism, system analysis and the modernization school in the study of politics (See Ake 1985).

New questions are posed, intellectual foci and emphases have shifted to underlying substructural forces which mainstream political science has deliberately obscured or mystified. In the words of the report of the *CODESRIA* Working Group on Social Sciences and Development, meeting in Port Harcourt, Nigeria in July 1980, an Afro-centric social science, of which political science is an organic part, should have as its focus a 'dialectical conceptualization of underdevelopment and development (which) should emphasize historical evolution, structural and sectoral transformation, the roles of social forces and conflict, the operational content of self-reliant development and global social democracy'.

While the focus of a substantial part of teaching and research in African political science is now generally on this political economy perspective, some new directions or priority areas must nevertheless be pointed out. This need arises from lacunae in the new perspective.

For example, concern with contemporary issues/problems has tended, by and large, to lead to what are essentially ahistorical analyses of these problems. Only fleeting attention is paid to political history, diplomatic history, political philosophy, and problems of constitutional change in teaching and research in the discipline. In short, the dissociation of history, philosophy, and law from political science must be corrected and new emphasis placed upon them by African political science.

A second problem in teaching and research in African political science is their insularity. By this is meant the preoccupation of political science in individual African countries with national politics, national development, and the nation-state.

This is due primarily to the scarcity of some of the resource material referred to earlier on, which has tended to force political scientists to focus on their immediate localities. The priority need in this respect is to provide encouragement and incentives for African political scientists to start studying other than their own countries. This can be done, for example, by strengthening network linkages within and between the various regions through the exchange of information, faculty and students, and the provision of fellowships and scholarships for this purpose.

Graduate/postgraduate training within Africa

A related priority need is graduate training within Africa. This need was underscored by the Conference of the *CODESRIA* Working Group in July 1980 and the Experts' Meeting in Kinshasa in October 1979, to which reference has been made above.

This need presupposes a view of training in political science not only to meet manpower needs for the public and private sectors but also to produce more academic staff and researchers. For indeed there is a correlation between a university's contribution to knowledge and the development and institutionalization of graduate education within it. In another respect, research is closely linked to the nature of graduate education.

For these reasons, the development and expansion of graduate education in political science and the other social sciences within African universities is crucial to the ability of the discipline to meet and serve the continent's need and help solve its problems.

Emphasis must now be placed on this aspect in training new academic staff and researchers in the discipline. There is already solid capacity for training at the master's and diploma levels. There is, however, much room for developing and improving upon the capacity for training at the doctoral and post-doctoral levels.

Because of this weak capacity at the doctoral and post-doctoral levels, prospective academic staff and researchers and even senior ones have tended to go abroad for further training or to spend their sabbatical leaves there. This way vertical links with institutions in Europe and North America are strengthened, to the detriment of much-needed and preferred horizontal linkages among African universities and research institutions. This state of affairs cannot but militate against an Afro-centric political science. It will lead to the entrenchment and continuing domination of mainstream political science in the West and perhaps, may also contribute to brain-drain from Africa.

In other words, the horizontal linkages resulting from training within Africa should engender a common perception of problems of development in Africa and exchanges of information about how they can be solved, and foster a critical attitude towards the dominant Western mainstream political science.

Professionalization of political science

The extent of the professionalization of political science in the three countries was indicated in the section above on the current situation (see page 256) The development of professional associations of political science is important for a number of reasons. Their establishment or strengthening where they already exist is therefore another priority area.

The functional role of such associations is multiple. First, they can provide a salutary and much-needed communication link between political scientists and the community they serve, particularly the policy-makers and bureaucrats, in African countries. Secondly, the annual meetings, conferences, seminars, and workshops organized by them, as well as their journals and newsletters, can provide their members and colleagues in other countries with useful avenues for the diffusion and exchange of information about the nature of ongoing research, as well as about critical issues in national and international politics. Above all, the associations can provide criteria for the assessment of substantive contributions to the advancement of scholarship in the discipline and therefore contribute to its progress.

NOTES

This is a revision of a paper presented at Cortona, Italy, September 1987.

REFERENCES

Ake, C. (1985) 'The social sciences in Africa: trends, tasks and challenges', paper presented at the Fifth General Assembly of the *CODESRIA* Conference on Utilization of Social Sciences in Policy Formation in Africa, Dakar, Senegal; mimeo, April.

Barongo, Y. (ed.) (1983) *Political Science in Africa*, London: Zed Press.

Coleman J.S. and Halisi, C.R.D. (1983) 'American political science and tropical Africa: universalism vs relativism', *African Studies Review* 26 3/4:25-62.

Dudley, B.J. (1975) *Scepticism and Political Virtue*, Ibadan: University of Ibadan Press.

Jinadu L.A. (1977) 'The development and role of political science as an academic discipline in Nigeria', paper read at CERDAS Conference on the State and Role of the Social Sciences in Africa, Kinshasa; mimeo.

— (1984) *The Social Sciences and Development in Africa: Ethiopia, Mozambique, Tanzania, and Zimbabwe*, Stockholm: SAREC.

— (1987) 'The institutional development of political science in Nigeria: trends, problems and prospects', 8(1):59-72.

Summerskill, J. (1970) *Haile Sellasie I University: A Blueprint for Development*. Addis Ababa: Haile Sellasie I University.

12 Political science in the United States

Past and present

David Easton[1]

Before we begin this overview of political science in the United States, it would be helpful to have some idea of what this discipline covers. How are we to describe its subject matter?

Political science has been defined in many ways — as the study of power, the study of the monopoly of the legitimate use of force, the study of the good life, of the state, and so on. If there is one thing that distinguishes Western political science, it is that it has not yet arrived at a consensus on how to describe its subject matter at the most inclusive level. For reasons that are elaborated at length elsewhere (see Easton 1981a), I have chosen to characterize political science as the study of the way in which decisions for a society are made and considered binding most of the time by most of the people. That is to say, to seek to understand political life is to address oneself to the study of the authoritative allocation of values (valued things) for a society.

Political scientists are, therefore, different from economists, anthropologists, sociologists, and other social scientists. As political scientists, we are interested in all those actions and institutions in society more or less directly related to the way in which authoritative decisions are made and put into effect, and the consequences they may have (See Easton 1981b). In effect, this is a description of what we may call any and all political systems. It is probably fair to say that this way of identifying political systems seems to have won the favour of many political scientists over the last quarter of a century.

With this conception of the study of politics, let us now turn to an examination of what has been happening in Western, especially American political science, during the twentieth century. It has passed through four stages. Each of these has been distinctive. Each has been incorporated in and, we hope, improved upon by each succeeding stage. I shall give the following names to the various stages: the formal (legal), the traditional (informal and pre-behavioural), the behavioural, and the post-behavioural. I propose to discuss each of these in turn.

THE FORMAL AND TRADITIONAL STAGES

Toward the latter part of the nineteenth century, political science started out with the conviction that once we have described the laws governing the distribution of power in a political system, we will have obtained an accurate understanding of how political institutions operate. Students of politics assumed that there was a reasonably close fit between what constitutions and laws said about the rights and privileges people held in various political offices and the way in which they acted in those offices (see Eckstein 1966).

Late in the nineteenth century, Walter Bagehot in Great Britain, followed by Woodrow Wilson in the United States (when he was a student and later a professor), made a major discovery. To everyone's surprise, they found that around the formal structure of political offices and institutions there were all kinds of informal behaviour and organizations in which power over decision-making might lie. Bagehot, Wilson, and others discovered them in the informal committees of their respective legislatures and in the political parties. Later scholars added interest or pressure groups to a growing list of informal institutions to be taken into account.

These findings introduced a new stage in the development of political science. They diverted attention away from the formal, legal structures to the informal practices surrounding them. This change, which had occurred toward the end of the nineteenth century, was in full swing by the 1920s. People who trained in the United States from the 1920s to the 1940s were exposed largely to what has come to be called traditional political science, the name for the second distinctive phase of political research in the twentieth century. During this period, training included a great deal of attention to the operation of political parties and their effect on Congress or Parliament and to the growth, in the United States, of pressure groups and other types of groups. The latter were drawn to our attention and analysed in depth, initially by Arthur Bentley (1908) who was ignored at the time; and later, in new ways, by Pendleton Herring (1929) and David Truman (1951).

Methodologically, this traditional period was one in which more attention was paid to mere description and the collection of information about political processes than to over-arching theories about how they operate. In fact, however, a latent theory unobtrusively guided research. Even though most of the scholars of that period were not conscious of it, they really saw the political process as a giant mechanism for making decisions. Decisions were, as one scholar, Merle Fainsod (1940:298), put it, a product of a 'parallelogram of forces'. This meant that when decisions were to be made, whether at the legislative or administrative levels, they were seen as being subjected to a vast array of pressures from groups in society — from political parties, from other parts of the bureaucracy itself, from interest groups, from public opinion, and so on. These pressures played against each other, developing a parallelogram of forces that, through bargaining, negotiation, adaptation, compromise, and adjustment (terms commonly used to describe the process), would arrive at some equilibrium point for that time and place. This equilibrium point would yield a particular policy, or the policy could be called the point of equilibrium among the various competing forces pressing against decision-makers. If at some time one of these social forces should change for whatever reason — as for example because of a change in the economic structure or in social attitudes, or in the occupants of decision-making roles — demands for modification of old policies or for the introduction of new policies might arise. Competition among the various groups for influence over the policy would then begin again, and a new point of equilibrium might be achieved (see Easton 1981a). As I have indicated, for the most part, this equilibrium theory remained only latent in the literature.

The characteristic methods of research during this traditional period were no less informal than their theoretical base. Little by way of special methods was used for the collection of data or for their analysis. Methods were not considered to be problematic, that is, as areas that required special attention or skills. Everyone was equally well equipped to collect and analyse information about politics. As a result, there were no formal or specified methods for testing the reliability of information acquired or of findings and interpretations based upon such information.

In addition, it was often difficult to distinguish whether the research worker was expressing his or her own preferences or was, in fact, describing how institutions operate and how people behave in political life. Statements relating what should be and what is were often almost inextricably intertwined. Facts and values played havoc with each other.

Finally, my own experience as a graduate student reflects the lack of theoretical coherence of traditional political science. At Harvard University, I took many different courses in political science. They covered the history of political thought, municipal or local politics, constitutional law, foreign policy, government regulation of industry, interest or pressure groups, international relations, the governments of specific foreign countries, and the making of laws in Congress. At the end of my graduate training my head was in a whirl. No one had ever tried to help me understand why my interests in politics required me to be exposed to such a wide variety of subject matters aside from the fact that, loosely, they all had to do with something called government. I gained no sense of a basis upon which I could argue that political science formed a coherent body of knowledge. There was no theoretical framework into which I could place all these courses or by which I could check their relevance.

Political theory might have been an area in which, because of its name, I might have expected to find the opportunity to address an issue such as this. But theory turned out to be devoted largely to the study of the history of political thought. Such history was, of course, interesting and important in itself, but it did not fulfil what might have been one of the functions of theory in, say, economics, chemistry, or physics, namely, the conceptualization of the discipline in part or as a whole.

The traditional stage then was one in which political science discovered the rich body of informal activities out of which public policy was formed. Yet it was a period during which description was often hard to distinguish from values, when theory did not measure up to the promise implicit in its name, and when method was so taken for granted that it was non-problematic.

THE BEHAVIOURAL STAGE

The formal-legal and traditional periods were the first two phases of recent times. They were displaced by the so-called behavioural revolution in American political science, which rapidly spread to many other parts of the world. This third phase began after World War Two though it had its roots in the earlier period. Without question, this is the central transformation that has occurred in Western political science in this century.

Despite the common root in the English terms, behaviourism and behaviouralism, the two words have little in common and ought not to be confused. Political science had never been behaviouristic even during the height of its behaviouralistic phase. Behaviourism refers to a theory in psychology about human behaviour and has its origins in the work of J. B. Watson. I know of no political scientist who subscribes to this doctrine. Indeed, I know of no political scientist, although there may be the occasional one, who even accepts the psychological theory of B. F. Skinner, the founder of the 'operant conditioning' school of psychology and the modern successor to Watson.

The only real relationship between the terms behaviourism and behaviouralism is that both of them focus on the human actor and his or her behaviour as the appropriate source of information about why things happen in the world as they do. Both also assume that a methodology based upon that of the natural sciences is appropriate for the study of human beings. Aside from this acceptance of the individual as the focus of research and of scientific method, there is little resemblance between these tendencies. It would be a mistake therefore to confuse behaviouralism in political science with behaviourism and its derivatives in psychology.

Behaviouralism in political science had the following major characteristics. These distinguished it from earlier stages in the study of political science (see Easton 1962).

First, behaviouralism held that there are discoverable uniformities in human behaviour and second, these can be confirmed by empirical tests. Third, behaviouralism showed a desire for greater rigour in methods for the acquisition of data and for their analysis. Methods themselves became problematic. They could no longer be taken for granted. Courses and books on methods for acquiring and analysing data became commonplace. Quantification, whenever possible and plausible, assumed an important place in the discipline. As a result, during the 1950s and 1960s, political science became adept at using a vast array of increasingly sophisticated empirical techniques — questionnaires, interviews, sampling, regression analysis, factor analysis, rational modelling, and the like.

Fourth, the behavioural movement committed itself to much greater theoretical sophistication than in the past. The search for systematic understanding, grounded in objective observation, led to a marked shift in the meaning of theory as a concept. Traditionally, in the distant past, theory had been philosophical in character, asking questions about the nature of the good life. In more recent times, it had become largely historical, seeking to explicate and account for the emergence of political ideas in past centuries. Behavioural theory, on the other hand, is empirically oriented. It seeks to help us explain, understand, and, if possible, predict the way in which people behave politically and the way political institutions operate.

A considerable amount of the energies of theoreticians in this period went into the construction of empirically oriented theory at various levels of analysis. So-called middle range theory has sought to build theories about large segments of the discipline, as in the case of power pluralism, which offers a theory of democratic systems, or of positive theory, which is found in game theory or public choice theory (see Riker and Ordeshook 1973).

In part, however, theory has been of the broadest character, called general theory. This type has sought to provide an understanding of political systems at the most inclusive level. Structural-functional theory and system analysis represent two major theoretical efforts of such broad scope.

Fifth, many behaviouralists felt that the values of the research worker and of society could be largely excluded from the process of inquiry. Ethical evaluation and empirical explanation were viewed as involving two different kinds of statements that clarity requires us to keep analytically separate and distinct. Behaviouralism adopted the original positivist assumptions (as developed by the Vienna Circle of positivists early in this century) that value-free or value-neutral research was possible. Although some of us, including myself (Easton 1981a:ch. 9), did not share this point of view, it is nevertheless correct to suggest that it was a dominant one during the height of the behavioural stage. As a result, moral inquiry receded far into the background among the priorities of interesting things to do.

Sixth, behaviouralism represented a new-found emphasis on basic or pure theory as against applied research. Its assumption was that the task of the social scientist was to obtain fundamental understanding and explanation. It was felt that only after we have reliable understanding of how political institutions operate and people behave politically would it be possible to apply such knowledge, with confidence, to the solution of urgent social problems. Understanding and explanation of political behaviour logically precede the utilization of knowledge for the solution of practical social problems. The period of behaviouralism, therefore, helped to divert the interests of scholars from social reform and encouraged them to set their sights on the needs of scientific development as a guide to research.

How can we explain the behavioural revolution of the 1950s and 1960s in the United States? It was clearly a product of a number of complex tendencies. It was part of the natural evolution of the discipline. The commonsense, proverbial style of traditional political science, with its dependence on historical description and impressionistic analysis, had simply exhausted itself. A developing mass industrialized society could not cope with its social problems with the degree of unreliability attached to explanations offered by traditional research. Too many difficulties in understanding political institutions and processes had been left unresolved. The epistemic successes of the natural sciences and of other social sciences such as psychology and economics, using more rigorous methods of data collection and of analysis, left their impact on political science as well. They suggested alternatives that led political analysis away from 'common' sense to 'scientific' sense where theoretical rather than social criteria set the problems of research and where technical skills took the place of mere description and commonsense methods.

In addition, however, there were social forces that encouraged a commitment to the introduction of science into the study of politics. During the cold war period in relationships between the United States and the Soviet Union, especially during the Korean War (1950-3), Senator Joseph McCarthy inaugurated and led a reign of psychological and legal terror against liberals and others in the United States. Scholars were selected as particularly vulnerable targets for attack. McCarthyism succeeded in driving underground an interest in social reform and critical theory.

From this perspective, objective, neutral, or value free research represented a protective posture for scholars. It offered them intellectually legitimate and useful grounds for fleeing from the dangers of open political controversy. This is perhaps an instance in the evolution of knowledge in which inadvertent gains may have been won for the wrong reasons. McCarthyism, of course, had nothing to do with the emergence of behaviouralism as a new approach to political research. It represented simply a historical circumstance that drove an interest in social reform underground. In doing so, it led scholars into the politically less dangerous grounds of basic research, an area that, as it turned out, had major benefits to offer for the development of political science.

In addition to McCarthyism, there was another important social condition that contributed significantly to the sustenance of behaviouralism. Post-World War Two prosperity, with its associated conservatism of the 1950s and the early 1960s, led to the prevalent view that ideology had indeed come to an end in the United States. Rapid economic growth offered material benefits to all segments of the population, even to the poorest. Critical social thought, including critical liberalism itself, all but disappeared in the United States and with it, all semblance of ideological conflict. D. Bell (1960) wrote a distinguished book entitled *The End of Ideology* that expressed this conviction.

In retrospect, it is clear that ideology had not disappeared. It seemed to have ended only because mainstream, liberal–conservative ideology was dominant and unchallenged for the moment. There were no major contenders. This situation, of course, changed during the late 1960s with the rise of the civil rights movement on behalf of the blacks. But prior to this period, contending ideologies did recede or go underground. The lack of challenge to established ideologies turned the social sciences away from social problems as a source of inspiration for its research toward criteria internal to social theory, derivative from the logic of the development of social science itself. This gave social science the appearance of withdrawing from society into an ivory tower of scientific research, at least if one took the rhetoric of social research at its word.

It is clear that what from a social point of view could be interpreted as a retreat from social responsibility by social scientists, from the point of view of science could be interpreted as a breathing spell free from social involvement. This had the effect of enabling political science to address, in a relatively undisturbed atmosphere, many technical aspects that have become central to its development — such as the place of theory in social research, the need for rigorous methods of research, the refinements of techniques for acquiring and analysing data, the establishment of standards of professionalism among political scientists and social scientists in general, and so on. In short, we can now recognize the behavioural phase as one in which the social sciences, for whatever historical reasons and fortuitous circumstances, were busy strengthening the scientific bases of their research. The cost was a significant withdrawal from an interest in social criticism and social involvement.

THE POST-BEHAVIOURAL STAGE

What I have called the post-behavioural revolution — a name now generally used for this next phase — began during the 1960s and is still with us today (see Easton 1969). It represents a deep dissatisfaction with the results of behaviouralism. It has not led to the abandonment of scientific method in political science. It is, however, leading to a substantial modification of our understanding of the nature of science and it is a movement that is still evolving.

Why did the post-behavioural movement arise? What were its sources? This movement accompanied the so-called counter-cultural revolution in the United States that, of course, has no direct relationship to the Cultural Revolution in China. The counter-cultural revolution arose in the West, and touched the East as well, during the later 1960s and early 1970s. It represented a period of worldwide social change. Much of the leadership came from large masses of students congregated in rapidly growing colleges and universities throughout the world. In the United States, it had its origins in the civil rights movement, especially after the 1954-5 Supreme Court decisions against educational segregation of blacks. It was accompanied by the growth of demands for the improvement of the condition of blacks and other minorities and by widespread protests against the Vietnam War during the Johnson and Nixon administrations. It was most clearly evident in new attitudes toward forms of dress, sexual behaviour, the place of women and minorities in society, poverty, respect for the physical environment (pollution, atomic waste, the dangers of nuclear energy), and social inequality. In its broadest meaning, it represented the awakening of the modern world to the dangers of rapid and unregulated industrialization, ethnic and sexual discrimination, worldwide poverty, and nuclear war.

This is not the place to describe this movement in detail. All we need to do is to draw attention to the impact that the counter-cultural revolution of the 1960s and 1970s had on the social sciences in general and on political science in particular. For the social scientists, it raised the question as to why we were unable to foresee the kinds of problems, just mentioned, that became salient in this period. In addition, even if the social sciences did foresee some of these problems, how did it happen that they did nothing about them? It appeared that the social sciences had simply withdrawn into an ivory tower. These kinds of questions led to large-scale debates on the nature of our discipline and what it ought to be.

From these debates several things are now clear. The original commitment to science during the behavioural period, that is, during the 1950s and 1960s, has been seriously questioned. Some of the criticisms of scientific method reflect well-known arguments inherited largely from the nineteenth century: human behaviour is composed of too many complex variables and therefore we are not likely to be able to discover any law-like regularities; unlike atoms, human beings are not determined. They have free will, and therefore can never be predicted even on a probable basis. Even if the methods of the natural sciences have manifested great epistemic success, this was a product of the fact that they deal with inanimate matter. Atoms, however, do not have feelings or intentions that, by their very nature, are unpredictable or inaccessible to observation or prediction.

Other criticisms of science were directed at its positivistic claims that behavioural research was value free. As I mentioned earlier, some social scientists had proclaimed 'the end of ideology'. With the counter-cultural movement came the argument that all social research is, on the contrary, really shot through with ideology. The point was advanced that the claim that social science was valuationally neutral was possible only because social science had assumed the ideological colouring of the status quo (bourgeois liberalism) and the existing power structure. Its ideological premises were at one with those of the establishment and disappeared into the received views of the day. This claim to false objectivity was seen as serving the interests of the establishment. It seemed to justify or excuse the withdrawal of social scientists from involvement in social issues, to divert social inquiry from urgent social problems, and thereby to allow the status quo to go unchallenged.

This attack on the ideological presuppositions of scientific method in the study of society broadened into a wholesale challenge of the epistemological and ontological bases of social research. In a widely read book, *The Structure of Scientific Revolutions* by T. Kuhn (1962), the view was advanced that all science, natural as well as social, is essentially an irrational process. In this book, scientific change is no longer seen as the product of a gradual accumulation of knowledge and understanding; change now represents only the shift of scientists from an existing paradigm or set of ideological and other presuppositions to a new one, for a variety of explainable reasons. The history of science, from this point of view, appears as a random shift from one set of premises (paradigms) governing research to another.

Despite the initial impact of this book, it is now realized that this criticism, in denying the possibility of any objective knowledge, went far beyond the realm of necessity or plausibility (see Suppe 1977). The criticism did however draw attention to the need to reconsider how we do manage to acquire valid understanding about the real world despite the fact that research may be saturated with evaluative presuppositions.

I have touched only briefly on the fierce attacks that have been launched against scientific method since the 1970s. They have, however, led to serious reassessments of the original commitment to the positivistic conception of scientific method prevalent during the behavioural period of the 1950s and 1960s. We can see the results of this in the far more diverse approaches to political inquiry available today than during the behavioural period. The earlier impressionistic methods have even regained some plausibility, as has the method of interpretive understanding (*verstehen*) put forward at the turn of this century by Max Weber. We have also witnessed the re-emergence of proponents of Marxism as an alternative way to develop a social science (see Poulantzas 1973; Ollman and Vernoff 1982).

Indeed, there are now so many approaches to political research that political science seems to have lost its purpose. During the 1950s and 1960s, in the behavioural phase, there was a messianic spirit and collective effort in the promotion and development of the methods of scientific inquiry even while there continued to be opposition to it. Today, however, political science has lost this sense of united purpose. There is no longer a single, dominant point of view or one that unmistakably catches the imagination, especially of younger members of the profession. Nor is there even a single defensive adversary. The discipline is fragmented in its methodological conceptions even though it is probably fair to say that scientific inquiry still represents the mainstream. However, it is not, as we shall see in a moment, only science in the old positivistic sense. Instead we are adding a new and more relaxed understanding of the nature of science itself.

In addition to losing its sense of a dynamic purpose concentrated on the pursuit of scientific validity, political science seems to have lost its core. There was once agreement that political science was a study of something, whether it was of power or of the authoritative allocation of values or of the good life. Also, if it will not seem self-serving on my part to say so, there was a dominant point of view. If there was any single comprehensive description of the subject matter of political science it was to be found in the notion that it studied the authoritative allocation of values for a society. This was a conception that I had put forward in my book, *The Political System*, in 1953, and it had found widespread acceptance.

Today, however, students are no longer so certain about what politics is all about. They may even be less concerned than they were in the past. Political science as a study of the state, a conception that, after World War Two had been driven out by the idea of the political system, has now been revived. It has accompanied the re-emergence, in American political science at least, of Marxist and quasi-Marxist points of view (see Easton 1981c) and in them, of course, the state is a central concept.

What, however, is being offered today to draw the discipline together, to give it a sense of common purpose, and to provide alternative methods, if any, for inquiry? Here is where the real difficulty arises. Political science is still trying to develop a new sense of its identity and a new drive or sense of purpose. We are clearly still in a transition phase, and it is difficult to predict just where we will end up. We look fragmented and display a great variety of objectives for the very reason that theories, methods, and perspectives are still being questioned, that is, they are still in the process of change.

We can get some flavour of the reconstruction taking place by recounting the different interests and approaches of American political science, at least at the present time. Marxism, after lying dormant in American social science since the 1940s (even though very much alive in Europe), was reintroduced during the 1970s. However, there is no single orthodoxy in the Marxist methods or theories that have been adopted. The fragmentation of European Marxism is reflected in its American renaissance. We find represented all schools of Marxism — critical theory, humanist, cultural, structural, as well as orthodox. These have all had some impact on American political science though structural Marxism, as developed by Althusser and Poulantzas, has probably been the most influential.

What is clear, however, is that in being absorbed into American social research the various schools of Marxism have been attenuated; most inquiry is only quasi-Marxist in character. Even in that form, however, the revival of Marxist thinking has brought to political science a renewed awareness of the importance of history and of the significance of the economy, social classes, and ideology as well as of the total social context (the social formation, as Althusser would phrase it).

The mainstream of American political science has, however, moved off in a variety of other directions. The interests of the behavioural period in voting, judicial, legislative, administrative, and executive behaviour as well as in interest groups, parties, developing areas, and the like have continued. During the post-behavioural period however, new topics of political research have arisen to satisfy the desire to understand the new concerns typical of this period — about environmental pollution, ethnic, racial, social and sexual equality, and nuclear war, for example.

In the search for answers to urgent social issues such as these, political science in this period has joined all the other social sciences in making an extraordinary commitment of its resources to the application of knowledge. We witness this in the rapid and widespread growth of the so-called policy analysis movement. Literally hundreds of institutes have arisen not only for the understanding of the way in which policies are formed and implemented but for the formulation of policy alternatives to help solve the urgent social problems facing all societies at the present time. These institutes ring the changes on all questions of policy creation and execution: what are the policies in various areas, how are they formed, what alternatives are neglected or rejected and why, what are the consequences, direct or indirect, of any policy, how do these compare with the ostensible objectives of the policies (contributing to the emergence of a vast subfield of policy evaluation), how does a given set of present policies influence subsequent policies (the feedback process), and so on. Because the effects of any policies are felt not only in the political sector but also in most other areas of society, policy institutes have typically been built around interdisciplinary curricula. In this way policy research has reawakened the hope of an earlier day for integrating the social sciences, at least in the application of its knowledge.

Another shift in interest that is part and parcel of this new policy orientation is reflected in the rebirth of the field of political economy. In the nineteenth century, as modern political science was evolving, economics and politics had already shown a close and natural affinity, as revealed in the work of John Stuart Mill, which he explicitly called political economy, and of Karl Marx. The revival of this link today is in part attributable, of course, to the revival of Marxist thought. But it has also blossomed independently through efforts to show the numerous relationships between the state of the economy on the one hand and political events and institutions on the other (see Frolich and Oppenheimer 1982; Monroe 1983).

Political economy is a return to a traditional combination of interests common in the nineteenth century. But perhaps the most dramatic shift in perspectives has occurred today in a different area, in what I shall call cognitive political science. The emergence of this approach reflects a movement away from the attempt to understand political phenomena as exclusively a product of non-rational processes, that is, as a product of social forces that influence decisions and actions of political actors and institutions.

The starting assumption of cognitive political science is that there is a strong rational component to political behaviour. This can mean one of two things: that human beings do act rationally, or that we can better understand their behaviour if we adopt such rationality as an assumption.

Whereas the outcome of empirical scientific research consists of generalizations about behaviour that are grounded in observations, the products of the cognitive approach are models about how human beings would or should act under varying circumstances if they were to act rationally. The product of inquiry takes the form of rational choice models, game theories, or other kinds of so-called rational actor models (see Riker and Ordeshook, 1973; Kramer and Hertzberg, 1975; Downs, 1957). For some, these models only tell us how persons might behave if they acted rationally. They are of value insofar as we can compare actual behaviour with the model in order to try to account for the deviance from the model. For others, however, these models represent the way in which people actually do behave. The assumption of rationality becomes a reality (Riker and Ordeshook 1973). For still others, however, the rational models represent ways in which people should behave if they are to conform to rational norms, and such norms are assumed to be desirable in themselves. Rational models may, therefore, depict formal calculi of rational behaviour, actual strategies of choice, or preferred strategies if one values rational behaviour.

Not only empirically oriented research but political philosophy also has been a major beneficiary of the rational approach. Rational modelling has breathed new life into political philosophy. During the behavioural period, moral research had all but died out for reasons already mentioned. Values were sometimes thought to be mere expressions of preferences, as in economics to this day. In the current post-behavioural period, renewed efforts are under way to demonstrate that there is a rational basis for moral argument and judgment. Most of the work in this area has been inspired by John Rawls's (1971) *A Theory of Justice*, itself influenced by economic modelling and game theory. In this book, the author attempts to develop valid and demonstrable criteria of justice derivable from the assumption of rational action. Using a similar convention about rational behaviour, others have turned to the task of developing moral theories about equality, freedom, international justice, legitimacy, and the like (see Fishkin, 1982; Beitz 1979; Lehrer and Wagner, 1981).

Political philosophy is not alone in this new approach. It was preceded by and has in turn reinforced the application of a rational actor approach in the area of voting behaviour and public choice, and is spreading as a technique to other fields of political inquiry. In its essence, it reflects the theoretical approach of contemporary economics and in fact even borrows economic theories for application to political situations (see Downs, 1957; Kramer and Hertzberg, 1975).

In substantive areas such as those just mentioned — policy analysis, political economy, and what I have called cognitive political inquiry (rational modelling and the new political philosophy) — there has been little difficulty in going beyond the range of interests characteristic of the behavioural period and in adding to its methodological perspectives. However, in the matter of actual methods of empirical research and in the fundamental premise that human behaviour is subject to scientific inquiry, despite the current pervasive criticism of scientific method, much less success has been met in finding an alternative.

Few people believe any longer in the value neutrality of science. That scientific concepts are value-laden can no longer be denied. But that this does not invalidate the search for objective knowledge and understanding is equally undeniable. Just how both these statements can be true is still the subject of much debate (see Lakatos and Musgrave, 1970; Suppe, 1977).

What, however, do the critics of scientific method offer as an alternative to the methods of science? This is where the real difficulty for the critics arises. The only formal alternative, that is, the only alternative that involves something that looks like a method that can be articulated, formalized, and communicated to succeeding generations is Weberian interpretive (*verstehen*) or empathic understanding. This method has been and continues to be discussed, and the interest in the writings of Max Weber has increased enormously in recent years. As yet, however, no one has been able to formalize, systematize, or standardize it in a way that makes it readily communicable to those who would seek to learn it. Despite this irreducible inexpressibility, strangely enough, many radical critics of conventional social science have adopted this method, implicitly or otherwise. This is especially strange as its inventor, Max Weber, has been called 'The Karl Marx of the bourgeoisie'.

THE PRESENT AND THE FUTURE

These many, often conflicting tendencies in post-behavioural political science in the West make it difficult to draw general conclusions about the state of the discipline. For the very reason that political science is still in process of change, we cannot speak of a single, dominant tendency or direction. If there is one, however, we can probably find it in the fact that most leading members of the discipline continue to accept the appropriateness for social inquiry of the scientific methodology found to be so successful in the natural sciences.

It would be misleading, however, to assume that our understanding of scientific method today is the same as it was during the behavioural period. Our conception of science has not stood still; it is itself undergoing change, wittingly or otherwise.

We no longer cast ourselves in the image of the positivist ideal of science. An incipient transformation is under way that may well displace that image with a new one. If so, this is probably the most dramatic thing that is happening in the social sciences though most social scientists may not be aware of it as yet.

Positivism as represented in the thinking of the Vienna Circle during the 1920s was largely subsumed, if not consciously articulated, as behaviouralism took shape, especially during the 1950s and 1960s. In this image, the ideal product of scientific inquiry would be a body of knowledge, based on axioms, with statements of relationships or generalizations that could be ultimately formalized, especially through the use of mathematics, and that would be well grounded in objective observations.

This model is still entertained by many social scientists. This is especially true for those who happen to be in an area where it can be either achieved or approximated, as, for example, in the areas of public choice and rational modelling. There, formal mathematization of propositions works well if only because it is intrinsic to the method of analysis in those areas. There are vast fields in political science, however, indeed most of political science to this point, that have not yielded this kind of intellectual product. Yet these areas of political science are clearly subject to rigorous inquiry through the use of the normal rules of logic, through careful acquisition of data consistent with the canons of science, and through equally sophisticated analysis of these data. The outcomes, though, do not measure up to the positivistic ideal of an axiomatized and mathematized set of propositions. Does this mean that they are not acceptable as scientific conclusions?

During the positivistic behavioural phase of political science, the answer might have been in the affirmative. Today, under the more relaxed understanding of science that is in process of growth within philosophy of science, a different answer can be offered, one that accepts non-axiomatized and non-mathematical statements as an integral part of scientific knowledge even in its ideal form.

Philosophy of science is that special discipline in the West that is concerned with understanding the nature of science — how it acquires knowledge (epistemology) and the nature of the world we wish to know and understand (ontology). As a discipline, the findings of philosophy of science itself are subject to change and, hopefully, improvement, no less than are the findings of any other discipline. Like other fields of inquiry it grows and changes. Although at one time philosophers of science, under the sway of early positivism, did indeed conceive of the appropriate outcome of scientific inquiry in the manner of the positivists of the Vienna Circle, today, most recent findings are moving in a far less monolithically mathematical direction. No longer do all philosophers of science see science as restricted to a single kind of formalized product in the image of classical positivism of the Vienna Circle. Rather, in a more sceptical mood, philosophers of science are now beginning to recognize that if we are to understand science we ought not to accept some abstract analysis of the nature of science as an adequate description of the way it operates to acquire valid knowledge. Rather, we are better advised to look at what scientists actually do.

When we do indeed look at the history of scientific practices we find a larger variety of research products that are accepted as useful and necessary than we would have guessed if we confined ourselves to the positivistic interpretation. Philosophy of science is now discovering that there are many varieties of outcomes with which scientists seem to be satisfied. These outcomes seem to answer the kinds of problems that are being asked in a particular area of science even if the outcomes do not look like the formal or mathematical models of early positivism. For example, systems of classification, taxonomies, conceptual frameworks, and qualitative generalizations about evolutionary processes that do not permit prediction need have little to do with formal models or mathematized propositions. Yet in the various sciences in which they are found, such as botany and biology, they are just as acceptable as final products (see Hanson 1969; Toulmin 1972; Shapere 1974; Suppe 1977).

If this is so in the natural sciences where the success of their methods cannot be denied, then it ought not to be any less true in the social sciences. In this view, then, systematic classifications of political phenomena, for example, or conceptual frameworks, as developed in my own thinking in systems analysis, would be just as normal a product of scientific inquiry as any generalization about politics or any mathematical model. The only question one must ask is whether at the time, the intellectual product satisfies the needs of a would-be scientific discipline, such as political science, in terms of rigorous and testable understanding. That is to say, if the knowledge we acquire seems to help us in attaining satisfactory explanation or adequate understanding of an empirically grounded sort, then that is the most that we can ask of the methods of science. The history of inquiry in the natural sciences now seems to reveal that there is no single fixed kind of intellectual project, as classical positivism would have us believe, that can be designated as appropriate and necessary to achieve understanding of any given phenomena.

As I have suggested, the post-behavioural state that we have just discussed is still evolving. It will be some time before a definitive statement can be made about how it finally differs from behaviouralism and about the new direction in which it may be leading political science. One thing is clear, however. It had its birth in efforts to cope with some of the unresolved problems generated by behaviouralism: the indifference to moral judgments, the excessive commitment to formal mathematized statements flowing from the use of scientific method, the focus on theoretical criteria to the neglect of social issues, the preoccupation with social forces as determinants of behaviour, overlooking, in the process, important cognitive (rational) elements, and a profound forgetfulness about the history of political systems that helps to shape their present.

In trying to cope with these kinds of problems bequeathed by behaviouralism, however, we can assume that post-behaviouralism is busily generating its own difficulties. Some of these are already obvious; others will undoubtedly emerge as new contemporary explanations exhaust their own potential. For example, in emphasizing the need to apply whatever knowledge we have to the solution of urgent social issues, we have already run into major difficulties in trying to reintegrate the various highly specialized disciplines. Descartes taught us that understanding requires decomposition and analysis of a subject matter. Application of knowledge to the solution of social problems, however, requires the reassembly of the specialized knowledge of the various social sciences. We are still at a loss about how to do this. Application of knowledge has also diverted scarce resources from the continued search for fundamental knowledge so that we are already being called upon to reassess the appropriate division between applied and so-called pure research. Computer technology will clearly change the character of major aspects of research in all the social sciences, including political science, in ways that we can only guess at the present time. And finally, the growing international character of research raises fundamental issues about the universality of concepts in the social sciences as contrasted with the culturally conditioned nature of most thinking about social problems. Can we develop a genuinely transnational social science when different national cultures approach problems of understanding social phenomena in such transparently different ways, often with such different concepts?

To enter into a discussion of issues such as these would, however, take us too far afield from our present purpose, an analysis of the four basic stages — formal-legal, traditional, behavioural, and post-behavioural — through which American political science has passed in the twentieth century. These issues may, however, foreshadow a fifth stage that we have not yet begun to enter.

NOTE

1 This article was originally prepared for presentation to a scholarly audience in the Peoples' Republic of China which previously had only limited exposure to Western social science. When reading this article, therefore, it is important to bear this context in mind.

REFERENCES

Beitz, C.R. (1979) *Political Theory and International Relations*, Princeton, N.J.: Princeton Univ. Press.

Bell, D. (1960) *The End of Ideology: On the Exhaustion of Political Ideas in the Fifties*, Glencoe, Ill.: Free Press.

Bentley, A. (1949) *The Process of Government*, Bloomington, Ind.: Principia, originally published in 1908.

Downs, A. (1957) *An Economic Theory of Democracy*, New York: Harper.

Easton, D. (1962) 'The current meaning of "behavioralism" in political science', Annals of the American Academy of Political and Social Science, mono (October): 1-25.

— (1969) 'The new revolution in political science', *American Political Science Review* 68:1051-61.

— (1981a) *The Political System*, New York: Knopf; originally published in 1953.

— (1981b) *A Framework for Political Analysis*, Chicago: University of Chicago Press, originally published in 1965.

— (1981c) 'The political system besieged by the state', *Political Theory* 9:303-25.

Eckstien, H. (1966) *Division and Cohesion in Democracy*, Princeton, N.J.: Princeton University Press.

Fainsod, M. (1940) 'Some reflections on the nature of the regulatory process', in *Public Policy*, Cambridge, MA.: Harvard University Press.

Fishkin, J.S. (1982) *The Limits of Obligation*, New York: Yale University Press.

Frolich, N. and Oppenheimer, J.A. (1982) *Modern Political Economy*, Englewood Cliffs, N.J.: Prentice-Hall.

Hanson, N.R. (1969) *Perception and Discovery*, San Francisco: Freeman Cooper.

Herring, P. (1929) *Group Representation Before Congress*, Baltimore, MD: Johns Hopkins Press.

Kramer, G.H. and Hertzberg J. (1975) 'Formal theory', in *Handbook of Political Science*, Reading, MA.: Addison-Wesley, ch. 7.

Kuhn, T. (1962) *The Structure of the Scientific Revolutions*, Chicago: University of Chicago Press.

Lakatos, I. and Musgrave A. (1970) *Criticism and the Growth of Knowledge*, Cambridge: Cambridge University Press.

Lehrer, K. and Wagner, C. (1981) *Rational Consensus in Science and Society*, Dordrecht, Netherlands: Reidel.

Monroe, K. (1983) *Presidential Popularity and the Economy*, New York: Praeger.

Ollman, B. and Vernoff, E. (1982) *The Left Academy: Marxist Scholarship on American Campuses*, New York: McGraw-Hill.

Poulantzas, N. (1973) *Political Power and Social Classes*, London: New Left Books.

Rawls, J. (1971) *A Theory of Justice*, Cambridge, MA.: Harvard University Press.

Riker, W.H. and Ordeshook, P.C. (1973) *An Introduction to Positive Theory*, Englewood Cliffs, N.J.: Prentice-Hall.

Shapere, D. (1974) 'Discovery, rationality, and progress in science', in K. Schaffner and P. Cohen (eds) PSA 1972: Proceedings of 1972 Biennial Meetings of Philosophy of Science Association, pp. 407-19, Dordrecht Netherlands: Reidel.

Suppe, F. (1977) *The Structure of Scientific Theories*, Urbana: University of Illinois Press.

Toulmin, S. (1972) *Human Understanding*, Princeton, N.J.: Princeton University Press.

Truman, D. (1951) *The Government Process*, New York: Knopf.

Index